Big Blue Java™

Complete Guide to Programming Java™ Applications with IBM® Tools

Big Blue Java™

Complete Guide to Programming Java™ Applications with IBM® Tools

Daniel J. Worden

Wiley Computer Publishing

John Wiley & Sons, Inc.
NEW YORK • CHICHESTER • WEINHEIM • BRISBANE • SINGAPORE • TORONTO

Publisher: Robert Ipsen

Editor: Carol A. Long

Managing Editor: Angela Smith

Text Design & Composition: North Market Street Graphics

Published by John Wiley & Sons, Inc.

Published simultaneously in Canada.

Library of Congress Cataloging-in-Publication Data:
Worden, Daniel.
    Big Blue Java : complete guide to programming Java applications with IBM tools / Daniel Worden.
        p.   cm.
    ISBN 0-471-36343-X (pbk. : alk. paper)
    1. Java (Computer program language)   2. IBM software.   I. Title.

QA76.73.J38 W666 2000
005.7'2—dc21
                                                                        99-089120

Printed in the United States of America.

10 9 8 7 6 5 4 3 2 1

I would like to dedicate this book to my real friends:

A man's mettle is measured
by his deeds
and his dreams
are entrusted to but few

Dark nights stole not smiling hope
your kind words never lessened
while you listened
to my tale of owes

We are not done, outdone nor done in
on this voyage
of challenge and discovery
And we will yet share in treasure true

Thank you. I get by with a little help from my friends.

—Daniel

CONTENTS

ACKNOWLEDGMENTS

A project like this can never be the work of just a few people, let alone one person. There are so many people who have assisted in the creation of *Big Blue Java*, I can only hope to mention a few. If your name is not here, don't fret—your contribution has been noted and is appreciated!

First, I have to thank a few people who contributed to the stuff that makes up this book. Thank you Jack Ladick and Russ Bunting for your respective chapters. And thanks are due to James Carslon, Declan Baker, and Bill Simpson for documenting their finding and "sharing the pain!" Our Big Blue Java applications are really something to be proud of and the way you pulled it off after others had tried and died is truly impressive. Thanks.

To Bill Dapp, the STARS team, and those WNS guys who just kept us up and running, also much thanks. Bill, I really appreciate the help with the DB2 stuff.

Without Emy Chu and Dominic Lam I would likely not have a relationship with IBM at all, let alone be a committed proponent of Big Blue Java in a technical sense. If we accomplish anything with this book, you guys deserve a full measure of credit. I'd also like to personally thank Joe Damassa, who sat next to me at the NC session during the BPEC 98 conference and was interesting enough to follow to his introductory session on SanFrancisco. Thanks. Sometimes, it's the slightest coincidence that makes the biggest change.

The book itself is the product of a collaborative effort. Thanks to Agent 99, Carole McClenndin, for knowing exactly who to talk to and getting this project off the ground. A million thank you's to my editor, Carol Long—it has been a pleasure to work with you and flying to Boston for lunch and a cappuccino was a memorable highlight of my career as a writer, even if the topic of conversation was constructive criticism.

I definitely need to acknowledge the Wiley New York staff including production, art, sales and *bien sur*, copyediting as delicately handled by Christina Berry. *Grazie, mille grazie.*

As always, Marie has been a paragon of virtue, and like the impact she has had on my life for more than a decade, her deft touch is clearly evident on this work as well. My boys, Alexander and Tristan, you have been long-suffering in giving up time with Dad.

To the Word N Wizards, you guys are the best. Thank you for sticking by me through the hard parts.

Finally, thanks to you the Reader. Without you, this book is just a tree fallen in the forest, with no one to hear it.

The idea for this book—*Big Blue Java*—was born during a discussion we were having at WNS, Inc., in the autumn of 1998. At that time, a great many things were still unclear about the way IBM intended to implement Java. As a San-Francisco Technology Licensee, we had already made the commitment to learning and working with IBM's Java business objects; however, the best way to accomplish this still loomed as unmarked territory. When we discovered in October of that year that the foundation and utilities layer of SanFrancisco was going to be replaced by WebSphere, we asked ourselves, "Hey, there must be a strategy behind all this; I wonder what it is?"

In conversations with Simon Phipps, IBM's Java evangelist who works out of Hereford on the Plate (or some such location) in the U.K., I became convinced that Java was much more than a passing fancy for IBM. Visits to the Rochester, Minnesota, development group reinforced that opinion. IBM has made a serious commitment to Java.

So I immediately went to my local computer bookstore to see if I could read up on what tools and techniques were available from IBM. Imagine my surprise upon finding that in the entire section, there was nothing addressing the IBM approach and tool set for designing and developing Java applications.

This is not to say that Java itself is in any way underrepresented in the third-party press. The vibrant and growing groundswell of support and interest in the language is evident from both the number and caliber of books published. Many of these books are highly detailed, in-depth treatments of design patterns and similar issues.

Aims, Objectives, and Audience

Our intent in this book is to clearly define and describe how to use the products available from IBM for the creation of Java-based applications. We will tackle this from an enterprise perspective, with a focus on how to use the products to solve real-world application problems. In fact, we will be profiling the challenges and techniques we used to successfully implement these technologies at our customer sites. This will help make the book relevant to those of you who want to work with the same technology and are looking for pointers on how to solve some of the problems we encountered.

Primarily this book is targeted at the technical developer or application architect level. It should also be of interest to any IT professional with a background in application development. We spend some time at the beginning laying the groundwork of why IBM has made this commitment. The first section deals with strategic issues such as the emergence of Java and e-commerce, as well as the relationship between IBM and JavaSoft and our interpretation of IBM's Java strategy.

The other four sections address development tools, servers products such as WebSphere Advanced and Enterprise, business and object modeling, and finally SanFrancisco as a development environment. We evaluate the features and functions of the product suite offered by IBM for Java developers to fit on a continuum of complexity. While a novice can use Net Fusion and the http server to create a rudimentary Web site, an escalation of expertise is required to work with Net.Commerce, WebSphere, Visual Age for Java, Rational Rose, and SanFrancisco.

We do address DB/2 from the standpoint of Java integration with legacy data, as well as exposing data held in objects to queries from outside the thin client world. In short, I pretty much try to take on the whole enchilada.

One of our objectives was to make the book comprehensible and useful to readers who have little or no Java programming experience. If you work in an AS/400 shop, for example, and you want to get an overview of what Big Blue is doing with Java and where you might start with the process, the first half of this book will be useful. On the other hand, if you are a down-and-in Java programmer and you're looking to get some pointers on how to implement a SanFrancisco prototype, the second half should prove very valuable. An IT manager looking for examples and case studies of where IBM's Java products have been used will have to skip a bunch of pages dealing with the technical specifics, but yes, there is something in here for you, too.

In many respects, this book is a chronicle of my organization's move into becoming a dedicated Java shop. Having become IBM business partners in 1996 and SanFrancisco TLAs in early 1998, we found ourselves struggling with the various components involved in designing, developing, and supporting Java applications. Originally, we had no real predisposition toward working only with tools available from IBM. Wherever practical we evaluated different offerings, in keeping with the multivendor stack approach left over from our days as client/server developers with a penchant for open systems.

At the same time, while we struggled with the how-to issues, we kept getting notices from IBM that products were now available that were integrated with each other. Our use of Merchant Server, for example, gave way to Net.Commerce because it talked to WebSphere, which replaced the utilities layer of SanFrancisco, and so on. As we evolved into working with the complete set of tools available from IBM, at some point the light went on. This is no accidental, haphazard rush to market of a bunch of unrelated tools marketed under one umbrella—this is an integrated tool set for delivering applications.

Please forgive my cynicism, but too often in the past we have seen vendors throw a bunch of products on the market, brand them with similar colors and logos, then declare with a straight face that these comprise an integrated development environment. This experience, I'm afraid, colored our judgment and kept us from seeing the forest while we worked in the woods.

The good news is that not only did we catch on (eventually), but we got so enthusiastic about our experience that we decided to share it with the Java development community at large. Hence this book—*Big Blue Java.*

Attendance at Solutions '99 and ongoing discussions with IBM managers, technologists, and partners have underscored our understanding of the Big Blue Java strategy. We have been barking up the right tree since 1998, and as the direction firms and the vision clears, it is becoming increasingly apparent that this portends a dramatic change in the way enterprise systems are going to be developed in the twenty-first century.

Last, as we have developed real-world applications for customers in 1998 and 1999, we have really seen the value of jumping on this technology and wrestling with it until we could get it to do what we wanted. Make no mistake, this is a significant new technology suite and tool set. As such it has tricks and traps, so to assist you as an IBM developer, we've tried to identify the gotchas that got us.

If you are a developer, work as part of a development team, architect applications, or design software, you should find this book targeted at your level. If you are interested in Java, and particularly if you want to learn more about IBM's Java products and how they work—this book was written for you.

CHAPTER 1

IBM's Java Strategy

I t is not every day that a company approaching $100 billion in revenue adopts someone else's product to be the cornerstone of its future. Yet that is exactly what Big Blue has done in making Java the single most important software product in its pantheon.

Of course, IBM has and will continue to make hardware, irrespective of Java. But every product that IBM makes is now certified to run a Java Virtual Machine, including the S/390 mainframe. IBM offers services, again irrespective of Java, but in 1998, 1999, and 2000, e-business television advertisements from IBM were shown everywhere. And at IBM, e-business depends on Java.

The Players

Several key companies, and their products, make up the horse race we call the Internet. Here's a program to help you tell the players, a little about their background, and where they fit. This background and our assumptions about the industry underlay much of the rest of the book. For those of you more interested in getting into immediate detail about IBM, please feel free to skip ahead to Chapter 2.

A Short History of Java

James Gosling, a Sun employee, initially developed Java as part of an X10 research project. Gosling's team was charged with responsibility for creating the *automated house.* The automated house in the case looks a lot like the Jetsons getting ready for work, if you remember your Saturday morning cartoons from years ago.

In order to meet this challenge, the toaster in the kitchen has to know that it's 7:00 A.M., and a workday. The alarm in the bedroom needs to go off, of course, but the real difference between the way you might organize your domicile with the technology of today and in an automated home is the high level of communication that would be required *between* appliances.

The word *appliance* is no accident. Like computers, appliances are made by a wide variety of manufacturers, but unlike PCs, for example, there is no unifying architecture for household appliances. The net effect of these options has been the inability of any one program to run on all of them.

So Gosling invented a new programming language.

It was designed to be small enough to run on a toaster. It was flexible enough to run on *any* toaster. Or to be run on a refrigerator, a coffee machine, a television, or a microwave oven. And it was robust enough that the same program could execute on this wide variety of hardware without encountering bugs.

After consulting with the marketing department, Gosling and his associates found that the word *Java* (as in a cup of Java, Joe, or coffee) had never been used as a product name. So, in 1995, Java the programming language was born.

But wait a second, is all this Internet excitement a direct result of Java? Maybe, but to really understand IBM's Java strategy, we need to put a few other things in perspective first.

Building Blocks of the World Wide Web

At a technical level, the TCP/IP protocol has been more important than Java in the rise of the Internet. It is easy to forget that the Internet, such as it was, has been ticking along quite nicely, thank you, ever since the sixties when it was launched as a Defense Advanced Research Projects Agency (DARPA) project to help universities share sensitive data.

The core enabling technology for the World Wide Web is the *hyperlink*, invented by Dr. Tim Berners-Lee. This is the technique that lets you click a word or phrase and jump to another location. Without hyperlinks and name resolution, the Internet is about as difficult to use as any other large cluster of Unix boxes, which is to say, difficult. The Internet, then, is like the lower levels of the ISO network model: It provides the physical, transport, and session services between the client and the server or servers.

The acceptance of the Internet by end users began when another newcomer to the equation arrived; the *Web browser*, invented as Mosaic by Marc Andreesen and others at NCSA, before Andreesen went on to found Netscape. The Web browser is the graphical hyperlink manager that sits on top of the Internet and asks, "Where do you want to go today?" Remember, all of these came on the scene in 1992 and 1993. The building blocks of the Web have been in place since that time. Java, on the other hand, was not invented until 1995.

Why Is Java Interesting?

When you start talking Java with IT people, they sometimes nod and say "Java, yes, applets." The applets concept—server-stored code downloaded and executed in a browser or other client Java Virtual Machine (JVM)—is something that most folks "get" immediately. But like the significance of hyperlinks, which put the http in anybody's address, it is the *consequences* of applets, not the feature itself, that counts.

Arguably, as we move into the third millennium (and the second half of the first century of commercial computing), there just isn't enough bandwidth to be moving applets across a network and executing them here, there, and everywhere. Local area networks with 100 mbs Ethernet? Okay, sure that's enough bandwidth. SONET and other metropolitan area networks, again, quite possibly. But the Web has emerged with this 56-kpbs, V.90 choke point that makes applets impractical.

So what's the fuss? Isn't everyone already sick to death of computing products with features that don't work as advertised and where CTRL+ALT+DEL is part of the social lexicon? The key value of the Web browser is its ability to support graphical user interfaces to widely distributed servers running on any client machine type or configuration.

This *is* a big deal. This is driving the popularity of the World Wide Web. Users anywhere can use anything, PC or Mac, Unix workstation or NetPC, to connect to a server and gain access with a point-and-click interface.

On some level it sounds almost too prosaic to be that dramatic a change agent. And please, do not misunderstand me to say that Java applets are useless or without a place. I'm only pointing to the ability to run xterm or windows functionality independent of client configuration as the single biggest enabler, working in conjunction with hyperlinks and the hypertext markup language. We would be seeing the Web emerge even without Java.

The Web Is Not E-business

From its inception, the Internet has been a place of information exchange. It was a powerful tool for researching and sharing research papers long before it went graphical. As you can also see, the Web has supported these activities since before Java was created by James Gosling at Sun Microsystems.

With the introduction of the Web browser came viewers. And correspondingly the counterforce was a move for the Web to become an advertising medium. No longer solely devoted to the exchange of academic ideas, the Web became commercialized. Today, one of the first steps any organization takes with these new technologies is to advertise its existence. In the trade, this has become known as *brochureware*.

The next evolutionary step (or revolutionary step if you feel that evolution should not be measured in weeks and months) was the first commercial transactions conducted over the Web. Paying for content online. The subscription model was introduced. Whether the content was proprietary analysis from a major consulting firm, or access to explicit pornographic pictures, the first e-business steps were taken.

The Web Provides *Access* to E-business

The World Wide Web, then, provides a means of offering content to any user, without his or her knowledge of anything but your address. It allows a business to present this content in a relatively uniform manner, and to extend and manipulate that content to include visuals, sound, and information. It is really mostly an unrestricted way to have a fundamentally spontaneous many-to-many relationship between those who want to see and those who want to show.

Naturally, this could include anything. And if you've taken a random walk through the Internet content recently, you would probably agree that it does. From photo galleries to Web-published novels and pop songs, the Web is becoming a means of distributing ideas in the form of art.

From Greenpeace to the National Rifle Association, the Web is used as a means to raise consciousness. In short, the Web can be used to display information from the divine to the depraved. It can be and is used to inform, to malign, to titillate, and to arrange. If the Internet provides the lower layers of the stack, for managing communications, the Web provides the top.

But the application that most interests IBM is conducting business.

Java *Enables* E-business

From our perspective, *Big Blue Java* is about the entire set of tools and techniques you need to do business on the Web. Java is truly the write-once, deploy-anywhere cross platform development language. It is inherently object-oriented. It is designed to support interaction with distributed objects. It is the language of e-business.

E-business is more than just offering products for sale and taking orders. It allows customers to view the status of those orders, or their accounts. It lets them help themselves, and more actively involves them in the process.

All of the stock market excitement (good and bad) about Amazon.com notwithstanding, you will see as you move through this section that e-business is much, much more than e-stores and business to consumer transactions.

In the same way that the Internet has radically changed the way a great number of people communicate over the world, e-business represents the changes to the way we do business. That includes shopping and balancing our checkbooks, but more than that, it includes the way business-to-business interaction is done.

Let's not forget that IBM is not the only company with the perspicacity to see this opportunity.

The Puzzle Pieces

So we can see that the computing landscape is vastly different at the end of the 1990s than it was even at the end of the 1980s. From desktop computing as the major growth driver at that time (especially when married to workgroup and local area network servers), to the Internetworking of these various servers through the Internet.

The rush to defacto standardize on MS-Windows as the GUI interface has given way to the general acceptance of the Web browser as a standard way to access content and services from different places and environments. Office automation as the killer application for business computing has stepped aside in priority and given it up to doing business on the Web, 7 days a week, 24 hours a day.

The Internet, the World Wide Web, and Java have become the three driving technologies for change in computers. They face the reigning champions of personal computers, MS-Windows/Office and Local Area Networking, which have dominated the agenda for the past 10 years.

It would be unreasonable to think that anyone is going to give up easily in the struggle for dominance over the next 10.

The Plans

Each of the players has their own view of the future. And why not—it's the difference of opinion that makes for an interesting horse race. Now that we have an overview of the various movements and drivers in the marketplace, it should be useful to consider how each of the major vendors is approaching these opportunities.

IBM versus Microsoft on the Web

Louis Gerstner, chairman of IBM since 1994, has said "We made a bet-the-company decision to back the Web and e-commerce." Bill Gates, chairman of Microsoft, has said, "Microsoft will be the most significant player on the Internet." Clearly, the Internet is the new market battleground, both now and looking forward into the mists of time.

It makes sense that with Microsoft's success in providing desktop windowing environments and end user software packages, that company would strive to be the dominant supplier of Web browser and Internet access software. Equally, it makes sense that with IBM's success in selling computers to business, it has chosen to focus on the servers and services to which those browsers connect. Microsoft has a front-end strategy, whereas IBM is focused on the back end. Microsoft has its roots as a personal computer software company, while IBM has built business machines.

This is not to discount Microsoft NT and Microsoft's Internet Information Server. Obviously, Microsoft wants as much of the pie as it can grab. But a Web server is only one small part of the equation, and as you will see as you progress through this book, IBM has developed and brought to market a comprehensive set of tools for building Web-based applications. As Little Red Riding Hood might be told, it's "all the better to do business on the Internet, my dear."

IBM is focusing on those people who are looking to sell over the Web, and Microsoft is focusing on those people who want to buy. Microsoft share prices aside, its business is where the money is made.

NOISE versus Microsoft

One of the interesting things about a company like Microsoft is that its people have created such a successful monolithic entity that it actually focuses its competitors together against it to form a unified front. As mentioned earlier in this chapter, the Internet is the market battleground, and there is more to the story than simply IBM versus Microsoft.

In this case, the "Allies" include Netscape, Oracle, IBM, Sun, and Everybody else—an alliance affectionately known as NOISE (or sometimes as VAM—Vendors Against Microsoft). By placing the Java specification in the public domain and ensuring a consistent cross-platform behavior through aggressive JavaSoft certification, Sun has set the tone for the technology. IBM's participation in the commercialization of Java through its work on the Enterprise JavaBeans standard has defined the technology for e-business.

Oracle has innovated with raw iron—a move to completely remove the necessity for an operating system. And Netscape has been busy with its AOL merger and focus on servicing the largest single install base of Web users anywhere.

Sun has taken an aggressive stand against Microsoft. Anyone who has ever read a quote from Scott McNealy, its president and cofounder, would agree that aggressive is a consistent way to describe Sun's approach. Oracle is no slouch in the anti-Microsoft department, either. And Netscape has gone on record with its complaints when it comes to competing with Redmond.

But it is Sun that has set the technical agenda by placing the Java specification in the public domain. We will get into exactly what this means, including caveats and constraints, in the next chapter, but for now let's just assume that in the same way anyone can create a browser, any vendor can adopt a Java strategy.

IBM's Java Strategy

IBM first shipped Java with an operating system in 1996—an operating system that ran on an IBM server. That, in a nutshell, is IBM's Java strategy. It's about the server. While other organizations grab the hearts and minds of consumers and users through the browser wars, IBM has been busy unifying its servers to run Java applications. We are talking about every single server that IBM makes—from the smallest Netfinity to the big RS/6000 boxes and S/390 clusters.

At the same time, the software folks have been busy creating an integrated tool set for creating those applications. Without which this book would have to have been called something else. Luckily for us, this tool set contains every software widget, utility, and service any developer could ask for when looking at a development environment. That's not to say it's perfect. But it is comprehensive.

So what do we have here—software development tools and servers on which to run the developed software. Interesting, but incomplete. Why would anyone want to adopt this development environment? Simply because they heard Java was an up-and-comer? Possibly, but as we've already seen, there are other players and they have their own offerings. So that leaves the key point: Why buy Java, and if you buy Java, why buy IBM?

Java is write once, deploy anywhere. Java is object-oriented. Java is faster, better, and cheaper than any other development environment. Strong words, but if they are true, they would certainly qualify as reasons to buy Java. So why buy *Big Blue* Java? Because IBM leads the pack in support of Java for business applications.

Co-opting Windows NT, Linux, and Novell

It's no secret that IBM's foray into desktop operating systems with OS/2 was not successful in undermining Microsoft in any significant way. IBM has continued to support and update OS/2, but NT, Linux, and Novell are also supported. This willingness to host all is a key to the IBM strategy for the future.

The main benefit to IBM in supporting these environments is establishing the customer relationship, if only at the hardware level. To insist that customers buy everything—hardware, software and applications—is obviously going to lead to fewer and fewer all-Blue shops. The one-vendor total solution is just not practical with today's bewildering array of options.

At the same time, there is a clear trend away from the character-based applications of the past. Users demand GUI-based access to their data and servers, which Microsoft has been more than willing to provide. By offering support for any of the main OS alternatives, IBM is showing its value as a hardware supplier.

But let's not forget that Java is inherently multiplatform. It can run—and run well—on a continuum of server environments. IBM has been busy ensuring that its Java development products can also run under multiple environments. In short, IBM is willing to give up the OS, as long as you buy its hardware, and it will give up the hardware as long as you develop software using its tools.

The Products

Since it's pretty clear that the deployment environment can and will consist of anything from a toaster to a mainframe, a natural next question would be: What applications will run in these environments? It's not so much that IBM wants to get into the applications business (unlike Oracle), instead it wants to continue to provide application development tools to software developers.

It is these application development tools that will make up the key software revenues for the IBM of the twenty-first century.

This book is titled *Big Blue Java*, so at this time I would like to introduce all of the products that make up the IBM suite of software for Java developers. Chapter 2 provides a brief description of each of the products, and the remainder of the book focuses on the features and how to use those products that we at WNS believe are the most significant ones across the board.

These products include the following:

VisualAge for Java. This includes the integrated development environment (IDE) for Java development as well as integration with other developer management tools such as TeamConnection for source code control.

WebSphere Studio. This is a set of tools for developing HTML and XML screens and Build IT for content assembly and management. WebSphere Studio supports a team-based repository that links to TeamConnection for managing multideveloper e-business projects.

WebSphere Application Server. This Java application server provides integration services for Web servers (Apache, IIS, IBM HTTP SERVER, etc.), Component Broker, TXSeries (for transaction management), and Lotus Domino.

Net.Commerce. This catalog, shopping cart, and secure transaction server provides the underlying features necessary to create and manage an online store.

SanFrancisco. This application business components framework provides the base objects and towers for creating enterprise Java applications for e-business.

DB2–UDB. This venerable relational database product has been updated to support Java integration and is a key component in developing database e-business solutions.

Taken as a whole, these products provide the entire set of developer tools, object framework, relational database, and site management services that any company needs to develop an e-business solution from the ground up. While there are other tools for managing and administering sites and servers, this will be treated as beyond the scope of our investigation.

The Pivot

While Windows NT may have been the fastest-growing server operating system to ship for the past few years, it is not the dominant installed environment by a long shot. It is estimated that 80 percent of Corporate America's data is still maintained in VM files on mainframe computers. This data is the raw content of many e-business applications.

In fact, the biggest single market opportunity facing any computer vendor is to get the largest piece of the business computing pie. That does not mean, however, that organizations will be throwing out their legacy applications wholesale and moving to Java, or to any other environment for that matter.

The money spent on Year 2000 fixes has taught corporations an important lesson. Proprietary code is hard to repair. At the same time there is a lot of investment tied up in these existing, functioning systems. The key will be the environment in which companies choose to write their new applications.

Clearly, IBM expects this to be Java. Whether it deploys on NT, Novell, Unix, or an IBM legacy system, customers can run these applications on their existing infrastructure. The e-business focus is a bet-the-company proposition for Big Blue. It is also the arena that most of us have worked in to get paid. Academic, defense, and personal investment in computer applications pales beside the sheer volume of money spent by commercial enterprises in pursuit of better computer systems.

E-business means taking advantage of the Internet; and it means Web-enabling applications; but most of all it means using computers to do business.

This is the pivotal point that IBM has chosen as the cornerstone of its strategy for the future. As should be clear from this chapter, it is one that has a lot of room for growth.

Why Java?

The reason for this chapter is, hopefully, to give you a better sense of the driving forces behind Java, including market trends and technological innovations. This is, naturally, a high-level treatment of these forces. Any one of them could be the focus for a good-size book.

The main conclusion you should draw from this investigation is that there is a future to working with IBM-based Java development products. It is our judgement that the alternate architectures will not prevail, and the other approaches or offerings can be folded into applications developed using the tools from IBM.

This is a technical book, not a marketing treatise or industry analysis. At the same time, it is always beneficial to have a grasp of the larger picture. So far this chapter has introduced you to the players, outlined some of their plans, and gone straight to the point. Java is critical to the future of computing—and IBM has a solid strategy on which to build.

The Importance of E-commerce and Java to IBM

From this section you should be able to see that Java is more than a technical innovation unifying the IBM hardware product suite. E-commerce and e-business is the future of Big Blue, and Lou Gerstner has drawn a line in the sand. We will look at the "when and why" that is driving the move to Java, from an overall business and organizational sense, as well as IBM's view of the opportunity it has to dominate this market space.

As technologists, we sometimes face a temptation to view the tools in isolation from the world that uses them. I believe that anthropologists are correct when they say two things set mankind apart from the lower primates—his or her use of sophisticated tools, and his or her ability to think conceptually. Information technology combines both of these uniquely human functions. However, it is important to understand the context in which these tools can be used and the framework in which our abstractions find their practical application. This applies not only to this book, where I will make every effort to show practical examples of new technology and techniques, but also to Java and object-orientation itself.

This segment will cover some of the sweeping changes facing the computer industry, in the form of Internet-based computing, and just as important will address the changing face of global business. *Big Blue Java* is about a lot more than new toys; it is a fundamentally new way to serve a newly emerging set of business requirements. The challenge we face is providing real-time, 7×24 global access to data and services from anywhere using cell phones, workpads, PCs, mainframes, Unix boxes, Macs, and even kitchen appliances. The challenge is creating the 24-hour-a-day stock exchange, the seamless integration of the supply chain from manufacturers in China, shippers in Hong Kong, and distributors in America. It is about customers buying your organization's goods and services around the clock and around the globe. In short, it is about creating systems that support twenty-first-century business practices.

You don't need to have me jumping up on a soapbox and telling you that the World Wide Web is great. You undoubtedly already have your own assessment of how it will affect your personal and professional life. But in this chapter you will be introduced to the tidal wave of business change anticipated by IBM several years ago, and this should help you understand the strengths and potential of the tool set we call Big Blue Java.

The E-commerce Revolution

If you follow the reasoning of several popular sociologists, you will see that we have had only a few major revolutions in the way humans organize the way they acquire and trade goods and services. Hunter-gathering societies gave way to the agrarian first wave, which lasted for a good many millennia, until finally giving way in the mid 1800s to an industrial society. The Third Wave articulated by Alvin Toffler has been gaining in strength for the past several decades, and we have the good fortune (I hope) to be living and working in an era of tremendous change.

There is an old proverb that says change means opportunity, and that is certainly the case when it comes to computers. The increasingly short lifecycles of hardware, as well as the rise and fall of popular tools, including desktop operating systems, translates into opportunity. IBM has seen this clearly and provided us as technologists with the tools necessary to meet that opportunity armed to the teeth.

So let's look at the opportunity as seen by the largest computer company in the world.

Metcalfe's law says that the value of any network increases exponentially with each node added to it. Of course, the Internet is also just a network and so this observation also applies to it. Let's look at the growth pattern of the Internet in the late 1990s (Figure 1.1).

Of course there weren't zero Internet hosts in January 1991, but the scale of this graph makes it impossible to show the number of Internet servers in any significant way prior to that year. As you can see, 1994 and 1995 were absolutely the best years to get in seriously and early on the Internet.

These servers are an important part of the equation. For several years the expression "Content is King" has been heard at Internet conferences, and content has to reside on servers. But to really get a businessman excited you have to talk about customers, and in our world that means Internet users.

The next figure (Figure 1.2) presents not only some interesting information about the user base on the Internet, but also makes a comment on the nature of Internet users themselves. This figure is taken from a Web site that counts the number of Internet users by the second. One-sixtieth of a minute is a meaningful number when considering the number of users

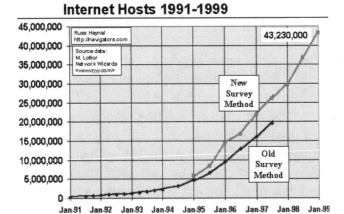

Figure 1.1 The growth rate of Internet hosts from 1991 to 1999.

who are actively signing up to be able to access the Internet and Web-based services.

So now you can see the kinds of numbers that get business people excited. Exponential growth—a gold rush in cyberspace and all that jazz. We are seeing server and user growth into the millions already. Let's call it 20 percent of the population of the United States is on the Web in 1999. But consider this 20 percent and what kind of market segment it makes up. People sophisticated enough to use a computer to do research are generally sophisticated enough to understand a secure transaction. And if they can understand a secure transaction, and they have some disposable income, well, does it not stand to reason that they could become Internet shoppers?

One of the things that interested me about the Web site shown in Figure 1.2 is the marketing slant provided by eMarketer eStats (by the way, I have no idea who these people are, and this is in no way an endorsement of them or their service). But like television and print media, there is a business in understanding who accesses which media, "all the better to sell you, my dear." The emergence of these kinds of statistics, services, and businesses shows that the Internet has not only a wires and pipes aspect but also takes on the characteristics of a communications medium.

I realize that I have not as yet said anything that isn't available here and there in magazines or books from other pundits. But stay with me, and I promise you that this line of thinking will take us to an interesting con-

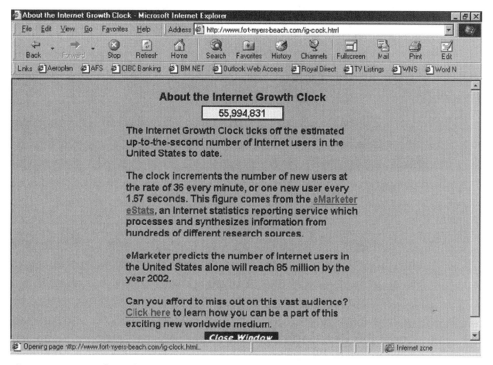

Figure 1.2 Number of Internet users in the United States on June 16, 1999.

clusion. Even more germane, let's imagine we are in the corporate head office of IBM a few years ago when wizards used their crystal balls and flip charts making these predictions. These had to be tough assumptions to swallow in 1996 and 1997, and yet that is exactly what IBM did. Its decision makers looked at the projections and bought in heavily. What we are seeing here is validation of those anticipated trends in 1998 and 1999.

But what about even further out? How long does the tidal wave go on? One of the more enthusiastic predictions for Web-based business is from Forrester Research. It is included as the next figure.

Figure 1.3 projects a dramatic leap in the value of goods sold over the Web between 1998 and 2003. From $51 billion total to just under $1.5 trillion. Now that's a growth opportunity! The most interesting thing that Forrester Research puts forward is the idea that the Amazon.com-type of opportunities represent only a sliver of the total value of e-commerce in the United States. The value of the business-to-business sector is already more than five-fold greater than consumer goods sold over the net. In other words, it's the extranet, not the Internet, that counts.

Figure 1.3 Forrester Research predictions for e-commerce.

But whether we are discussing a Web site, Internet, intranet, or extranet means of communications between businesses and consumers, there is a huge shortfall in the ability of organizations to service all of this demand. The Net-based services, no matter who they are targeted at, require investment and experimentation. New tools are needed to migrate traditional business services to the Web. Naturally, this was anticipated and predicted by the good folks at IBM before they decided to jump into e-business with both feet.

International Data Corporation, another market research firm, provided the graph displayed in Figure 1.4.

In 2003, the same year Forrester Research predicts that $1.3 trillion worth of goods will be moved over the Internet, global IT spending on Web-enablement is anticipated to be $1.5 trillion. It takes money to make money!

In a way, I am comparing apples to oranges and calling them fruit. By 2002, IDC sees the U.S.-based IT expenditures at $500 billion, and the projections for goods and services in 2003 are essentially three times that. The main point is that for the next few years, either more money, or a healthy percentage of revenues, will be invested and reinvested by organizations into the Web technology that allows them to make that revenue. Correspondingly, there will be reductions in operating costs associated with the more traditional means of generating income. Paper handlers, admin staff, telephone support folks—all of these jobs will undoubtedly be cut as part of the business case for investment in e-commerce. For the next few years, however, it will likely be a messy combination of the two models; traditional means of providing goods and services alongside new systems

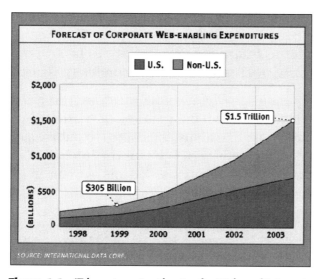

Figure 1.4   IT investment estimates for Web and Internet-enabled technologies.

with a growing customer base. The major point here is that companies that wish to take advantage of the growth potential of e-business will need to invest heavily in infrastructure and tools to allow them to do that.

IBM has foreseen this requirement, and has been busy for the last few years of the 1990s developing and debugging these goods and services just in time for customers to incorporate them into their new way of doing business. This is good news for anyone wanting to work with these technologies.

IBM's Mission: First, Protect Our Install Base

With the failure of OS/2 to counter the migration to Microsoft operating systems, IBM became at risk in its hardware business. In the same way that Windows NT began to seriously threaten Novell's NetWare Operating System, it became obvious that the AS/400 market was also beginning to evaluate NT as an alternative solution.

Mainframes had already been exposed to the threat of market erosion as a result of Unix boxes and client/server systems from the early 1990s. This, of course, later slowed and rebounded as organizations began to experience the instability problems that marked a great many custom-designed client/server solutions. Open systems are a very attractive theory, but with the introduction of components from many vendors also comes an inherent complexity. Different versions of everything from software release levels to firmware versions have to be accommodated in an open system. A natural result of all this complexity is instability.

This same argument applies to Windows NT. Anyone who has installed and administered Windows NT 4.0 on a variety of hardware platforms can report a wide variety of anomalous behaviors (to put it kindly). IBM banked on the technical superiority of OS/2 for the Intel platform, but it didn't fly. The market wanted applications, and lots of them, imperfect or not.

IBM estimates that two-thirds of the world's legacy applications are installed on Big Blue gear. This means that of all the organizations who stand to gain from integrating legacy systems with new technology, IBM is very much at the front of the line. Big Blue, and customers, will not win much if every application has to be scrapped in favor of something new. IBM recognizes this and has co-opted the upstarts and newcomers and folded them into an architectural framework for e-business.

With the release of their Java development suite—Net.Commerce, Web-Sphere, and SanFrancisco—IBM did something it had never done before; it released software that ran only on a competitive platform. In this case, the platform was Windows NT. A classic case of "If you can't beat 'em, join 'em."

How does this make sense? Is IBM throwing in the towel and giving up on its ability to compete and win in any computer market space? I don't think so. In fact, if you look beyond the superficial, there are some interesting and subtle implications to IBM's decision to incorporate Microsoft products into its solution set.

Next, Grow the Business Disproportionately

Unlike Microsoft, IBM is not solely a giant software company. In fact, IBM has within it three distinct organizations; a software business, a hardware business, and a services business. While Windows NT and other Microsoft products do in fact compete head to head with the software organization (and let's include Lotus in that category), Microsoft products run quite well on IBM hardware from Netfinity servers to ThinkPad notebooks. All of which equipment provides a nice return to the shareholders, thank you very much. In that market space IBM is not competing with Microsoft, but instead is leveraging sales of their hardware to capture as much market as possible.

At the same time, there is a huge install base of existing IBM customers who are using other operating systems. In the midrange space there is of course the AS/400, but also the RS/6000. On top of this is the emerging Windows NT/Netfinity market.

The challenge for Big Blue was to come up with a strategy that would provide a unified theme and an engine to drive growth in all of the markets in which IBM plays. This was a very big job for a very big company. Under John Akers, IBM often adopted a "my way or the highway" approach to sales. There was no cooperation with competitors; IBM wanted as much of any deal as it could get. That attitude taken to its conclusion saw a very shaken up IBM, with losses and layoffs for the first time in its history. Under Mr. Gerstner, the company adopted a "kinder, gentler" approach that has obviously worked in turning the company around and restoring it to the position of leader in the computing industry that it had previously enjoyed for decades.

One component of the turnaround solution, in my view, was the communication to the sales force that any IBM participation in a customer solution was better than none at all. The all-or-nothing mandate was overturned in favor of a foot-in-the-door strategy. This set the stage for a more open IBM, especially in its product offerings. From this, I believe, you see a significant investment in working with Microsoft in order to ensure that the Netfinity/NT working relationship does just that—works.

This is the long way of explaining why IBM would choose to offer Microsoft operating systems and even promote them as a platform for development. But it doesn't explain the unifying theme for growing the business in all the other segments.

Before getting to that, I'd also like to point out that IBM is making every effort to ensure that customers have the choices they want. At the time of this writing, many of the products that make up the Big Blue Java development environment are also available under Linux. IBM has quietly admitted that it will be working on releasing more. It will prove interesting if by giving up the operating system on the development boxes, IBM secured its ability to successfully sell hardware and software for applications development. It would be a classic case of choosing your battles well.

E-commerce Is the Market and E-business Is the Theme

You would have to have been locked in a Turkish prison without TV privileges to not have noticed the IBM advertisements promoting e-business. IBM has been very serious about spending money and getting mind share in this area. Consumers and businesspeople alike have been exposed to concepts like scalability ("Lock the Door") and the Web as more than presentation graphics ("Flaming logos and spinning logos").

In my opinion, the strategy is brilliant in its simplicity: Sell the infrastructure that business will need to use the Internet. Not just routers like Cisco. Not just portals like AOL and Yahoo! The whole ball of wax. The servers, workstations, networks, software, consulting—everything, except applications.

IBM sells solutions, yes, and an application is a necessary part of that solution. So, IBM has opted to leverage business partners, independent software vendors, and customers to develop applications that use its tools. The technology driver in all of this—Java.

By offering a unified development environment that addresses the opportunity customers see in the Internet, incorporating Java as the most rapidly growing language since Mandarin, and running on any hardware that supports a Java Virtual Machine, IBM has come up with a single approach that leverages each of its divisions.

This approach protects the installed base of equipment that can become Java servers while still running existing applications. It feeds consulting revenue as customers struggle with the design and implementation of an entirely new systems infrastructure, and it attracts developers to learning and using tools that result in applications that IBM can promote to other customers.

No other organization has the experience in communicating business benefits of using information technology to business people like IBM. No other organization has the clout and deep pockets to commercialize Java like IBM. And there is no other organization that can dominate the e-business market space like IBM.

Look at how it all comes together. You have a significant new way of doing global business in the Internet. You have an enabling technology with an unparalleled growth rate in Java. You have a global vendor used to providing hardware, software, and services. And all IBM had to do was give up on the idea that it could have the entire pie. As it is, only two pieces of the solution come from other vendors: the development station operating system is from Microsoft, and the application development language is from Sun.

The corresponding benefit is that software developed using the business tool set (what I have been calling Big Blue Java) can run not only on all IBM servers from PCs to the mainframe, but can also be deployed on HP, Sun, and other vendors' gear. IBM can now obtain revenues from customers that don't have a single IBM box in their shop.

IBM Going Forward

The IBM of the twenty-first century is very different from the one of the early 1960s. Somehow, the largest computer company in the world saw the need for change, came up with a strategy, and implemented it. I would like to point out that my editor wanted me to minimize the discussion of market strategy and positioning, on the basis that it might seem too pro-IBM. I hope that flavor does not come across.

I think it's worth noting that as a computing professional for more than 18 years, I have at various times in my career been highly negative toward Big Blue. SAA, OS/2 EE, and even TopView did little to warm my feelings. It has only been during the last few years—with IBM's change of emphasis on business partners and the move toward its own interpretation of how Java can be used by business partners (and customers)— that my position has changed.

Everything covered in this chapter was originally something I had to puzzle out for myself. The IBM organization didn't share their strategic thinking with me until the Solutions '99 Conference. Having been designing and deploying systems since 1982, I had not previously attended a conference like it. The best news, from my point of view, was that my suppositions about the IBM strategy were not in error. Incomplete, yes, but not wrong. I am pleased to be able to say that IBM has been very vocal about its commitment to Java and why it is good for it, good for its customers, and good for us techies.

As technologists, we invest a good portion of our life in understanding tools and how to make them do what we want. Applied information technology is the key for most of us—not creating tools for their own sake.

Over the years the one thing that has been consistently true about our industry is that there is always a better mousetrap, always a faster gun in the West. We don't try to stay abreast of changes in computing; we try to slow the rate at which we fall behind. Then, with a supreme effort, we push ourselves into learning a whole new way of doing things, or we retire.

I believed that IBM has a plan to accomplish this as an organization. After evaluating its tools and direction, my company and I have decided to do the same. After attending Solutions '99 in Las Vegas, it was explicitly stated by IBM that it has a plan and we were pretty close in seeing it.

Most of this book is devoted to how to make the technology work. In this chapter you should have really seen the reasons why you would want to do that.

IBM and JavaSoft

As you have seen in the two previous sections, Java is integral to IBM's strategy for e-business. This is the first time in the history of IBM that such an important and significant technology was neither developed nor owned by the corporation. Instead, ownership of Java is maintained by Sun Microsystems, a key competitor in the Unix workstation and server marketplace.

In order to better understand why Big Blue has adopted Java as the fundamental language in developing new software solutions, we will look at some of the characteristics of Java as a language, and relate these to changes in the way software is being developed and used worldwide.

In this section I will introduce you to JavaSoft, the Sun Microsystems subsidiary responsible for stewardship of Java. Also, we will look at the strategy Sun has for Java, including participation of key partners like IBM for commercialization and enhancement of Java as a language.

The committee structures, priorities, and directions to date will also be covered, in order to show the differences between Java's evolution and other languages.

Drivers Behind Java

Let's not forget what gave rise to Java in the first place. Sun, as part of its ongoing search for new markets and products, launched an initiative to get into consumer electronics. This was in the form of set-top devices for bringing movies and other multimedia content to households through the display mechanism of the television set. At the same time, the goal of the technical group exploring this area was to extend the umbrella of devices to include personal digital assistants and household appliances.

When C++ proved impractical to accomplish the goal of supporting many different microprocessor types, team member James Gosling developed a new language to address the requirement. First called *Oak*, it was quickly renamed *Java* when product name infringements were discovered.

At about the same time that Sun realized that consumer electronics was not going to be a growth area for the company, Netscape released its first browser. In 1994, Java was repositioned as the language for Web applications by Sun.

The very features that allowed Java to function well in the automated house environment distinguished it from other languages for building Web client applications. Specifically, it is platform independent, secure, robust, and small. Equally significant, Java was built from the ground up in compliance with the object-oriented model.

From its roots in consumer electronics, Java inherited a basic practicality. From the assumptions on which it was built, Java embodies the principles of good computer science. Specifically, Java as a language reflects some of the most recent thinking on the nature and behavior of computer languages in general. Its very newness is a critical factor in its ability to apply theory in a working language.

Object-Oriented Java

While developing Oak, James Gosling referred to what at that time was the most recent thinking about the nature of programming languages. This included the need for any newly developed language to incorporate the principles of object orientation. The object-oriented model puts the emphasis on three major characteristics. These are:

Inheritance. A new class can inherit fields and methods from an existing class. This link is maintained so that changes to the existing class can be made available to the new class in the future.

Polymorphism. As in real life, the offspring of an ancestor object can have different data and behaviors than its siblings while still sharing the link back to the originator. Polymorphism is shown where a newly defined subclass overrides the behavior inherited from an ancestor.

Encapsulation. An object can encapsulate or hide methods and data from programmers who use it. Complexity is masked and productivity increased through the principle of encapsulation.

This superficial introduction to the major features of Java as an object-oriented language is intended only to set the stage for understanding the need to manage its ongoing evolution. From this you should be able to see that the construction of Java itself is based on a programming paradigm much different from other languages, which frequently have significant intellectual debts to 4GL techniques or more traditional transaction-oriented thinking.

Java is different from other programming languages. It was created for a different deployment environment, and it was designed under a different language model. These differences uniquely position it as the language of choice for e-business applications in an Internet environment. But perhaps I should leave the conclusions for the end of the chapter!

The Importance of Components

As part of the ongoing development of programming languages and techniques, object orientation is just now beginning to become commercially popular. The combination of a need for a language to lend itself well to multiplatform deployment, as well as the rise of the Web browser as a platform-independent client, provided the impetus for Java's acceptance.

More than just riding the rising tide of the Web, Java is also inheriting trends in corporate software development techniques. Earlier in this chapter, we looked at a quick definition of object-oriented software characteristics and recognized that Java was written with this model in mind. It did not have to be adopted after the fact.

Another trend in systems development is the move toward components. These may be software applications (a Java applet, for example, is potentially a component) or they can be complex combinations of hardware, software, and communications, wrapped together and presented as a single component. Large-scale legacy applications, for example, running on traditional mainframe hardware and incorporating data that can only be accessed through a CICS application, might be handled as a component.

By using components, application architects can now effectively mix legacy or existing applications in the context of a new systems architecture. Because Java is object-oriented, it lends itself to being the language of choice for systems based on a component architecture.

The Role of JavaSoft

Since Java as a language is continuing to evolve, to ensure ongoing compatibility between previous implementations and future ones, a structure had to be put in place to manage the evolution of the language itself.

JavaSoft is an operating company of Sun Microsystems that is responsible for the Java Development Kit (JDK). While the Java specification itself is placed in the public domain, Sun has the right to veto any proposed changes to the language and rigorously controls the certification process.

It is possible for a company to pay a nominal sum for the documentation of Java and to do a clean room implementation of the spec, resulting in a proprietary Java variant that owes no royalties to Sun. This is in essence what Microsoft did with their its enhancements in J++.

However, in order for a company to use the name Java and display the by-now-famous calligraphic coffee cup, Sun must certify that the implementation of Java is actually compliant with the specification. In Microsoft's case, Sun was unwilling to do this. Hewlett-Packard has implemented its own clean room implementation of embedded Java, and the jury is still out on whether Sun will litigate or not.

JavaSoft has been accused of not being impartial when it comes to administering the Java certification process. Clearly companies like Netscape, HP, and Microsoft will want to differentiate their offerings and in some cases will be forced to do so in order to address weaknesses in the specification as it is at any given time.

All in all, however, JavaSoft should be commended for bridging the disparate views and approaches that competitors take. Java has been very successful in gaining acceptance across a large number of vendors. And to be fair, Sun is not taking a "not developed here" stand on changes proposed by other parties.

In fact, the Enterprise JavaBeans specification itself resulted in large measure from work done by IBM staffers on the SanFrancisco project.

With so many different ways in which the product can be used, it makes sense that differentiation will occur first at the level of to what use the product is put. IBM has determined that commercialization of Java in the form of e-business and e-commerce applications is of the highest priority. Others are focusing on the potential to run Java on embedded systems.

In each case, the role of JavaSoft is that of arbiter and facilitator. No doubt experience with incorporating the collaborative/competitive dual nature of Unix and NFS qualifies Sun better than any other firm for leading this effort in the Java arena.

The Future of Java

Java is a young, vibrant, and rapidly evolving language. It has found its feet and is learning to walk (or run!). There is significant change still on the horizon, but the course is clear. Java is moving toward a component architecture based on the standards defined by JavaSoft for Enterprise JavaBeans.

Enterprise JavaBeans

Enterprise JavaBeans (EJB) was announced at the JavaOne conference in 1998. IBM has said to expect it to be incorporated in products like San-Francisco by mid-2000. For companies looking for a way to standardize development of applications across a complex organization, incorporating both new and legacy systems, EJB clearly provides a viable path. If you add to that requirement a need to run on and support multiple platforms, and support truly object-oriented component development, it is the *only* path.

Sensibly, IBM has chosen to co-opt the EJB standard and commercialize it, rather than fight a more open standard with its own proprietary approach. Embracing a philosophy that was unthinkable ten years ago, Big Blue would rather switch than fight. And this makes a great deal of sense for all involved.

The Common Programming Model is the only way that IBM can get developers to write in a single language, yet deploy that code on any piece of gear offered by Big Blue. When the potential market for components and software development tools is factored in, it hardly seems surprising that IBM is also eager to take advantage of EJB support of other competitive platforms.

This approach to programming offers many major advantages over traditional approaches. Where other enterprise software development approaches such as Corba's COS or Microsoft's DCOM have been essentially oriented to run only on their environments, Sun developed the EJB specifications to be able to work on any enterprise system infrastructure services already in existence. Interoperability of applications was a paramount requirement.

In this case, Write Once Run Anywhere (WORA) does not just apply to hardware platforms. Using EJB application programming interfaces (APIs), any vendor can choose to support Enterprise JavaBeans, allowing developers to code their application and simply take advantage of whatever infrastructure services are implemented in the run-time environment.

The Enterprise Java APIs are completely platform- and vendor-neutral. The APIs are designed to layer on top of heterogeneous infrastructure services from any vendor. Each API provides a common programming interface to a generic type of infrastructure service. If a vendor who offers this type of service implements the Sun API, then an application could access any service provider through the common interface.

If this is true across multiple vendors, then it follows it is also true across multiple product lines from a single vendor—in this case, IBM.

Embedded Java

In terms of scalability, if EJB represents the largest of all possible deployment environments—the World Wide Web and global business-to-business integration—then embedded Java leads us to the economies of small. Smart cards, Java rings, personal digital assistance, bar code scanners—if it holds a microprocessor, it will support a JVM.

Embedded Java allows any device, however small, to run a Java-compliant application. There are multiple Java implementations now for any number of devices. Think of embedded Java as a generic replacement for Application-Specific Integrated Circuits. Instead of putting your automobile's antilock braking logic on a dedicated chip, the microprocessor will support a JVM and the application will be written (and maintained) with Java.

If it sounds like we're saying that Java will take over the world, in a way that's exactly right. Java has the ability to run on so many different plat-

forms—to be embedded in appliances; automobiles; anything, really—
that for the first time not only can you write once and deploy anywhere,
but you can now write once in one language.

The potential gains that Java presents for IT departments in terms of
managing the creation and maintenance of logic is astounding. The same
programming techniques and tools used for decision support and administrative systems will also be used to add value to the products produced
by the organizations in which they run. Instead of running multiple
teams of IT professionals with differing skills and languages, people can
move from one assignment to another, whatever the scale, and be immediately productive.

Jini

Beyond Enterprise JavaBeans and embedded Java, Jini is another major
evolution in the Java interpretation of how computer programs should
behave. No doubt influenced by Sun's "the network is the computer"
thinking, Jini is a Java-based implementation that does not incorporate
the notion of a central control. In fact, Jini applications can roam around
the network, looking for a JVM on which to run, based on performance
characteristics established for the program and measures of machine
availability and performance.

Imagine a process or program that can detect an idle machine and take
advantage of its resources while that machine's owner is out for coffee
or lunch. This is the ultimate freedom from hardware that Jini offers.

Jini is a set of APIs and network protocols that lets you build and deploy
distributed systems organized as federations of services. A service in this
case can be anything available to the network. Hardware devices, software,
and communications channels can all be treated as services. A federation
of services is a set of services, currently available on the network, that a
client program can bring together to help it accomplish its desired goal.

Jini addresses the need to raise the level of abstraction for distributed
systems programming from the network protocol level to the object
interface level. Embedded Java means there will be a proliferation of
devices available on the network, from many different vendors. Jini
makes it unnecessary for vendors of devices to agree on network level
protocols in order for their devices to work together, supporting a TCP/IP
or netbeui interface, for example. Instead, vendors can agree on Java

interfaces. The Jini processes of discovery, join, and lookup lets devices locate each other on the network. Once located, devices are able to communicate with each other through Java interfaces.

Microsoft and Sun Struggle over Java's Future

Sun and Microsoft have very different ambitions for Java. Sun wants Java to serve as a platform-independent solution for building distributed applications, while Microsoft wants Java to serve as a platform-dependent solution for building Windows applications. As a result of these competing visions, developers must choose which flavor of Java to use, and wonder if the outcome of this struggle will benefit them.

Obviously for the purposes of Big Blue Java, the Microsoft view of the future is not consistent with IBM's plans for Java. Nor is it consistent with the historical trends in the industry. Platform dependence is marketable only so long as the platform offers something that no other competitor can provide. In the case of Microsoft, arguably an easy-to-use GUI-based platform with inexpensive software components (applications) made for a clear winner. The browser-based Java applications now emerging are effectively competing with the Microsoft fat client approach.

Implementing thin client on Microsoft will no doubt appeal to many developers. However, the choice for these people is not so much which Java variant to use, but rather why not Visual Basic? Microsoft C/C++? Why not implement thin client as part of a WinTerminal architecture? The number of options Microsoft provides means that Java is an also-ran strategy for them. There is certainly no commitment to enhancing Java as a language for allowing developers to write and maintain one set of source code while deploying on as many environments as desired.

HP and Microsoft

Hewlett Packard has allied with Microsoft on the Java issue. The clean room implementation of Java means that HP now has control of its own Java Virtual Machine, and it is likely that it will be Microsoft friendly.

By providing this JVM to Microsoft, it is possible for Redmond to implement its own Java without homage to Sun. Of course, this Java variant would not likely be compatible with Sun's JVM standards (meaning developers would be locked into a Microsoft solution), but this is consistent with Microsoft's strategy anyway.

With a legal JVM for its Windows CE operating system, Microsoft can ignore Sun's objections and push out its own Java development agenda. HP in this case stands to sell hardware, whether that is HP handhelds running CE, such as the 600 LX, or servers that support Microsoft's NT.

ISO Standardization

Any criticism that you read here about Microsoft is not meant to imply that Sun is without flaw or weakness. Sun has been trying to get the International Standards Organization to adopt Java—while leaving Sun as the steward of the Java standard.

Sun has been actively seeking the official standardization of Java by ISO. Official standardization would eliminate the chance of Java fragmenting into multiple standards, which would result in it becoming obsolete or blunting its momentum.

To propose a standard to the ISO, a company must undergo the lengthy and costly process of becoming a Publicly Available Specification (PAS) submitter. Sun successfully completed this step. However, the ISO changed the maintenance rules of a standard. These new rules require the submitter to give up some control over the future maintenance of any product it wishes to have standardized. Sun refused to do this, arguing that a key body needed to be responsible for ensuring appropriate long-term development—specifically themselves.

The net result of this was the refusal of the ISO to standardize Java.

Sun has tried to go around the ISO refusal by approaching the European Computer Manufacturers Association (ECMA) for approval. Whether this will ultimately push Java into a standard format that Sun can accept and still accomplish the goals of a public standard remains to be seen.

In the interim, Sun is the arbiter of what is or is not Java, and it has clearly demonstrated its willingness to fight for this right in court.

Visual Basic and C++ Competition

As if competition within the Java family wasn't enough, what about the other languages on the market? Visual Basic is hardly an object-oriented language, and while ActiveX components may have some of the marketing features of Java beans, ultimately it comes down to the single environment on which VB applications can be run.

C++ is, of course, an object-oriented language, but it is showing its age and it still contains the weaknesses that were specifically designed out of Java. Real-world Java applications are beginning to show they can outperform similar logic implemented in C++. If performance is not an issue, cross platform deployment and developer productivity put Java way ahead on the attraction curve.

This is not to say that C++ is dead, or has no attraction. In fact, as a developer using the same object-oriented analysis and design techniques, combined with code generators like those from Rational Rose, you could hedge your bets. With a thorough approach to object modeling, code could be generated for either Java or C++. For obvious reasons when we generate code from Rose you will see that it is for Java.

Summary

Java is hot stuff. We wouldn't be seeing the investment and jockeying for position surrounding Sun, HP, Microsoft, and IBM for the product without there being some real fire under all the smoke.

The future of the language ranges from a single development environment good for everything from programming cellular phones to writing enterprise applications. Add to that the potential of Jini to free programs from designated deployment configurations, and the whole thing takes on a new dimension.

We have seen industry pushes and purges in the past. In some ways the vendors are getting more aware of the laws of cause and effect, ultimately becoming smoother while at the same time more manipulative.

From a Big Blue Java perspective, nothing changes. The IBM focus on a Sun-compliant JVM is still the most likely winner in any of the scenarios previously mentioned. But the real bottom line is that if you want to ensure that your programs are written once and will deploy on any IBM gear—Java is absolutely the way to go.

CHAPTER 2

The IBM Java Product Suite

C learly IBM wants you, as a software developer, to be using its integrated Java development environment. This is not terribly different from the approach taken by Oracle or Microsoft. It makes sense that a single vendor—especially one with deep enough pockets to fund or acquire each of the components—should be able to cover the range of tools necessary for a complete solution.

The only other approach that you could adopt would be to review every tool on the market, picking and choosing, and eventually assembling your own tool kit. This was, of course, the theory behind the client/server best-of-breed approach. The problem with this methodology is that vendors do not actually implement standards consistently (as we have seen even with the JavaSoft standards). The resulting hodge-podge of products may have the ultimate in features, but in my experience the lack of integration causes so many practical problems between incompatible releases, upgrades, bugs, and so forth that it simply doesn't work.

The question then becomes: Which vendor do I back? In Chapter 1, we explored our reasons for selecting IBM. I hope our rationale made sense and that you could follow our logic in deciding that Big Blue Java is indeed the right vendor at the right time.

In this chapter I would like to introduce you to the main features of each of the products that make up that tool kit. This should serve more as a dictionary than an encyclopedia. In subsequent chapters we get into the details and examples of each product. Here you will find in one place a brief description of each product on the entire Java development continuum, as well as where and when you would choose to use it.

Common Programming Model

As discussed earlier, IBM has selected Enterprise JavaBeans as the component architecture for the future. One practical implication of this decision has been to support a common programming model across all servers. Whether you are working with CICS, IMS, TPF, Component Broker, Domino, or DB2, with the new model you can choose to develop and deploy using a single application development suite—specifically Java.

Component Broker provides the necessary translation services between newer Java-based applications and legacy programs running on S/390, AS/400, and Unix servers. In this way you can bridge the gap between legacy applications and the newer development tools and methodologies, allowing for incremental migration of applications over time.

The lack of a common way to write applications even within the same dialect has long been an Information Technology problem. Developers might all be writing applications in C, for example, but end up re-creating code that was already available to the team. Reuse requires a tremendous amount of knowledge about existing code, as well as a highly disciplined approach to project management.

By exposing services to developers through an integrated product suite, as well as providing repositories and linked models in tools like Visual Age for Java, it is now much easier to expect developers to take advantage of services and code that already exist. In some cases this will occur because the developer is made aware of that existence; and in others it will be, for example, because direct access to the database is not possible and the only way to obtain the desired data is through a specific component call.

If this is in fact the architecture of the future, IBM has already begun to provide products that support it. The last part of this chapter goes into more detail about the new programming model and the frameworks that support it.

The Range of Tools

Even with a program it can be challenging to tell the players apart. For a quick look up on the various products that make up the IBM e-business development suite and servers, the following product dictionary is provided. IBM has segmented its tool set into four main categories; Front-End Development, Servers, Application Integration Middleware, and Components. The Big Blue e-business tools covered in this book are listed here, and the way they fit together is shown in Figure 2.1.

Front-End Development Tools

VisualAge for Java—Professional Edition. Provides drag-and-drop visual programming support for building Java applets, servlets, Java-stored procedures, and JavaBeans, as well as tracking source code changes.

VisualAge for Java—Enterprise Edition. Has all of the features of Professional and also includes team management features for multiple programmer projects and automatic code generation for RDBMS and transaction servers.

WebSphere Studio. Provides a visual development environment for Web-based e-business applications. Includes site mapping, team assignments, code generators, and tools for constructing and integrating Web front ends to databases and servers.

Application Integration Middleware

MQSeries. Message Query handling supports publish/subscribe capabilities, dynamic workload distribution for improved scalability, and failover for high availability.

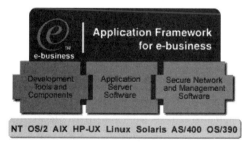

Figure 2.1 IBM's Java Solution Continuum.

MQSeries Integrator. Routes, translates, and exchanges messages between applications.

MQSeries Workflow. Integrates messaging with mail and document processing for complete workflow solutions.

Component Broker. A scalable runtime environment for distributed component-based applications. Supports EJB.

Servers

WebSphere Application Server, Standard Edition. Supports Java servlets and connections to various databases.

WebSphere Application Server, Advanced Edition. Supports higher degrees of clustering, scaling, and better integration with existing transactional systems.

WebSphere Application Server, Enterprise Edition. Supports much higher transaction loads through load balancing, and supports CICS, Encina, and Component Broker (CORBA) programming. In this edition, a common infrastructure (logging, locking, two-phased commit, etc.) supports multiple styles of programming.

CICS Transaction Server. Provides high-volume, high-availability transaction handling services for legacy IBM environments. It is accessible through Component Broker.

Net.Commerce—Start. Is aimed at first-generation e-business sites. Supported on many platforms including Windows NT, AIX, AS/400, Sun, and HP. Provides catalog and payment services for Web-based shopping.

Net.Commerce—Pro. Is scalable to higher levels of transactions than those supported by the START product. Intended for second-generation Web sites, it features advanced catalog tools to create intelligent catalogs, as well as support for back-end integration to SAP, EDI, IBM MQ Series, IBM CICS, and IMS.

Net.Commerce—Hosting. Is offered for service providers who use Net.Commerce to support a virtual mall with many different merchants operating under one umbrella. Hosting provides the necessary licensing to use START and PRO features across multiple e-businesses running on one server. Payment services based on SET, and Euro currency support are included in this version.

DB2–UDB. This relational database engine offers all of the features and performance available from a leading SQL database, including the ability to run Java applications in the database. Scalable to the largest data stores in the world, DB2 has a large install base and runs on many different platforms.

Components

SanFrancisco Application Business Components for Java. Provide prebuilt, reusable components that help developers create Java-based e-business applications. SanFrancisco Version 1.4 supports a migration plan to convert SanFrancisco's components to Enterprise JavaBeans. Migrating SanFrancisco to EJBs enables SF applications to run on any EJB server, including IBM's WebSphere Application Server. Advanced functionality called *Towers* supports General Ledger, Accounts Payable, Accounts Receivable, Warehouse, and Order Management.

Lotus Products

One of the things that we wrestled with when contemplating the scope and detail of this book was whether to include Lotus products as part of the topics covered. Ultimately, we decided not to do this. For one reason, Lotus is positioned as a separate organization within the IBM Corporation. It is a wholly owned subsidiary with its own products, support network, and, for that matter, color (yellow, as opposed to blue).

Therefore, as you progress through this book, don't expect to find much coverage on Domino and other Lotus products, which you may be working with as part of your Java solution set. On the other hand, since this is a quick lookup chapter on resources that are available through IBM, it made sense to include at least a brief note on the Lotus options:

ESuite. This product was the first fully implemented Java applet-based suite of office tools. Based on the Lotus Smart Suite style functionality, in 1998 Lotus moved aggressively into position as a supplier of general office software capable of running on thin clients. Performance has been an ongoing problem, probably due to the applet architecture, and market reaction has been tepid at best. The eSuite product is based on the concept that 80 percent of users only need 20 percent of the features. To keep the footprint as small as possible, eSuite does not provide the high end features of an MS-Office or Smart Suite. However, if you need office applications that run in a true Java thin-client environment, you might want to check this out.

Domino. Domino is a modular server platform that delivers messaging and Web application functionality with the scalability, availability, and reliability demanded from large enterprise customers.

Domino Mail Server R4.6. Internet messaging. Web access, calendaring and scheduling, collaborative workspaces, newsgroups, and discussions.

Domino Application Server R4.6. Integrated Web-based messaging and application server.

Domino Enterprise Server R4.6. Builds on the functionality of Domino Mail and Domino Application Servers with high availability services.

Tool Features and Integration

From the product profiles you can see that every major facet of application development has been addressed. VisualAge for Java competes with products like Jbuilder from Borland or PowerJ from Sybase. But Visual-Age for Java offers higher levels of integration for component services like SanFrancisco.

SanFrancisco provide the most comprehensive set of Java objects for business available from any body. There are, of course, competing frameworks for development, but these are typically based on C/C++ or a 4GL. IBM has given independent software developers a head start by providing objects which may represent as much as 60 to 80 percent of the finished application logic.

At the same time, SanFrancisco services are supported by a WebSphere foundation and utilities layer. While earlier versions of the product had their own server and services strategy, as IBM released a more integrated set of tools, this was converted to WebSphere Application Server in 1998. WebSphere of course supports much more than SanFrancisco objects. WebSphere is really the core server around which all the other Java servers revolve.

Since e-business means Web-based business, IBM put the development tools necessary for large project Web site creation into WebSphere Studio. This includes NetObjects Fusion and Build-IT, which would be comparable to Microsoft's FrontPage with extensions. In all of the development tools, IBM has been careful to support integrated source code control and check-in/check-out-type programming team management tools. Many of the other Web development environments available are built with a single developer in mind and have a loose integration with a lightweight source control system.

All of the development tools are designed to allow you to more easily create Enterprise JavaBeans, and in many cases wizards are provided to help you migrate existing objects to that programming model. These are the tools that back up the strategy of a Common Programming Model.

Server Side Support

With the variety of products listed, you should be able to see how the components can be integrated to create an across-the-board solution consisting of messaging, database services, data translation, and Web and e-commerce services. IBM is focusing on providing servers that drive e-business, recognizing that the thin client model is much easier to roll out to the world at large, given the massive telecommunications infrastructure upgrades required in some parts of the world to get sufficient bandwidth. If "thin is in," then servers are where it's at, and the range of servers and services offered in the previous list should allow any solution designer to find a way to get the job done. Figure 2.2 shows how IBM has assembled the four major servers into an application framework. As discussed in Chapter 19, IBM is moving MQSeries under

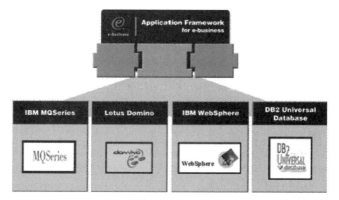

Figure 2.2 IBM's view of how servers integrate at the highest level.

WebSphere Enterprise and combining it with other server integration technologies such as TX Series and Component Broker.

We believe the ability to link Enterprise JavaBeans to legacy applications through products like Component Broker will be the key to incremental migration of those applications to newer technology over time. There is a tremendous amount of data and logic in legacy applications, representing significant financial investment by organizations everywhere. While the potential inherent in an object-oriented framework like SanFrancisco and Enterprise JavaBeans is highly attractive, the dilemma has always been what to do about the existing stuff. For the first time it is now possible to have all information technology assets accessible in a coherent architecture that allows fast adaptation and evolution as future requirements emerge and change.

Big Blue Java Programming Model

One of the things that should be clear at this point is IBM's commitment to Java as the underlying language for development of systems from this point forward. That being said, there is no piecemeal approach being taken to adoption of this language as a standard.

Instead of pursuing the Microsoft approach of flooding the market with CDs that encourage "basic" programmers to start coding first, IBM has put together a comprehensive and cohesive model for developing Web-based applications.

If it sounds like I prefer the IBM approach; well—guilty as charged. In my organization we frequently run into disgruntled customers who are disillusioned by the computer industry in general and software people in particular. It is very regrettable that one consequence of being involved in such a rapidly changing business is a resulting lack of discipline and structure. I firmly believe that what IBM is offering is exactly where business computing needs to go. On a less preachy note, it is also exactly where my business needs to go, and I see tremendous value in the combination of tools, techniques, and services that Big Blue is offering.

In short, IBM has created a framework for developing solutions that incorporates these new technologies. That framework consists of more than software tools and hardware on which to run them. It also codifies an approach, and relies on modeling and diagramming tools as well as adhering to standards. The solution is a greater whole than the sum of its parts.

Well, that's nice. It's been tried before with SAA (Systems Application Architecture) and even the client/server development tools like Power-Builder and SQL Windows took their shot.

What Makes Java So Different?

It's the Web. The combination of a truly universal front-end GUI environment (the browser), a global naming service (URL), and distributed communications (the Internet) have resulted in an infrastructure that provides dramatically new capabilities. At the same time, evolution and acceptance of object-oriented software development techniques promises to radically change the way software is written. Java pulls it all together with the published open standards for the way distributed enterprise computing can be accomplished through EJB.

These things are indeed different. The drivers for change have never been more powerful. The opportunities presented have never been more attractive. And the challenges we face as software developers has never been greater.

Leading into this chapter on frameworks, I wanted simply to stress that, to use Bob Dylan's wording, "the times, they are a-changin'." As you get more exposure to frameworks-based development you may sense, as I did, that there is a light coating of the theoretical around these new techniques. They are computer science-ish. For those of us who have taken the phone calls and meetings of impatient executives and had to soothe irate users, it might be tempting to dismiss these theories as impractical.

We found that people who are successful in adopting these new technologies use frameworks for developing systems. There is simply too much complexity in the new environment to "hack and slash" one's way to a new system. At the end of the day, to provide value to your customers, your system has to perform a useful function; it must do it efficiently; and it cannot be difficult to maintain or change. As well we know from legacy or heritage systems, this is easier asked than answered.

The Lego Approach

Perhaps it is no accident that the people inventing new development techniques today are from the generation that grew up playing with Lego and Mechano sets. The idea that complex objects could be created from interchangable components is one that many of us were first exposed to as children. Modularity was probably too esoteric a word for most of us to use back then, but the concept is dead-on, and it applies equally well (if not better) to building software.

Several years ago, n-tier client/server architecture was all the rage. The n was to indicate that there could be two, three, or more discrete elements in the system. Three-tier was for the adventurous who wanted to not only segregate their business logic, but run it on a completely different server than that managing the presentation of the user interface or the database server being used by the application.

With the introduction of the Web, n-tier computing got a new face but with the introduction of Enterprise JavaBeans, the architecture really went exponential.

Classic Model-View-Controller Development Approach

Each of the tools and approaches you can take to developing Big Blue Java applications maps well to the established Model-View-Controller (MVC) definition of systems behavior. Originally developed as part of the object-oriented development techniques used by Small Talk, the MVC model has been incorporated deeply into the way IBM sees programming will be done using Java and their tools.

A definition of the Model-View-Controller approach follows:

Model. Contains all data to be manipulated and handles the computations on that data.

View. Presents the data to the user.

Controller. Interacts with the user and notifies the model and view as appropriate.

A graphical depiction of this process is shown in Figure 2.3.

One way to think of the model is to consider that all variables and procedures, essentially the data and the methods of an object, belong to the model. The view is the GUI or screen that is used to display the data, while the controller does what its name implies: It translates user requests for action into specific behaviors in the GUI or model. A right-mouse-click on a screen element, for example, is handled by the controller and a menu might be presented to the user. That menu item might be to perform a summary on a selected set of data. The controller translates the request to the model, which in turn performs the work and pre-

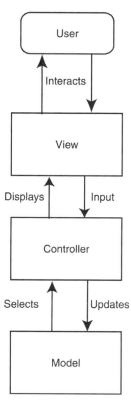

Figure 2.3 Model-View-Controller and how they interact.

sents the result (or status) back to the controller for subsequent presentation to the view.

Once again, the theme is separation of concern. Using the Model-View-Controller design approach, it is much easier to segregate the assignment of work to different people and tools.

The problem domain, consisting of the logic and the data, belong to the model. The controller addresses the user interaction between the model and the view. The view is more concerned with the aesthetics of the application and the logical grouping of data and options for presentation to a user.

In short, the model is *what the application does;* the controller is *how the application does it;* and the view is *what the application looks like* while it is doing it.

Working with the Model-View-Controller Paradigm

As we discuss in the chapter on Team Java, several distinct skills are required to appropriately address the unique requirements of each aspect. The complexity of multitier applications, even without introducing legacy systems integration, is a formidable challenge.

By breaking up each of the disciplines required to address the development of an entire application, a more manageable approach can be undertaken. For something as simple as a comic book tracking application, it may not be necessary to assign multiple people to the various aspects of development. You see this frequently with PC application developers who want to tackle all aspects of the delivery from top to bottom.

Unfortunately, very few people are well-rounded enough to excel at each aspect of software development. The rigor and discipline needed to design and write logical code is not consistent with an appreciation for the look of the application, including colors and sizing of screen elements. Expecting both taste and insight as attributes of a single developer is asking a great deal. Not to mention that as well as understanding what the application does, the controller requires that it be organized in a way consistent with the user of the application. Generally the best person to define this is someone who has experience working in the problem domain area.

The good news is that by breaking the application design and development into these three parts, it is much easier to handle the development of larger applications, with multiple technical resources assigned to each area.

One such area that is vital to IBM's business strategy is to provide tools that support the development of e-commerce applications.

The E-business Framework

As part of the push to e-business, IBM is providing more than just software and hardware tools. Big Blue recognizes that IT solutions developers are going to be facing more than just a new set of tools, that we were facing a whole new way of building systems. To help the adoption process, IBM has defined a set of techniques, called frameworks, for using these tools.

The major building blocks of Web applications using the IBM e-business frameworks include:

- Web Clients
- Infrastructure Services
- Web application Servers
- External Services

Taken together, these four components allow designers and developers of Web-based applications to create truly enterprise-wide systems. When combined with the object-oriented analysis and development approach, a completely new way to design, develop, and deploy applications comes to light.

Web Clients

As discussed in the previous chapter, Java runs on toasters, cellular phones, personal digital assistance, car phones, and cars. The concept of a client is not just a PC running MS-Windows (although it can be). Think Dick Tracy and you will be closer to the mark.

The enabling technologies of these clients include Java, but they also rely on the presentation languages made up of all flavors of html, dhtml, xml, and http. Additionally the communications and mail protocols are core client components including; TCP/IP, smtp, IIOP, and X.509.

As soon as you starting thinking about running applications on your watch, it becomes apparent that downloading large Java applets, or requiring local storage and execution of the software, is just not feasible. As part of the scalability of Big Blue Java, we need to remember that scale also means down, as well as handling the big jobs. To support this smaller scale, the development framework insists on server side handling of most, if not all, of the processing of business logic. From this we get "thin client" rather than "dumb terminal."

The role of the client is to present information to the user and to elicit input that is then passed back to a server for subsequent processing.

There are, then, two distinct flavors of thin client computing.

HTML Clients

Okay, so I went on record saying you would always use HTML and not applets. If we have learned anything from working with technology it should be to *never* say never and *always* say "it depends"!

HTML clients are the lightest-weight client model to which you can develop. You can be sure that whatever client connects to your application, the results will be displayed, whether red, or green, or black and white. For fastest execution over a potentially slow link to the server, we strictly stick to HTML on the client, and the work is done in Java Server Pages or servlets.

Applet Clients

Applet clients make more sense for applications where you know you have available bandwidth, such as an Extranet, linking corporations over T1 lines, or an Intranet for a cross-departmental application. The key advantage to using applets is the ability to provide screen controls. HTML applications do not behave in the way now familiar to many users of MS-Windows. Also, programmers who think two-tier client/server can more easily adapt to the idea of using Java to work as just another language, running on a client connecting to just another server, even if it is a Web-based application server.

As a rule of thumb, when contemplating the applet approach, ask yourself if the problem you are considering would support an X-Windows terminal. The download and boot time required to run an X-term is analogous to downloading and executing applet code. If you have no experience with X-terminals, you may want to count yourself lucky. However, as part of the framework approach, try to do it in HTML first, and resort to applets only to accomplish something vital.

Infrastructure Services

Any application will have some requirement to incorporate security and authorization for different uses. It is also usually important to have some means of accessing resources outside the application. If this includes access to file systems or users, directory management services are needed. In the IBM programming model, these functions are handled as part of Infrastructure services.

If only it was as easy as looking up a user profile and determining their local directory!

Enterprise systems have grown into complex jungles of interconnections. Databases alone contain enough idiosyncratic behavior to require months of training and years of experience to understand how to work with them well. Network services, whether across a wide or local area, down to the level of something as prosaic as identifying printers, is a discipline in its own right.

Web Application Servers

With WebSphere, IBM has pulled together various other servers such as Component Broker, TX Server, and Apache (relabeled IBM HTTP server). Like any application server, these Web application servers take user requests, parse them for logic, and then pass them on to the appropriate server for subsequent processing.

The key distinction with a Web application server is the requirement to format results and hand them back to a client in the form of a Web page. There are many ways to accomplish this, including Java Server Pages, and applets and servlets; however, the Web application server is required to manage the process beyond the simplistic serving of static pages.

External Services

At the end of the twentieth century, integrating with existing computing infrastructure had become a highly complex, generally unplanned, time-consuming nightmare for anyone trying to write new applications.

As part of the IBM programming model, the requirements for managing integration with existing and external services has been isolated to a set of services to support application integration. It is not reasonable to expect developers working with new tools to maintain a down-and-in competence with various heritage architectures, let alone syntax. By isolating existing and external systems into connectors, new systems can take advantage of these services.

These connectors provide access to Web application servers through protocols specific to the desired service. Application messaging services ensure that e-mails and other notifications are passed to the appropriate servers with guaranteed delivery. Workflow services are extensions to messaging that includes translation and brokering of messages across multiple systems. Component integration supports the wrapping of an existing application with the features and services of a Java-based object. This allows developers to use the same method of component interaction, even with legacy applications that do not natively support those methods.

The separation of integration of external services from application developers is a key concept underlying the new development model. The architecture for doing this is Enterprise JavaBeans, and the IBM products are WebSphere Enterprise and MQ Series. The last section of this book provides more detail on these services and functions. For the time being, let's continue identifying the overall lay of the land.

Applying the Model-View-Controller Approach to E-business Tools

Within an application, the model-view-controller approach is quite easy to grasp. The model is the application logic; the view represents the screens with which the user interacts; and the controller manages the events as directed by the user and passes parameters and results to and from the model.

It's important to understand that the model can be scaled to the highest levels of enterprise systems integration. The objects that contain the data and methods represented by the notion of model may actually be legacy applications that are accessed by new Java-based systems integration techniques.

That in no way changes the way it would look to an application developer responsible for developing a new user interface. By segregating out the need to manage users to one group and logic to another, the application development team can focus on the nuts and bolts. In turn, the user interface folks need not be burdened with how the application works; they only need to focus on what it does.

Object orientation and enterprise systems integration is tricky, complicated stuff. At the same time, IT is under tremendous pressure to quickly develop relevant, user-friendly applications. The frameworks make it possible to meet these two seemingly contradictory requirements. These frameworks represent a unification of many different tools and techniques.

One way to refer to the changes addressed by these new tools is EAI— *enterprise application integration*. The Model-View-Controller paradigm allows us to evaluate several means of interconnecting applications, whether they are small-scale departmental applications, or if tying applications together across a large organization.

EAI Drivers

There are several key reasons why organizations are looking at EAI. These include:

- Expanding relationships with suppliers and customers
- Integrate disparate technologies to achieve best-of-breed
- Move past restrictions of traditional systems
- Deal with mergers and acquisitions
- Speed up the development cycle

These are the kinds of demands that commercial IT organizations are facing from their own customers—the operational and corporate managers who expect IT to support them, not the other way around.

There are several advantages to placing a great degree of emphasis on integration of existing pieces instead of replacing everything. Advantages include:

- Make development budget go further
- Extend the period of return for existing systems investments
- Develop capability to integrate with foreign systems of customers and suppliers

The push to integrate applications is one with which many non-IT executives have little patience. The explanations of the difficulties are dismissed with a curt "That's why we pay you people the big bucks," or (worse) a suggestion that it could all be implemented in two days with Microsoft Excel.

Approaches to EAI

There are four distinct methods that can be used to integrate applications. These include:

- Data level EAI
- Application interface level EAI
- Method level EAI
- User interface level EAI

These approaches are currently used to varying degrees in every organization today. Database integration, whether based on two-phase commit, or simply synchronizing the contents of one server's database from another, is a commonly used way to get information from system *a* to system *b*.

Application interfaces can range from custom programs that call single or multiple APIs to handling the interface through a messaging server like IBM's MQ Series. We look at how application interface EAI can be accomplished as part of the review of WebSphere Server Enterprise and some of its companion products.

User interface integration is frequently the updating of an old application with a new look, so-called *screen scraping*. Users may prefer these results, but this is not generally considered a very elegant way technically to integrate applications.

At the other end of the sophistication spectrum is method level EAI. This is where application logic is exposed in a manner that lets objects outside that logic take advantage of it. In our view, method integration involves distributed objects and component brokers to coordinate access and transactions across the enterprise.

This kind of sophisticated architecture requires a framework that is shared across all applications. Fortunately for us, IBM has adopted just such a framework in EJB and extended it with SanFrancisco.

Object-oriented Integration

It should be pretty clear to all of us that the proprietary systems of the past have led us to the silos of systems that have definite boundaries and borders. The net effect of these silos (as you have no doubt experienced firsthand) is the chafing restriction of moving organizational data from one to the other.

Even solving the data problem with meta-data servers and data transformation servers doesn't begin to address one of the key problems uncovered by work done to make systems Y2K-compliant. That is the value of the business logic that is maintained in legacy systems.

In many cases, the people who worked through the original logic and business rules for these systems are no longer employed with the organization. The only residual value the company has is in the form of program logic, which is not easily changed or even maintained.

Somewhat ironically, to my way of thinking, all of the emphasis on change and responsiveness to new opportunities is still representative of only a small percentage of the organization's business. Much of the operations and administration of any organization actually survives from one decade to the next. If it didn't, it would undoubtedly be easier to get executives to scrap one set of systems and replace them with another.

In this, we need to be able to expose legacy system interfaces to other (newer) applications within several key constraints and while accomplishing specific objectives. These include:

- Do not break the legacy application.
- Ensure transaction integrity (rollbacks across multiservers).
- Performance counts.
- Abstract infrastructure complexity from developers.
- Move toward a consistent programming approach (framework).

Depending on the time and money budgeted to accomplish this Herculean task, it could be done, albeit not quickly or easily. The specific goals, abstracting complexity and a consistent framework, are definitely outcomes usually associated with an object-oriented approach to software development.

In this case we are taking an object-oriented approach to systems integration.

Can't Build Everything from Scratch

Frequently I see recommendations from technical people that maintain that the entire suite of legacy applications needs to be rebuilt from the ground up. There are many arguments for this, virtually all of them technical in nature, such as better performance, easier maintenance, elegance of design, and so on. These arguments are very difficult to make to a chief executive or finance officer, however, when they do not share the mindset of "technology for the sake of technology." They are looking for working solutions to real-world problems.

No doubt there will be a move to replace systems entirely within organizations over time. I expect this will be a lot like the way the human body replaces itself—one cell at a time. In the same way that replaced cells must conform to a DNA blueprint in order to be successful, new systems need to adopt the architectural constants that will allow them to work together in an integrated fashion.

Java Is the Key to the Architecture

Across all of the aspects of multidisciplinary application development, Java has been chosen by IBM to be the key unifying language for not only new applications, but for applications that integrate with existing data stores.

Every resource, whether data or logic, is covered by a product suite or technology that fundamentally supports access by a Java programmer. As we have already seen, the objective is to unify the organization without requiring migration to a single standard application platform. To give that approach a name; Windows NT.

Of course, it is unrealistic to think that organizations are willing to throw out investments in existing systems. At the same time, the advantages of a lingua franca across the board are readily apparent. Visual Basic for Applications works for unifying a small organization with Microsoft products. This facility is available for all other platforms in a more robust, open and scalable version—it's called Java.

There is no question in my mind that IBM has made an astonishing change in the organizational culture from even that of the early 1980s. To provide ongoing support of traditional products while incorporating a means to gain productivity and efficiencies is a masterstroke of meeting many needs with one strategy.

At the technical level, Java provides a consistent means of writing cross-platform applications. By taking advantage of the object orientation underlying Java, IBM has been able to package that language into a set of services that make it easier for traditional programmers to make the leap to Java. These are called *application frameworks*.

Application Frameworks

The separation of concerns is fundamentally no different than the division of labor that radically changed the productivity of the manufacturing sector at the turn of the twentieth century. The difference is that instead of dealing with physical things, an information system addresses representations of physical things.

"The map is not the territory," said Alfred Korzybski, and while manufacturers were revolutionizing the way things were made in the early 1900s, artists created paintings of smoking appliances entitled "Ce n'est pas une pipe," and thinkers wrote essays on abstraction. You might be asking yourself, "What does this have to do with software development?" In fact, these underlying notions are at the heart of the changes in the way we can develop software solutions using new products and techniques.

With these new approaches, however, comes some of the difficulty inherent in giving up the old. I believe it is vital for anyone advocating the move to new software development models to acknowledge that traditional programming is neither dead nor mortally wounded. There is a place for it in the same way that there has always been a place for writing assembler programs. (Interestingly, you can see the revival in what is essentially assembly programming for the WorkPad and Palm Pilot PDAs). The percentage of development work may shift dramatically, but it will not eliminate, or render obsolete, the skills that many have worked hard and long to acquire.

The point is that what we see now is a new way to do computing, and it is not the be-all and end-all replacement of software technology, methodologies, and practice. There is a role to play for the traditional, and what was the challenger ten short years ago is now lumped into that category. Relational database applications are considered legacy. Two-tier client/server applications are consider traditional. Adabas/Natural applications are also heritage or legacy systems.

Not only has IBM adopted an approach to technology that deals with legacy code, but also legacy *coders*.

I can't stress enough that my intention here is not to irritate or annoy anyone, nor in any way undervalue the contributions to software development made by those of us who have worked with lower-level languages and traditional approaches. These new approaches to developing software are not so evolved that they are without risk or flaw. It will take time before it is clearly evident that some approaches consistently yield the best results.

My point is simply that we are moving in this direction, and that as professional systems people, we must look for the good we can take out of these new tools and techniques.

That being said, we are living in an object world or we will be soon.

The IBM frameworks have been laid out at many levels: systems level, e-business frameworks, applications, and integration frameworks. There is a great deal of literature and talk on the subject. Yet, when I first encountered the material I found that there was no clear statement of exactly what a framework was. Leveraging one, yes; building one, certainly. But an accessible definition was not so easy to find.

At WNS, we have a small development team that frequently pulls in younger and less experienced developers. Our folks are characterized primarily by an eagerness and willingness to learn, as well as a lack of preconceived notions often called *baggage*. I personally prefer to think of it as experience. At the same time, it is necessary to actually explain these tools, directions, and strategies in a way that will enable these more junior people to quickly incorporate them into their daily work.

To that end, we were talking about frameworks, and I explained this concept as an analogy. It seems to fit pretty well and has been validated as essentially correct by object folks who know far more than I do about such matters. So in the interest of clear communication, I will use this analogy to define how we at WNS think of frameworks.

The Mass Transit Analogy

A software framework is very much like a public transportation facility. One of the first flags of independence a young person in the city experiences is his or her first solo bus trip. You get on the bus at one stop; you ride the bus for a while; and when you get close to your stop you ring the bell and then get off.

You don't need to know how to drive a bus.

You don't need to know the rules of the road.

You don't need to know how much fuel the bus has left.

You don't need to know where the bus goes next.

You don't need to know anything at all about the service, the infrastructure, the interconnection of routes, the rotation of tires, or any of the other myriad things that someone must look after to make it possible for you to take the bus.

The bus arrives and leaves at a particular time. You go to the stop and wait for the bus. Your job is to know where you are and where you want to go. This is the same as understanding the business logic of an application to be written.

The bus system is running all the time. So is the framework. The services exist, and in some cases they might be actively listening for you. (Taxi!)

You are a unique passenger. An object is a unique combination of data and methods. Polymorphism is the way many different objects can take advantage of the same set of services. The bus will pick you up no matter where you work, no matter what you wear, and no matter what the color of your hair.

Services can interact. You can take a bus, the subway, a trolley, or the El. You can take one of these to the airport, and then catch a plane with a different group of passengers. In a similar manner an object can tour around the infrastructure, changing domains to get to where it needs to be, based on its unique set of requirements.

In every example, the services exist independently of the object. The object might initiate contact and take advantage of a planned route, but the route is already mapped out, and the bus is moving along its predesignated route.

The Advantages

It is easier to take the bus than to drive the bus. And it is much easier to drive the bus than to organize a mass transit system. By aligning the "job of work" to be done with a particular individual's skill set and interest, project managers can be sure that appropriate progress will be made. Leveraging the domain expertise of a developer who knows the business of writing business logic without concern for either infrastructure calls or control-of-flow translates into a tremendous potential productivity gain.

Additionally, it is much easier for a developer with a long-term grounding in traditional programming to focus on development work within a single part of the framework than it is to overhaul and update his or her complete understanding of hardware, software, operating systems, protocols, programming syntax, and GUI conventions—not to mention performance tuning and systems integration.

The e-business application framework provides for a logical breakout of technologies and techniques to be used by various members of a development team. The development tools provided by IBM are designed to work with and fully support this approach to application development. The framework itself is a head start on developing applications.

Using application frameworks such as SanFrancisco is even more of a head start than the e-business framework, since it contains completed code that fully handles a particular set of business functions. This is covered in detail in the section on SanFrancisco, but it is worth noting here that IBM supports the framework approach itself on many levels.

The Disadvantages

To move to an object-oriented development approach is a radical shift away from traditional client/server programming, let alone developing character-based host/slave applications. This means there is a learning curve as steep as any other a developer will likely encounter in his or her career.

The reliance on the framework to do the job implies that the framework is well developed, stable, and efficient. Many of the tools and techniques that we use to create Big Blue Java applications are far from completely developed. There is ample room for improvement, and in the same way that some folks would rather walk to work than use an inefficient mass transit system, there may be those who would prefer to create an entire application from scratch than use the framework in its current form.

The Value Proposition for Frameworks

Like everything else in the systems business, the choice of when to use the framework and when to write from scratch will depend on the nature of the challenge you face. At WNS, we decided to do the first iteration of a self-contained application using the e-business framework, and then to move to using an application framework like SanFrancisco.

The key to our way of thinking when using an application development framework is the gap analysis between what the framework offers and what the business requires. With a good understanding of these two elements, we can readily identify what percentage of the application must be customized.

If the nature of the problem to be solved is not well-defined, or if the understanding of the capabilities of the framework is thin, the map will be incomplete, and productivity gains will give way to frustration and disappointment.

Frameworks provide a great deal of groundwork on which to build, but they also represent overhead. The tradeoff is future maintainability versus design discipline now. Where a large team will be working on a complex problem, the framework approach can be a savior. For small applications, the resulting overhead can blow your budget for time and money right out of the water.

So, like so many other things, it depends on the specific situation.

IBM Application Frameworks

There are several application frameworks to work with that have been supplied as part of SanFrancisco. These are defined in more detail in the chapter on SanFrancisco application components for business, but it is useful, as part of our exploration into the definition and role of frameworks, to describe the options at a high level here.

SanFrancisco contains the common business objects needed for designing almost any application. These include:

- Company
- Business partner
- Etc. (We have a section on SanFrancisco that details these.)

The specific frameworks that provide application functionality, or the model side support in keeping with MVC terminology, are referred to as the *SanFrancisco Towers*. These Towers include:

- General Ledger
- Accounts Payable
- Accounts Receivable
- Order Management
- Warehouse Management

As described earlier in the general definition of a framework, the intention is to deliver a fully functioning set of already constructed and tested Java objects that can be used by developers to create customized applications.

Yes, developer productivity was one goal of introducing the framework—but the vision for SanFrancisco is considerably greater than that. The design objective from the outset was to provide a set of common objects so that independent software vendors and customers' organizations could use the same objects across multiple applications, developed in isolation of each other.

That, in a nutshell, is the potential power of a framework. IBM has announced that beginning in the year 2000, support for Enterprise Java-Beans will be included in all of their Web servers, and the SanFrancisco frameworks are being re-implemented for version 2.0 as Enterprise Java-Beans.

Summary

IBM has gotten its Java act together and offers a range of servers and tools to help you build an e-business. From the most straightforward Web site development, to more challenging integration of databases and e-store shopping services, all the way up to the highest-scale customer self-service applications, IBM has products that have been made to work in the field.

The strategy for multiplatform support and a common programming model as well as a write-once, deploy-anywhere orientation are manifested in the tools. Just as important as the features of each tool is their ability to work together, leveraging the skills learned and functionality offered by an environment like VisualAge for Java across many different types of projects.

In each case, the emphasis is on providing tools to developers who can go out and create real world e-business applications that can grow to whatever size their success takes them. Whether you are an architect, a designer, or a plain old-fashioned programmer, there is a Big Blue tool for you to use in creating your next Java or Web-enabled application.

IBM has done significantly more than assembled a product suite or tool set and brought it to market. Recognizing the incredible learning curve for these technologies, IBM has facilitated the background materials, the training programs and examples needed to show what the technology can do. This is pretty much what the market expects and requires from a vendor that wants people to use its tools.

The architecture, frameworks, and components provide a much greater head start on making this new technology useful immediately. Rather than take a slow-paced evolutionary approach to moving to e-business and Java, IBM has created a whole new way to leverage legacy systems.

The potential returns to any organization using the combination of methodology and tools, while keeping existing investments in technology where appropriate, is highly attractive to management and IT organizations alike.

CHAPTER 3

Team: Java

G iven the complexity of the tool set and the scope of the technical unfamiliarity that the great majority of software developers face with Big Blue Java tools, a team of people is required to create a working application.

We have pointed out that the new design paradigm has four views—design, deployment, process, and logic. These four are crossed by use cases in an object-oriented methodology. Unfortunately, for business applications this is not sufficient. Building Big Blue Java applications is an inherently complex proposition.

We found as we began grappling with the technology that it was not going to be possible for any one person to understand the entire application in its entirety and depth. The challenge became one of mapping individual team members with their skill sets to roles, then in turn determining which tools to assign to the roles. Just as important was our discovery that the tools provide overlapping functionality. It is possible to build user interface screens in VisualAge for Java as well as in WebSphere Studio.

To alleviate some of the confusion, we had to find a way to specify exactly to what use a particular tool would be put, the input that each role had a right to expect would be provided to them before they started work, and the resulting output from their efforts.

Understanding the Problem

Throughout the short history of software development there have been people who intuitively knew how to use information technology to create a system that worked. They promoted methodologies, modeling techniques, and tools. The problem has been, and I believe continues to be, that these approaches are not directly transferable to other individuals not possessing the same levels of skill and experience.

These techniques are not interoperable among different people and teams.

A superior analyst can quickly and completely document an understanding of an organization from interviews. This understanding can take the form of a business process map, a data model, UML model, or text-based narrative. The point is that this one individual can accomplish the goal.

The purpose of the models and diagrams is to communicate that understanding to the other people involved in designing and developing the application. On one level this is simply common sense. But take it as the objective of the modeling process. Your models are good if they communicate a full and complete understanding of the problem *and* the solution.

This is where my own difficulties with object-oriented (OO) design emerge.

In theory, traditional approaches modeled the solution with a bias toward the *computer* and what it wanted—predictability, consistency, and hierarchy. The object-oriented approach, however, emphasizes modeling of the solution with a bias toward the *environment* in which the system operates. Most user environments want the opposite of what a computer needs: They want flexibility, customizability, and options.

Most OO training scenarios involve a real-world problem, like the classic bank machine example. In other words, a real-time system, or another electromechanical real-time system. E-business, however, is about data-based systems. Which is a different animal than real-time applications.

This is not to say that we should not incorporate OO analysis and design techniques into our development process when using Big Blue Java tools. Taking a position of that nature would likely lead to big problems for me, especially with the SanFrancisco crowd in Rochester!

The key point underlying the way we, at WNS, constitute projects and assign responsibilities is that we are dealing fundamentally with business data. That data is almost certainly maintained in a legacy data store. There is no way we can assume that we will be given control or ownership of that data so that we can tightly bind methods to it. In short, we have to deal with objects that ultimately will not behave like objects.

There are several general steps that we follow in order to arrive at a set of requirements, produce a systems specification for meeting the requirements, design an appropriate application from the spec, develop and then test it, and finally deploy a systems solution. If this sounds like the familiar old waterfall approach to developing software, don't worry. It isn't.

Of course, it is possible to warp any technology to function the same way the earlier obsolete technology did. People have written Java classes that manage memory the way that you do with the C language, for example. The intent here is not to warp or defeat OO analysis and design techniques as part of the way we develop applications using Big Blue Java. The objective is to fold OO thinking into the collection of tools and techniques that we already have and use, to ensure we get the full picture of what needs to be done, as well as recommending a general approach to developing software that can be used by others.

Business Process Map

First, we must understand the business in which the system will operate. This first-level understanding is reflected in a business process map. Ideally, the map will include a definition of the events and resources that are used by each unit and role within the scope of the system. The key deliverable here is to identify all of the discrete units, groups, and users, and to understand the flow of activity from one to another. These represent the tasks to be automated or supported with automation.

An example of a high-level scope and context diagram is shown in Figure 3.1.

Business systems always have existing data. They generate or take in, process and pass on information as part of their value. Occasionally, one finds a process that lends no value to the organization, but for our pur-

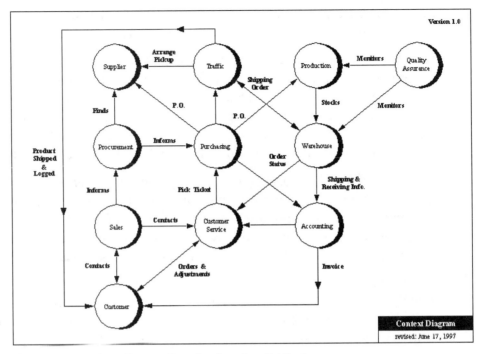

Figure 3.1 Context diagram for a food service distributor.

poses we will assume that the analyst or corporate management has eliminated these long before we have to develop systems to support them.

After defining the scope of the business processes and the context of the system to be automated, it makes sense to model the data that is used by the business already. The data modeling discipline for this is called *entity relationship diagramming*. And there is no reason to throw it out the window simply because we have Rational Rose and UML on board. In fact, as we progress through our Team Java examples, you should be able to see that it makes life easier to model objects once the business process map and logical data models are complete and validated.

In the case of Deal Manager, the first Big Blue Java software product from WNS, a fundamental design feature of the application is that the data is pulled from various legacy systems into a shared relational database. Usually this is DB2, but we can support SQL Server and Oracle when necessary.

It's in the Data

As part of the application development efforts, we had to break down the data to be retrieved from various existing sources and normalize it. This is a highly useful exercise for validating the completeness of the logical data model, among other things.

The high-level entity relationship diagram (ERD) for Deal Manager is shown in Figure 3.2.

The key relationships and constraints for ensuring data integrity are also defined at this point. An e-business application without data integrity is not long for this world.

However, it was never our intention to turn our Big Blue Java development team into a bunch of SQL programmers. In fact, with all the other pieces of technology to come up to speed with, putting the business logic in SQL-based stored procedures seemed to be a low-value proposition (at least for the other members of the team).

Isolate the Database

To get past that, we decided to abstract the database into highly accessible, discrete views of the data and to publish those definitions as part of

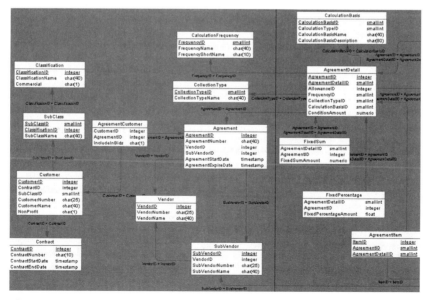

Figure 3.2 Entity relationship diagram.

the project. The data dictionary we published for the team included the view definitions to allow the creation of the other application components to provide the business logic, screen handling, and functionality that the application required.

The purpose of each view is to provide a table consisting of all the columns needed for a particular screen or application function. This could, of course, be written by the developer as a SQL Select statement, or the SQL wizard could be used when creating a bean. However, we wanted to be sure that we were getting the right data, and by using views we could drop and re-create the underlying table object if needed without stepping on the application code.

The select beans written in data access builder in turn called the views. We ended up with dozens of views, in some cases as simple as v_vendorname, a view that provided a single result, the vendor name from a supplied vendor number. That idea was that the resulting single column could be bound to a single screen control, such as a text field.

A First Glimpse

The next step was to create a few sample screens that could be demonstrated to our customer advocate prior to showing the end user what the application would look like. Our customer advocate is the domain expert responsible for making sure the team is working on problems that the customer actually encounters. In our case, the domain expert had created some paper forms to demonstrate the basic functionality the application would have to incorporate.

While these paper forms did include places for things like drop-down lists and table results, we actually didn't feel bound to build the form exactly like the domain expert indicated. This is because the real value in the paper prototype was to get some idea of what menu flow of related screens the users would want. Not to mention an inventory of what data and functions needed to be expressed.

One of the developers had a real problem with our emphasis on the screens prior to the creation of the object model in Rational Rose. Rather than fight about it, we let the developer go ahead and create a first-draft object model in Rose. During the first walk through of the paper prototype with the domain expert, it became obvious that the Rose diagrams would have to be completely reworked, as there were several assumptions made about the business that were exposed as incorrect.

This is one key reason why WNS insists on having some of the more traditional GUI client/server analysis pieces done prior to developing the object model. An inventory of the data lets you know what resources you have to work with and a first-level set of screens lets you understand what the visible functions will be taken on that data.

Risks of This Approach

The use of data-aware controls to connect to a relational database has two very real implications. First, this is essentially a two-tier client/server system using Java, and it is not object-oriented. This means that we lose the advantages of encapsulation. In our approach, even though we are taking pains to limit the amount of knowledge a developer has to have about the implementation details, there is still a requirement to understand at least the interface and results of the data access or screen controls.

Second, this approach requires fundamentally more maintenance. Or at least it would if our strategy was to support rather than replace. Given the small scope of the number of installations we have of the product, we were confident that version two would be adopted by all existing customers and that it would be a fundamentally different object-oriented implementation of the application.

Proceeding with the New Tools

We decided to architect the application using JSPs to manage the presentation of the results and screens to the user through a Web browser. Since our JSPs were being created in WebSphere Studio, we also decided to take advantage of the database wizards for creating beans that called the data from the database and subsequently created a Java Server Page.

Our visual programmer was working at this time on creating data access beans that would connect to the database and could be tied to screens. The forms development functionality of VisualAge for Java is somewhat limited, so we delegated the creation of basic form elements to a graphic designer using NetObjects Fusion. The designer created a set of generic pages that are called into VisualAge for Java and used as the templates for developing application screens.

Roles, Responsibilities, and Tools

The team consisted of the following roles and used the tools shown in Table 3.1.

These are the essential areas of responsibility that we found had to be assigned and coordinated in order to build a working Big Blue Java application using WebSphere Studio, VisualAge for Java, WebSphere Application Server, and DB2.

Graphic Design

The objective of this project was to come up with an application for commercial resale. The number of target customers was small, and we were expecting to customize and enhance each one. We were not shooting for shrinkwrap.

A consistent, professional look and feel was a key ingredient to being able to sell this application. Unfortunately for us, in 1999 this translated into looking like a Microsoft Windows application.

The tools provided by IBM had some rock-solid integration, team control, and performance aspects. They also had the traditional weaknesses

Table 3.1 Team Roles and Tools

ROLE	RESPONSIBILITY	TOOLS
Database designer	Logical data model and objects	DB2, PowerDesigner
Graphics designer	Consistent look and feel through creation of windows, objects, and backgrounds	Net Objects Fusion, Photoshop, Fireworks, Dreamweaver
User interface specialist	Screen flow, menu hierarchy, right-mouse button support, help files	WebSphere Studio, Java Server pages, Homesite
Domain expert	Responsible for documenting and explaining user requirements	Word, PowerPoint, Visio
BuildMaster	Pull together all most recent versions of components and packages	VisualAge for Java, Team Connection, Visual Source Safe
Visual programmer	Pull application together in VisualAge for Java	Data access beans, Visual-Age for Java

around building cosmetically attractive applications that we had come to expect.

The graphic designer used Adobe Photoshop and other graphic tools to create discrete Windows elements that we wanted to include in our application.

Push buttons are a good example. In WebSphere Studio, you can drop a push button onto your HTML form and assign it properties, like *ifclicked* or *dblclick* to execute a particular Java Script. This is good.

What is not so good is that each button redefines its size on the basis of the amount of text on the button. The result is that a push button that says GO is smaller than one that says SUBMIT. To make each button the same size, it would have been necessary to find a consistent number of letters for each button and use synonyms for the text labels. BACK and NEXT make sense from that point of view, but we didn't care for OKAY as the submit button and DOIT just wasn't going to work.

For those of you who have little familiarity with GUI programming, please trust me. Different-sized buttons on the same screen scream *Amateur!* Also, don't use red unless you have a button for "Fire Nukes." These are mistakes that have already been made by countless Windows application programmers since Windows 3.0. It would be a shame if we had to repeat their experience as we moved to the creation of Web-enabled applications.

The main specifications provided by the graphic designer included:

1. **Size of work area.** We chose to develop for 800×600 screen resolution, because a number of our customers were working with older technology that did not support 1024×768. A screen that is defined for a higher resolution will make it necessary for scroll bars to be used to get from one side to the other on a system with lower resolution. This makes for a very frustrating user experience. We could have decided to be ultrapessimistic and design for 640×480, but this did not give us enough real estate on the screen.

2. **Screen templates.** Look-up screens, master detail screens, and multicolumn table screens were all laid out by the graphic designer prior to building the first set of screens. These did not include any of the controls necessary for handling the data; the templates simply specified the size of border and relative positioning.

3. **Screen widgets.** Tool bar icons for Print, Save, Cut and Paste, push buttons, image buttons, and Back and Next buttons were all predefined and supplied to the development team as .GIF files.

4. **Splash screen.** Naturally the application had to have a splash screen and logo. This was one of the first graphics developed, and we used it extensively at the beginning of the project for the team to get a sense of the product it was building.

5. **Buttons.** Examples of the buttons defined by our graphic designer are shown in Figure 3.3. These widgets are also provided on the attached CD for those of you who are beginning to work with Big Blue Java application development.

These buttons look identical to the ones used in standard Visual Basic development of Windows applications. As much as I would like to be able to say "Let's do it differently and better!" the user interface standards for more than 80 percent of the GUI-based applications in business today have already been determined. Stick with the basics if you want your application to be readily accepted by users who are used to PC-based applications.

Even those who work extensively with green screen applications have still been exposed to the ubiquitous MS san serif font. I strongly recommend picking one's battles, and personally I'd rather have the lower administration costs of a browser-based application than argue whether the application looks good. If it makes you feel any better, Microsoft lifted the whole notion of GUI interfaces from Apple, which had taken it from Xerox. Thank you, Doug Englebart!

Creating a Screen Form

After we defined our basic look and feel from a widgets and layout standpoint, we still didn't have a screen form.

Remember, this was one of the first steps in validating our tool set and our understanding of the problem domain. It was not the beginning of application development or coding. Still, understanding the division of

Figure 3.3 Sample buttons for HTML applications.

labor was a challenging first step, and we were much more comfortable with addressing visible objects rather than nonvisible ones first.

Our user interface specialist first laid out the menu flow and hierarchy in a menu flow diagram. This helped identify what screens were expected, as well as which ones were to be used in several places.

One of the first things we did was to look for screen-handling widgets that provided more functionality than the default ones shipped with VAJ and WSS. It turns out there are some nifty widgets available from IBM themselves at www.alphaworks.ibm.com. We logged onto the site and helped ourselves to some of the more advanced swing beans.

One of the first widgets we knew we needed was an equivalent to Jtable from the swing palette. Of course, we could have just used the Jtable control if we were developing an applet. But the objective of this application was to create as thin a client as possible, while still providing the full functionality that would be familiar to the user of a fat client application.

Laying Out the User Interface Space

It is vital to validate the logic contained in the model by asking "what will the users be doing with this application?" In my experience, the best way to pose those questions is to work through a set of screens and walk through them with a representative of the users.

Before putting anyone to work on the UI control functions, however, it is important that the guidelines be established in order to reduce wasted effort. In spite of the practice of disposal of the paper prototype or hand-drawn interface, the next level of implementation of the User Interface should actually contain some valid control characteristics. To ensure that our developer responsible for this wasn't taxed with too many aesthetic issues, we first provided a template illustrating how screens for this application would be laid out.

As you can see in Figure 3.4, the areas are defined and labeled. This allows anyone on the team to quickly refer to the area the controller will be connected to for any given operation.

Each member in an experienced team of developers will have some appreciation for the contribution of each of the other members of the team. There is no room for religiosity or obstinate dismissal of the role of any aspect of the development process. To trivialize pretty screens or to say "the data is irrelevant" gets people fired in my organization.

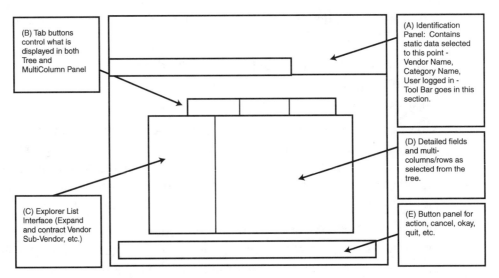

Figure 3.4 A definition of a selection screen.

This may seem like a strong position to take, but I am convinced that when applications must be developed by a team of people, each member of that team must be prepared to understand, accept, and support the contribution of the other members.

This is vastly different from the notion of software development as a black box. It is human nature to care more about the effect of one's actions on a known person than on a complete stranger. As we tried (and in some cases failed) to successfully develop solutions using these Big Blue Java technologies, I came to understand that first, no one person can successfully perform all of the necessary roles in the development effort, and second, the team has to have an identity of interest that embodies itself in the application being developed.

First Draft Online

In order to assist the user interface developer, who was made responsible for the development of the controller logic, the graphic designer provided the sample screen shown in Figure 3.5.

Please note that the screen developed here has absolutely no functionality. The cancel button does not cancel, and the filters do not work either. This is a representation of the view of the application.

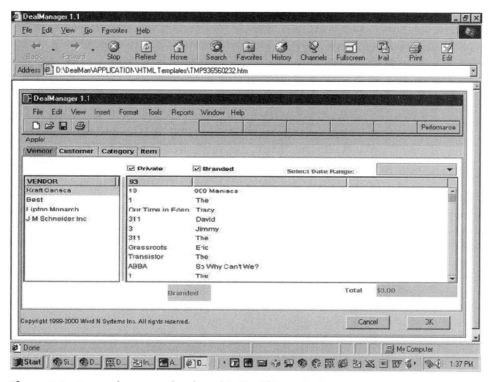

Figure 3.5 A sample screen developed in NetObjects Fusion.

The objective was to create a depiction of the areas that could be used regardless of the specific tabs, buttons, data displayed, and so on. From the work done in graphic design, it soon became a consideration that we would have preferred to develop in 1024 × 768 screen resolution. This was rejected after a review of the customer site showed that the majority of users were at 800 × 600.

For those of you working with similar constraints, you may be interested to know that the applet region is 750 pixels wide × 292 pixels high. If you accidentally create an object larger than that, your applet will get scroll bars inside the Web browser and require the user to use the mouse in order to get to the right or bottom of the screen.

Additionally, note that the D panel (isn't it handy to have worked out a quick way to refer to the screen areas!) contains 10 rows. In the event that a request returns more rows, a scroll bar is added by the control. This was allowed for by the graphic artist to ensure that the sizing of the D panel was sufficient to show the contents of the retrieved data.

Team Review

It is essential that the members of the team get together frequently to walk through the progress made by each contributor. The separation of concern should not be treated as an abdication of interest.

During a recent session that we held at WNS, the data analyst called into question our entire approach to the user experience through the menu flow. It turned out that what we had thought was a dozen or so fields that could be handled through an explorer like tree control was in actuality many thousands of records, which would overload the control. Even if the control could have handled that workload, it was obvious that we needed to narrow down the search parameters prior to displaying the result set.

The data analyst on our team had a tour of duty in a previous life as an interface builder, so we had the benefit of a GUI interface specialist correcting our misconceptions. The point I took away from the session was just how easy it is for assumptions to creep into the design phase, and the need for frequent validation or correction.

Team Use of VisualAge for Java

Once any given user of the shared repository (see the chapter on Visual-Age for Java) has registered a particular set of classes, they become available for other users of the repository.

To access the complete set of available resources, click on the palette and select Available. The lists of resources not currently included in your workspace are then presented.

We discovered a few very interesting things during our initial work with SanFrancisco and VisualAge for Java. First, if you neglect to include the source files, your environment will blow up when you try to work with it, meaning you have to go back and include the files later. This registration process, by the way, is not trivial, either in terms of elapsed time or network bandwidth utilization.

I suppose it was good news to the development group that after several false starts I got so frustrated with the lack of progress that I went out and acquired a 100-mbs hub and kicked everybody up a notch for network performance. Make no mistake, working with this technology will show every flaw or weakness that may exist in your network architecture!

Another thing we learned is that if you accidentally kick the power plug out of the wall (Bill said it was an accident!), when you restart your session your computer will take some time to resynchronize your workspace with the repository. When the SanFrancisco object registration process failed the first couple of times, we were appalled to realize that it was going to actually take an hour and a half to synch, even with 500 MBs of RAM and a fully functional 10/100 network bursting to top speed. **Tip:** Let it finish. Go for coffee. Start it at night if you have to, but let it do its thing. It will eventually work.

On the other hand, be very careful that no one has changed the administrator's password on the shared repository. Unfortunately, our team hit a bit of turbulence and we lost a few nonbelievers. This of course necessitated a change in the admin passwords. However, since a reboot of NT is necessary for a password change of this magnitude to take effect, a few days went by before it kicked in. I know, it's hard to believe that NT was up for several days running, but I guess that was the good news part!

Anyway, the system administrator had to do a restart in the middle of the day, and presto, three people lost six hours worth of work apiece, since a change in the password of the repository means that the workspaces are out of synch and get corrupted. Too bad, so sad—but we lived and learned.

Once we had finished with the perils of Pauline, we did indeed manage to get the various workspaces synchronized with the repository and the SanFrancisco classes loaded to boot.

New users configuring their workspace were presented with a list of available options, as shown in Figure 3.6.

We had to use the VisualAge for Java import utility the first time in order to see these SanFrancisco assets in the list. Most of the others were already there, as part of the defaults available with VAJ.

The main point here is simply that someone needs to be assigned the responsibility for including assets in the repository, backing up as well as managing the checking in and out of objects. In our shop, we make the BuildMaster responsible for including or deleting objects from the repository.

Corrupting the Workspace

This is a sad but true tale of how we lost several developer days of work, due to some strange and unpredictable dependencies within the Visual-Age for Java repositories and the way they work with workspaces.

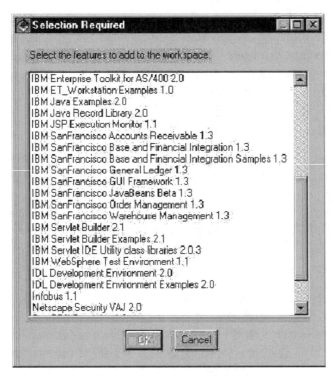

Figure 3.6 Adding assets to your workspace.

On one occasion, my development team came in frightfully early in the morning in order to have something ready for demonstration to the marketing team. After working for five or six hours apiece on several application modules, they tried to exit VAJ and save their work back to the repository.

Unfortunately, unbeknownst (which, by the way, is actually a real word!) to them, the NT administrator had rebooted the server on which the repository was stored. This in and of itself is not a problem, but in this case the administrator password was also changed.

When the team tried to synchronize their workspaces, it turned out they no longer had permission to access the repository. Their save failed, and with it the changes made in their workspace were gone, history, toast.

Summary

With the introduction of this new technology comes a requirement for teamwork that is actually unparalleled in the Big Blue software world.

Don't get me wrong—I understand that IBM has coordinated huge software development projects in the past. Where these projects differ is the need for tremendously effective *interdependencies* among developers.

It is impossible for any one person to handle the end-to-end aspects of developing Big Blue Java applications. When we tried, the individual charged with the task ended up having a nervous breakdown!

It is much more reasonable to approach this huge technical challenge as an exercise in delegation, teamwork, and coordinating tools. Luckily for us, IBM foresaw the need for this and has worked hard to bend the tools into a framework of controls and techniques to assist in this process.

Last, the use of Visual tools for development is absolutely critical to the successful outcome of working with these products.

CHAPTER 4

Introduction to Using VisualAge for Java

V isualAge for Java (VAJ) 2.0 Enterprise professional is the integrated development environment (IDE) to be used when developing Big Blue Java applications. The key reasons behind this are the level of integration with other IBM-related Web tools, such as WebSphere Application Server and SanFrancisco Java components.

VAJ2 has been rated one of the top developer toolkits available in 1999. The visual approach to component integration and the ability to share components and modules among several members of a development team are the reasons you would select VisualAge for Java instead of other IDEs such as Jbuilder or Power J.

While there are other IDEs on the market, some with different and arguably better features, there is much to be gained from having a consistent developer environment for Java product development.

Most of this chapter is oriented toward how to use the VisualAge for Java IDE, not the reasons for using it.

Basic VAJ Project Creation

When you launch VisualAge for Java, you are presented with options that step you through creating particular Java objects, such as an applet or a class. Generally, you would want to go immediately to your particular work area that is the consistent desktop for navigation around your project. This is the developer's workbench, and all of the particular projects associated with that developer will be registered within that area. The launch options are shown in Figure 4.1.

If you decide this is a little too much coaching from your development environment, you click off the show windows at startup option and go right into VisualAge for Java. You can still access the Quick Start menu

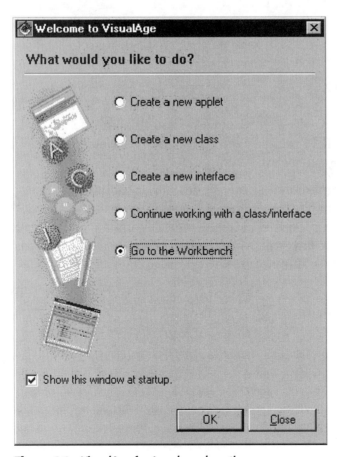

Figure 4.1 VisualAge for Java launch options.

by selecting it from under file. (See Figure 4.2.) As you will see, VAJ provides a wide range of development options with associated support.

From the Quick Start menu you can use wizards, move directly to creating Java objects, or manage the repository. The repository is a container for projects.

All of the code and resources of a programming effort belong to a project. The difference with VisualAge for Java is that the project is intrinsically something that it shared across multiple contributors. In fact, the very first step you must take when working with VAJ is to either open or create a project.

Projects are always kept in the repository. Whether it is a simple one-screen online code application that makes up the entire project or the work of dozens of people laboring for months on end, every project is kept in the VAJ repository.

The shared repositories themselves act as a source control package. Each developer owns his or her source code. Should another developer decide to check out that object, it is versioned as a separate project. Only the owner or creator of a project can release it for view or modification.

As well, VisualAge for Java detects all available source control applications installed on your computer and offers these as options on a drop-down menu when you want to access other objects, such as externally developed servlets or html pages, in or out of the source control system.

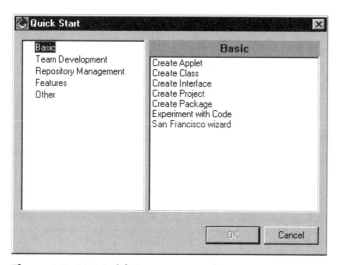

Figure 4.2 VAJ Quick Start menu options.

Team Connection from IBM and Visual Source Safe are two of the many popular source control environments that are supported.

You can see in Figure 4.3 the first screen presented to a developer working with VAJ 2.0.

Each developer has his or her own unique workspace or workbench that consists of projects checked out of the repository.

It is important to understand that the lists of projects that show up in the project section are only the ones that you have added from the VAJ repository. If you delete a project from VAJ 2.0 you have removed it only from the list of projects available to your particular workstation. To truly delete it, you must go to the repository.

Figure 4.4 shows the list of available projects in the Repository Explorer. This feature is available only with VAJ enterprise and professional versions. The downloadable VAJ standard does not give you Rep Explorer.

After browsing the available projects through Repository Explorer and selecting one, you can begin working with VAJ 2.0. This assumes you

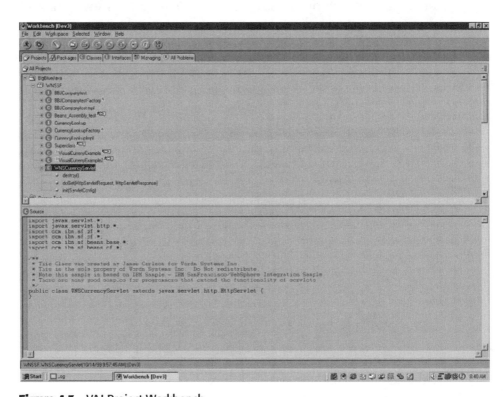

Figure 4.3 VAJ Project Workbench.

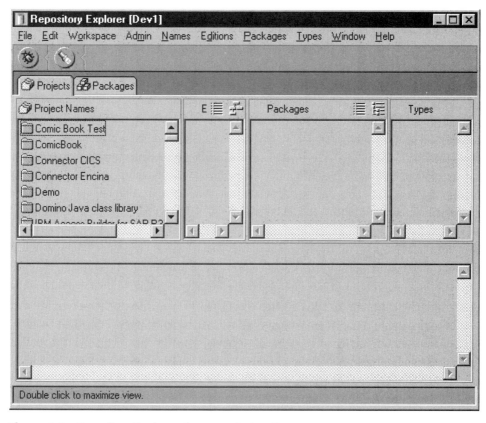

Figure 4.4 Repository Explorer shows project options.

didn't want to start one from scratch. One of the advantages of using the repository is the ability to create template projects, which you can then modify and save as customized documents. In this way, standard VAJ project options can be put into a project once and be immediately available to any developer of a new project.

Working with a New VAJ Project

Having successfully navigated your particular source code control system and the VAJ repository, you are ready to begin work on your Java project. After creating a new project or selecting an existing project, a developer is presented with a description of the project resources, as shown in Figure 4.5.

Projects include the packages, classes, and interfaces associated with the project as well as descriptions of the problems encountered (even

Figure 4.5 VAJ 2.0 Project resources.

with Java there are bugs and behavioral anomalies) and project management notes.

I have always believed it is important to define terms when introducing new concepts, even when dealing with more advanced material that assumes certain prerequisite information and knowledge. For this reason I will take a moment to define the basic elements of a Java application, even though you no doubt already know this!

Packages are similar to the executable modules of more traditional code. You can think of a package as all of the resources needed to execute the Java application. Objects, executable or not, are combined into Java packages that can be referenced by other objects or run as applications in their own right. An applet or servlet is a deployment on the client or server side of a particular package. For example, to run a particular Java application, you might call something like com.ibm.test.hello.class, which is directly analogous to calling c:\com\ibm\test\hello.exe on a DOS command line, or #.!/usr/com/ibm/test/hello to execute an application in Unix.

Because the Java application executes within a Java virtual machine, all of the resources must be contained in the path defined as part of the package name. As in the preceding example, typing com.ibm.test.hello .class will invoke the Java virtual machine and pass to it all of the byte-code that is to be executed.

The reason I mention this is to distinguish between the VAJ concept of a project and the more general Java concept of a package.

Packages are in turn made up of *classes*, which are the essential building blocks of any Java application. Classes are a template for creating objects. Readers are a class; readers of Big Blue Java might be considered a subclass (that's supposed to be amusing, not insulting!); and you would be considered an object—an instance of the class. When using VAJ 2.0 to develop applications, you deal exclusively with classes. It is only at runtime that the instantiation of classes turns the application into something that works.

Interfaces define how the classes interact. From a commercial applications development perspective, an HTML screen form on its own, for example, is not of much use unless combined with the necessary logic for accessing a data store. The interfaces map out how the classes talk to each other and the methods that are exposed for that interaction. In the same way that a traditional stored procedure or CICS application will take parameters and then perform functions on tables or files, the exposed methods of a Java class allow other users and objects to pass messages to the class. The class (or object, because it has to be instantiated for those messages to be passed back and forth) then processes the messages passed to it from the interface in the form of its internally defined methods.

To use a somewhat silly example, you, the instantiated object of the class reader, get a message that you are at the end of the page. The method invoked is to turn to the next page. This is quite a bit different than a traditional "Do Read While 'End of Page? = NO" style of programming.

Figure 4.6 shows an example listing of the various resources, in the form of packages, available as part of a project.

If you look carefully at the icons at the end of the Employee Panel, you can see a depiction of a running person, or jogger. The jogger indicates that this class is runnable. At least this is true for applets and console applications. We had some difficulty getting servlets and JSPs to actually execute within VisualAge for Java 2.0. Our workaround was to export the servlets to WebSphere and test them externally. Additionally, you can download JSDK 2.1 and spend some time configuring VisualAge for Java to run servlets. This is to be fixed in the Java Developer Kit 1.2.

Let's get back to developing applications using VisualAge for Java. Below the panel you see the components that make up the class. This is the way that resources such as screens and application logic are associated to make up an application using a visual development environment, in this case VisualAge for Java.

User Interface Components

While it is possible to develop user interfaces and Web browser screens with HTML in VAJ 2.0, our approach is to have these developed using graphics tools such as WebSphere Studio and the Macromedia suite of products. This means VAJ must check in the HTML screen source and

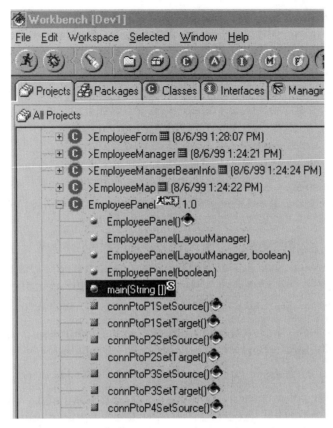

Figure 4.6 VisualAge for Java Project Resource List.

associate user actions with it. Unfortunately, these screens are treated as nonvisible objects and must be run in debug and test modes to see how the application looks and behaves.

You might have noticed in Figure 4.3 that many of the packages were prefaced with a *C*. This indicates that they are visual compositions. Using VAJ 2.0, you as a developer can create screens and user interface elements that have the traditional characteristics of any GUI application environment—checkboxes, radio buttons, drop-down lists, and so on.

One way to accomplish this is through the use of the Visual Composition Editor. An example of this screen is shown in Figure 4.7. The icons on the left of the screen indicate the controls that are available to a developer. On the right you can see the beginnings of a dead simple label and data area for display of data retrieved from a database or captured from a user entering the data into the form.

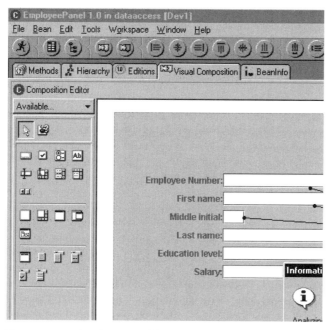

Figure 4.7   Visual Composition Editor for creating UI screens.

Now we are ready to use some of the features of VisualAge for Java 2.0 to create a functional application. In our case, we have been consistently working with the comic book collection to be sold through a Web site.

Beginning with the Quick Start menu, you could decide to use VisualAge for Java to create an applet. The SmartGuide takes the developer through the process of creating a project for the applet. (See Figure 4.8.)

As discussed earlier in this chapter, to work on any Java application the developer must define the project and package that is to contain it. For our example, let's go through the basic steps of creating an application that supports rating of a particular comic book title. For purposes of authenticity, the UI components will look an awful lot like a four-year-old did them.

On selecting the project and package names from the lists, you are dropped directly to the Visual Composition Editor. The VAJ Visual Composition Editor is shown in Figure 4.9. You might want to take note of a few things going on in Figure 4.9. Again, if you are experienced with visual development tools, this might seem like a basic introductory overview. However, I strongly believe that moving to Java is requiring a

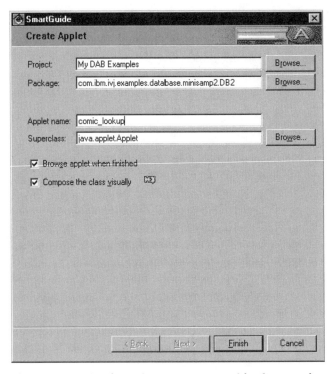

Figure 4.8 VisualAge for Java SmartGuide for creating applets.

great many development shops and experienced IT people to work with new tools and techniques. The objective of this overview is not to teach VisualAge for Java, but to cover the essential points of working with the entire Big Blue Java tool set.

On the left side of the Composition Editor panel you see various windows widgets for creating screens. They are the usual radio buttons, text labels, checkboxes, and so on. Select one by clicking on it, then click on the white space (work area) to position it. (Drag-and-drop is not supported in VAJ 2.0.) Each screen element has properties and behaviors. Right click to view the options. Then select properties. Under text, you can see that it is called Label1. Clicking inside the Label1 area within the properties box will allow you to edit it. The properties options are shown in Figure 4.10.

Alignment of multiple elements is handled by clicking once on a particular widget, then holding down the control key and clicking another screen element. A right mouse button click brings up the layout option from which you can align left, right, or center. You cannot lasso a group

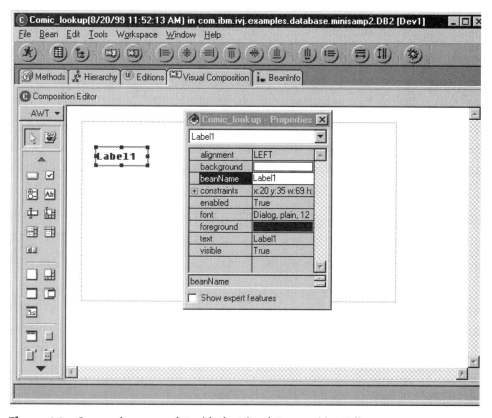

Figure 4.9 Composing an applet with the Visual Composition Editor.

of objects to select them in one fell swoop as you can with other graphical development environments. Figure 4.11 shows the alignment options for screen layout and design control.

You can accomplish the same thing by selecting the elements and clicking on one of the icons above the Visual Composition tab. Like the left, right, and center button in MS Word or PowerPoint, this toolbar lets you align selected screen widgets without accessing the pull-down menus. No big deal.

Once you have developed a particular view of the applet you can test it by clicking on the jogger. This converts the screen elements into runtime Java code and executes it within VisualAge for Java. This is shown in Figure 4.12. The Applet Viewer shows how the applet will look if distributed to an external browser.

That concludes the README.1ST description of working with VisualAge for Java 2.0 for creating applets.

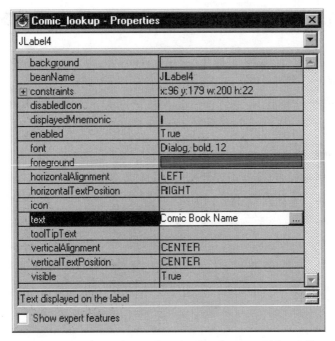

Figure 4.10   Properties options in Visual Composition Editor.

I think it is fair to note that graphic design controls are not one of the important distinctive advantages of using VisualAge for Java 2.0. Instead, visual programming support is what makes this a usable tool for a development team. The preceding examples are provided not only for those of you who are unused to visual programming of GUI applications, but also to show some of the limitations of the IBM tool set.

However limited the graphics layout options may be, VisualAge for Java does a great job of stepping you through what the applet does and where it does it. For example, even though the applet builder option dropped us right into the Composition Editor, you can see there are several other tabs representing views of this applet. This is where you start to see the power of VisualAge for Java.

First, let's look at the information collected about the beans we have used in the creation of this applet.

In Figure 4.13, there is only one bean used—Comic_lookup. To get details on the methods that are associated with this particular applet, we select the Methods tab. (See Figure 4.14.)

To manage the classes that make up the applet, the developer can look at the hierarchy, as shown in Figure 4.15. The hierarchy of packages,

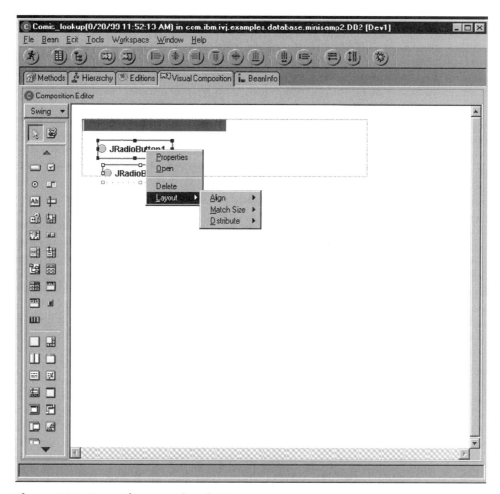

Figure 4.11   Screen layout options in VAJ 2.0.

classes, and subclasses lets you visually determine how the application is using various pieces of general and customized Java code.

The three-panel view (in Figure 4.15) of each class, applet, and the panels, containers, and components that make up the object in which they reside allows a developer to quickly look at the methods associated and source code.

These are the various views of the object hierarchy, layout, and appearance of visual components as well as display of all associated source code. Considering that this ties back tightly to the repository for shared development, you should be able to see the benefits of VisualAge for Java, not only as an integrated development environment, but also as a team tool.

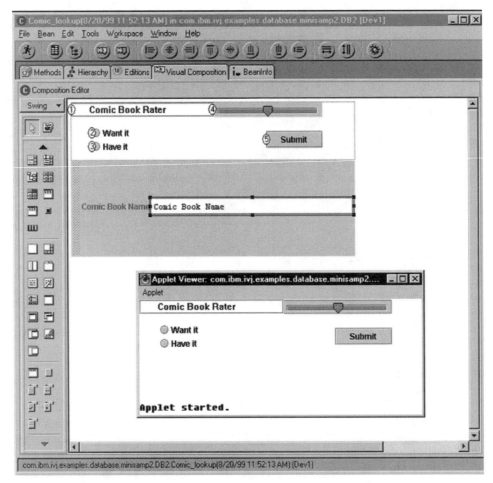

Figure 4.12 Previewing an applet created by the Composition Editor.

If that isn't enough (and, given the demands of developing these applications for enterprise deployment and support, it probably isn't) it turns out there is quite a bit more to VisualAge for Java.

For example, there are additional utilities for creating applets, beans, and other Java executables that integrate tightly with existing data stores such as DB2 or, for that matter, anything you can connect with over ODBC.

Data Access Builder

To create the application that supports this process, we used VAJ 2.0 and, specifically, the data access bean builder feature that is supported

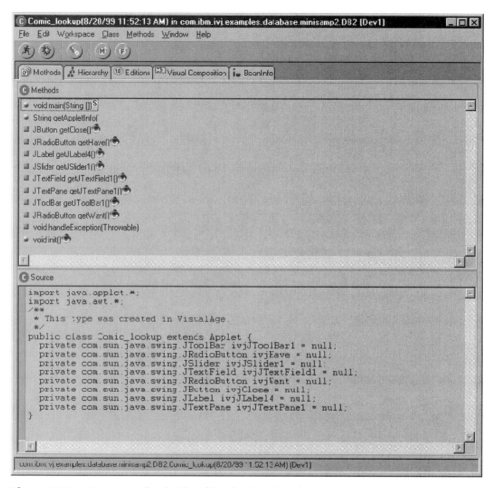

Figure 4.13 Bean counting in VisualAge for Java 2.0.

with the professional and enterprise versions of the development environment.

There are many techniques for populating a Java application with data from a persistent data store such as DB2 or SQL Server. The technique we have decided to use first is the bean builder approach.

Figure 4.16 shows how the workspace begins to look after you have created a project, defined some resources for it, used the Visual Composition Editor to create a user interface object, and started to connect that UI widget to a database.

When working with VisualAge for Java, you tie the screen properties to a particular access method. In Figure 4.16, you can see a line tied to

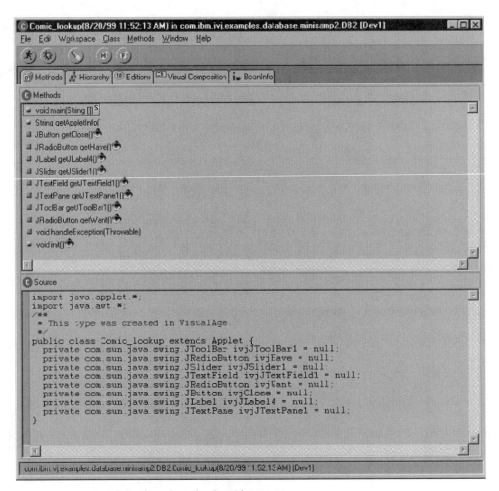

Figure 4.14 Visual display of methods with VAJ 2.0.

Middle initial. That line was drawn, and the drop-down list box containing Swing, AWT, Servlet, and other data access methods was activated. To use the bean builder approach, the developer will select Database.

It is worth noting the Available option. As always in Windows, the ellipses (. . .) indicate that other screens or options are available. Understandably, options are available through the Available option, but the point I am trying to make is that other ways of accessing data can be added to the option list from this point. In fact, prior to using these screens, we selected Available and Servlet in order to make that data access method part of our standard list.

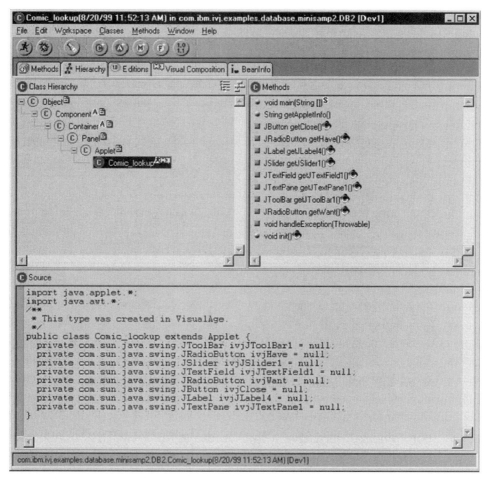

Figure 4.15 Viewing the hierarchy of Java classes.

Data Access Techniques

As I have stated at various points throughout the book, Big Blue Java is about e-business systems and systems that mean business use data. VisualAge for Java has a couple of very neat features for accessing data through JDBC.

Like its cousin Open Database Connectivity (ODBC), Java Database Connectivity has database-specific drivers that are mapped to connection names. Using JDBC, the developer doesn't even need to enter a login or password to get access to his or her own test database. Of course, this information has to be provided to the JDBC connection when it is first

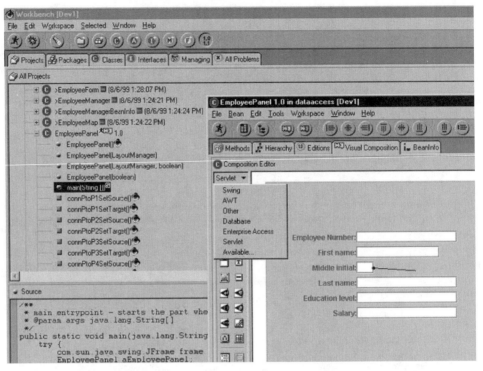

Figure 4.16 Populating a form with data using data access beans.

configured. Alternatively, the VisualAge for Java JDBC connection can be configured to prompt for a user name and password each time it is used.

The JDBC connection configuration is covered in Chapter 10. At this point, we do not want to get sidetracked from explaining how VisualAge for Java is used to create Java applications.

Using the Swing widgets as we did in the examples earlier, you create the basic look and feel of the user interface. Text labels, panels, and backgrounds are all added to create that user-friendly look and feel. When it's time to get the application to do some real work, however, you click where it indicates the Swing palette is loaded and change it to Database. If Database is not available to you, you must go to Available and register it with your VisualAge for Java workbench.

There are two widgets with the Database palette: select and dbnavigator. We are going to use these to tie a live database query to a display area in our applet. From this you will get a sense of exactly how easy it is to create database-enabled applications using VAJ 2.0.

Figure 4.17 shows a sample window ready to be database enabled. You can see how the developer used a Jtext label to create the Comic Name. A background and JscrollPanel were used to create the area for navigating around the returned results. Finally, a Jtable widget was added on top of the panel.

Using the database widgets, we added the dbnavigator, which allows controls for displaying and moving through results returned from a database. The worker bean in this example is labeled Select1. This is a query bean dropped on the workspace and tied to the dbnavigator bar. (See Figure 4.18.)

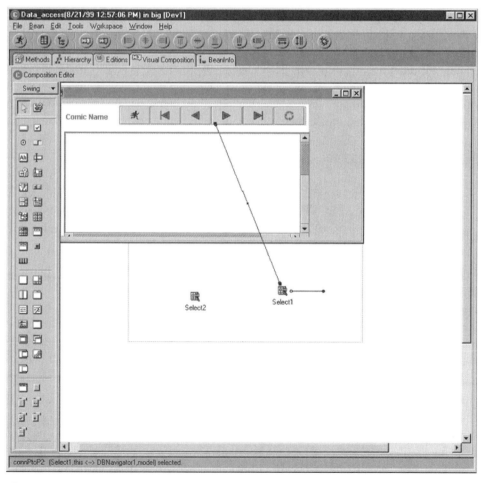

Figure 4.17   Using VAJ to connect an applet to a database.

Figure 4.18   Dbnavigator bean.

The properties of this control have to be modified from the default to be able to work properly with a simple select. The properties changes are shown in Figure 4.19.

For purposes of our applet, we do not want to show transaction behavior such as showCommit, showDelete, or showRollback. All we are interested in having dbNavigator handle is the returned results themselves.

A developer must go through several steps in order to get the select bean to behave in the desired manner. From a project manager's standpoint, the developer of the application at this level does not have to understand SQL or database access at all. Instead, a database administrator could set up views and provide a dictionary of view names and results to the developers so they do not have to handle join logic.

In this example, we are going to retrieve a few results from the comic database that we promoted to DB2 from Access just for the occasion.

Defining a Database Select

The select bean is handled in the same manner that any other widget is managed within VisualAge for Java. You right click on it to get to the properties. To make the select work with dbnavigator, the properties were set as shown in Figure 4.20.

The Query property lets us do the work of connecting to the database and getting results back. Let's go through the process for our comic book info lookup applet. (See Figure 4.21.)

Dropping down the list box will provide a list of the available packages in which you can contain this database access class. Clicking on Add brings up the next dialog box, as shown in Figure 4.22.

The connection name can be anything you want. It is always a good idea to test the connection before proceeding. Selecting the id and password prompt will generate a login screen for any user of the deployed applet.

Once you define the connection, you must then determine which SQL you want passed to the data store. To do this within VAJ, select the SQL

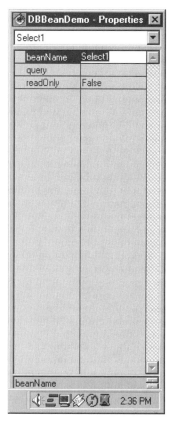

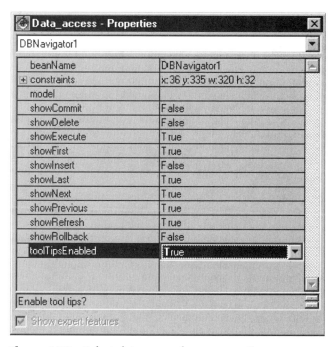

Figure 4.19 Dbnavigator bean property

Figure 4.20 Select data access bean properties.

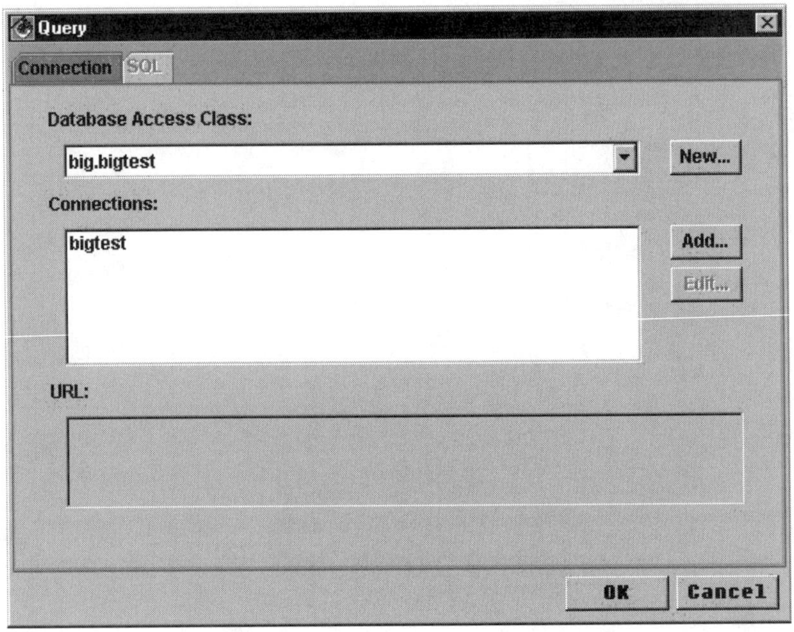

Figure 4.21 Connection properties to link an applet to a DB2 table.

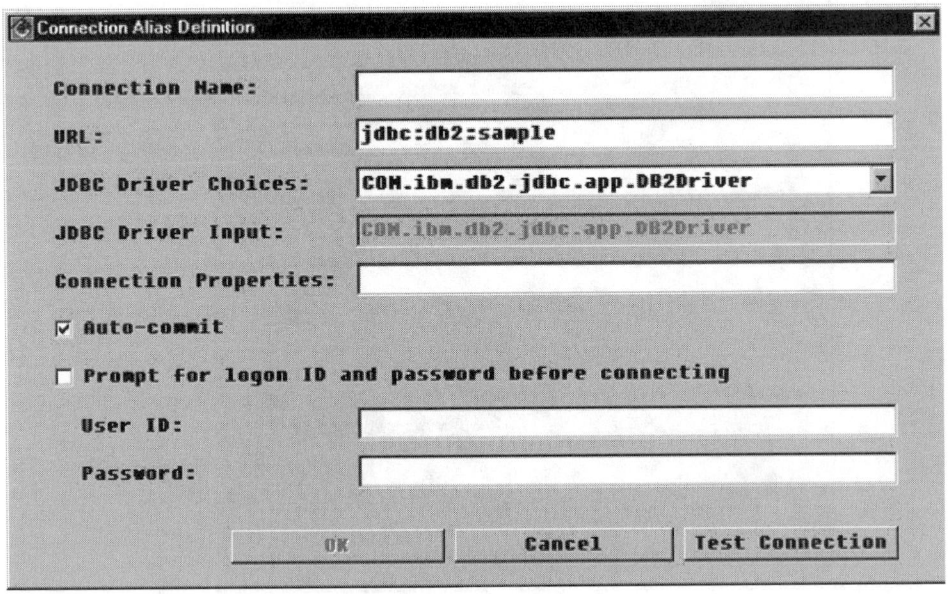

Figure 4.22 Setting the JDBC connection parameters.

tab at the top of the dialog box shown in Figure 4.23. You will then be able to look at the existing SQL and edit it.

As you can see, the existing statement is displayed to help the developer choose an existing SQL statement to modify or otherwise use as a template. An eagle-eyed reader will notice that I did not actually use the comic book SQL for this example.

Selecting Add will take you to the dialog shown in Figure 4.24. The OK button is grayed out until you give the SQL spec a name. In this case, we are going to step through the SmartGuide to arrive at the SQL statement itself. (See Figure 4.25.) This displays the contents of the database to which we connected using JDBC. All of the tables and views are displayed and can be selected to be included in the generated SQL statement.

To define the specific data that you want the select bean to pass back to the applet, click on the Columns tab. The options are displayed in Figure 4.26.

You can view the SQL, map data types, and define the ascending or descending sort order for any given column. Select Finish to return to the workspace.

Once you are back in the workspace and have finished defining your complete SQL connection, you bring up the dbnavigator1 bean, right

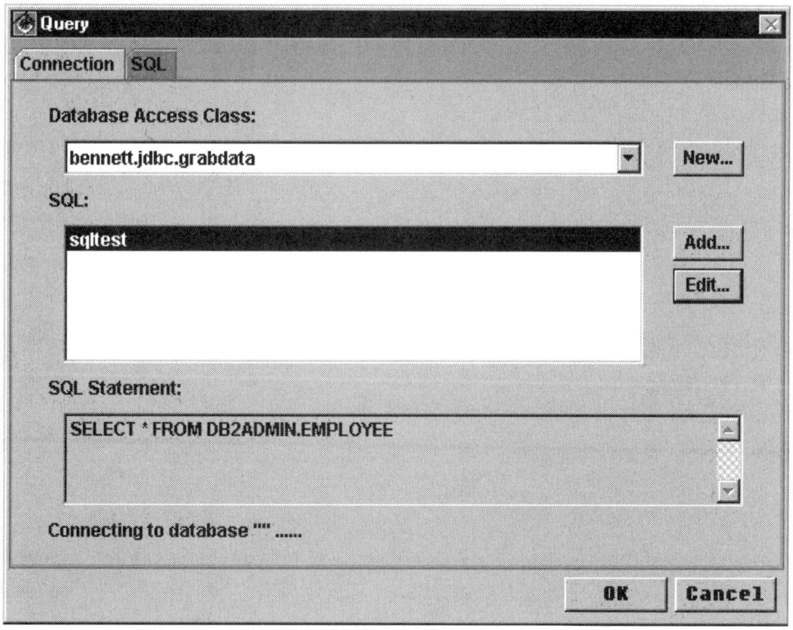

Figure 4.23 Creating an SQL statement.

Figure 4.24 Options for creating an SQL statement.

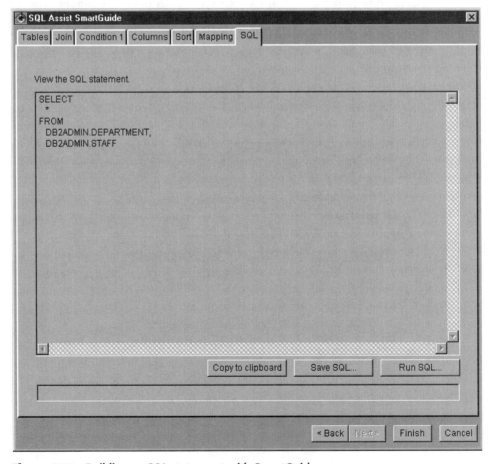

Figure 4.25 Building an SQL statement with SmartGuide.

click, bring up connect, and select model. Click on the select bean, right click, and select this. The select bean is linked to the dbnavigator control. Perform the same operation between the dbnavigator control and the Jtable widget to display the results passed by dbnavigator from the select bean. (See Figure 4.27.)

Again, eagle-eyed readers will notice that I have not described the purpose of the dotted line or how we got there. Using the same techniques as connecting the select bean, I took advantage of the exception properties to write any error messages generated when using dbnavigator to a test field at the bottom of the window.

Click on the jogger, under file at the top of the window, to test your applet. One problem with the SQL SmartGuide is the lack of right mouse button support and an annoying tendency to display the fully qualified

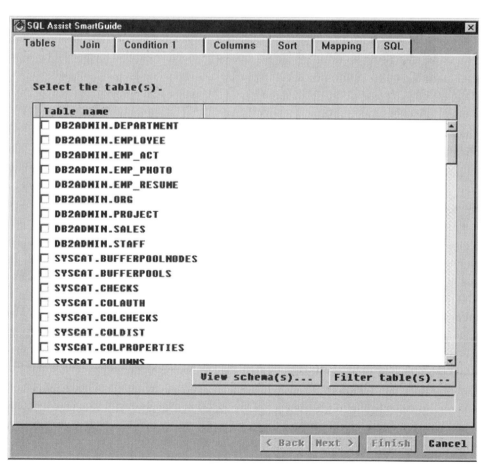

Figure 4.26 Selecting specific columns using SmartGuide.

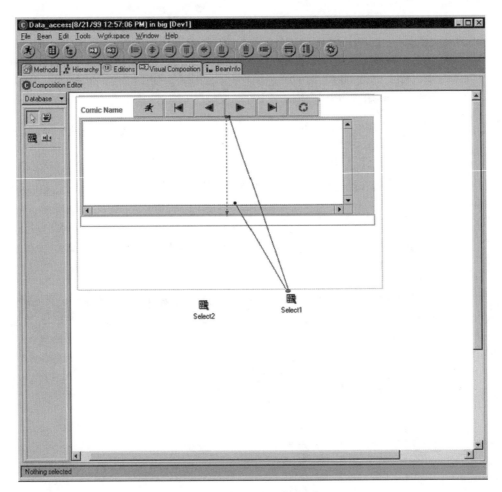

Figure 4.27 Integrating the data controls in Visual Age for Java.

table names as the column names on retrieval. This is a problem when you want to have a nice autosized column presented to your browser and to just let the data access bean handle the connection to the database. Because I have an SQL background, I thought to simply rename the column to title=db2admin.sampledb.title, and so forth, but editing is not supported even though you can view the SQL code that is generated by the Wizard.

To get around this you have to copy the SQL to the clipboard or save it to an external file. Edit it there and reimport it through a magical means (cut and paste).

The applet results in our test window are shown in Figure 4.28.

Problems with VAJ

In spite of the enthusiasm with which we may have embraced or endorsed the whole VisualAge tool set, there are occasionally problems. This should be expected from any software tool (unfortunately), but I've included a few sample troubleshooting suggestions here because, first, you may encounter them and, second, it will give you an idea of the quality of the implementation.

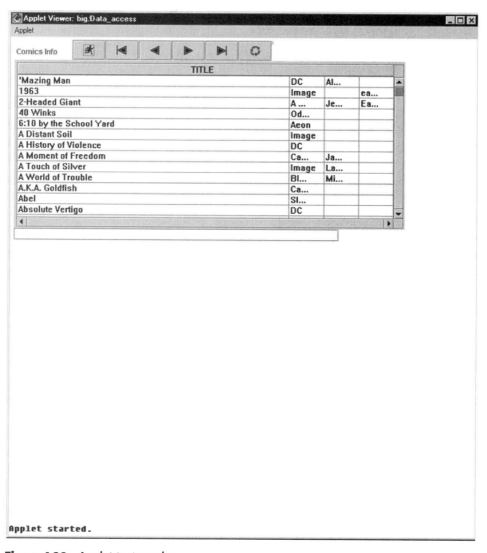

Figure 4.28 Applet test results.

Speeding Up the Loading of Java Applet

Run your applet using Sun's Java plug-in. The plug-in already has all of the swing classes local to itself, so you don't have to put them in your applet jar file. You can then just put your applet and its supporting classes in the jar file. This could save you up to 2MB in size in your jar file.

The only drawback is that anybody who wants to run your applet has to first download the plug-in.

Class Loading Problems on the DefaultLayoutManager and plaf MetalLookAndFeel

This class is supplied as a class and often not included when exporting. You will find that the applet viewer will be able to view the applet just fine; however, a browser pointing to a jar or directory structure will not be able to find the plaf. This can be overcome by manually adding the classes at export time.

Data Access Builder: Notes

I am not allowed to generate a schema mapping for the DB2 database unless I am logged on as db2admin. This causes some problems if I am logged on to my account. Does the problem lie in the fact that the default userid and password are assigned to the db2admin account? Can I avoid this difficulty by creating another DB2 user account for my personal account? (See Table 4.1.)

Trouble Doing More Than Selects with the Data Access Beans

This is a restriction of working with this type of bean. Although you can connect to a database, retrieve a record set, successfully navigate the records, and delete records, you are unable to add or update records in the database. This is a problem inherent in the beans themselves. Look at software.ibm.com/vaj to see if a fix pack is available.

Problems with VAJ When Using Swing

Many times, your VAJ will not want to swing. The error message shown in Figure 4.29 will be seen in the debugging tool. To correct this, right click

Table 4.1 Data Access Class Library Reference

CLASS NAME	DESCRIPTION
DatastoreJDBC	Manages database connections, providing client connection to the database, disconnection from the database, and the ability to commit and roll back database transactions.
PersistentObject	Provides interfaces for adding, deleting, retrieving, and updating a row from a table.
PODataId	Base class for objects that uniquely identify rows in tables.
DAManager	Provides the ability to work with a collection of rows from a table and facilitates movement through a collection of rows via a database cursor.
DAIOStream	Used for handling Large Object (LOB) input and output by using streams.
DAException	Defines exceptions thrown by the Data Access Builder and its generated code.
Data Access Property Editor classes	A group of classes that let you use a GUI to edit the property values for a variety of data types. Useful when writing apps with the Visual Composition Editor.

on your class, go to properties, and analyze the class path. This will create a new class path, which will allow you to execute swing applications.

Crashing and Lost Workspaces

Due to subtle network problems, periodically VAJ cannot connect to the repository. If you exit VAJ, you will lose your workspace and will have to attempt to rebuild consistency. To avoid this, you should save your workspace and then exit the program by choosing not to save your workspace when the connection error is displayed.

Summary

In this chapter you have been taken through the basics of working with VisualAge for Java. The intention was to provide a README.1ST level of introduction to the tool, because this is the starting point for creating Big Blue Java applications.

There are many advanced features within VisualAge for Java, and using the tool to create servlet and JSP has its own unique challenges. How-

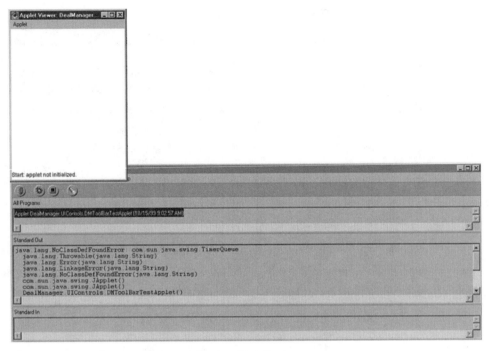

Figure 4.29 Swing error message in VisualAge for Java.

ever, as a multideveloper tool for visual programming of Java-based applications, it is truly outstanding.

Over the next few releases, the idiosyncratic behavior will no doubt give way to a smoother developer experience, but for our money, VisualAge for Java is a highly useful tool right now.

CHAPTER 5

Introduction to WebSphere Studio

I was originally going to call this chapter "Developing Wizzy Wowie Web Sites," but the more I poked around with WebSphere Studio, the more I came to appreciate its uses for creating deep content, not just flashy sites.

Historically, IBM has not been well known for its attention to the user interface. Scalability, robust and reliable hardware, yes, but a pretty face, not so much.

With WebSphere Studio, IBM has gone to great lengths to give us as developers a toolkit that allows you not only to create as attractive a site as you can come up with, but to do so in the context of a site development team.

Make no mistake, whereas most Web graphics are created by over-worked, underpaid graphics' types in the basement, designers of commercial Web sites are not going to be using the same techniques (unless of course they look better!).

At WNS, we originally gravitated to NetObjects Fusion simply because we were looking for some site templates and the box had been shipped to us as part of our software development partner license. Not the most researched of technology directions, I admit, but after all, it was *only* the site creation software. Because we specialize in back-end work and are working hard to bring our EJB solutions to market, we didn't want to get sidetracked with something as trivial as the user presentation development environment.

The foregoing is meant to be somewhat tongue in cheek. As any successful developer of GUI-based client/server software can tell you, the look and feel of the application is vital to its user appeal. And user appeal is where your application can win or die.

So, for this part of the investigation into Big Blue Java tools, we're going to take off our enterprise, future-oriented, scalable, and robust technical architecture hat and put on our party hat. That's right—settle in and prepare to have a little fun with technology.

Because it *is* fun. The flaming logo and the spinning logo are now the stuff of sardonic commercials, especially as early Web site developers thought the sizzle was the steak. Still, advertising works, and advertising on the Web is no exception. Without a cool theme, a hot image, and plenty of eye-catching movement, all your efforts won't get the recognition they deserve.

Luckily for me, my best friend is a longtime graphic artist. In fact, we collaborated on an entirely PC-produced video production in the mid-1990s (back when 1-gig scsi disks were hard to find). If I remember correctly, our video took up 72 gigs of space.

It was with some trepidation that I brought the WebSphere Studio materials to him to evaluate with me. After all, Gustav is, was, and will remain a dedicated Mac guy. I shouldn't have worried. Good technology has a way of winning over even the most skeptical, and it turns out the WebSphere Studio is not only a terrific product from a team management standpoint, but as a creation tool as well.

The Studio Toolkit

As currently shipped, version 3.0 of WebSphere studio works with the following:

- VisualAge for Java (standard)
- NetObjects Fusion
- NetObjects Script builder

- NetObjects BeanBuilder
- NetObjects Build-IT
- Allaire Homesite
- WebSphere Application Server

Notice the preponderance of NetObjects references in the product list? NetObjects is a privately held company, partially funded by IBM. Perhaps this semi–arm's length arrangement has allowed IBM to get access to some hot site development technology.

In any case, as well as supporting VisualAge for Java as the integrated development environment, WebSphere Studio also has an interface between the Studio's workbench to VisualAge TeamConnection. This provides development teams with a way to access any component under development, including models and EJB components. Yes, that means the GUI developers are an acknowledged part of the enterprise development team.

From within the workbench, developers can launch applications that are not included as part of WebSphere studio. For example, at our shop we have standardized on Macromedia's Dreamweaver as the html development tool of choice, and we work with Fireworks and some of the other Macromedia plug-ins to good effect. Adobe Photoshop is another staple for image construction and enhancement.

Who Works with WebSphere Studio?

Studio was intended to be used by the following:

- Page designers
- Graphic artists
- Programmers
- Webmasters

Essentially, anyone involved in the creation of content for display on a Web server, whether these pages are static or dynamic, can use WebSphere Studio.

What Makes Up WebSphere Studio?

All of the design and publishing aspects of dynamic Web pages are supported in WebSphere studio. WSS provides a graphical display of all files used in a project and their links. This visual site map is updated automatically whenever the files change or move.

Third-party editing tools are declared and launched from within WSS, but a page design facility is included for creation of HTML and JSP files. Additionally, wizards greatly simplify the process of creating pages that are fed from databases and JavaBeans.

The real advantages of WebSphere Studio can be found in the utilities for publishing pages created by multiple developers to multiple servers. As mentioned earlier, WebSphere Studio supports integration with source control systems, including the following:

- Team Connection
- Visual Source Safe
- PVCS
- Rational ClearCase
- Lotus Domino

Three designer tools are included for creating complex pages:

Applet Designer. A visual tool for authoring Java applets.

WebArt Designer. Supports creation of masthead images, buttons, and any other graphic you might use on a Web page.

AnimatedGif Designer. Used to assemble, you guessed it, animated .gif files.

Working with WebSphere Studio

After launching WSS for the first time, you must create a new project. You can choose a blank site or work with one of the template sites provided with WSS. On launch of the product, you see the basic workbench as depicted in Figure 5.1.

The servlet, theme, and Web folders are consistent resources required for all WebSphere Studio projects. You use these to store the resources used in the creation of the site. Servlet, for example, is where you would store all beans and Java code, whereas Web is a natural folder for storing images and other site-related files. Theme holds changes you might make to the overall style sheets used in the various screens. An example of this is shown in Figure 5.2.

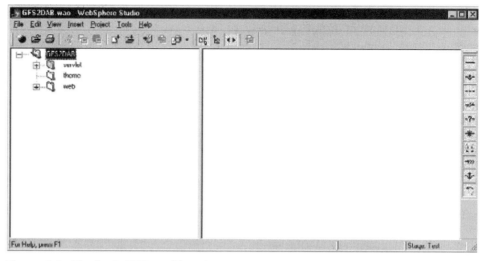

Figure 5.1   The basic WSS workbench.

To import a project developed using other tools, select a blank site and explicitly add the files through the import wizard. Theoretically, you can drag and drop the desired files through the Explorer interface, but we found that occasionally this leads to problems with the program hanging or corrupting the workspace. Of course, we were using the beta 3 ver-

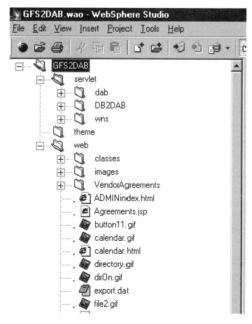

Figure 5.2   Displaying resources in WebSphere Studio.

sion of the program, so perhaps this was fixed. In any case, I recommend using the officially sanctioned import method.

Importing Resources into WebSphere Studio

As you define your WSS project, you will want to associate beans and other resources with it. To accomplish this, select the servlet folder for beans and class files and the Web folder for your html, gif, and jpg resources. Right click on servlet, select insert, and follow the dialog boxes to associate the desired classes and servlets with the WSS project. These are shown in Figure 5.3.

This can be done by pointing to entire folders, as shown in Figure 5.4, or by explicitly naming a file. You use this technique to ensure common resources are available to anyone who works with WebSphere Studio.

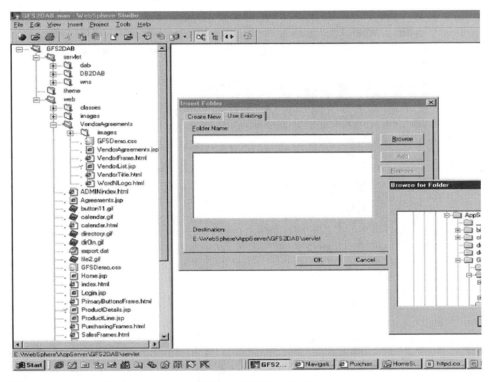

Figure 5.3 Associating resources with your WSS project.

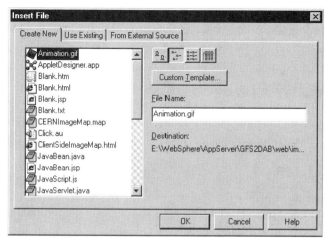

Figure 5.4 Inserting specific resources.

The insert file dialogs step you through associating the specific files you want to include with your WebSphere project. Once you have completed this step, you are ready to configure your WSS environment for ongoing operation.

Configuring WSS to Work with Plug-Ins

As part of your ongoing work with WebSphere Studio, you are likely to want to call up the various programs you like to use to manage html and gif resources, as well as editors and viewers for Java Server Pages. To tailor this to your individual taste, you must associate the default program to a particular file extension, much the same way that clicking on a .doc file in the Microsoft world generally will launch WordPad or Word unless explicitly changed to another program.

To do this in WebSphere Studio, you must first choose Tools and then Tools Registration to get the dialog box shown in Figure 5.5. This brings up the Tools Registration window. From Tools Registration you select a particular file extension to activate the edit option, then click on edit in order to get to the list of options for editors or tools you wish to use. You can see this in Figure 5.6.

I recommend setting up Allaire Homesite as the default tool for editing your Java Server Page. You will see from our examples in this chapter

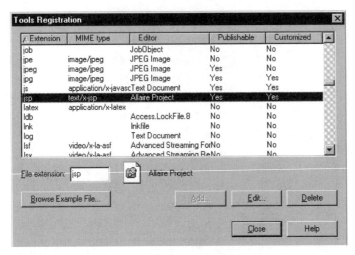

Figure 5.5 Defining default tools in WebSphere Studio.

that there are several advantages to working with Homesite. Besides, it's included as part of the WebSphere Studio package, so why not use it?

Now that your WebSphere Studio environment is configured to your liking, it's time to get down to work. In terms of the Model-View-Controller approach to developing systems, we assigned our Controller duties to our WebSphere Studio developer.

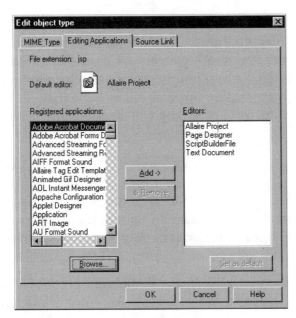

Figure 5.6 Editing the tool definitions.

One of the key technologies we wanted to use in the implementation of Deal Manager was Java Server Pages. At one point, we thought we could do the entire application using JSPs, but we soon found that we needed some more applet functions to get a fully satisfactory user experience.

Having said that, JSPs are a critical component to virtually all e-business development efforts. In the following examples, I'll take you through the steps we used to create and modify JSPs as part of an actual application. Once you have associated all of the various widgets with your WebSphere project, you can finally get down to work. The basic workbench is shown in Figure 5.7.

A checkmark appears in the explorer list to indicate that you are working with a particular page or resource. By right clicking on the object—in this case a Java Server Page—you can choose to preview it with your default Web browser. This sends the Java Server Page to the WebSphere Application Server, where it is processed and the results sent back to your browser exactly as for a production user.

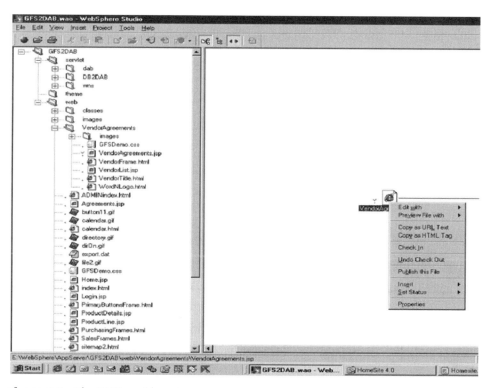

Figure 5.7 The WSS workbench.

Figure 5.8 Viewing JSPs in Homesite.

You will get a chance to see the output of this page in just a minute. In some situations, for example, working into the wee hours of the morning on the home system, you may not have access to WebSphere Application Server and its services.

Double click on the JSP and Allaire Homesite will handle the Java Server Page. (See Figure 5.8.)

Working with Allaire Homesite

Homesite gives you three main views of your page: edit, browse, and design mode. The edit mode allows you to view and change your actual

HTML code, whereas the browse mode brings up the internal homesite Web browser and displays that code as best it can. Design mode allows you to move through links and change relationships of the pages.

The Java Server Page defined as a starting point for our Deal Manager application was intended to supply vendor, item, and agreement information in one screen. The look of the screen as developed by one of our developers is shown in Figure 5.9. As you can see from the diagram, the Homesite browser lets you see all of the html functions processed properly. However, none of the Java code executed. To see that, the developer would click on WebSphere Studio on the taskbar at the bottom of the window and right click to preview, with the option to submit the page to WebSphere Application Server. When we did this with the same Java Server Page viewed in Figure 5.9, we got the results you see in Figure 5.10.

You can see in Figure 5.10 that there is actually data displayed from the Java Server Page. Homesite was unable to process the Java script that attached to the database and submitted a query, whereas WebSphere

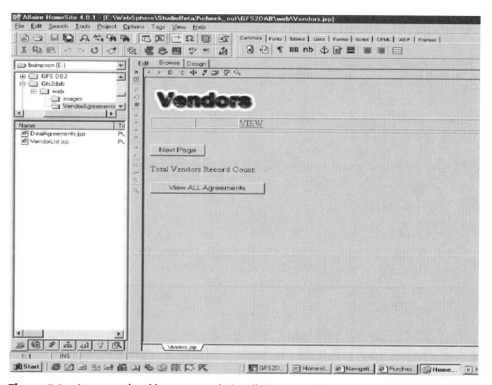

Figure 5.9   An example of browse mode in Allaire Homesite.

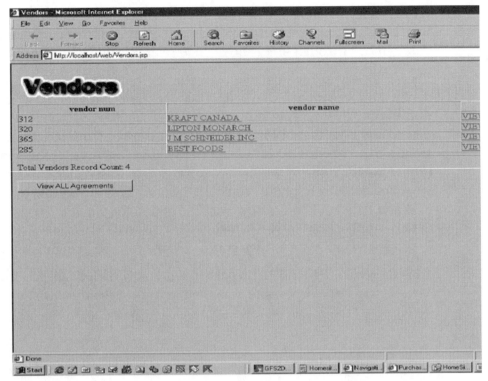

Figure 5.10 The same JSP processed by WebSphere Application Server.

Application Server was set up to do just that. The specific code to be processed by WebSphere Application Server is as follows:

```
// connect to the DB
   theVendorDs.connect();
   theVendorDs.setAutoCommit(true);
   dab.VendorManager theVendorMan = new dab.VendorManager(theVendorDs);

// Set the SQL suffix
theVendorMan.open("");
```

The key point here is that Homesite does not choke on the code, even though it can't process it. Homesite is used to check the visual aspects of the page, whereas WAS is used to check under-the-hood processing. Naturally the page looks quite a bit different with test data than with no data at all.

In Chapter 3 you can get a better idea of what this particular screen turned into once we got a user interface specialist involved. I wouldn't want to be overly critical of our development team, but you should be able to get a sense of why good programmers don't necessarily make good user interface people. The form shown in Figure 5.10 is an adequate JSP from a functional standpoint, but it is hardly the best example of good layout and design.

Using Homesite and WebSphere Studio, however, gives a developer a good handle on what the page is doing, regardless of how it looks. In our particular case, we used WSS to develop and test some reasonably complicated Java Server Pages. In Figure 5.11 you can see the view of multiple JSPs and their interrelationships.

When the PurchasingFrames.html is previewed using Internet Explorer (meaning processed by WebSphere Application Server), the screen comes up as shown in Figure 5.12. This should give you a pretty good overview of the process of creating a Web site that uses dynamic pages with WebSphere Studio.

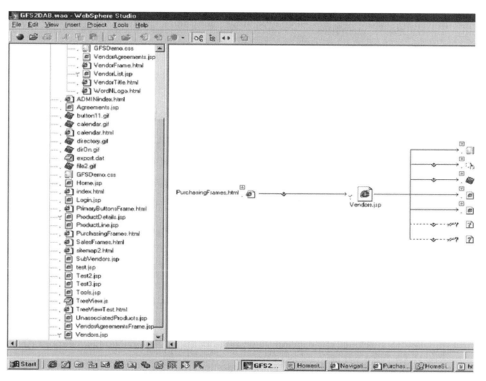

Figure 5.11 Managing multiple JSPs in WSS.

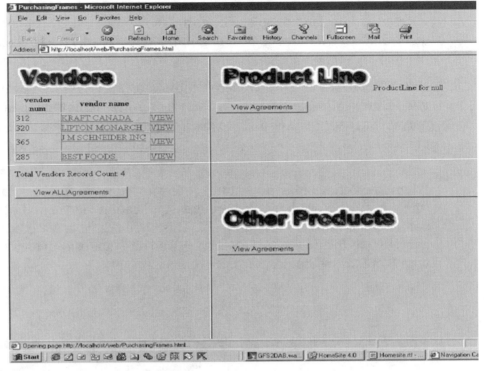

Figure 5.12 Displaying multiple JSPs using frames.

Advanced Editing Options in WebSphere

The Universal Attribute Editor is used to navigate through the site structure and change the attributes of any tag. These tags allow you a tremendous amount of control over the look and feel of your site. An example is depicted in Figure 5.13.

Using the attribute editor, you can change background colors, size, orientation, and so on for any of the elements of a Web page anywhere in the site. The biggest advantage is that these can propagate throughout the site, so you apply the change once and see it everywhere—a global search and replace for an entire Web site, if you will.

Using the autopublish option, you can view the up-to-date behavior of your site as soon as you make a change. Better yet, your users can be looking at the site as it evolves in test without you having to explicitly copy files and make them available for preview.

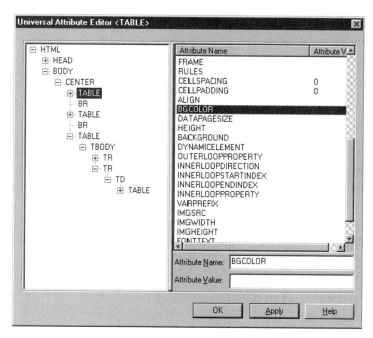

Figure 5.13 Using the Universal Attribute Editor.

Autopublish usually points to a local or test server, and WSS will manage the copying of files and changing of links for the local directories. This is done in the background for each file you change, and the results are immediately viewable on the test Web server.

The real power of this control is evident when you have more-involved creation processes than just develop, test, and publish. For example, you can customize the assembly stages into many discrete steps, pointing to a different server for each stage. When you are ready to move from, say, test to user acceptance, WSS looks after the ftp'ing of all files from your development server to the target servers. These logical publishing targets make it much easier for the Web site development team to coordinate work and minimize site administration.

All of the check-in and checkout process is handled automatically through the project file menu. When you install WebSphere Studio, any version of control software you have already installed shows up on the Tools → Version Control → Add to Version Control menu.

Once activated, any checked-out files will show a tiny red checkmark to the left of the name. Each time you, or someone else, opens that file, it is automatically checked out to you.

For graphics designers and other folks who are not necessarily used to the rigors and discipline of multiteam administration, this feature is a lifesaver. Ask anyone who has had to go back to older versions and make changes because his or her work was accidentally overwritten!

WebSphere Studio not only gives you pretty much all the features of a great Web site design tool, but you can fold in your favorite third-party applications. What's not to like? The real value comes from the wizards, for masking the complexity of working with Java Server Pages and Java-Beans, and the multiserver, multideveloper support features.

In short? Mikey likes it!

CHAPTER 6

NetObjects Fusion

The first technology anyone needs when considering developing Web-based solutions is a Web page creation program. There are, of course, many on the market to choose from: FrontPage is the Microsoft offering for beginners; Macromedia offers Dreamweaver for the artsy crowd; and IBM rounds out its Big Blue Java solution set with NetObjects Fusion.

Those of you who have watched and worked with IBM over the years recognize that for all its excellence in marketing, management, product development, and other disciplines, IBM has never been accused of being all sizzle and no steak. Image counts for a lot less than thirst when it comes to the user interface. On the other hand, the lessons from OS/2 were hard won and not to be ignored. People like to buy pretty things. Given a choice between an ugly but functional thing and a pretty but useful thing for the same money, pretty wins most of the time.

To ensure that we Big Blue Java solution developers weren't caught up in the age-old argument of function over form, IBM made it possible for us to have both. By taking an equity position in NetObjects, IBM has been able to tightly integrate an existing third-party product into the lineup while ensuring that investment in this technology won't go the way of many other alliances.

NetObjects Fusion provides a development environment for the creation of Web pages that is recognized as being a first-class offering quite capable of standing on its own, even without the rest of the Big Blue Java tools to help out. Considering the way it can be integrated into the development of multideveloper projects, it is the first choice at my organization for developing pages.

In this chapter we will go through the creation of a basic Web site and introduce you to the features of NetObjects Fusion.

Getting Started

Installation of this application is quite straightforward. You will need a license key, however, so keep it handy. When you first launch NetObjects Fusion, you are asked if you want to import an existing site, work with a template, or simply create a new site from scratch.

The Sun StarOffice 5.1 suite was just made available for download as I was writing this. I decided to evaluate it in my spare time while I was resting. The results of that review I intended to make available to folks on the company Web site. To maximize *my* reusability, I thought it would be interesting to document the process of creating Web pages using that example. Perhaps you'll get two benefits from this chapter: (1) You will have an opportunity to go through the creation of a Web site using NetObjects Fusion, and (2) you will be able to get some insight into another product, even if it is from Sun.

Creating a Site

In Figure 6.1, you see the startup screen asking if you want to create a site from scratch or use a template. In Figure 6.2, you see the listing of the template assets, which is actually a pretty reasonable selection.

Of course, few programs these days insist that you do everything from scratch. The key point I would like to make is to discourage you from opening up notepad and going to town writing your own html. It only feels productive for some programmers. In fact, one of the strengths of this environment is the ability to include corporate image standards into standard templates and ensure that everyone who develops a Web site under a company's roof is complying with the look and feel mandated by management (not to mention that it's faster and easier).

For this particular case, it made sense to work with a minimalist site, so I chose blank on the basis that you just can't get more minimalist than that.

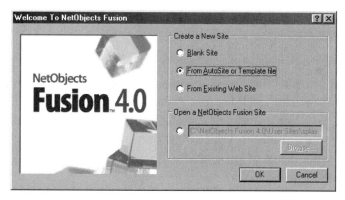

Figure 6.1 The create site dialog box in NetObjects Fusion 4.0.

The workspace in NetObjects Fusion starts with a site representation, a properties box, and a standard list of function buttons across the top of the window. This view of the site is one that you continually come back to as you work with the site. If I had selected a more complex template, a number of pages and page relationships would already

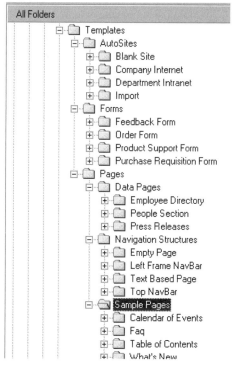

Figure 6.2 The directory structure of templates in NetObjects Fusion.

have been defined. By building on this one, I will have to add them myself and define their properties as I go. (See Figure 6.3.)

By double clicking on the page with which I want to work, I bring up the working view of the site. This provides the developer with access to the NOF tools as well as the background, color, and layout properties. Each element represented on the page has its own associated properties, not dissimilar to the way in which Visual Age for Java associates application elements with collections of properties that can be accessed by a right mouse click. (See Figure 6.4.)

Let's say the first thing I want to do is lay out some text and add an eye-catching graphic. By selecting the text button from the left-hand panel, I can drag the text rectangle into whatever size and position is desired. Then, doing what all writers do, I can type some words for posterity.

In Figure 6.5, you should be able to see the text rectangle I created (in this case, for the headline) as well as the properties box next to it. A critical notion to keep in mind when working with NetObjects Fusion is that

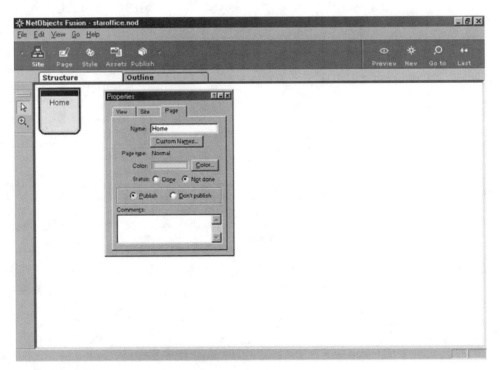

Figure 6.3   The site view of NetObjects Fusion.

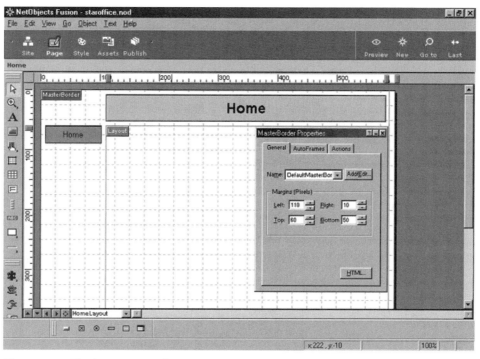

Figure 6.4 The layout page view.

the properties box will change depending on where you have clicked. It brings up a single properties box and then flips between the objects as you select them. It took me four tries to capture this image, as I neglected to ensure that I clicked inside the text rectangle to activate its property box. That said, you can see that the properties box allows you to select the font size, bold, italic, underline, and all other font-control characteristics that are available in NetObjects Fusion.

By using the text and picture tools from the tool bar on the left of the panel, I can do some basic layout of what I think I want my home page to look like. Then, to really see what it will look like in a browser, I have to preview the site. This is done by clicking on the big blue preview button at the top right of the workspace. At that point, NetObjects generates a preview of the site and calls up your default browser to display the page. The amount of time needed to generate a preview is directly proportional to the number of pages and complexity of your Web site. This is one of the reasons I started with a simple, single-page example. The

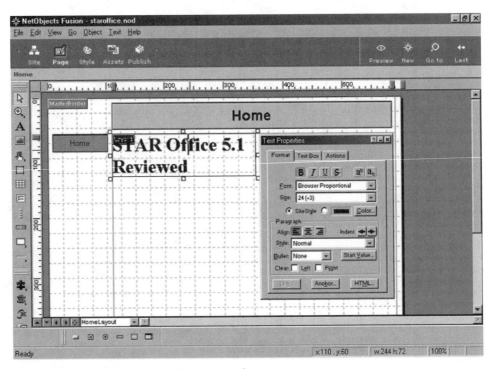

Figure 6.5 Text placement and font control.

strategy is to build your site in small, discrete blocks, then assemble them into a completed Web site when you are happy that the individual pages are exactly what you want.

In Figure 6.6 you can see what the page looked like in preview mode. As soon as I saw it, I realized that the graphic stuck out too far on the right and that I truly hated the banner and home buttons. This struck me as a good time to use one of the really neat features of NetObjects—the ability to change the view of tagged screen elements.

By letting NetObjects Fusion manage the creation of the HTML, one of the benefits is that a Web site developer can quickly and easily go into the site and change the look and feel of all banners, backgrounds, buttons, and fonts. This is applied to the site as a whole and means that updating the look of your intranet page (or whatever it is you choose to use NOF to build) is not a time-consuming task. In fact, we use NetObjects Fusion to create our own internal company news site, and we apply the style changes at least once a week, if only to keep people coming back for more.

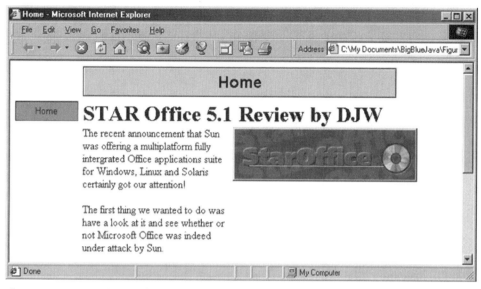

Figure 6.6 A preview of the page from NetObjects Fusion.

The real dilemma of the Web is quality not quantity. With so much information, data, and noise available on the Web, the question becomes one of attracting and keeping people on your site. There is tremendous competition for attention out there, and a good Web site has to beat the competition to keep folks coming back for more. This means you need a content strategy, naturally, but you also need to remerchandise your site, making it look constantly fresh and new.

To change the styles of buttons and other objects, go back into the page and select the Style option from the menu at the top of the page. This brings up the select list and examples shown in Figure 6.7.

For purposes of the StarOffice Review, I kind of thought Professional was the most appropriate. After double clicking on the style name to ensure it was selected, then clicking site, a message box popped up to ask me if I wanted to apply the new style name to the site, which, of course, I did. I guess this ensures that you didn't hit that name solely by accident.

You might think it would be more intuitive to have an Activate button there at the list, but once you're used to the behavior, it's pretty straightforward. Still, I thought it was a good idea to mention it in case you're working with NetObjects Fusion for the first time.

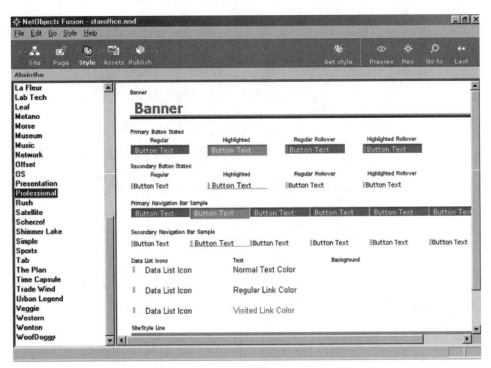

Figure 6.7 Default style sheets provided with NetObjects Fusion 4.

Adding Pages

Once you have NetObjects Fusion up and running, and you have defined your home page, it is reasonable to expect that you will want to add a number of pages underneath home. After all, navigating through a site is what most Web designers are hoping for, although statistics tell us that the home page is by far the most visited and first left.

Adding a page to the site is actually quite straightforward. From the site map view of NetObjects, select edit and new page. The keyboard shortcut is Ctrl+N. Somewhat annoyingly, the right mouse button doesn't bring up a menu list. In fact, right clicking on the workspace in site view mode seems to do nothing at all. A definite oversight on the part of the tool developers, this.

Having Ctrl+N'd a new page, click on it to select and choose the page option from the menu. This will allow you to work with the page itself. As mentioned earlier, this is the consistent model for working with NOF. You look at the site and select a page with which to work.

The properties for a new page that is added in this fashion gives you three options. These include View, Site, and Page. View lets you lay out your pages vertically or horizontally, while Site gives you the basic page count, create date, and other such trenchant details. The Page view, however, has a couple of useful things you might want to activate to save time in development.

The Page properties under site view is shown in Figure 6.8. Specifically, I would like to draw your attention to the Publish/Don't publish radio buttons. When I first started working with NetObjects, I found the amount of time taken to compile an entire site was onerous when all I wanted to do was view a changed page. One of the people at work walked by while I was cursing under my breath and quickly pointed to this great tension reliever. Selecting Don't publish suppresses the compilation of that page in preview mode, and it lets you keep working on it in draft mode while still rolling out completed pages to the http server.

Because one of the first things I wanted to do with this page was to create a data template, I thought it would be a good idea to create the layout first in a more generic form. I was looking for a standard background that would be a light watermark or backdrop for the site. I knew I had to be very careful about this kind of graphic because it adds size to the site

Figure 6.8 Overall properties of a page belonging to a Web site.

and can easily become visually overbearing. At the same time, you probably want to know what your options are, so I thought it was a perfectly appropriate addition to the site from a Big Blue Java perspective.

That said, the layout properties box lets you select background and choose to work as part of the style sheet for the site (usually, you would define a consistent background in a new style, but let's take this one step at a time). You can choose to color the page, or you can browse your .jpg and .gif graphic assets to provide a picturesque background, somewhat like the graphics a lot of folks put on their PCs at home.

Because we were reviewing the StarOffice product, it occurred to me that perhaps that graphic might make a good visual anchor throughout the site. Once selected, however, you can see in Figure 6.9 that the default behavior of the insert was to tile the graphic, repeating it many times, which was not actually what I had in mind.

To get around this, I had to use a graphics package. Personally, I find that MS Photoshop pretty much meets my requirements for image manipula-

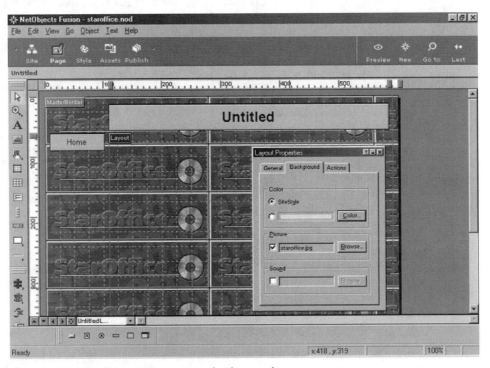

Figure 6.9 Including a JPG as a page background.

tion (as long as I don't want to add text), where my more professional graphics fiends (no that's not a typo), prefer Adobe products such as Photoshop. It occurred to me that using the little Sun logo on a white or clear background might provide some cool visual interest without burdening anyone downloading the page with too large a file. Every byte adds up, ultimately translating to a long page-load time from a user perspective, which can be painful at 56-kbps and excruciating at 28.8-kbps modem speeds.

For similar reasons, it is usually a good idea to avoid embedding sounds in a page. If you wish, of course, you can, and this is the property box where you define that asset.

This might be a good time to point out the frame labels that show you how the page is constructed. Every page must have a master border, which defines the area in which the other page assets fit. As you can tell from the earlier coverage of adding a page, there is also a layout region. Figure 6.10 shows the rectangles in the construction view where these page elements are shown. In this example, you can see the banner and the home button, which both show up on the page when previewed or published. However, you can also see the master border rectangle and the layout rectangle. Click on either of these to activate the property box associated either with the entire page frame or the layout section. You can add or edit master border frame definitions. The layout options are covered in the previous section of this chapter.

Labeling Pages

To change the name of a particular page after you create it, you must click on the name in the site view and edit it there. This is similar to the way

Figure 6.10 Labels for master border and layout objects.

you change the name of a folder or document in Windows. That title then shows up on the title bar when you want to work with the page itself. Interestingly, there is no way to change the text property of the bar from within the page view. Seems a little restricted, but there you have it. To change the name of the page, you must do so from the site view. (See Figure 6.11.)

For purposes of this site, I wanted to first create the navigation and then add the graphic image that I had already captured when working with StarOffice. The figures became the representation of the site, and I wanted to make sure the flow was right before bothering with the finer detail of arranging type, selecting font sizes, and basically ensuring that the copy fit.

Aligning Objects

Once you have defined your images, tables, text rectangles, and other assets, you can use NetObjects Fusion utilities to distribute and align the assets relative to each other. These are accessed from the menu bar at the top of the NetObjects Fusion screen and are shown in Figure 6.12.

Inserting Text

This is a pretty straightforward operation. On the toolbar located by default on the left-hand side of the page you will find a button with a

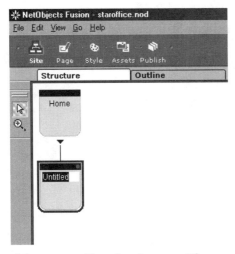

Figure 6.11   Changing the page title.

large letter *A* on it. This stands for, you guessed it, *alphabet*, and it allows you to draw a text rectangle on the Web page.

For purposes of this Web site I had copied some text directly from Word, and the Ctrl+V keyboard shortcut deposits the text into the rectangle. As you might hope, the rectangle automatically resizes to accommodate the amount of text pasted into it.

If you want to update text without having to cut and paste or otherwise touch the page, you should import a file into the text rectangle. This is accomplished by selecting import page under the file menu and browsing the filenames until you get to the one you want to include.

As with cut and paste, the rectangle automatically resizes to accommodate. When I tried this with my review of StarOffice, I found that I could just pick an MS Word 97 filename and StarOffice imported it directly. The only difference in the way the text looked within NetObjects Fusion was in the paragraph spacing. It wasn't necessary to have additional carriage returns to separate paragraphs. Other than that, everything looked as it had in the original document. Mind you, I didn't have complex objects such as tables and the like. When I tried importing an Excel spreadsheet, it understandably complained and tried to convert the document to ASCII text. Not much came through, however. After writing this, I realized that

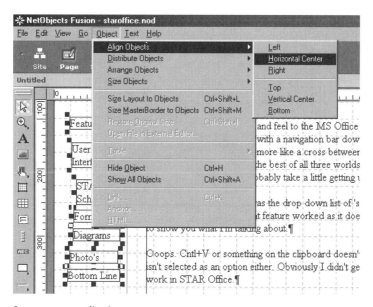

Figure 6.12 Aligning text.

you probably would want to know whether you could import complex word documents directly into NetObjects Fusion, so I gave it a try.

It did not like that at all. The text values themselves were converted to ASCII and imported, but I got the same corrupted text messages that appeared when I imported a spreadsheet. Oh well.

From the text and image assets you have imported into your site, you can start defining the links and navigation behavior you want.

Linking Objects and Pages

To create text links to specific areas on a page, you must first define anchors. This is done by clicking on the specific place on the page you want your anchor to be located, then selecting Anchor from the properties box. The dialog for defining the anchor and for listing already defined anchors then comes up. This is shown in Figure 6.13.

Once you have defined your anchors, you can select and link the activators you want to have clicked in order to land the user at the destination.

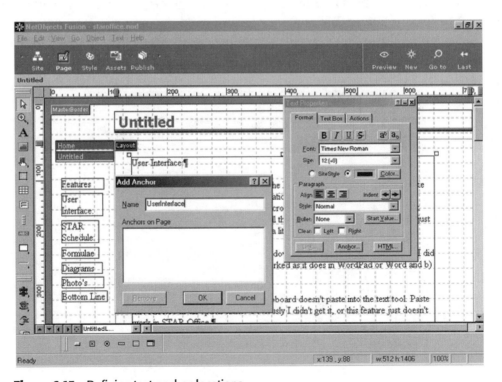

Figure 6.13 Defining text anchor locations.

Double click on the text rectangle to get into edit mode, highlight the text you want to make clickable, and select link from the properties box. As you can see in Figure 6.14, this brings up the destinations available to you, including the anchor we just defined. This is the process you use to create a Web site.

Of course, in and of itself this is not all that much more impressive than FrontPage. Where the power of NetObjects Fusion comes in is in the tools for administering the site, the component add-ins, and the ability to support data access. The components that are provided with NetObjects Fusion include the following:

- Media plug-in
- Data lists
- Data controller
- Java
- ActiveX

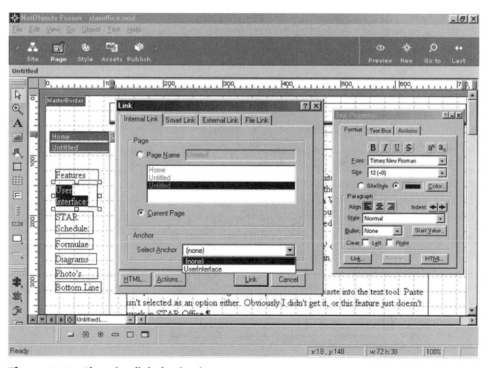

Figure 6.14 Choosing link destinations.

This makes for a pretty powerful combination of components when added to the built-in capabilities provided by NetObjects Fusion itself.

For example, one of the components that we like to use is the data plug-in. This widget allows you to define internal or external sources of data for the Web site. Normally, we try to keep our data in SQL databases, although some of our customers have data sources such as FoxPro or even dBASE applications. There is native support for these data sources built into the data component of NetObjects Fusion. In fact, the default supported list of data sources includes the following:

- Microsoft Access
- Paradox
- Text files
- dBASE
- Excel
- FoxPro

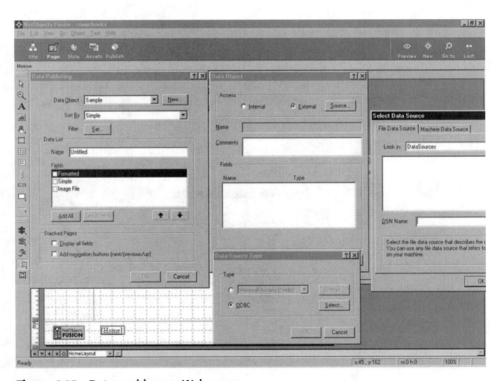

Figure 6.15 Data-enable your Web pages.

As well, you can see from Figure 6.15 that the capability to define ODBC links to any database that supports it is also supplied. This pretty much includes anybody you can imagine.

Summary

I find it interesting to talk with graphic development people specializing in the creation of Web sites, who tend to be a bit artsy and are more concerned with aesthetics than, say, scalability issues. This is probably a good thing, as someone should be concerned with what looks good.

When I am speaking with these people, I usually mention MS FrontPage as a development environment. I do this more to see how they'll react than from any real interest in the MS product. We went through a Front-Page phase until the Web site designers got tired of all the additional overhead generated. Most of the time, people who work professionally with Web site development react like mashed cats to the idea that MS FrontPage is a suitable environment.

NetObjects Fusion, on the other hand, is considered respectable. Perhaps from a graphics standpoint you might like the layering and visual control you can get from Macromedia Dreamweaver or Fireworks, but NetObjects Fusion will not only meet the needs of even demanding graphics people, but it supports a large-scale multideveloper approach.

When you add in the data access components, it adds up to one thing—NetObjects Fusion is a very strong element of Big Blue Java. Use it to get your first Web-enabled database applications going even if you don't have access to some of the other sophisticated tools.

It is easy to use and it is powerful. We had a summer intern from UCLA who learned the product in a matter of days and within three weeks had a very slick demo site, complete with Java application add-ins and database access.

CHAPTER 7

Servlets and Java Server Pages

Like applets, servlets are Java programs that perform useful work. Well, depending on the purpose of the application, *useful* might be too strong a word, but in any case they execute a desired function. In our case, we are specifically interested in data-handling capabilities, as e-business is primarily about commercial transactions that involve the exchange of data at some level. Hopefully, they exchange money data.

A great deal of Web-based application development uses graphic images, not only to enhance the user's experience, but also to communicate goods (and potentially services if you can find a comprehensible way to represent them) for e-stores and e-tailing.

The purpose of this chapter is to help you gain a better understanding of exactly what a servlet is, especially in contrast to an applet, and the role of Java Server Pages. For many of you, the introductory part of Java programming will be old hat, but in my experience it's always best to introduce a concept from the ground up. We will not be spending a lot of time on basic Java programming here. One assumption underlying this book is that you either have that skill or are interested in Big Blue's tool set from a design, architecture, or planning perspective—which means that someone else gets the job of actually writing the programs.

Servlets Defined

In the beginning there was the Java Web Server from JavaSoft. This product has supported servlets as defined in the JavaSoft Servlet API 1.0. Other Web servers, such as WebSphere, support this API as well.

Servlets are Java software components that are protocol- and platform-independent because they execute inside a server-side Java Virtual Machine. These components support a request/response model of computing that allows us to extend the capabilities of the Web server, as the components can integrate with other files, applications, and data stores. Servlets let you reach outside the Web server or application server and access other system resources. Because they execute on the server side, there are fewer problems encountered with bandwidth and other performance considerations when the applications are deployed.

How Servlets Work

The process flow of a generic servlet would encompass the following (see Figure 7.1):

- Web client passes request to the Web server.
- The server invokes the servlet, passing the client request as parameters.
- The servlet executes accordingly.
- A response is constructed and passed back to the server.
- The server forwards the request to the Web client.

Servlets explicitly manage the interaction between themselves and the external resources. They may invoke additional Java applications, or even other servlets, to form a chain of work. Or instead, servlets can invoke external applications in other languages, allowing calls to legacy data stores such as rdms or CIC applications.

One key difference between applets and servlets is that servlets may be nonvisible objects. Roughly analogous to a stored procedure in a relational database application, the servlet is invoked by name, passes parameters, and returns results.

However, increasingly we are finding that for the express purpose of retrieving database results and passing those back to calling applica-

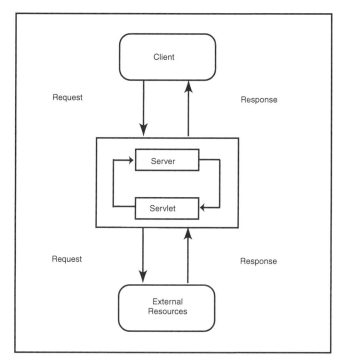

Figure 7.1 Servlet process flow.

tions in the form of browser-based clients, Java Server Pages are a more effective solution.

Advantages of Using Servlets

Security. The servlet can contain or obtain validation and security logic for accessing resources outside the Web server.

Performance. Servlets are multithreaded and can run within one background operating system process. This advantage may be offset by the interpreted nature of any Java application.

Java-based. Quick and robust application development is a feature of Java compared to C++ and other development tools.

Portability. Again, due to the features of Java, servlets can be deployed and executed on any compatible JVM.

Robustness. Poorly designed servlets cannot bring down a server due to a memory fault.

Separation of concern. Servlets allow you to portion out work to appropriate sources and provide the name of the servlet to an html developer, who can use the servlet to generate dynamic results without understanding how those results are generated.

Advantages of Servlets over CGI-BIN Applications

Servlets function very similarly to CGI-BIN applications. However, there are several advantages to working with servlets. First, parameter passing is easier to grasp for new programmers when developing servlet-passed applications. Experienced CGI programmers can accomplish the same result, but the technical expertise required is somewhat higher than implementing in Java.

More important, CGI-BIN applications are not portable across various platforms. As a CGI programmer, you need specific technical knowledge about the deployment environment. This is very different than the objectives for writing an application for cross-platform deployment. Using Java servlets allows the programmer to adopt the write-once, run-everywhere approach, as opposed to the effort needed to port CGI applications.

Last, servlets use a different threading model than CGI applications. As with a CGI application, the first request from a client initiates a process, or thread, on the server. However, once spawned, a servlet request is destroyed only when the Web server itself is bounced or when the servlet explicitly completes and quits. Otherwise, the process runs in the background, waiting for another request.

Using a telephone book lookup application as an example, once requested, the servlet fires up, passing the last name parameter to the external data source where the demographic data is maintained. Once retrieved, the result or result set is passed back to the browser for review. The servlet remains running and does not require the same initialization overhead when the next request for a phone number is sent from either that user or any other.

Drawbacks of Servlets

For every pro there is a con, and servlets are no exception. While programming a task in servlets is quite clean, the difficulty comes in displaying the results. To display retrieved results through a servlet, you must take a request from the browser (no problem), execute the logic (no problem), generate the response (again, no problem), and then send a response to the browser, including the necessary HTML or XML tags. This is a problem.

To accomplish this, the whole page must be created as part of the functionality of the servlet. If you want to change the look and feel of the page, you have to change and recompile the servlet. It is a messy business to get an icon moved or updated. To get around this, Java Server Pages were defined.

Java Server Pages

Another approach to providing results from server-side Java programs is to use Java Server Pages or JSPs.

Servlets and JSPs have Java-based logic in common. However, as covered previously, servlets can be nonvisible. It is not necessary for them to deal with layout and user interface issues. In point of fact, it is actually quite a lot of work to incorporate user interface and presentation logic into a servlet.

For this reason, Java Server Pages incorporate many of the same features as servlets, but support much easier presentation management through the use of XML and HTML tags.

Java Server Pages are intended to display dynamically generated content to a Web browser. They are all visible. HTML alone, of course, would have been sufficient if the world had been content with static Web pages. Beyond publishing white papers and so-called brochureware, this was only a phase in the development of the Web as a communications and commercial medium. Updated and ever changing content is what it is all about. To combine data access with Web browser layout, we use Java Server Pages.

If you have ever written or come across an Active Server Page (ASP) from Microsoft, then you have some familiarity already with the technology. The problem is, of course, that Microsoft has opted for a proprietary API to its Microsoft IIS or Personal Web Server. Pages developed using ASP technology are not scalable beyond the restrictions of those products, and they are not portable to other Web servers such as WebSphere.

Advantages of Java Server Pages

There are several key reasons that you would use Java Server Pages to create an application:

- Separates content creation from its presentation
- Enhanced reusability
- Simplified page development through tags

Who Develops Java Server Pages?

In the beginning, there was the page, and the page was created by a Web page developer. By referring to tags or scriptlets for the content creation, page designers need to be more concerned with the look and feel of the layout than with the logic needed to generate the contents. They know how the page is expected to ask for results, and, of course, they need to know what the results will look like in order to format the results page appropriately. They are ultimately most concerned with the user experience than with the business logic.

Enterprise JavaBeans can also be called from Java Server Pages, which clearly shows how reusability is enhanced. Not only is content generation separated from the presentation logic, but through the use of beans business logic is separated from the underlying infrastructure and system calls needed to successfully run the bean.

Using this division of labor, JSPs may be developed by nonprogrammers. While this may cause some to gasp, it is becoming a well-known fact that good system programmers with a sense of visual style are a rare and much-sought-after breed. It simply makes more sense to allocate programmers to logic and graphics forms' designers to the pages.

Critical to the success of the team management process are the naming conventions, object services, and libraries, as well as typical result set examples.

When to Use Java Server Pages

If servlets are used primarily to perform back-end processing, JSPs are used when those results must be passed to a Web browser for user review and action. On the continuum of skills, JSPs are less complicated. Although they are written in Java, they may be created and maintained by people with more junior programming expertise. Given the development of dynamic graphic products from CD-ROMs to kiosks and video games, finding a graphics-savvy developer with a modicum of programming experience is not that difficult.

How Java Server Pages Execute

When invoked, any JSP page is executed by the JSP engine running on either a Web server or JSP-enabled application server such as WebSphere. The server takes the client request, pulls up the JSP page, and passes the resulting response back to the client.

Java Server Pages are usually compiled into servlets. For this reason, JSPs and servlets are treated in much the same way. If they do not exist when first called, they are compiled into a servlet class and cached in memory. The most basic implementation of this process is demonstrated in Figure 7.2.

As stated earlier, this is fine for your basic dynamic Web application with a small number of anticipated hits and preferably a discrete database

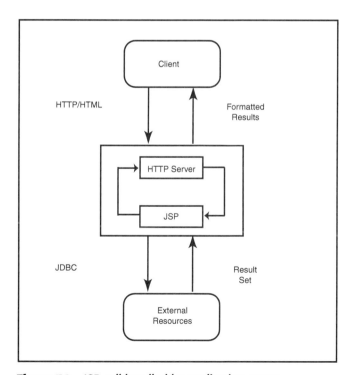

Figure 7.2 JSP call handled by application server.

accessed by JDBC. However, it does not scale terribly well into the hundreds of users and millions of rows that make up a real-world Web-based application for a great many people.

One of the reasons for this is that each user may create a new connection to the database, which requires initialization overhead and puts strain on the database server itself. In order to break out the logic to the staff with expertise most appropriate to address the problem, you can combine servlets and Java Server Pages.

As the implementations of JSPs become more complex, we have started to look for ways to let JSPs handle the user interface for returned results while taking advantage of the components available in Enterprise Java-Beans. These beans are called from the JSP using Remote Method Invocation (RMI) or IIOP.

Through the services of the EJB components, JSP programmers can take advantage of services regardless of complexity of location. There is no way for page programmers to know if an EJB component they are using is executing on a server halfway around the world or right next door. And the power of this technology is not only do they not know, they don't have to know. Managing the results returned from the call to the servlet or the bean is the only consideration that a JSP programmer needs to address.

XML Compatibility

Java Server Pages can generate both XML and HTML pages, and XML tools can usually pull in JSP pages. These can be run under any server that supports JSP. The simplest way to generate XML is to include the XML tags and the static template definitions of a Java Server Page. Server-side beans that generate XML can be called instead of servlets to create dynamic XML pages.

Using a Java Server Page as a middle tier as part of the Enterprise Java-Beans architecture is supported in the Java 2 Enterprise Edition platform.

How They Fit Together

Unquestionably servers are segregating into areas of concern and responsibility. Gone are the days when an enterprise (or even departmental) solution could be handled by one or two programmers.

Writing Java applications for the World Wide Web opens up tremendous potential for cross-platform deployment. For the first time in the history of computing we can create applications that are virtually write once, run anywhere. Perhaps it is to be expected that there is a tremendous complexity inherent in that capability. The Java approach to managing this complexity is to separate the areas of concern into technology that exposes and calls services from others.

You should by now have a better sense of exactly where servlets and JSPs fit into the application architecture. From here we create some specific examples of Web-based applications using both servlets and JSPs.

Application Scenario

Let's say we want to open an online store. Throughout Big Blue Java we consistently use the example of a Collectibles Store. The idea is that everyone can relate to collecting something, whether of commercial value (e.g., stamps or coins) or of a strictly personal nature (e.g., rocks or butterflies). In any case, the Web is the perfect place to present your collection to the world and to look for opportunities to trade, sell, or buy.

In this scenario, we have a collection of comic books left over from days gone by. As most people now know, well-preserved rare editions of comic books can be worth a considerable amount of money. A first edition *X-men* from 1963 was listed on the Web for $700—and its condition was only fair!

For purposes of exploring servlets and JSPs, let's consider our vintage collection of comic books stored for years in the attic and ready for the enjoyment of a new owner or owners.

The first order of business would be to register a domain name, set up a static Web site on a server (ours or rented), and get listed on a few search engines. This parallels what most folks were doing with the Web in the mid-1990s. Assuming we have the basic infrastructure available to us, let's look at two scenarios for generating a simple interactive Web site dedicated to our comic book collection. Let's also assume we have entered all the specifics in an Access database, so we'll want to do a little integration from Web site to external database.

In the interest of maintaining a consistent focus, we will use the Web site generated with WebSphere Studio and NetObjects Fusion for our site navigation and the static html. Let's assume that our more graphically gifted spouse did this, which in my case is absolutely true. I only wish I actually had some of these comics to sell! For those of you who outgrew the comic book stage long ago, wait until we do the international fine wine exchange site using Enterprise JavaBeans. In any event, we have a Web site to create and some comic books to sell. The basic topology for our site is shown in Figure 7.3

In this case we are not concerned with credit card transactions or any aspect of a commercial site other than a straightforward listing of the comic books available, their condition, and price. To order, an e-mail is initiated that conveys the name, address, and telephone number of the person requesting more information or looking to place an order.

Each of the three approaches will use the same html generated from Web-Sphere Studio. The only differences will be in how the data is obtained and the result screens populated. The screen is shown in Figure 7.4.

The Applet Approach

At the Solutions99 conference, almost everyone was promoting the servlet and Java Server Page approach. The applet approach was very unpopular.

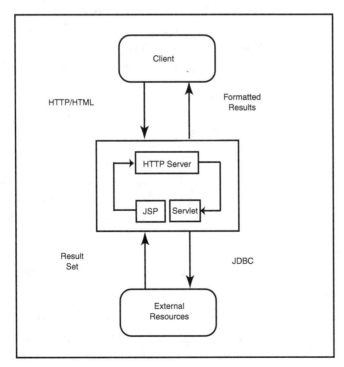

Figure 7.3 JSPs and servlets combined.

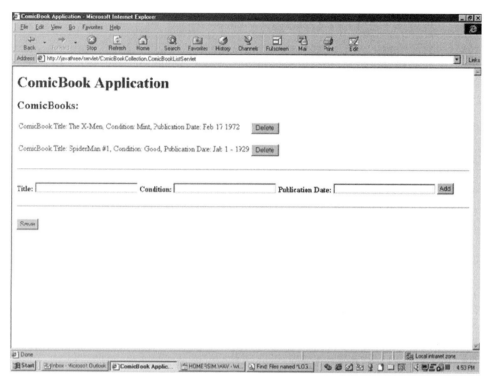

Figure 7.4   A simple servlet-based application viewed in a browser.

We found that applets can be a functional way to build Java applications, but there are a few things that have to be established about the environment in which they will be running. For example, a casual dial-in user of a Web-based service is not going to very interested in the wait required to load a large applet. For that matter, people will often quit and move on if their screen takes more than a few seconds to load. This is where servlets and Java Server Pages make a tremendous amount of sense.

On the other hand, if you have a dedicated group of users with T-1 access or a local area intranet, the amount of time to load the applet may not be much greater than the time it takes to fluff up Outlook98 from the hard disk.

Additionally, you may have slow connections. Still, a dedicated group of users, perhaps folks who dial in and work from home, may not mind downloading or even installing a few plug-ins from CD.

Because of differences in the applet approach and a server-side approach, I have addressed applet development in separate chapters. For now, let's carry on with how we develop server-side applications.

The Servlet Approach

We can very easily code the connection of the html screen to the Access database using servlet tags. The servlet is called in the html through the following code:

```java
package ComicBookCollection;

/**
 * This type was created in VisualAge.
 */
public class ComicBook implements java.io.Serializable {
    private String fieldTitle = new String();
    private String fieldCondition = new String();
    private String fieldPublicationDate = new String();
/**
 * ComicBook constructor comment.
 */
public ComicBook(String title, String condition, String publicationDate) {
    setTitle (title);
    setCondition (condition);
    setPublicationDate (publicationDate);

    }
/**
 * Gets the condition property (java.lang.String) value.
 * @return The condition property value.
 * @see #setCondition
 */
public String getCondition() {
    return fieldCondition;
}
/**
 * Gets the publicationDate property (java.lang.String) value.
 * @return The publicationDate property value.
 * @see #setPublicationDate
 */
public String getPublicationDate() {
    return fieldPublicationDate;
}
/**
 * Gets the title property (java.lang.String) value.
 * @return The title property value.
 * @see #setTitle
 */
public String getTitle() {
    return fieldTitle;
}
/**
 * Sets the condition property (java.lang.String) value.
 * @param condition The new value for the property.
 * @see #getCondition
```

```
 */
public void setCondition(String condition) {
    fieldCondition = condition;
}
/**
 * Sets the publicationDate property (java.lang.String) value.
 * @param publicationDate The new value for the property.
 * @see #getPublicationDate
 */
public void setPublicationDate(String publicationDate) {
    fieldPublicationDate = publicationDate;
}
/**
 * Sets the title property (java.lang.String) value.
 * @param title The new value for the property.
 * @see #getTitle
 */
public void setTitle(String title) {
    fieldTitle = title;
}
}
```

The next program deals with a particular comic book, an instance of the comic book class. One of the reasons for instantiating a particular object of the class in this way is to support persistence. In the old days we called this *saving to disk*.

```
package ComicBookCollection;

import java.io.*;
import javax.servlet.http.*;
import javax.servlet.*;
import java.util.*;
import ComicBookCollection.ComicBook;

public class ComicBookListServlet extends javax.servlet.http.HttpServlet{
    private String SerializedComicBookFileName="d:\\ComicBooks.ser";
    private String ServletURL=null;
    private Vector fieldComicBookList = new Vector();
/**
 * ComicBookListServlet constructor comment.
 */
public ComicBookListServlet() {
    super();
}
/**
 * This method was created in VisualAge.
 * @param title java.lang.String
 * @param condition java.lang.String
 * @param publicationDate java.lang.String
 */
public synchronized void addEntry(String title , String condition, String
```

```
publicationDate) {
    getComicBookList().addElement(new ComicBook(title, condition,
publicationDate));
    return;
}
/**
 * This method was created in VisualAge.
 * @param Title java.lang.String
 * @param condition java.lang.String
 * @param publicationDate java.lang.String
 */
public synchronized void deleteEntry(String title, String condition,
String publicationDate) {
    Enumeration e = getComicBookList().elements();
    ComicBook c = null;
    while (e.hasMoreElements()){
        c=(ComicBook)e.nextElement();
        if (c.getTitle().equals(title) &&
c.getCondition().equals(condition) &&
c.getPublicationDate().equals(publicationDate)){
                getComicBookList().removeElement(c);
                return;
            }
    }
    return;
}
/**
 * This method was created in VisualAge.
 */
public void destroy() {
    saveList();
}
/**
 * This method was created in VisualAge.
 * @param req javax.servlet.http.HttpServletRequest
 * @param resp javax.servlet.http.HttpServletResponse
 * @exception javax.servlet.ServletException The exception description.
 * @exception java.io.IOException The exception description.
 */
protected void doGet(HttpServletRequest req, HttpServletResponse resp)
throws ServletException, IOException {
    sendList(req, resp);
}
/**
 * This method was created in VisualAge.
 */
protected void doPost(HttpServletRequest req,
                      HttpServletResponse resp) throws ServletException,
IOException
{
    boolean sendTheList = true;
```

```java
        String action = req.getParameter("action");
        String title = req.getParameter("title");
        String condition = req.getParameter("condition");
        String publicationDate = req.getParameter("publicationDate");
        if( action.equals("add")){
            addEntry( title, condition, publicationDate);
        }
        else if( action.equals("delete")){
            deleteEntry( title, condition, publicationDate);
        }
        else if( action.equals("save")){
            saveList();
        }
        else{
            sendTheList = false;
            log("Bad request");
        }
        if( sendTheList){
            sendList( req, resp);
        }
    }
/**
 * Gets the comicBookList property (java.util.Vector) value.
 * @return The comicBookList property value.
 * @see #setComicBookList
 */
public Vector getComicBookList() {
    return fieldComicBookList;
}
/**
 * This method was created in VisualAge.
 * @param config javax.servlet.ServletConfig
 * @exception javax.servlet.ServletException The exception description.
 */
public void init(ServletConfig config) throws ServletException {
    try {
            FileInputStream fIn = new
FileInputStream(SerializedComicBookFileName);
            ObjectInputStream in = new ObjectInputStream(fIn);
            setComicBookList((Vector)in.readObject());
    }
    catch(FileNotFoundException e){
            setComicBookList(new Vector());
    }
    catch(Exception e){
    log("Error initalizing servlet: " + e);
    throw new ServletException("Error initalizing servlet: " + e);
    }

}
/**
```

```
 * This method was created in VisualAge.
 */
public synchronized void saveList() {
    try{
        FileOutputStream fOut = new FileOutputStream(
SerializedComicBookFileName);
        ObjectOutputStream out = new ObjectOutputStream( fOut);
        out.writeObject( getComicBookList());
    }
    catch( IOException e){
        log("Error saving list: " + e);
    }
}
/**
 * This method was created in VisualAge.
 * @param req javax.servlet.http.HttpServletRequest
 * @param resp javax.servlet.http.HttpServletResponse
 */
private void sendList(HttpServletRequest req, HttpServletResponse resp) {
    PrintWriter pOut = null;
    ServletURL = req.getScheme() + "://" + req.getServerName() + ":" +
        req.getServerPort() + req.getServletPath();
    try{
        resp.setContentType( "text/html");
/*
        pOut = resp.getWriter();
        The Domino Go Webserver does not support the getWriter method
*/
        pOut = new PrintWriter( resp.getOutputStream());
        pOut.println("<TITLE>ComicBook Application</TITLE>");
        pOut.println("<H1>ComicBook Application</H1>");
        pOut.println("<H2>ComicBooks:</H2>");
        pOut.println("<TABLE>");
        for( int i = 0; i < getComicBookList().size(); i++){
            String Title =
((ComicBook)getComicBookList().elementAt(i)).getTitle();
            String Condition =
((ComicBook)getComicBookList().elementAt(i)).getCondition();
            String PublicationDate =
((ComicBook)getComicBookList().elementAt(i)).getPublicationDate();
            pOut.println("<TR>"
                    +"<TD VALIGN=TOP>");
            pOut.println(" ComicBook Title: " + Title + ",
Condition: " + Condition + ", Publication Date: " + PublicationDate);
            pOut.println("</TD>");
        pOut.println("<TD>");
            pOut.println("  <FORM ACTION=" + ServletURL + "
METHOD=POST>");
            pOut.println("   <INPUT TYPE=HIDDEN NAME=action
VALUE=delete>");
            pOut.println("   <INPUT TYPE=HIDDEN NAME=title VALUE=\""
```

```
        + Title + "\">");
            pOut.println("   <INPUT TYPE=HIDDEN NAME=condition VALUE=\"" +
Condition + "\">");
                pOut.println("   <INPUT TYPE=HIDDEN NAME=publicationDate
VALUE=\"" + PublicationDate + "\">");
                pOut.println("   <INPUT TYPE=SUBMIT NAME=DeleteButton
VALUE=Delete>");
                pOut.println("  </FORM>");
                pOut.println("</TD>");
                pOut.println("</TR>");
            }
            pOut.println("</TABLE>");
            pOut.println("<HR>");
            pOut.println("<FORM ACTION=" + ServletURL + " METHOD=POST>");
            pOut.println("  <INPUT TYPE=HIDDEN NAME=action VALUE=add>");
            pOut.println("  <b>Title:</b>");
            pOut.println("  <INPUT TYPE=TEXT NAME=title SIZE=30>");
            pOut.println("  <b>Condition:</b>");
            pOut.println("  <INPUT TYPE=TEXT NAME=condition SIZE=30>");
            pOut.println("  <b>Publication Date:</b>");
            pOut.println("  <INPUT TYPE=TEXT NAME=publicationDate
SIZE=30>");
            pOut.println("  <INPUT TYPE=SUBMIT NAME=AddButton VALUE=Add>");
            pOut.println("</FORM>");
            pOut.println("<HR>");
            pOut.println("<FORM ACTION=" + ServletURL + " METHOD=POST>");
            pOut.println("  <INPUT TYPE=HIDDEN NAME=action VALUE=save>");
            pOut.println("  <INPUT TYPE=SUBMIT NAME=SaveButton
VALUE=Save>");
            pOut.println("</FORM>");
            resp.setStatus( HttpServletResponse.SC_OK);
            pOut.close();
        }
        catch( IOException e)
        {
            log("Error writing to browser: " + e);
        }
    }
}
/**
 * Sets the comicBookList property (java.util.Vector) value.
 * @param comicBookList The new value for the property.
 * @see #getComicBookList
 */
public void setComicBookList(Vector comicBookList) {
    fieldComicBookList = comicBookList;
}
}
```

This calls a Java Server Page from within the html when the user clicks submit on the form.

```
<!DOCTYPE HTML PUBLIC "-//W3C//DTD HTML 4.0 Transitional//EN">
<!-- Login Page Version 1.0 Written by: James Carlson August 9, 1999-->
<!-- Login Page Updated by: Bill Simpson August 17, 1999-->
<!-- Login Page Updated by: Bill Simpson Sept. 28, 1999-->
<!-- This JSP takes quires the user for username and password and   -->
<!-- passes these parameters by the post method to XXXXX.class       -->
<!-- If the username and password are not approved then this JSP     -->
<!-- will handle the error qury the user for a valid username        -->

<html>
<head>
 <title>DealManager Login Screen</title>
  <link rel="STYLESHEET" type="text/css" href="GFSDemo.css">
</head>
<BODY><center>
<img src="images/DM_Splash.jpg" width=500 height=300 border=0
align="absmiddle">
<BR>
<BR>

<% if (request.getParameter("login") != null ) {
       wns.gfs.UserManager users = new wns.gfs.UserManager();
       boolean loginPass;
       loginPass = users.verify( request.getParameter("login"),
request.getParameter("pwd") );

       if (! loginPass) {%>

           <!-- Hacker Bait!!! -->
           <FORM method=POST action="Login.jsp">
           <table cellspacing="2" cellpadding="2" border="0">
               <tr>
                   <td>Login Failed Please re-enter your login
information.</td>
               </tr>
               <tr>
                   <td>Login</td>
               </tr>
               <tr>
                   <td><INPUT TYPE="text" NAME="login" Value="<%=
request.getParameter("login").toString() %>" SIZE="20"
onFocus="select()"></td>
               </tr>
               <tr>
                   <td>Password</td>
               </tr>
               <tr>
                   <td><INPUT TYPE="Password" NAME="pwd" Value="Re-Enter
your password here" SIZE="20" onFocus="select()"></td>
               </tr>
               <tr>
                   <td><input type="submit" value="Submit"></td>
```

```
                </tr>
            </table>
            </form>
        <% }
        else { %>
            <!-- Recognized User! -->
            <BEAN Name="mySession" TYPE="wns.gfs.UserSession" INTROSPECT=NO
CREATE=YES SCOPE=SESSION></BEAN>
            <%
                mySession.setName( request.getParameter("login") );
                mySession.setValid(true);
            %>
            <SCRIPT LANGUAGE="javascript">
            <!--
                location = "toolbar.htm";
            //      -->
            </SCRIPT>
<%      } %>
<% }
    else { %>
        <!-- First Time Vists... I swear! -->
        <FORM method="POST" action="Login.jsp">
        <table cellspacing="2" cellpadding="2" border="0">
            <tr>
                <td>Login</td>
            </tr>
            <tr>
                <td><INPUT TYPE="text" NAME="login" Value="Enter your login
here" SIZE="20" onFocus="select()"></td>
            </tr>
            <tr>
                <td>Password</td>
            </tr>
            <tr>
                <td><INPUT TYPE="Password" NAME="pwd" Value="Enter your
password here" SIZE="20" onFocus="select()"></td>
            </tr>
            <tr>
                <td><input type="submit" value="Submit"></td>
            </tr>
        </table>
        </form>
<% } %></center>

<APPLET CODE=TabbedControl.CheckHD.class ARCHIVE=CheckHD.jar WIDTH=285
HEIGHT=125 ALIGN="MIDDLE">
        <PARAM NAME = "REDIRECT"
value="http://turing/Gfs/GFS_OCT4/installPage.html">
</APPLET>

</body>
</html>
```

A Combination Approach

Using a the combined services of the servlet for gathering data from Access and the JSP for representing it back to the user, you can see the increased maintainability in architecting even the simplest Web/db applications this way.

There are other ways to provide data back to a calling form, including data access beans, which is covered in the section on Visual Age for Java and through Enterprise JavaBeans. EJB is addressed conceptually in this section, but samples of beans and how these components are used in larger systems are addressed later.

At this point you should have a clear understanding of the basic rudimentary steps when linking html forms with a back-end database using applets, servlets, and Java Server Pages. Our comic book collection might be juvenile, but it shows a few techniques for how just about anyone can get a dynamic Web site up and running. One of the most interesting things about this example is that although the code and approach are not sophisticated, they are scalable. This application can run on an NT server, AS/400, Unix, or an OS/390 mainframe—with the exception of Access as a data store, of course.

As we progress to more-complex business problems, we'll use more-powerful techniques to address them. But you should now be comfortable with both what a servlet or JSP is and how it can be used.

To create a server-side application, you use either servlets or Java Server Pages. It is generally faster and easier to write JSPs. An additional advantage to using JSPs is that you can include html generated from a page designer such as NetObjects Fusion or even FrontPage from Microsoft.

The login screen is shown in Figure 7.5. There are two ways to create this login screen: either by using Java Server Pages (JSP) or directly through a servlet.

```
// This file was generated by IBM WebSphere Studio Release 1.0 on 30-Sep-
98 6:32:29 PM.

package XtremeTravel;

/**
* Login Servlet for the XtremeTravel sample
*/
public class LoginServlet extends com.ibm.servlet.PageListServlet
implements java.io.Serializable
{
```

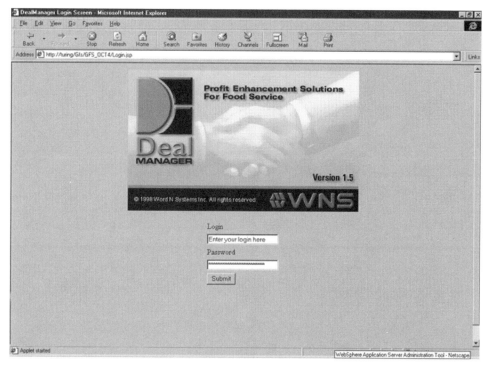

Figure 7.5   Login screen.

```
    /******************************************************************
**********
     * Process incoming requests for information
     *
     * @param request Object that encapsulates the request to the servlet
     * @param response Object that encapsulates the response from the
     * servlet
     */
    public void performTask(javax.servlet.http.HttpServletRequest
request, javax.servlet.http.HttpServletResponse response)
    {
         try
         {
              javax.servlet.http.HttpSession session =
request.getSession(true);

              // instantiate the bean and store it in the request so it
              // can be accessed by the called page
              XtremeTravel.LoginBean Login = null;
              Login = (XtremeTravel.LoginBean)
java.beans.Beans.instantiate(getClass().getClassLoader(),
"XtremeTravel.LoginBean");
              // store the bean in the session so it can be accessed by
              // other servlets as the user navigates the site
              session.putValue("Login", Login);
```

```
                        // Initialize the bean city property from the parameters
                        Login.setCity(getParameter(request, "city", true, true,
true, null));

                        // Initialize the bean firstname property from the
                        // parameters
                        Login.setFirstname(getParameter(request, "firstname",
true, true, true, null));

                        // Initialize the bean lastname property from the
                        // parameters
                        Login.setLastname(getParameter(request, "lastname", true,
true, true, null));

                        // Initialize the bean state property from the parameters
                        Login.setState(getParameter(request, "state", true, true,
true, null));

                        // Initialize the bean street property from the
                        // parameters
                        Login.setStreet(getParameter(request, "street", true,
true, true, null));
                        // Initialize the bean zip property from the parameters
                        Login.setZip(getParameter(request, "zip", true, true,
true, null));

                        // Call the output page. If the output page is not passed
                        // as part of the URL, the default page is called.
                        callPage(getPageNameFromRequest(request), request,
response);
                }
                catch (Exception theException)
                {
                        handleError(request, response, theException);
                }
        }

        /*****************************************************************
**********
        * Returns the requested parameter
        *
        * @param request Object that encapsulates the request to the servlet
        * @param parameterName The name of the parameter value to return
        * @param checkRequestParameters when true, the request parameters
        * are searched
        * @param checkInitParameters when true, the servlet init parameters
        * are searched
        * @param isParameterRequired when true, an exception is thrown when
        * the parameter cannot be found
        * @param defaultValue The default value to return when the parameter
        * is not found
        * @return The parameter value
        * @exception java.lang.Exception Thrown when the parameter is not
        * found
```

```
    */
    public java.lang.String
getParameter(javax.servlet.http.HttpServletRequest request,
java.lang.String parameterName, boolean checkRequestParameters, boolean
checkInitParameters, boolean isParameterRequired, java.lang.String
defaultValue) throws java.lang.Exception
    {
            java.lang.String[] parameterValues = null;
            java.lang.String paramValue = null;

            // Get the parameter from the request object if necessary.
            if (checkRequestParameters)
            {
                parameterValues =
request.getParameterValues(parameterName);

                if (parameterValues != null)
                    paramValue = parameterValues[0];
            }

            // Get the parameter from the servlet init parameters if
            // it was not in the request parameter.
            if ( (checkInitParameters) && (paramValue == null) )
                paramValue =
getServletConfig().getInitParameter(parameterName);
            // Throw an exception if the parameter was not found and it was
            // required.
            // The exception will be caught by error processing and can be
            // displayed in the error page.
            if ( (is ParameterRequired) && (paramValue == null) )
                throw new Exception(parameterName + " parameter was not
specified.");

            // Set the return to the default value if the parameter was not
            // found
            if (paramValue == null)
                paramValue = defaultValue;

            return paramValue;
    }

    /******************************************************************
**********
    * Process incoming HTTP GET requests
    *
    * @param request Object that encapsulates the request to the servlet
    * @param response Object that encapsulates the response from the
    * servlet
    */
    public void doGet(javax.servlet.http.HttpServletRequest request,
javax.servlet.http.HttpServletResponse response)
    {
            performTask(request, response);
    }
```

```
    /*********************************************************************
**********
    * Process incoming HTTP POST requests
    *
    * @param request Object that encapsulates the request to the servlet
    * @param response Object that encapsulates the response from the
    * servlet
    */
    public void doPost(javax.servlet.http.HttpServletRequest request,
javax.servlet.http.HttpServletResponse response)
    {
            performTask(request, response);
    }

}
```

This is a servlet that has been compiled from login.jsp from within Web-Sphere Application Server.

```
package pagecompile;

import java.io.*;
import java.util.*;
import javax.servlet.*;
import javax.servlet.http.*;
import java.beans.Beans;
import com.sun.server.http.pagecompile.ParamsHttpServletRequest;
import com.sun.server.http.pagecompile.ServletUtil;
import com.sun.server.http.pagecompile.filecache.CharFileData;
import com.sun.server.http.pagecompile.NCSAUtil;

import wns.gfs.UserSession;

public class _Login_xjsp extends javax.servlet.http.HttpServlet {
    private static final String sources[] = new String[] {
        "d:\\websphere\\appserver\\web\\login.jsp",
    };
    private static final long lastModified[] = {
        934317558000L,
    };

    public void service(HttpServletRequest request,HttpServletResponse
response)
        throws IOException, ServletException
    {
        response.setContentType("text/html");
        PrintWriter out = response.getWriter();
        CharFileData data[] = new CharFileData[sources.length];
        try {
            for (int i = 0 ; i < data.length ; i++)
            data[i] = ServletUtil.getJHtmlSource(this,
                        sources[i],
                        "8859_1",
```

```
                                    lastModified[i]);
        } catch (Exception ex) {
            ex.printStackTrace();
            throw new ServletException("fileData");
        }
        // com.sun.server.http.pagecompile.jsp.LiteralChunk null-null
        Object tsxResultObject = null;
        HttpSession tsxSessionHolder = null;
        {
            String url = HttpUtils.getRequestURL(request).toString();
            if ((request.getAttribute("__XXcallPageXX__") != null) &&
!url.endsWith(".jsp")) {
                out.println("<base href=\"" +
                        url.substring(0, url.indexOf("/", 8)) +
                        request.getPathInfo() + "\">");
            }
        }

        // com.sun.server.http.pagecompile.jsp.CharArrayChunk
d:/websphere/appserver/web/login.jsp 1,1-
d:/websphere/appserver/web/login.jsp 18,1
        data[0].writeChars(0, 614, out);
        // com.sun.server.http.pagecompile.jsp.ScriptletChunk
d:/websphere/appserver/web/login.jsp 18,1-
d:/websphere/appserver/web/login.jsp 23,26
                if (request.getParameter("login") != null ) {
                    wns.gfs.UserManager users = new
wns.gfs.UserManager();
                    boolean loginPass;
                    loginPass = users.verify(
request.getParameter("login"), request.getParameter("pwd") );
                    if (! loginPass) {
        // com.sun.server.http.pagecompile.jsp.CharArrayChunk
d:/websphere/appserver/web/login.jsp 23,26-
d:/websphere/appserver/web/login.jsp 35,60
        data[0].writeChars(873, 406, out);
        // com.sun.server.http.pagecompile.jsp.ScriptletChunk
d:/websphere/appserver/web/login.jsp 35,60-
d:/websphere/appserver/web/login.jsp 35,107
        out.print(ServletUtil.toString(
request.getParameter("login").toString() ));
        // com.sun.server.http.pagecompile.jsp.CharArrayChunk
d:/websphere/appserver/web/login.jsp 35,107-
d:/websphere/appserver/web/login.jsp 48,6
        data[0].writeChars(1326, 428, out);
        // com.sun.server.http.pagecompile.jsp.ScriptletChunk
d:/websphere/appserver/web/login.jsp 48,6-
d:/websphere/appserver/web/login.jsp 48,20
                } else {
        // com.sun.server.http.pagecompile.jsp.CharArrayChunk
d:/websphere/appserver/web/login.jsp 48,20-
```

```
d:/websphere/appserver/web/login.jsp 50,8
        data[0].writeChars(1768, 42, out);
        tsxSessionHolder = request.getSession(true);
        wns.gfs.UserSession mySession = (wns.gfs.UserSession)
tsxSessionHolder.getValue("mySession");
        if ( mySession == null ) {
            try {
                mySession = (wns.gfs.UserSession)
Beans.instantiate(this.getClass().getClassLoader(),
"wns.gfs.UserSession");
                if ((Object)mySession instanceof Servlet) {
                    ((Servlet)
(Object)mySession).init(getServletConfig());
                }
            } catch (Exception ex) {
                throw new ServletException("Can't create BEAN of class
wns.gfs.UserSession: "+ ex.getMessage());
            }
        tsxSessionHolder.putValue("mySession", mySession);
    }
    if ((Object)mySession instanceof Servlet) {
        ((Servlet) (Object)mySession).service((ServletRequest) request,
(ServletResponse) response);
    }
    // com.sun.server.http.pagecompile.jsp.CharArrayChunk
d:/websphere/appserver/web/login.jsp 50,104-
d:/websphere/appserver/web/login.jsp 51,8
    data[0].writeChars(1906, 9, out);
    // com.sun.server.http.pagecompile.jsp.ScriptletChunk
d:/websphere/appserver/web/login.jsp 51,8-
d:/websphere/appserver/web/login.jsp 54,10

                mySession.setName( request.getParameter("login") );
                mySession.setValid(true);

    // com.sun.server.http.pagecompile.jsp.CharArrayChunk
d:/websphere/appserver/web/login.jsp 54,10-
d:/websphere/appserver/web/login.jsp 60,6
    data[0].writeChars(2029, 132, out);
    // com.sun.server.http.pagecompile.jsp.ScriptletChunk
d:/websphere/appserver/web/login.jsp 60,6-
d:/websphere/appserver/web/login.jsp 60,13
        }
    // com.sun.server.http.pagecompile.jsp.CharArrayChunk
d:/websphere/appserver/web/login.jsp 60,13-
d:/websphere/appserver/web/login.jsp 61,1
    data[0].writeChars(2168, 2, out);
    // com.sun.server.http.pagecompile.jsp.ScriptletChunk
d:/websphere/appserver/web/login.jsp 61,1-
d:/websphere/appserver/web/login.jsp 61,15
        } else {
```

```
    // com.sun.server.http.pagecompile.jsp.CharArrayChunk
d:/websphere/appserver/web/login.jsp 61,15-
d:/websphere/appserver/web/login.jsp 82,1
    data[0].writeChars(2184, 625, out);
    // com.sun.server.http.pagecompile.jsp.ScriptletChunk
d:/websphere/appserver/web/login.jsp 82,1-
d:/websphere/appserver/web/login.jsp 82,8
        }
    // com.sun.server.http.pagecompile.jsp.CharArrayChunk
d:/websphere/appserver/web/login.jsp 82,8-
d:/websphere/appserver/web/login.jsp 85,0
    data[0].writeChars(2816, 20, out);
}
}
```

When to Use Servlets

When debugging JSPs, the error messages refer to lines of code in the servlet itself. This means you have to review the source code, which can be either Java code or class files. The JSP is compiled into a servlet that in turn is compiled into bytecode and executed directly by a JVM. This conversion occurs the first time the JSP is invoked.

For debugging and performance you would tend to evaluate servlets.

When we went into the JSP code and renamed an invoked beans package to the wrong name, then called the JSP through our Web browser, we got the error messages displayed in Figure 7.6. The error points to Java code, which can be very misdirecting when debugging a large or complex page. Because you are pointed to the line on the servlet code, you have to map that line of code manually back to the lines on your JSP in order to determine exactly where the error occurred. This is a trivial example, but trust us, it can drive you bonkers!

More important, you can see an implementation of a well-crafted servlet in the following.

Introduction to JavaBeans and EJB

Beans was originally the somewhat cute term that Sun chose to refer to the specification of Java components that ran on the client in a client/server implementation of the language—the JavaBean as applet, if you will.

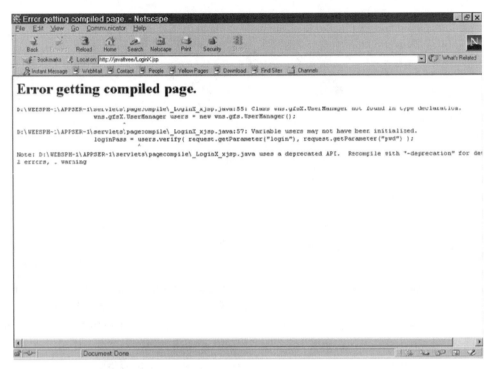

Figure 7.6 Servlet Runtime Error Message.

First announced in March 1998, Enterprise JavaBeans, defined in the EJB specification 1.0, is quite a departure from that model. Far more than just a component, the ambition of the EJB spec is to form the basis of the all-encompassing application architecture for using Java. Addressed by this architecture is the need for applications that are

- Scalable
- Multitier
- Distributed
- Object-oriented
- Open (third-party extensible)
- Multiplatform
- Dynamic

As well, Enterprise JavaBeans squarely faces the reality that client-side Java programming has tremendous practical restrictions. EJB addresses the complete set of requirements for architecting solutions that execute on the server.

In short, Enterprise JavaBeans provide a framework for access to those services used by developers writing server-side Java components. These include the following:

- Naming
- Persistence
- Directory
- Security
- Transaction
- Messaging
- CORBA integration

The objective is to provide access to these services so the developed components will take advantage of their sophistication without having to understand their intricacies in order to develop Enterprise JavaBeans. Encapsulation of complexity is a key theme to developing Java-based solutions, and EJB is no exception to this principle.

As client/server systems moved from basic two-tier implementations to n-tier client/server, integration of application servers increasingly became a key problem to solve. In most cases, these servers are not identical, either in the underlying platform or in the language in which the business logic was implemented. In fact, the n-tier client/server computing model became the way you would pull together an integrated system from combinations of new and old systems.

Object-Oriented Developments

About the same time, the value of taking an object-oriented (OO) approach to development was making itself apparent. The desire for code reuse, resulting in developer productivity as well as the need for an integrated systems architecture, kept pointing to OO as a better way to get things done.

The Object Management Group (OMG) defined CORBA (Common Object Request Broker Architecture) as a means of accomplishing these lofty goals. Microsoft countered with its Common Object Model (COM), then realized it was missing a key element and refined it to the Distributed Common Object Model (DCOM). Through the late 1990s, there was considerable confusion in the minds of architects and developers about which one would become dominant.

Enterprise JavaBeans draws on many of the CORBA implementation strengths while offering its own unique set of functions and services. As in many three-way races, while the top two contenders are struggling, an upstart third party comes flying by on the outside to take the win. To put it more plainly, when we looked for a component architecture to accomplish the goals set out at the beginning of this chapter, we determined that EJB is the best bet.

Now that we have quickly reviewed the market drivers for and competitors to EJB, let's look a little deeper at what Enterprise JavaBeans provide.

If you accept that Java is the language of the Web, then it is no great leap to assume that the client for any Java application will be a Web browser. It's not, strictly speaking, necessary, of course. The model-view-controller paradigm allows the separation of the GUI environment that presents the data from the work of the application itself.

Enterprise JavaBeans form the basis for the components running on the server that handle the complex transactions and integrate with legacy applications, as needed, while providing results for display in a Web browser.

Of course, Enterprise JavaBeans can be used to communicate server to server, but the ultimate goal is to interact with a user, regardless of how many beans were used to arrive at that point. But the most universally cross-platform client handler is still the Web browser, so let's proceed with the assumption that this is the environment of choice.

EJB Goals and Objectives

The key notion here is that Enterprise JavaBeans are the components that extend the capabilities of a Web server, where a Web server is treated like an application server would be under the more traditional client/server architecture. The following are the major objectives of Enterprise JavaBeans:

- Facilitate creation of application by abstracting low-level systems programming for transaction management, load balancing, thread creation, and so forth.

- Define the structure of an application development framework and the contracts that exist among them.

- Support integration of components from multiple vendors by defining a standard way to build applications.

- Allow creation of complex, integrated solutions made from components from various sources that can be run on any compliant server platform without recompilation.

- Integrate with non-Java applications and CORBA-compliant objects.

A lofty set of goals indeed, but as experienced developers of software solutions that had minimal reuse, ongoing maintenance headaches, and one-off systems integration requirements, we got very excited about EJB.

How Enterprise JavaBeans Work

There are two major elements to an Enterprise JavaBean. There is the bean itself, which can be considered a *component*, and there is the environment in which the component executes, which is referred to as the *container*.

Components

As a component, an EJB executes from within an EJB container. Containers are executed on an EJB server (EJS). Hosting of EJB containers has been supported by many vendors since Java was first released, and moving to support of an EJS is not a dramatic change. Most vendors are upgrading their servers to support EJS execution as well. WebSphere Server is the product provided by IBM for this service.

The EJB itself is a nonvisual component that is basically a Java class implementing business logic. Any EJB component is extensible to the point of providing support for distributed transactions across an enterprise. All other classes within the system exist to provide client access or manage the deeper services such as persistence for the EJB component.

These nonvisual components are intended to be snapped together like Lego blocks to make complex applications quickly and without the need for infrastructure programming.

Containers

The container is where the component resides as well as where the component gets services like transaction handling, resource management, security, persistence, versioning, scalability, and mobility. The component developer can focus on the creation of the component knowing these services will be made available when their code is moved to its home—the container. In this way, a developer does not need to handle the rollback of a transaction in the event of a problem, because this service is already resident in the container.

Given that multiple EJBs are resident in a single container, the developer does not care what the other components are doing, because execution is also handled within the container. The runtime requirements of the component are defined by the deployment descriptor, which tells the container what services the component needs to execute successfully.

Enterprise Java Servers

This is the highest-level application providing a runtime environment for containers of EJB components. IBM's WebSphere Advanced and WebSphere enterprise are both Enterprise Java Servers. The services provided by the EJS are shown in Figure 7.7.

The Enterprise Java Server manages the activation and deactivation of components and services, load balancing, and failover support for high availability. Security is handled through the JMAPI, transaction services through JTS, and naming and directory services through JNDI; interop-

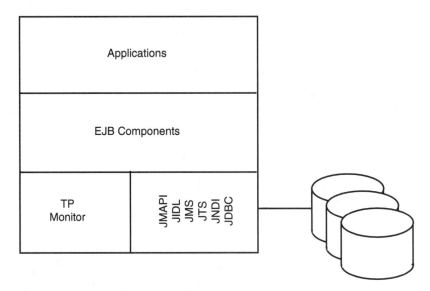

Figure 7.7 Enterprise Java services.

erability with CORBA IDL programs is supported by JIDL; messaging services are provided by JMS and database connectivity through JDBC.

Let's discuss the two fundamental kinds of Enterprise JavaBeans.

Session Beans

As you might expect, session beans are created only for the duration of a particular user session. There are two kinds of session beans, stateful and stateless, for two discrete purposes.

A *stateful* session bean exists only while the Internet session, the connection between the browser and the server, is up. A *stateless* session bean, on the other hand, is best described as a pool of connections to a database or another server. Yes, they exist only for the purpose of a user session, but once that session is completed, the processes themselves do not disappear. Instead, they are available to be picked up by a new session. A stateful session bean is useful for reducing initiation time for a dynamic pool of connections. Twelve database connections, for example, might service two dozen users who connect and drop their pages on a frequent basis.

Session beans are not usually persistent and do not have to call transactions. However, they can be persistent and they could call transactions. A classic behavior of a session bean is that if the plug is pulled on your server, the objects die.

Entity Beans

Entity beans, on the other hand, have persistence and will be re-created on the resurrection of the server. To relate to entity beans more easily, consider them equivalent to a row in a database table.

Entity beans also come in two flavors, though the emphasis for an entity bean is not on state, but rather *persistence*. Persistence describes how the data is used by the bean. Some beans manage their own persistence explicitly. This is referred to as *bean-managed persistence* (BMP). This logic is coded by the developer and maintained as part of the bean.

More frequently, persistence is delegated to the container. This is known as *container-managed persistence* (CMP). To take advantage of different storage mechanisms and maintain fully flexible deployment options, CMP entity beans are used.

Enterprise JavaBean Interfaces

There are two kinds of interfaces to any given EJB: home and remote. The *home interfaces* define the methods for location, creation, and destruction of instances of any EJB classes. Every instance of an EJB must have a home interface. The home interface is the way an EJB for our comics collection would create a listing for a new comic, retrieve the details and attributes of an existing comic, or remove a comic from our collection. Collection in this case is not the Java-specific term, but instead refers to our boxful of old comics from the attic.

The *remote interface* defines the business methods associated with the Enterprise Java bean. Any given calling application does not access the EJB directly, but instead must access the remote interface using an EJBObject instance. Remote interfaces are the exposed methods that ensure the object is used only in the manner intended by its creator. For our comic collection, remote methods might include list comic, describe comic, and delist comic. A more complicated bean could extend the methods to include value comic, which could be a way to associate the list, asking, or bid price for a particular comic.

Each and every bean has a unique identifier. In an entity bean the identifier points to the information, similar to the way a unique primary key in a database table uniquely identifies the row. Beans need not derive their identifier from valid data they represent, but could be hash numbers or a random number assigned to that object.

Executing Enterprise JavaBeans

A calling program connects to an EJS and requests that an EJB do some work on its behalf. The server then creates the object on the server side (it instantiates the object); however, instead of letting the calling program work with the object directly, the EJS provides a proxy object with the same interfaces as the EJB component. This proxy works with the remote interfaces of the EJB object, while the client program treats the proxy as if it were a local object. This allows the EJB to run on the server, while allowing the proxy to be used by the local program, wherever it may have been invoked from.

The container is responsible for managing this process. Each EJB component class was created with a home interface that forms the contract between the component and the container. As discussed earlier, this contract extends to the way instances of the bean can be created, found, or destroyed.

To create an EJB on a server, the client uses the Java Naming and Directory Interface (JNDI) to find the home interface of the desired bean. This JNDI is a standard extension to Java that provides a global service to all Java environments later than 1.0. EJB takes advantage of JNDI to maintain compatibility with other APIs.

Our calling application now knows the home interface of the target bean. A create( ) method is then called on the home interface, resulting in the creation of a server-side object. On the client side, the remote method interface is directed to the EJB container, which in turn creates the actual EJB component and returns an EJB object (the proxy) to the client. The client can then access the EJB objects methods as if they were local but are in fact directed to the container. The container passes the method invocation to the EJB component, where it is implemented.

Sound complicated? Actually, it is. But such is the price we pay for true portability and object reuse. The process is depicted in Figure 7.8.

The proxy, or EJB object, runs on the client and passes remote interface calls to the EJS and on to the container holding the bean. The EJB com-

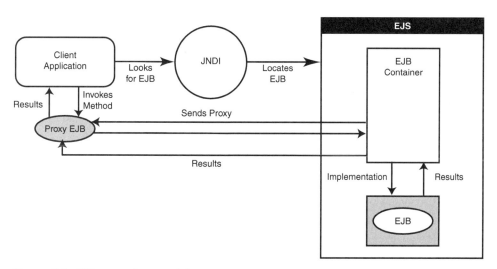

Figure 7.8 EJB execution model.

ponent actually performs the business logic. One of the most intuitive examples of this I've seen is the VCR and remote control. The buttons are labeled the same on both, and pressing the right button on either will result in the fast-forwarding of your tape, but it's the VCR that actually handles the tape.

This seems like a lot of overhead in the case of a single EJS, container, and bean. But it shouldn't take a lot of imagination to see the advantage this has when scaled to dozens, hundreds, and thousands of users, each hitting the EJS, looking for beans across the enterprise.

Getting a Handle on EJB

For a longtime relational systems developer like me, it takes some getting used to the idea that each instantiated object could be a row, with attributes and properties consisting of nonnormalized data.

Dr. Verlyn Johnson, who has worked with the SanFrancisco project since its inception, told me that rdbms folks tend to pick up quickly on the notion of Enterprise JavaBeans, especially when they think of objects as normalized processes with the data built in. Where the EJB uses container-managed persistence, its own treatment of data is similar to using views. Views act like tables but don't actually contain data. Perhaps it's ironic that the container-managed persistence might refer the retrieval of the data belonging to an EJB component from a relational database like DB/2.

In talking with many AS/400 developers, it seems that the separation of concern might be a very easily adopted concept, because that platform already has some operating system and hardware abstraction in the form of the machine interface (MI). To write effective RPG applications, you simply took for granted many of the services of the machine. One key value of Enterprise JavaBeans is the abstraction of infrastructure coding from the client application programmer.

IBM estimates that 40 percent of all application programming done today in C, C++, and other languages directly addresses the infrastructure. Even relational database programming with Sybase SQL Server (my old alma mater) consisted in large measure of managing transactions. This is now delegated to the container and/or subsequently offloaded to a TP monitor like Encina.

As you will see in the chapters on WebSphere Enterprise and SanFrancisco, tremendous combinations of reusable components are possible when you choose to work with an Enterprise JavaBeans Framework. For the first time in computing history it is truly possible to create applications that focus on your understanding of what the application must do for the business without becoming a specialist in every computer discipline to do it.

Multidisciplinary Development

Legacy data stores, existing business logic, and sophisticated user interfaces are all capable of being turned into components. Is this a brave new world? Well, it's certainly a complicated new world—and complex enough that no one person can follow it top to bottom and across the board.

The Big Blue Java approach offers a wealth of tools, and for the first time they can be pulled into a single comprehensive architecture, existing side by side with legacy applications. *Scalable* can mean down as well as up, and at my firm we have been working with companies from $1 million in sales to those with sales figures in the billions.

As software solutions developers, we are seeing for the first time a single approach to solving problems of scale: browser-based interfaces and Web servers extended with Enterprise JavaBeans. Add to that the boost from using SanFrancisco EJB components and it makes for a compelling story.

No, we are not as yet impressed with application performance, nor are we comfortable with the demands on bandwidth generated by this approach. But over the years, have we not all seen that hardware first catches up with and then surpasses the demands software puts on it? It is not my intention to be Pollyannaish about the difficulties and challenges of this new technology.

Following through the simple example of the instantiation of one EJB from an application is highly complex, especially compared to generating 5250 character-based applications running in RPG. There is a great deal to learn, and just as important, a great deal to forget, or unlearn, when addressing an EJB solution.

The purpose of this description is to give you an idea of how the architecture works and some of the terminology for creating Enterprise Java-

Beans. At this point, you should be ready to build and deploy a bean using VisualAge for Java 2.0.

Summary

IBM has pulled out the stops and completely committed itself to providing tools that support development of Java-based software solutions. The scope of this solution set requires an organization the size of IBM, because the expense and coverage is large and global. Enterprise computing requires an Enterprise computing company.

Sun has done a terrific job in defining a language and creating a specification for the development of objects using that language. The Big Blue Java approach to twenty-first century systems is to make those objects business oriented at the enterprise level. To support this, IBM offers not only servers, but software tools and prebuilt application frameworks to give organizations a head start on new applications using new technology.

Enterprise JavaBeans delivers on the capability for multiple teams of developers to reuse code in the creation of scalable, multitier, secure, robust, extensible software quickly.

The requirements driving the move to new technology address the pressure that has increasingly been placed on IT organizations for rapid development and deployment of systems that support the business. In my opinion, the tools and techniques offered by IBM for the implementation of Enterprise JavaBeans is a considerable step in that direction.

The best structure is not only modular—it must be organized by function. For example, if you are writing logic in Java, create beans. Call the beans from within a Java Server Page if you expect to display results to users or to accept input from them.

If the processing is all on the back end, you might as well invoke the beans from a servlet, because a JSP compiles into a servlet eventually anyway and debugging is more straightforward.

Server-side processing is becoming increasingly acknowledged as the key means to develop e-business applications with IBM technology. The guaranteed high bandwidth required to run applets successfully is frequently not available. This can lead to unacceptable application performance and failed Java projects.

Of course, the whole point to the diversity of techniques for Java application development is choice: You will have to decide which approach makes the most sense for your applications. I hope that in this chapter you have gained a sense of where and how you can take advantage of servlets and beans to get the job done.

CHAPTER 8

WebSphere Application Server

As we discussed in the first section of the book, Windows NT as an application server is strategic to IBM. In fact, all of the servers that we are working with, as well as the VisualAge for Java development environment, run on Windows NT.

Generally speaking, Windows NT is an interesting phenomenon. Microsoft spent years and millions of dollars in a committed approach to taking on the workgroup server OS market, at which objective it has largely succeeded. Novell certainly no longer enjoys the prominence it once did as the 60 percent market leader in the LAN server marketplace, and don't get me started on OS/2. It made a great deal of sense for IBM to choose Windows NT, as it seems that corporate America has already voted for this platform.

Then along came the Linux phenomenon—just in time to challenge Windows 2000. As it turns out, if you are looking to install Big Blue Java development services, you will be working with either Windows NT 4.0 or with Linux. Support for Windows 2000 has not even been announced as I write this, nor would I be looking to jump on that bandwagon very quickly. We have enough instability with betas, conflicting dynamic link libraries, and just plain old Windows flakiness.

That's right, the development environment we created at WNS for all these servers was not one of the greatest testaments to robust, reliable, and predictable behavior. Oh, don't get me wrong, I'm not saying it didn't work most of the time. There was just a high degree of frustration on the part of the developers who were struggling at various times with new technologies, techniques, and other challenges.

The good news from your point of view is that we discovered several important tricks along the way, and we actually got to the point where we were good at quickly and correctly installing (or reinstalling) the entire environment. In this chapter I will take you through those considerations for WebSphere Application Server, DB2, and HTTP Server. This is the core set of services for Web-enabled applications.

Prerequisites: The Hardware Platform

We standardized on IBM Intellistations with PIII 500-MHz processors and 512 megabytes of RAM as the minimum configuration for development machines and services. There were times when we strongly felt this was not enough engine to pull the servers through, even in development mode.

If you want to take the software for a drive around the block without trying to develop anything with it, I once shoehorned it onto a 64-megabyte 200-MHz machine. I was able to start the services and look at the documentation, but that was about it. When it comes to Big Blue Java, *hardware counts*. Get as much of it under the software as you possibly can.

Another key point we found out the hard way is to stay away from clones. While I did have one reliable installation on a generic machine, others would crash at some point during the use of the products, never to be worked with again (until reinstalled). This is a time-consuming and annoying effort. My point is that if you have to compromise, first make sure you have sufficient RAM (a functional minimum of 196 megs will work), but the processor speed is where we found the bottleneck.

Getting Started

When you first pop in the CD for WebSphere you are greeted with the typical splashy screen. Over the next several pages, I'll walk you through the installation screens, but to make it more interesting we'll throw in a collection of the error messages we encountered at various times. From these you should be able to get a sense of how the process works and what can potentially go wrong. The helpful part will be the discussion of how to address that problem and move forward to a successful installation.

WebSphere installation was the first step taken to create the full Big Blue Java development environment.

The AutoPlay kicked in as soon as the CD was inserted and warned that the Web server needed to be quiesced prior to installation of the WebSphere Application Server. Because I had decided not to install IIS as part of the Windows NT installation, I was very curious to see how the installation routine handled that particular exception. Of course, I could have decided to install IIS 2.0 at this point, but the need to experiment was just too irresistible. I wanted to see if curiosity killed the server! (See Figure 8.1.)

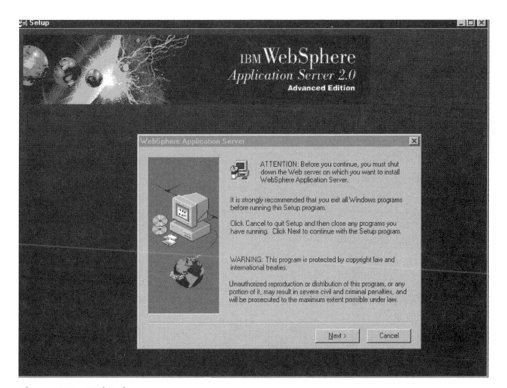

Figure 8.1 WebSphere.

After a couple of warnings about directory names and really, really, *really* shutting down the Web server and any other open programs, the installation options finally displayed.

As you can see from Figure 8.2, WebSphere offers a bunch of functionality beyond some listener process that just sits there intercepting Java calls from an http server. That is, essentially, what it does, but this Web Application Server is the heart of deploying Web-enabled e-business applications. Don't cheap out on the disk space when it comes to installing WebSphere. You want all the options. Trust me.

JDK and JRE Compatibility

One of the most significant underlying components of WebSphere is the JDK used. In our case, we chose to implement 1.1.6 for compatibility with SF 1.3 rather than the newer JDK 1.1.7. Actually, that was true for the installation session from which we captured this particular JDK selection dialog box. Later, when we moved to SanFrancisco 1.4, we had to upgrade the JDK to 1.1.7 and then to 1.1.8 for other servers.

You may choose not to install the entire Java Development Kit in any of these cases. However, to work properly, WebSphere requires at least the Java Runtime Environment. We never did restrict any of our servers to just the JRE, so I won't comment on how well that works.

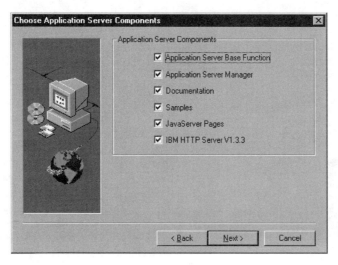

Figure 8.2 The installation options.

For planning purposes, you will want to install WebSphere on a box where you do not have a dependency on a different Java Developer Kit environment. Our problems typically came where we wanted to install SanFrancisco, VisualAge for Java, and WebSphere Application Server all on the same box. SF is quite picky about the JDK version it gets, whereas WebSphere allows you to set it as an option. (I guess that explains the dialog box shown in Figure 8.3).

In some cases, our developers were downloading and working with the latest JDK available from Sun. This is just something to keep an eye on as part of the installation planning process.

I love the way that software vendors (and some book authors) assume you are always starting out with a fresh box on which to install the package under discussion. With WebSphere, you will get a consistent sense that this product is going to be installed on a box that is already being used for something. This is reflected in the way you can point to an existing service or can install it at that time.

The JDK installation routine is straightforward. Since it is a required part of all the tools we use, I've decided to include the step through here for those of you who would like to read about it before trying it at home. (See Figure 8.4.)

More from superstition than anything else, I chose the Java sources as well. Frequently, the IBM setup routines will let you opt out of something

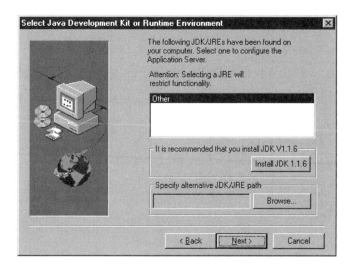

Figure 8.3 Specifying the JDK or JRE release.

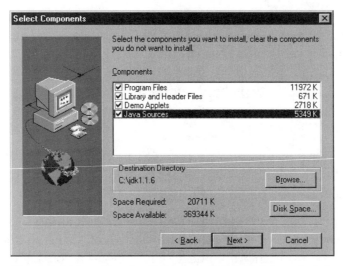

Figure 8.4 Installing the JDK from within WebSphere install routine.

needed later on. Rather than do the installation twice, if you have room on your disk, I recommend installing everything.

Note that if you have not set the classpath previously, the installation routine will do it for you. However, if you have already set it to an early JDK version, you will have to update it manually. About halfway through the installation of DB2, I got the error message shown in Figure 8.5. I'm including it for your enjoyment.

Ah, the old big red X OK dialog. Sure wish I had an idea what that was about.

When I tried to save the WordPad file that I was using to document the installation message, I got the error message shown in Figure 8.6. I think it explains the big red X.

Figure 8.5 The big red X—king of error messages.

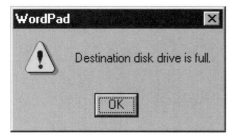

Figure 8.6 Showstopper error message.

Obviously, the installation routine will not tell you if you have sufficient disk space for all the files it wants to install. I went back and started over, this time specifying a clean disk.

The install went without a hitch, except for the need to back out of the entire thing. I mean that I stepped through the install process screen by screen, files copied, and then bleep showstopper. DB2 had to be preexistent on the machine. I backed out of the process again, installed DB2 first, and carried on.

HTTP Server Dependencies

WebSphere Application Server works with—it does not replace—the Web server. This isn't a big deal, but it is important to recognize that the services provided by WAS extend the Web servers you already have in place—it does not step on top of them.

Similar to many shops, we already had a few servers dedicated to server html, and in our case a couple of database servers supporting Net.Commerce implementations. We had gone down that path prior to deciding to work with WebSphere. The last thing I wanted to do was interfere with an existing online store (customers being the touchy folks that they are).

WebSphere can work with existing servers across a network. For development purposes, it is actually easier to put them on the same box rather than try to troubleshoot the connectivity issues when they arise. However, if you already have some experience with running a particular http server environment, terrific, stay the course. The options supported by WebSphere are shown in Figure 8.7.

In keeping with the start-from-scratch tradition, I'll take you through the http server installation process. This is, by the way, exactly how it occurs

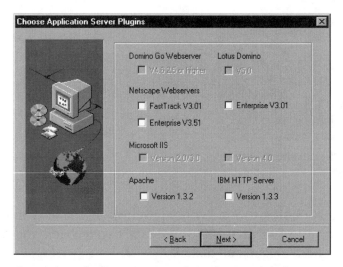

Figure 8.7 The HTTP Server options presented during WAS installation.

during the WebSphere install. (See Figure 8.8.) You take time out in the middle for the installation of dependent servers like HTTP and, as we'll see a little later, DB2.

For those of you who are unfamiliar with HTTP Server, this is the very unappealing name under which IBM decided to remarket Apache. If you, like me, prefer to minimize your technology risk by standardizing on market leaders for base products, this one fits the bill. After clicking through the usual warnings, you select the custom installation and the options shown in Figure 8.9.

Personally, I can't figure out why anyone would want a server without security or icons, but these options are obviously part of the HTTP Server install. During the course of more than a year, we did not once find a situation where we required anything more of the Web server than to install the defaults. We did have some difficulty getting our traffic-reporting software to sort out the difference between our IIS, Domino, and HTTP servers, but I suspect that was more related to the Market-Wave software than to IBM's server implementation.

User Account Options and Implications

For all of these servers, there are several implications to the user name and password that you choose to install and run them under. Ultimately,

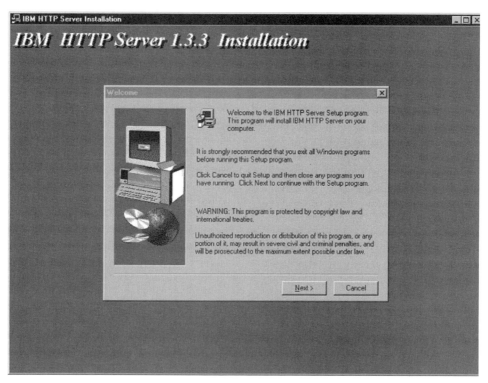

Figure 8.8 The HTTP Server process as part of WAS installation.

it took us several tries to sort through which server liked what account. For a couple of them, such as DB2, we ended up just sticking with the default installation account, since they fired up services no matter who rebooted the server.

One of the key things you have to decide first as part of your installation is what role the server will have relative to other servers on your network. To work through this issue first requires that you have an understanding of the role of Windows NT user account validation through Primary and Backup domain controllers.

In our case, all of our user accounts are authenticated through a master (primary domain), and other servers are set up to authenticate from that server. This turned out to be a real problem with the installation of HTTP Server, for example.

While you are installing the Web server, you are presented with an innocuous message like the one in Figure 8.10.

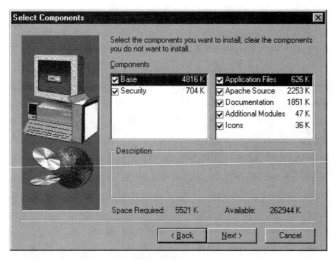

Figure 8.9 HTTP Server installation options.

For the sake of convenience, I decided to use the DB2 administrator account (I was already logged in with that ID after having installed DB2). That didn't work, and I got the big X from the message displayed in Figure 8.11.

When you can't beat 'em, join 'em, so I opted for the administrator. Interestingly, it didn't like that, either, so I had to go out to the local machine and create a webadmin account. As it turns out, you can't use an address

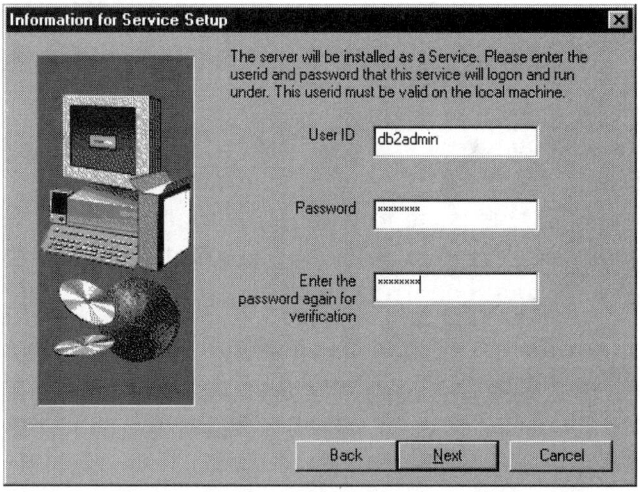

Figure 8.10 Setting the user account for the HTTP server.

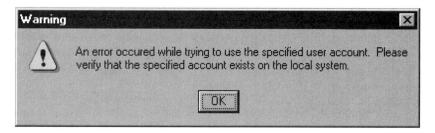

Figure 8.11 User account error message from HTTP installation.

that is supplied by the PDC. You must have a local account. The default account to use is Administrator. This is a bit of a nuisance, since I have been using the domain logins and passwords as supplied from the primary domain controller. This works fine for DB2, but apparently WebSphere is looking for local accounts.

From a planning perspective, you may decide to do exactly what we ended up doing for our development team, which was to allow them to create their own Primary Domains, complete with access to Administrator privileges.

The net effect of this is requiring people working on those servers to administer a completely different set of users and passwords, as well as having to set up trust relationships between the servers if you want them to be able to access shared services. However, in most cases the developers are running Windows NT workstation or server on their own machines, and they simply connect to the server name and port for the service running on the PDC. The WebSphere, HTTP, and SF servers are isolated from the rest of your administration and have only administrative users set up on them.

After installing the second time (reinstalling?), I found that the http service just wouldn't start after saying it had been successfully installed. The http service is vital to be able to get WebSphere going, so I poked around a little and finally found a solution.

You have to manually set the password for the http service in order to allow it to successfully start up on boot. To do this, you go into the control panel services, where you will see the screen shown in Figure 8.12. Select startup, and the dialog box shown in Figure 8.13 is displayed. You can also

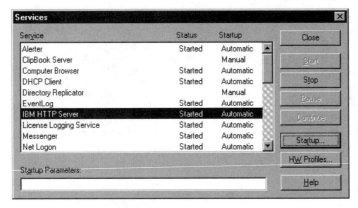

Figure 8.12   Selecting the HTTP Service.

double click on the service to get to the dialog in Figure 8.13, which is where you make the changes. Change the password, or if you prefer not to widely distribute Administrator roles for services, enter the account you wish to use for administration of the http server. After restarting the service, it came up just fine.

Windows NT Installations

I think it is worth noting that after several years of administering various servers and services under Windows NT 4.0, the process described

Figure 8.13   Setting the HTTP user account and permissions.

here is not unusual. There are a great many false starts in getting familiar with any new server, let alone something as significant as WebSphere.

For those of you who are more familiar with environments like the AS/400, I can only offer these words of encouragement: You're not alone. Coming from a Unix/Novell environment was a real shock for me, too. The pretty administrative interface wears off quite quickly and leaves you wondering how on earth an application server could refuse to start a service that was working only hours ago—unless you reboot it three or four times, at which point it runs fine for a few days until you get a blue screen of death, and the dance continues.

Windows NT is not, in my professional opinion, a reliable or stable application server. I would never use it for a real-time life-and-death application such as operating-room support for surgeons. On the other hand, it is (or was) relatively cheap, and it's everywhere. So, from a development perspective, it's good enough.

I offer this at the risk of incurring the wrath and ire of all those who are in love with NT as an environment. Having become OS jaded and cynical through my own experiences with everything from CPM/80 to CTOS, SunOS, Solaris, HP-UX, Novell 3.x, and even MacOS, I think it's worth noting that working with NT has its own unique challenges. These include fixing things that have been working for ages and having to reboot continually to start services. *Illegitime non carborundum.* (Don't let it bother you.)

Diatribes aside, as my http server was now installed, up, and running, I was able to get logged on to WebSphere, where I was presented with a myriad number of options. This is where this book should really start to provide some value for those of you unfamiliar with this particular server. In the rest of this chapter, I'll take you through the basic features and services of WebSphere Application Server, so you should be able to get it up and running at your site.

When you choose IBM WebSphere Application Server Administer Server from the cascading menus under the Start Programs option, you are presented with the login screen shown in Figure 8.14. The interface for managing the WebSphere server is entirely based on html pages and servlets, which is kind of cool. The server that we are going to use to generate Web-enabled applications is itself Web enabled. This is how things should be.

Administering WebSphere Application Server

Once you have installed your server and its dependent services, you can finally get down to the business of configuring WebSphere for your environment. In our case, we were looking to install an application server to support the training and development of some new developers. Or I should say developers new to Java and the IBM tool set. I think it's interesting to note that this book is the documentation that came out of that process. The things we discovered and the approach we took to training are reflected in the examples in and structure of *Big Blue Java*. If the success we have enjoyed with the technology is any indication, you should find that it is a functional and intuitive way to go about adopting this tool set.

Setting Up WebSphere for Developers

The first programs we needed to register with WebSphere were NetObjects Fusion and WebSphere Studio. From the chapters dealing with

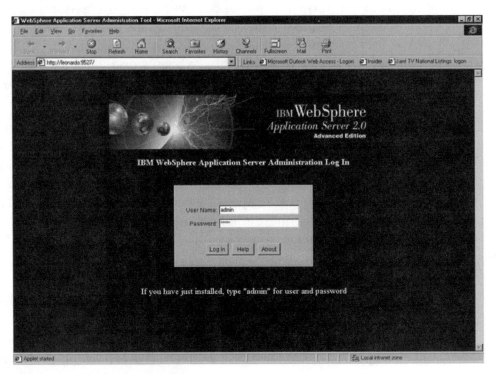

Figure 8.14   WebSphere works.

these programs you should recognize that creating front ends is really a small part of what you can build. Through Data Access Beans and Persistence Builder, both of which depend on WebSphere Application Server to function properly, you can create functional Web-enabled applications.

First, let's deal with how WebSphere handles that support.

To perform any administrative function in WebSphere, you go to the admin option and log in. That leads you to the screen shown in Figure 8.15. This interface shows you the kinds of things an administrator can do with WebSphere. For our purposes, the first thing we want to do is register a servlet. This is accomplished by selecting servlets from the tree view, as shown in Figure 8.16. Here you see the panel for managing servlets. Unfortunately, you cannot just list the directory contents of the servlets the way you can for html screens and look them over that way. By registering your servlets, you can see the names and properties of each one. Shown in Figure 8.16 are the default servlets that come with WebSphere Advanced.

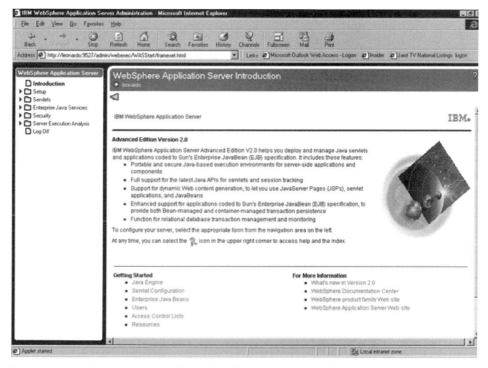

Figure 8.15 Administration options of WebSphere advanced server.

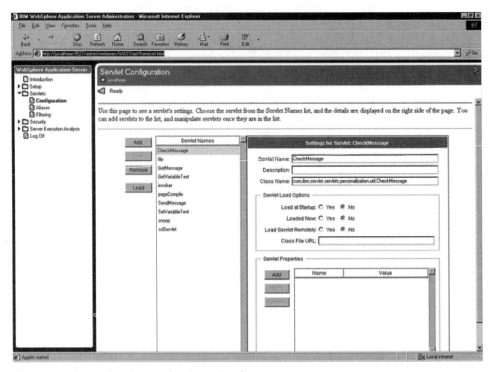

Figure 8.16 Configuring servlets in WebSphere.

To register your own servlets, you must press the Add option, which brings up the dialog box shown in Figure 8.17. In this dialog, you add the name you want the servlet to be known by as well as the precise package and class name associated with it. We've filled out our ComicBookList-Servlet for this example and, to test that we correctly filled out the form, pressed Test. Figure 8.18 shows what we want to see.

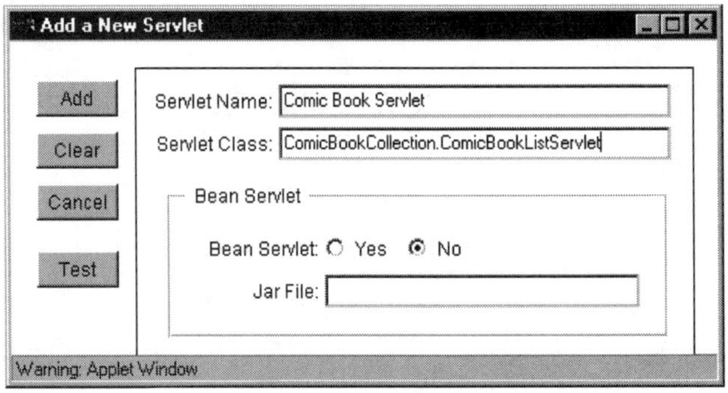

Figure 8.17 The Add Servlet dialog.

Figure 8.18 Servlet registration test result.

Having registered our servlet successfully, we can now set properties for it. Going back to the original servlet administration form and selecting our servlet name sets this. The options allow us to load the servlet immediately or to schedule it for the next reboot. (See Figure 8.19.)

The servlet is available as soon as you press Add, and at that point you can load it into memory or schedule it for running on reboot.

We created a quick servlet application (ComicBookListServlet) in the section on Java Server Pages and Servlets. After registering it, you can

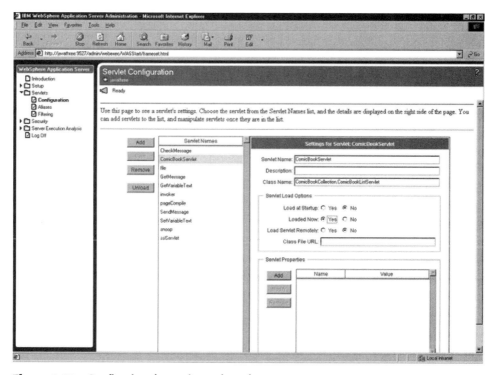

Figure 8.19 Configuring the registered servlet.

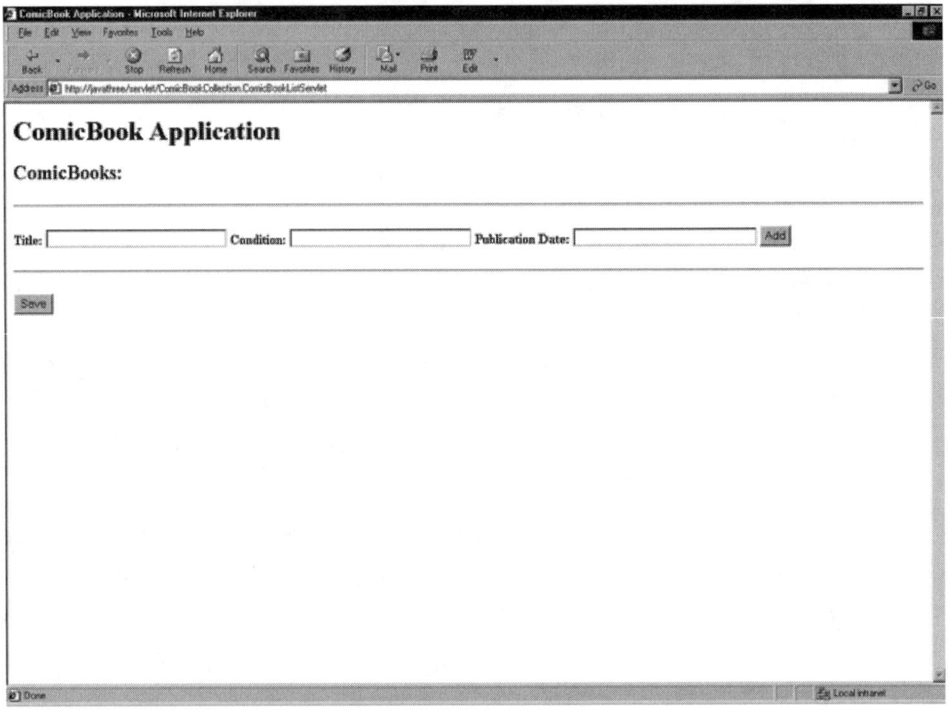

Figure 8.20 The comic book servlet runs.

execute it by hitting the URL of the IBM http server associated with WAS. The http server passes the request off to the WebSphere Application Server for execution. The returned application is shown in the browser capture in Figure 8.20.

Agreed, the functionality of this particular servlet isn't anything to write home about. Still, it's good to see the end-to-end process taken from creating a servlet running on the application server we just installed and displaying results to my browser.

Summary

WebSphere Application Server is the shape of things to come when you are talking about IBM-backed e-business applications. The key is the server-side support for Java programming, which extends the functionality available to a Web browser and http server tremendously.

This is the real three-tier application server for an *n*-tier client/server architecture when it comes to applications running Java. The thing that impressed us most here at WNS was our ability to create so many variations of programs, from beans to servlets and Java Server Pages, all of which are managed by the WebSphere Application Server.

The installation is a little tricky the first time, and I expect that it will get smoother over time. But for anyone who had doubts about the practical effort IBM is putting into this Java product line, look closely at WebSphere. You should be able to see clearly that these products let you develop and deploy applications large and small, with the emphasis on server-side processing, but using the new language of Big Blue applications: Java.

CHAPTER 9

Net.Commerce

O ne of the key pieces of technology for development and deployment of e-business solutions is the online shopping server. IBM provides Net .Commerce to address the basic requirements of creating an online store, which include the following:

- Shopping cart services
- Catalog management
- Secure credit card transaction support

The objective of Net.Commerce is to allow an experienced developer to get new sites up and running in a matter of a few days. Our experience at WNS indicates that IBM has succeeded with Net.Commerce. While there are a great many quirks and constraints in the way Net.Commerce has been implemented by version 3.2, the product has evolved into a capable tool for creating Web stores quickly. Version 3.2 offers many benefits over previous versions that mandate a closer look. Improved and added features include the following:

Java integration into the product advisor. This allows users to conduct advanced searches and allows applications designers to integrate the Java team into the NC development process.

Integration of eNetwork Dispatcher. This allows for load balancing across multiple servers.

Region-specific tax codes. This allows true worldwide sales ability.

It is important to properly configure your JDK for all the Big Blue Java products that we cover. Make sure you download and set up IBM's JDK1.1.7 in keeping with the install instructions before you install any of the IBM products.

In many implementations, shopping cart software has been created as a set of cgi-bin scripts. In keeping with the objectives of the Big Blue Java strategy, IBM has ensured that developers are not limited to the restrictions of cgi but can create applications that run on the same kinds of environments that are supported by WebSphere. Additionally, Net.Commerce integrates with a number of Web servers, such as Domino, Apache, and IIS, and provides linkages to different data stores.

There are three distinct areas for creating a Web store that must be managed. These include the creation of a graphics-rich site through Web development tools such as NetObjects Fusion, the development and modification of the store through Net.Commerce, and the handling of data from the store back and forth to the operational systems for billing, inventory, and shipping.

Creating a Web Store

Our first Net.Commerce site to go into production was called SportOptics. The main objective of this site was to offer high-quality scopes and binoculars to hunters and bird-watchers. This demonstration is to show the basic manipulation of the supplied store. Advanced topics such as load balancing are not covered. However, an in-depth library can be found at IBM's Web site.

Customization of the supplied stores requires differing levels of knowledge depending on the changes in functionality that you require. The following is a list of skills and the changes that you can make with that skill set:

DB2/SQL. This will allow you to prepare customized order-retrieval systems, and it simplifies catalog management. It is important to note that most of the order retrieval and management can be very efficiently handled by IBM's Catalog Architect.

Net.Data and HTML. This will allow you to change the appearance of the store. How to do this will be demonstrated in our example in this chapter.

C++ and Java. This skill set will allow you to customize any portion of the command process. This generally is not required, as virtually all functionality has been covered with the supplied command structure.

Our first step was to create a Web site using what is now considered traditional means of generating HTML from a visual page designer.

Setting Up the Store Server

Net.Commerce contains its own scripting and development functionality. These tools are provided in the form of the template designer. This tool proved difficult to use because any document we modified could not be modified with any other editor (including notepad). It has been our practice to use a simple text editor, and we can allow for pretty much any customizations to be carried out by novice programmers with some knowledge of the flow control commands in Net.Data.

Commands, tasks, overridable functions, and macros are the customizable portions of the framework, which allow for full control over logical flow, processing, database connectivity, and visual appeal.

Function Model

The four main components to the model are the *commands, tasks, overridable functions*, and *macros*. (See Figure 9.1.)

Commands

A *command* performs a specific business operation such as adding an item to the shopping cart, processing an order, or displaying a specific product page. All commands are executed as HTTP requests (or, less often, internally by another command), which generate responses in the form of WebPages. Each command is imbedded in a URL, and, when transmitted, the command parameters are passed to the Net.Commerce system for processing. Based on the function a command performs, it is classified as either a display command or a process command. A *display command* retrieves information from the database, whereas a *process*

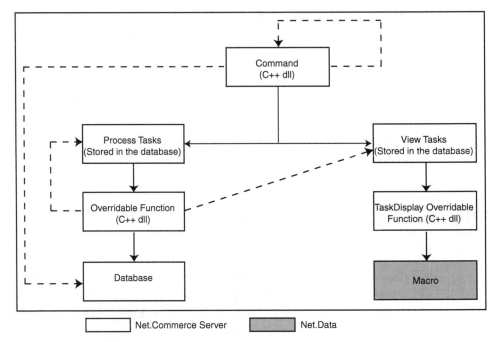

| | Net.Commerce Server | | Net.Data |

Figure 9.1 Net.Commerce function model.

command writes information to the database. In summary, a command either executes a display command or a chain of process commands followed by one display command.

Commands are stored as DLLs and are loaded by NC when the server starts. If they aren't loaded correctly, the function will not be loaded and an entry in the error log will be made. You can find the logs in d:\IBM\ NetCommerce3\instance\<storename>\logs\.

Tasks

A *task* is an association between a command and an overridable function or between two overridable functions. It defines the process that the overridable function is to perform, the parameters that the caller passes, and the expected output of the function.

Overridable Functions

An *overridable function* (OF) is a piece of program code that implements a task. Specifically, it implements a behavior that is expected by the task and handles input and output parameters as defined by the task. The input parameters that are passed by the calling command must be a subset of those defined by the task that the function implements. This allows the programmer to write an overridable function that doesn't use all of the parameters and return more than are expected. This allows for reuse of overridable functions.

When an OF is called, a task name and a merchant reference number are provided to the overridable function manager. The function manager then selects the assigned OF on the basis of the calling task and the merchant reference number. This allows you to customize the command structure for each merchant and each merchant's store.

Macros

Macros are files that are executed by Net.Data. They contain information that retrieves information from the database and displays the results as a formatted Web page. In Net.Commerce, they provide three important store functions:

- They extract and display database information.
- They provide an interface for collecting information.
- They display the results of processing.

Macros are executed by either calling a command that sets a view task or calling the ExecMacro command. All of the view tasks call the TaskDisplay overridable function that determines from the database the name of the macro to execute. The ExecMacro command is designed to call macros that are not assigned to a view or exception task and therefore aren't stored in the database (like the special page in SportOptics). The command structure outlined in Figure 9.1 demonstrates the relationship between commands, tasks, and views.

Modification of the Function Model

The modification of the function model requires the modification of all of the aforementioned components. The command structure is adequate for most business functions. However, all the functions that are called from a command can be changed by modifying supplied overridable functions and modifying the tasks. If additional commands or extensive modifications of existing commands are required, a new command must be built in C++ and stored as a DLL. The server will then load this DLL at runtime.

Tasks are very easy to customize with the existing NC task assignment operation. This allows for different overridable functions to be assigned to tasks.

Overridable functions are quite easy to create, the major problem being the C++ compilation settings. The supplied classes are easy to understand; however, there are many error codes, which become difficult to rationalize.

Macros are extremely simple to customize, as they are based on simple if-then flow control, SQL statements, and HTTP coding. Modifying these macros can change all aspects of the store appearance.

Sample Macro

The Net.Data macros contain SQL queries to retrieve information from the database and HTML sections to display the information as WebPages. In our store, we wanted to allow users to change their passwords if they had forgotten them. For instance, at registration, the user inputs a challenge phrase and a challenge answer. The following example uses the Challenge question: "What is the name of my dog?" The correct answer is "Bernoulli." This screen was implemented in our initial Net.Commerce site, SportOptics.

Before we look at the formatted WebPage that the macro implements, let me explain about our SportOptics project.

In 1998, we met with a distributor of recreational accessories who wanted to open up shop on the Internet. Until that point, we had mostly been kicking the tires of the various shopping cart technologies, but this represented a real opportunity to do business on the Web.

After trying and discarding Merchant Server, we settled on Net.Commerce as the chosen vehicle to implement the site. Part of this chapter is a high-level treatment of that experience and the capabilities we uncovered. When you first log on to SportOptics, you are greeted with a splash page that will take you to a view of the products suitable for either bird-watchers or hunters. While many of the same accessories can be used by these two groups, apparently they don't mix all that much. Go figure.

In any case, Figure 9.2 shows the home page of SportOptics, which is where a customer would look up what's new and then potentially look up the status of his or her order or account.

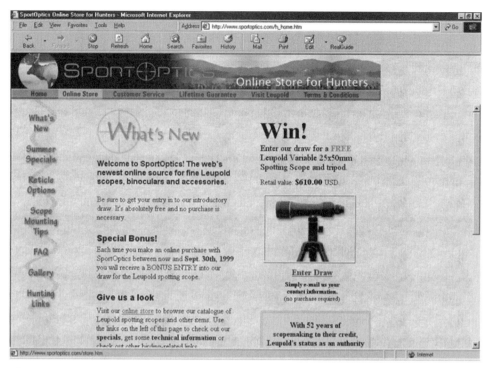

Figure 9.2 SportOptics home page.

Once ensconced in the site, our intrepid customer could then choose to enter in his or her frequent buyer number. The Web generally, and Net.Commerce specifically, supports promotion based on buying patterns that are available on the basis of shopper identification. By rewarding loyal customers with awards and promotions, we found that the Web site could generate higher return traffic. The key is to avoid anonymous buyers, which, come to think of it, makes sense—if people are going to give you their credit card numbers, you need to have at least their name, and if you are going to ship them stuff, you'll need their address. (See Figure 9.3.) (By the way, the SportOptics site carries no munitions or arms of any kind. Just thought I should mention it.)

The formatted WebPage that the macro implements is displayed in Figure 9.4.

Net.Commerce is fully customizable though the modification of the supplied commands, tasks, overridable functions, and macros. This customization allows for changes in the business processes, the appearance, and connection to remote databases. The main limitations of Net.Com-

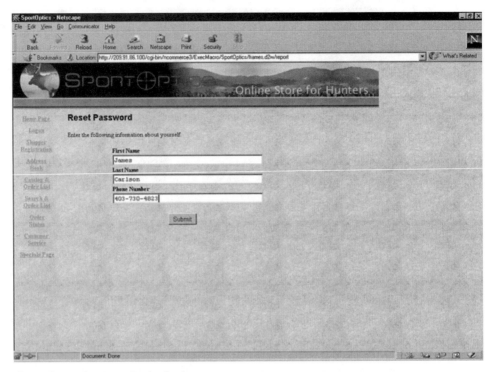

Figure 9.3 The SportOptics login page.

merce out of the box are the order management and product input interfaces. These limitations can be overcome with Catalog Architect and customization of the back-end databases. Although connections to multiple databases are supported in Net.Commerce, using DB2 database servers should provide a turnkey e-store solution.

To implement the logic behind the screen shown in Figure 9.3, the following Macro was written in Net.Commerce:

```
Net.Commerce Macro Code for Password Challenge

%include "SportOptics\SportOptics.inc"
%DEFINE{
     b_success = "true"
     s_loginid = ""
%}

%{ b_success is used a flag to determine if the getQuestion function has
found a person matching the users input %}

%{ getQuestion takes the input salname, safname, saphone and returns the
challenge question and header for the page in a table format. If no user
is found the user is told and the b_success flag is "false" %}
```

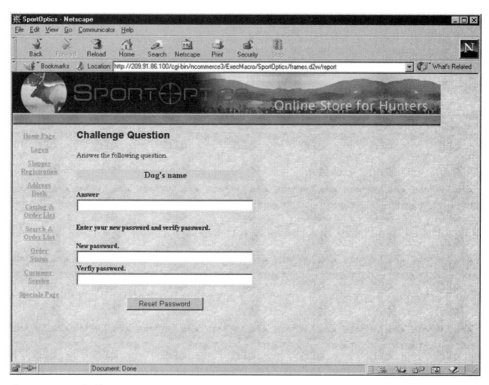

Figure 9.4 Challenge question for password setting.

```
%FUNCTION(DTW_ODBC) getQuestion() {
      select shchaque, shlogid , sashnbr
      from shopper, shaddr
      where salname = '$(salname)'
            and safname = '$(safname)'
            and saphone1='$(saphone1)'
            and sashnbr=shrfnbr
            and saadrflg='P'

%report {
        <TABLE WIDTH="300" CELLPADDING="0" CELLSPACING="0" BORDER="0">
            <TR>
<TD ALIGN="LEFT" VALIGN="CENTER"><FONT FACE="helvetica"
COLOR="$(TitleTxtCol)"><H3>Challenge Question</H3></FONT></TD>
        </TR>
        <TR>
        <TD><FONT COLOR="black" SIZE="2">Answer the following
question.</FONT></TD>
        </TR>
        <TR><TD><BR></TD></TR>
%ROW {
            @DTW_ASSIGN(s_loginid, V_shlogid)
```

```
            <TR>
                <TD ALIGN="center" BGCOLOR="pink">
                <FONT COLOR="$(TitleTxtCol)" Size="3">
                <B>$(V_shchaque)</B></FONT><BR></TD>
            </tr>
        %}
%}

%MESSAGE {

    100 : {
            <TR>
            <TD><B>Your Shopper record was not found in the database.
Please try again.</B></TD>
            </TR>
            <BR><BR>
            @DTW_ASSIGN(b_success,"false")
            %}:continue

        DEFAULT : {
            <B>An unknow error occoured in the getQuestion()
(pwdreset.d2w).</b>
        %}
%}
%}
```

%{ The input block gets the users first name, last name, and phone number
and puts them in NVPs. These NVPs are passed to the report section
below.%}

%HTML_INPUT {

```
<HTML>
<HEAD><TITLE>Reset Password</TITLE></HEAD>
<BODY BACKGROUND="$(BodyColor1)" TEXT="$(TextCol)" LINK="$(LinkCol)'
VLINK="$(VLinkCol)" ALink="$(ALinkCol)">

<TABLE WIDTH=500 CELLPADDING=0 CELLSPACING=0 BORDER=0>
<FORM METHOD=post ACTION="/cgi-
bin/ncommerce3/ExecMacro/$(STORENAME)/pwdreset.d2w/report">
        <TR>
            <TD Align="left" VALIGN="center" COLSPAN=2><FONT
FACE="helvetica" COLOR=$(TitleTxtCol)>
            <H3>Reset Password</H3></FONT></TD>
        </TR>
        <TR>
            <TD ALIGN="left" COLSPAN=2><FONT COLOR="black" SIZE="2">Enter
the following information about yourself.</FONT></TD>
        </TR>
        <TR><TD><BR></TD></TR>
        <TR>
            <TD><SPACER TYPE="block" WIDTH=80 HEIGHT=10></TD>
            <TD><B><FONT SIZE="-1">First Name</FONT></B></TD>
        </TR>
```

```
    <TR>
        <TD><SPACER TYPE="block" WIDTH=80 HEIGHT=10></TD>
        <TD><INPUT TYPE="text" NAME="safname" SIZE="40"
MAXLENGTH="30"></TD>
    </TR>
    <TR>
        <TD><SPACER TYPE="block" WIDTH=80 HEIGHT=10></TD>
        <TD><B><FONT SIZE="-1">Last Name</FONT></B></TD>
    </TR>
    <TR>
        <TD><SPACER TYPE="block" WIDTH=80 HEIGHT=10></TD>
        <TD><INPUT TYPE="text" NAME="salname" SIZE="40"
MAXLENGTH="30"></TD>
    </TR>
    <TR>
        <TD><SPACER TYPE="block" WIDTH=80 HEIGHT=10></TD>
        <TD><B><FONT SIZE="-1">Phone Number</FONT></B></TD>
    </TR>
    <TR>
        <TD><SPACER TYPE="block" WIDTH=80 HEIGHT=10></TD>
        <TD><INPUT TYPE="text" NAME="saphone1" SIZE="40"
MAXLENGTH="30"></TD>
    </TR>
    <TR>
        <TD><BR></TD>
    </TR>
    <TR>
        <TD Align="center" COLSPAN=2><INPUT TYPE="submit"
VALUE="Submit"></TD>
    </TR>

</FORM>
</TABLE>
</BODY>
</HTML>
%}

%{ The report section calls the PasswordReset command if getQuestion finds
a person matching the users input. The NVPs and URL are passed for the
mandatory parameters to password reset. %}

%HTML_REPORT{
    <HTML>
    <HEAD><TITLE><Reset Password</TITLE></HEAD>
    <BODY BACKGROUND="$(BodyColor1)" TEXT="$(TextCol)" LINK="$(LinkCol)"
VLINK="$(VLinkCol)" ALINK="$(ALinkCol)">

    <FORM Method=POST action="/cgi-bin/ncommerce3/PasswordReset">
        <INPUT Type = "hidden" Name="url" Value="http://$(HOST_NAME)/cgi-
bin/ncommerce3/ExecMacro/pwdok.d2w/input" >
    @getQuestion()

    <INPUT TYPE="hidden" Name="merchant_rn" VALUE="$(merchantRefNum)">
```

```
        <INPUT TYPE="hidden" NAME="login_id" VALUE="$(s_loginid)">
%IF(b_success == "true")
        <TR>
                <TD><BR></TD>
        </TR>
        <TR>
        <TD><B><FONT SIZE="-1">Answer</FONT></B></TD>
        </TR>
        <TR>
                <TD><INPUT TYPE="text" NAME="chal_ans" SIZE="40"
MAXLENGTH="254"></TD>
        </TR>
        <TR><TD><BR></TD></TR>
        <TR>
        <TD><B><FONT COLOR="black" SIZE="2">Enter your new password and
verify password.</FONT></B></TD>
        </TR>
        <TR><TD><BR></TD></TR>
        <TD><B><FONT SIZE="-1">New password.</FONT></B></TD>
        <TR>
                <TD><INPUT TYPE="password" NAME="new_pass" SIZE="40"
MAXLENGTH="16"></TD>
        </TR>
        <TD><B><FONT SIZE="-1">Verfiy password.</FONT></B></TD>
        <TR>
                <TD><INPUT TYPE="password" NAME="newver_pass" SIZE="40"
MAXLENGTH="16"></TD>
        </TR>
        <TR><TD><BR></TD></TR>
        <TR>
                <TD ALIGN="center"><INPUT TYPE="submit" VALUE="Reset
Password"></TD>
        </TR>
        </TABLE>
%ENDIF
        </FORM>
        </BODY>
        </HTML>

%}
```

The preceding code demonstrates the four sections of a Net.Data Macro:

Define section. Defines global variables.

Function section. Retrieves and displays information from the database and passes variables to other macros, commands, and overridable functions.

Input and Report sections. Points of entry for Net.Data into the macro.

Define Section

The define section is delineated by the %DEFINE { *statement1*, *statement 2*, . . . } statement, which allows for the use of global variables. There can be multiple define sections, providing they are at the outermost level of the macro and before any section that calls the variables continued in the statements. If a variable is called that isn't defined, then it is replaced with the NULL character.

To call a variable you simply use the following reference $(*variable_name*). The variable identifier can be any alphanumeric combination and the underscore providing that it begins with the underscore or a letter. It is important to note that Net.Data is case-sensitive; thus the identifier *Shopper* is different from *shopper*.

All variables in version 1.0 of Net.Data are strings. This proves to be tricky when using comparison and assignment operators. Although Net.Data version 2.0 has different variable types, this functionality is not supported in Net.Commerce 3.1.2.

The following piece of code shows our define section:

```
%DEFINE{
b_success = "true"
s_loginid = ""
%}
```

This section has two global variables, called b_success and s_loginid. As you will see in latter sections, these values can be called by referencing $(b_success) and $(s_loginid).

You may have noticed the %include "SportOptics\SportOptics.inc section, which simply includes a file with a large define section. This file defines certain global constants that control the appearance of all the WebPages.

Function Section

Functions retrieve information from the database and pass values to commands, overridable functions, or other macros. There can be many functions, which must be defined before the input and report sections. The % FUNCTION(DTW_ODBC) FunctionName () { . . . } statement defines the function. Because Net.Commerce uses ODBC to connect to the database, the language environment must be defined as DTW_ODBC to provide an interface between our function and the database.

The function selects the information to display via a SQL statement which is passed to the database. Let's look at the first section of our getQuestion( ) function.

```
%FUNCTION(DTW_ODBC) getQuestion() {
      select shchaque, shlogid , sashnbr
      from shopper, shaddr
      where salname = '$(salname)'
            and safname = '$(safname)'
            and saphone1='$(saphone1)'
            and sashnbr=shrfnbr
            and saadrflg='P'
```

The select statement is parsed by Net.Data, and the $(salname), $(safname), $(saphone1) variables are replaced with the values-associated NVPs as inputted in the input section. (This is discussed later.) This SQL statement will return rows for each matching record with the shchaque, shlogid, and sashnbr columns.

If the SQL statement returns rows, the report section of our function will be executed. The report block will be executed, and for each row returned it will execute the row block. The code for these sections is as follows:

```
%report {
          <TABLE WIDTH="300" CELLPADDING="0" CELLSPACING="0" BORDER="0">
               <TR>
<TD ALIGN="LEFT" VALIGN="CENTER"><FONT FACE="helvetica"
COLOR="$(TitleTxtCol)"><H3>Challenge Question</H3></FONT></TD>
            </TR>
            <TR>
            <TD><FONT COLOR="black" SIZE="2">Answer the following
question.</FONT></TD>
            </TR>
            <TR><TD><BR></TD></TR>
%ROW {
               @DTW_ASSIGN(s_loginid, V_shlogid)
          <TR>
               <TD ALIGN="center" BGCOLOR="pink">
               <FONT COLOR="$(TitleTxtCol)" Size="3">
               <B>$(V_shchaque)</B></FONT><BR></TD>
          </tr>
     %}
%}
```

As you can see from the HTML, the coding *challenge question* is the title of the page, followed by the prompting to answer the challenge question. In the row block we find two new items: the DTW_ASSIGN statement and the V_shlogid variable. The DTW_ASSIGN is one of many built-in Net.Data functions, which can be referneced in the Net.Data online manuals. The DTW_ASSIGN function copies the string from V_shlogid to s_loginid. In this row section the V_shlogid is the value of shlogid returned for the current row. You will also notice the use of $(V_shchaque) in the bolded text field tag. This tells Net.Data that this statement isn't simply text but it should be parsed and replaced with the associated value before being written to a WebPage.

If the SQL statement doesn't return any rows, the message block is executed. The error code returned by the database is used to determine which section of the message block to perform. The message block is revisited as follows:

```
%MESSAGE {

     100 : {
           <TR>
           <TD><B>Your Shopper record was not found in the database.
Please try again.</B></TD>
           </TR>
           <BR><BR>
           @DTW_ASSIGN(b_success,"false")
           %}:continue

     DEFAULT : {
           <B>An unknow error occoured in the getQuestion()
(pwdreset.d2w).</b>
      %}
%}
```

If no rows are returned, the error code is 100, and the 100 block is executed. The HTML coding shows that the shopper is informed that the shopper wasn't found in the database. The b_success variable is assigned a value of false and used as a control statement in the report section (discussed later). The continue modifier after the 100 block indicates that Net.Data should continue execution if the 100 block has been executed. If the error code is anything else, the default block is executed. This section is generally used for debugging, and thus it is advisable to provide explicit error messages.

Input Section

The input section is a point of entry into the macro. The define section and the function section are parsed and compiled at runtime before the input section is reached. The following is the first portion of the input section:

```
%HTML_INPUT {

<HTML>
<HEAD><TITLE>Reset Password</TITLE></HEAD>
<BODY BACKGROUND="$(BodyColor1)" TEXT="$(TextCol)" LINK="$(LinkCol)'
VLINK="$(VLinkCol)" ALink="$(ALinkCol)">

<TABLE WIDTH=500 CELLPADDING=0 CELLSPACING=0 BORDER=0>
<FORM METHOD=post ACTION="/cgi-
bin/ncommerce3/ExecMacro/$(STORENAME)/pwdreset.d2w/report">
```

The title of the page is Reset Password, as seen in the HTML coding. This Web page uses a table as defined in the table tag. The FORM tag is very important, as it specifies the next command. The action associated with the form calls the ExecMacro overridable function to execute the pwdreset.d2w macro with the point of entry in the report section. Let's look closely at the input fields in the next section of our macro:

```
<TR>
    <TD><SPACER TYPE="block" WIDTH=80 HEIGHT=10></TD>
    <TD><B><FONT SIZE="-1">First Name</FONT></B></TD>
</TR>
<TR>
    <TD><SPACER TYPE="block" WIDTH=80 HEIGHT=10></TD>
    <TD><INPUT TYPE="text" NAME="safname" SIZE="40"
MAXLENGTH="30"></TD>
</TR>
```

The rows of the table are easily visible through Net.Commerce. The coding responsible for the first name text field and the input box that follows are carefully crafted to allow the values to be passed to the report section of pwdreset.d2w. Net.Data will pass the name value pairs (NVP) associated with the form to the overridable function. The overridable function called in this case is ExecMacro, which displays the report section that follows. In our example, one of the name value pairs is *safname* and *James*. These values are automatically passed by Net.Data and can be referenced in the downstream macro by $(safname). This will be demonstrated in the report section of the macro.

Report Section

The report block of the macro is simply another point of entry; it has no impact on the types of functions carried out or the information retrieved from the database. A portion of the report block is reproduced as follows:

```
%HTML_REPORT{
      <HTML>
      <HEAD><TITLE><Reset Password</TITLE></HEAD>
      <BODY BACKGROUND="$(BodyColor1)" TEXT="$(TextCol)" LINK="$(LinkCol)"
VLINK="$(VLinkCol)" ALINK="$(ALinkCol)">

      <FORM Method=POST action="/cgi-bin/ncommerce3/PasswordReset">
        <INPUT Type = "hidden" Name="url" Value="http://$(HOST_NAME)/cgi-
bin/ncommerce3/ExecMacro/pwdok.d2w/input" >
      @getQuestion()

      <INPUT TYPE="hidden" Name="merchant_rn" VALUE="$(merchantRefNum)">
      <INPUT TYPE="hidden" NAME="login_id" VALUE="$(s_loginid)">
```

The FORM tag indicates a different kind of action than seen in the preceding input section. This action references a command called *PasswordReset*. This command is passed to the login_id, the merchant_rn, and the url values in NVPs. These values are not inputted by the user but are assigned in the code itself via the hidden type input tag. This allows for values to be passed to macros and overridable functions without input from the user.

The @getQuestion() reference calls the getQuestion function, which was reviewed in the function section. Recall the function's SQL statement, which refered to $(salname), $(safname), $(saphone1). These values are from the input section, which were passed via NVPs when the report section of the macro was called. It doesn't matter that the report section is in the same macro as the input section; the NVPs would have been passed to any macro that was called.

The b_success variable is used as a flag to control program flow. It is set to True in the define section, and set to False if the getQuestion( ) function cannot find the user's challenge question.

The complement of the hidden, text, and password input fields provides the PasswordReset function with its mandatory parameters.

Connecting to Databases

The limitations of Net.Commerce are the product information input and the order retrieval systems. Product information requires three separate information pages. The required information is the path name of the picture of the product, such as /sggifs/SportOpticsPictures/vx3254.gif, the pathname of the template macro, the price precedence, and description. When inputting the data you must also remember the hierarchical structure of the catalog, as the node number must be inputted manually. Screen captures of the product input screens are shown in Figures 9.5 through 9.8.

Figure 9.5 shows the screens that allow you to define a product and its characteristics such as shape, size, weight and associate a graphic to display with the product. These are the default entry screens provided by Net.Commerce.

Figure 9.6 shows the screen you use to define price and sale price for a given product. Here you set the date range for which the sale price is effective.

Figure 9.7 shows the screens Net.Commerce uses to associate the layout used for text and graphics layout, including center, right and left justify. You can also suppress either the graphic or text information to organize the way a group of products is displayed. Net.Commerce comes with several default templates you can use.

Figure 9.8 is a screen capture of the order reporting feature supported in Net.Commerce. Using this feature you can determine order name, date last updated, subtotals, tax and shipping charges associated with any given order.

These input procedures represent the most basic way to get data into Net.Commerce. Catalog Architect is a more sophisticated companion product and provides the ability to publish your product information with advanced features.

Catalog Architect

The order retrieval system provided with NC is limited to showing one order at a time, without the ability to print a list of completed or pending orders. The store is selected and the search button is pressed. The user then scrolls through the windows and at the bottom clicks on an order to retrieve. Once the order has been retrieved, there is no ability to print the order.

These limitations can be easily overcome with the integration of MS Access. Access can connect to the database using DB2's Client Applica-

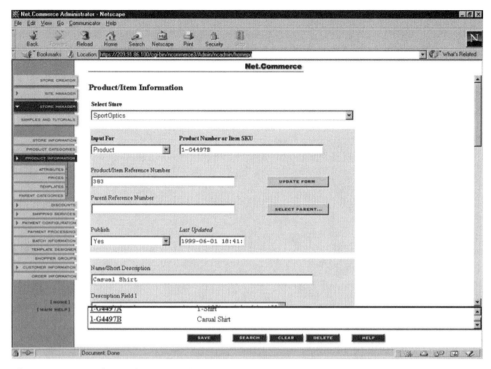

Figure 9.5 Product information input screen.

tion Extender (CAE) product. CAE allows ODBC clients to connect to and interact with the database. A few simple screens will allow for the user to retrieve orders of any given status.

Catalog Architect is IBM's solution to the catalog management problem associated with the input screens. This product requires Windows NT and CAE. We have not employed this as we require a more lightweight order retrieval and catalog management system that can run on a client's Win95\98 Box.

Connection to Multiple Data Stores

Net.Commerce allows for connections to multiple databases, through ODBC connections. The connections can be implemented through the commands or overridable functions. There is a supplied class, which can connect to remote ODBC databases and retrieve information. This solution is difficult to implement as issues arise such as multiple initializa-

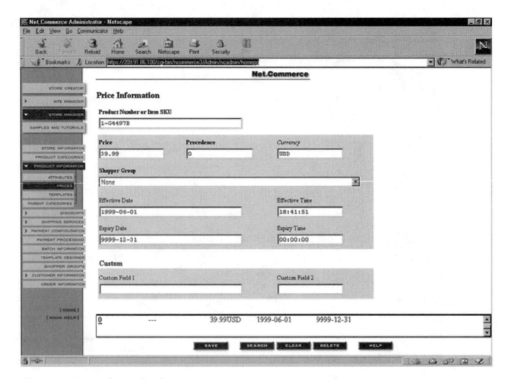

Figure 9.6 Product price input screen.

tion of the same overridable functions, which would create multiple connections to the same source. This can be overcome with the use of flag variables; however, this can become more complex if there are multiple stores, which may initialize the function in another server pool.

One possible solution is to integrate a middleware product like IBM's DataJoiner, Component Broker, or MQ Series as part of WebSphere Enterprise. This allows for single-point integration of multiple heterogeneous BackOffice systems. The role of Net.Commerce in this case would be to manage the presentation of catalog information and provide a secure session for a customer using the Web to browse, select, and pay for items. Other servers tied in to the inventory and billing operations would support the backend processes.

Net.Data

Anyone who has browsed IBM's Web site will be familiar with the Net.Data logo used on Big Blue's own e-stores. Net.Data is the key means

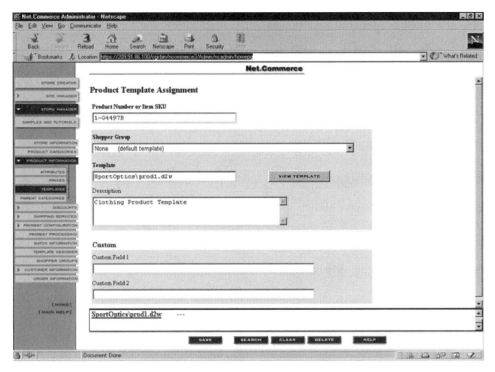

Figure 9.7 The product template assignment screen assigns a Net.Data Macro.

used within Net.Commerce to manage and display HTML pages, as well as to provide modifiable functionality through macros.

Net.Data is integrated into the Net.Commerce daemon and is loaded as a Windows NT DLL or an AIX shared library. It combines functions, simple control statements, SQL, and HTML to produce dynamic Web pages. When Net.Data is called, it searches for the macros using the MACRO_PATH statement in the db2www.ini file.

This component is rather transparent when you deal with the NC server. The macro that we created to display a challenge question is a Net.Data macro. However, Net.Data provides much more functionality than suggested here. Net.Data enables Internet and intranet access to relational data on a variety of platforms. The most prevalent databases can be data sources for your Web application: DB2, Oracle, Sybase, DRDA-enabled data sources, and ODBC data sources, as well as flat file and Web registry data.

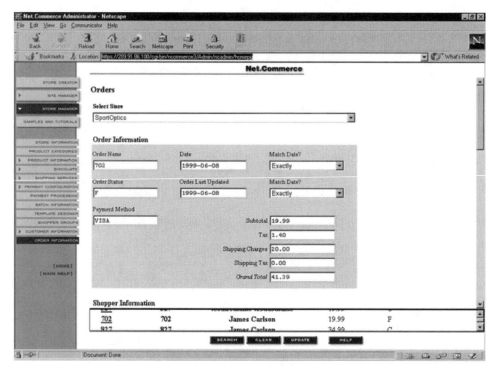

Figure 9.8 Inputting product info to Net.Commerce.

Summary

Net.Commerce is a complete and powerful combination of shopping cart software and e-store management utilities. When combined with the Java programming capabilities available with version 3.2, it is another strong entry in the Big Blue Java tool kit.

There is some overlap in the capabilities of Net.Commerce (Net.Data), WebSphere, and SanFrancisco. How you choose to implement the technology should be driven by your specific requirements. It's nice to know that there are options.

From this chapter you should have gained a sense of where Net.Commerce fits into the tool kit. Also, you should see how you can go about customizing the default Net.Commerce implementation to handle your special site needs.

CHAPTER 10

DB2 UDB 6.1

IBM's roots in the relational world are long and deep. It was an IBM research fellow—Dr. E.F. Codd—who made the necessary discoveries and advances in mathematics to allow the creation of the first relational database. Dr. Codd's rules of normalization are still adhered to by anyone wishing to take full advantage of the capabilities of an RDBMS.

It is fascinating to consider that the term *legacy system* now applies to two-tier client-server applications built using relational technology. Perhaps that is in part due to the human tendency to not want to grow old. The early relational applications are now closing in on 20 years of age, and the great boom in client/server systems is now 5 to 10 years in the past. You would think that this would be more than enough time to get some return on investment out of them.

Like all technological innovations, there was a considerable struggle in the relational world, first to get people to understand the value of the new technology, and later to differentiate features, functions, and benefits. I first worked with Ingres from Relational Technology in 1985 and later moved to working with Sybase in 1990. More recently, WNS played with Microsoft's SQL Server and ultimately standardized on DB2 as the scalable relational database of choice.

There are a number of reasons for this move to DB2, and it is somewhat gratifying to see that as of the time of this writing, DB2 has officially moved into the role of number one installed relational database, eclipsing Oracle. One of the reasons behind this is the native DB2 support provided as part of any AS/400 installation. When you buy an AS/400, you get DB2 as part of the package. There are, of course, upgrades to the AS/400 native DB2 offering, but when you are counting installations, 600,000 AS/400 sites certainly go a long way in helping make your database number one.

DB2 and Trying Harder

In the late 1990s there was a tremendous upheaval in the relational database market. RDBMS engines rapidly became a commodity. As a result, the previously strong contenders such as Sybase and Informix were left struggling to stay in the black, let alone innovate or take market share.

Microsoft, of course, grew the sales of its SQL Server product, but mostly through the provision of Back Office and not through leveraged applications or solutions. Oracle got drawn into the NetPC arena and, as it is wont to do, took its eyes off the core business of providing database engines and tools.

IBM, on the other hand, had quietly mandated a major upgrade to DB2, moving through versions 5 to 6.1, and the DB2 Universal Database initiative had all the force of a significant product overhaul. The key new feature set introduced support for Java in the database.

Persistent Data Stores

One of the key weaknesses of the object model from a practical standpoint is captured in the expression "The data is irrelevant." Object-oriented designers and developers are sometimes blinded by the brilliance of their own tools and techniques. A business system doesn't just use data—it depends on it. So it stands to reason that the mechanism for storing that data must be a strong functional component of any solution.

IBM recognized this early and folded its DB2 development initiatives into its overall Java strategy. The net result is that we have access to a strong database environment in which to keep our vital organizational data. The difference is that instead of the data being stored in flat POSIX files (heaven forfend), we can take advantage of all of the features and functions of a mature relational database.

The key services you want from a relational database are:

Data integrity. Usually implemented through constraints, stored procedures, and triggers, data integrity is paramount. Only the right data can be changed, inserted, or deleted.

Recoverability. In the event that a transaction fails, whether through network error, computer failure, or simply a bad process, the initial state of the data must be restored. Transaction logging is an essential part of this recoverability. Backups taken without compromising performance of a production system are also an important requirement. No one wants to bring down the online store in the middle of the day in order to do a backup. When you offer 7×24 services to a global market, it's always the middle of the day somewhere.

Scalability. Developers need small-footprint, lightweight databases with all the features found in their larger cousins in a production environment. The same software needs to run in cheap and cheerful Linux boxes as in big iron shops that never sleep.

Interoperability. Database environments must run on multiple operating system and hardware platforms. There is no one right answer for all situations. At the least, your data store must be able to run on NT, Linux, AS/400, RS-6000, and the mainframe. Throw in the PalmPilot, and DB2 makes a clean sweep!

Object Databases

I'm going to go out on a limb here and say unequivocally that object databases are not going to replace relational databases in the next five years. The reason I say this is simple—there is too much experience and too large an install base for RDBMS to go away. Instead, the relational databases will take on support for more object-oriented features—themselves becoming more object-oriented. But don't look for that silent but deadly newcomer in the database world to pop up and knock everybody else out of the water. Datastores provide value, but this is not the arena where the real action takes place.

The problem with most of the object databases on the market is that their features do not provide a compelling business case for anyone to buy them. Interesting—yes; practical—perhaps; but where's the beef? Why would anyone facing all of the choices in the systems market today, along with the very compelling changes in languages and communications architecture, turn around and swap database environments as well? To me, it just doesn't make sense to do that.

Database Basics

When the original RDBMS (okay, from here on let's just refer to DB2) hit the market, the key feature that people wanted was the ability to store data in less disk space. Disk space was not cheap in the 1980s—far from it. The real value of relational technology went undersold or unsung, while we all focused on storing just the data we had to, and restricted duplication to foreign keys.

I'm going to try to cover the essential concepts of the practical value you gain from using a relational database, while at the same time drawing parallels to the adoption of object technology. If this takes a bit of jumping around before it all comes together, please bear with me.

In a relational database everything depends on the key. The primary key of any given table is the unique identifier on which the other data elements in that table depend. In the U.S. government's database, for example, my name depends on my Social Security Number, which is the unique identifier the government has given me, to keep track of my taxes. No data is duplicated across other tables if it is directly related to the primary key. A foreign key, on the other hand, is the primary key of one table but has a dependency on another table's primary key. My employee ID is a primary key for occupation data, but it is still dependent on my Social Security Number, which is, after all, the real me.

With a relational database, everything comes down to sets. Even in a query to the database that results in one row being returned, that row is not a single item; it is a set consisting of one row. This thinking underlies everything about relational databases.

Adopting Relational Technology

One of the problems with the set orientation of relational technology is that there have been times when it simply didn't work well with what the programmers wanted to accomplish. For example, in some cases you might have wanted to go through a list of employees to determine which ones had been with the company for more than two years, and to give them a 5 percent salary increase. This is no problem using Structured Query Language (SQL) syntax, as you simply update the salary column with a 1.05 times multiplier for anyone with the appropriate start date.

Where this gets a little trickier is where you have multiple raises depending on the length of service (e.g., 5 percent for 2 years, 7 percent for 5 years, and 10 percent for 10 years). With SQL this is three separate update passes, which does not appeal to many programmers—especially those used to walking through an ISAM file and simply calculating the right salary increase based on the value of the start date. To do that requires that you take on row-at-a-time processing, which breaks the relational model.

Well, guess what? In order to sell their products, the vendors had to support that capability in the form of row-at-a-time processing. While they were at it, the vendors added all kinds of other bastardizations of the model in the form of extensions to their implementation of SQL. Cursors, If-statements, Go-to and branching support—all kinds of icky stuff. Naturally, the relational theorists were outraged.

But it worked. And it continues to work to this day.

In the same way that some of the traditional file-handling capabilities of ISAM needed to be supported in relational processing, the object model needs to take advantage of relational capabilities. Even if it violates the theory, in practice it just makes sense.

N-tier Client/Server

When Sybase came out with stored procedures and triggers in 1988, the database world was set back on its haunches. The ability to connect to a relational database engine using an application programming interface and to call a precompiled back-end set of commands was innovative, to say the least. It fixed performance problems; it provided for reusability of codes and functions; it increased security. It was revolutionary. Triggers, on the other hand, made sure that if any data item was updated, inserted, or deleted, a particular set of functions would be guaranteed to take place, or the entire transaction would be rolled back. This was great stuff.

As people worked more with relational databases, the straightforward connection of a client to a server in the two-tier fashion gave way to the idea of increased separation. If it made sense to separate the data layer from the client that displayed the data, then maybe it was a good idea to separate the logic that ran the application from both the client and the data server. Presto! You now have the n-tier client/server computing.

N-tier client/server is essentially what we are working with in the model-view-controller paradigm. The point I want you to take away from this diatribe is that in the same way that the relational folks had to incorporate the value of the previous era's technology and techniques, the object world will also have to make that accommodation. That extends to more than simply adopting relational technology as part of the new architecture.

A great deal of data still exists in virtual sequential access method (VSAM) files. CICS applications specifically use these puppies to a great extent. The integration of data is something that folks from the relational world have been working on, lo these past 10 years. One of the approaches to moving traditional or legacy applications into this new world will be at the database integration level. Other approaches include component brokering and messaging; these are covered in the chapter on WebSphere Enterprise (Chapter 20).

For now, let's look at how DB2 works, and where you might position it to fit into the Big Blue Java world.

It's All Relative

Personally, I don't believe that the heading for this section is true. In fact, to say "it's all relative" is an absolute statement. Semantics aside, however, when it comes to application development, you definitely need to be able to relate two things together and present those as meaningful information to a user.

IBM as well has a deep commitment to relational technology. As we have covered in the section on strategy, the heart of the Big Blue Java approach is to provide a unifying lingua franca to all aspects of existing technology as well as Java- and Web-enabling new releases. DB2 has not been left out of this process.

With the introduction of DB2 UDB 6.1, powerful new Java-enabled features have been incorporated into the RDBMS.

The Control Center

With Release 6.1, the DB2 Control Center is now itself a Java application. Web-based administration, or for that matter execution of Control Center, can now be invoked on any platform that supports a JVM. As we know from our investigations to date, this is pretty much everything.

In our tests with Control Center, we found that 6.1 opened up doors that previously had been closed. For example, it is now possible to connect to a server, and, provided you have the correct permissions, to connect to databases known to that server. It is not necessary to have direct access permissions to administer a particular RDBMS.

The largest value to this is the promotion of single-site administration of distributed database servers. In our work at WNS with database support, we have found that a single DBA can handle 20 or 30 servers, depending on their size, transaction load, and state of maturity. This becomes much more problematic where databases require involved remote log-on procedures, or where the tools available are strictly character-based.

The Control Center in UDB 6.1 is clean, user-friendly, and effective. It allows you to view the resources and objects of DB2 servers from previous versions as well. In short, it works very well. Let's go through some of the features and functions of Control Center. (See Figure 10.1.)

Control Center uses a tree for database objects on the left, while the detail is displayed on the right. This is quickly becoming the standard way (if it's not already) to depict master-detail relationships of long lists.

One of the most frequent transactions anyone uses a visual database browser for is to determine the size and growth of transaction logs. The tran logs are wonderful things when it comes time to undo or roll back transactions, but they do require some degree of management if you don't want their devices to fill, leaving your database hung in limbo. To provide a useful example of the capabilities of a generic Java application, as well as of Control Center in particular, I now propose to take you through some of the basic administration functions of UDB 6.1.

Adding users, changing passwords, and assigning permissions are the prosaic functions that make up a database administrator's life. The NT-based SQL Server administration tools have gone a long way toward making SQL/NT a popular database environment for smaller applications. With

Figure 10.1 Initial login screen using UDB 6.1 Control Center.

UDB 6.1, you not only do not have to give up the ability to use a visual administration tool; you can use the same tool to connect to UDBs large and small.

To give you an idea of how this works, Figure 10.2 shows how Control Center manages a user account.

Figure 10.2 shows how you can quickly look at a list of users defined for a particular database. In our example, we want to add a new developer, give him a working database that he has full permissions for, and provide select access for a production 5.1 database running over the network on a Unix server. An administrator can do all this from within the same Control Center session. See Figure 10.3.

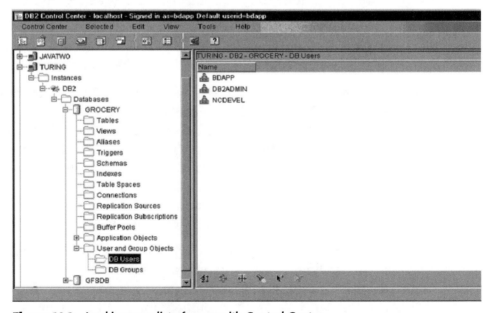

Figure 10.2 Looking up a list of users with Control Center.

Once you have the user defined you can then move on to creating a new database. In this case, we are allocating 20 megabytes of space to the database on a personal computer. The particular version of UDB that we generated these examples from was UDB 6.1 personal DB2 for Windows NT. This product directly competes with the small user database implementations of SQL Server, Personal Oracle, and Adaptive Server Anywhere.

Figure 10.4 shows the smartguide definition for the database name and location.

Figure 10.5 shows a control center session that identifies the DB2 instances running in the local network.

Figure 10.6 shows the administrative screen used to define users and associate permissions for them.

This will be treated as the home database for the developer. All permissions are vested in that user identity. To make things a little more challenging, now we are going to provide access to a production database and then use UDB to pull over some of the data to allow the new user to

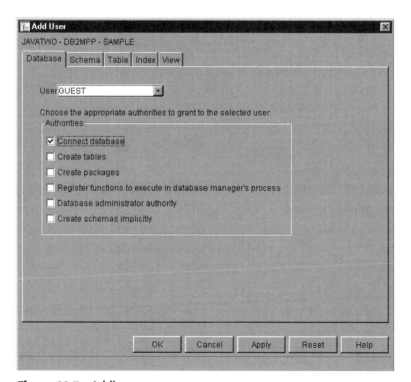

Figure 10.3 Adding a new user.

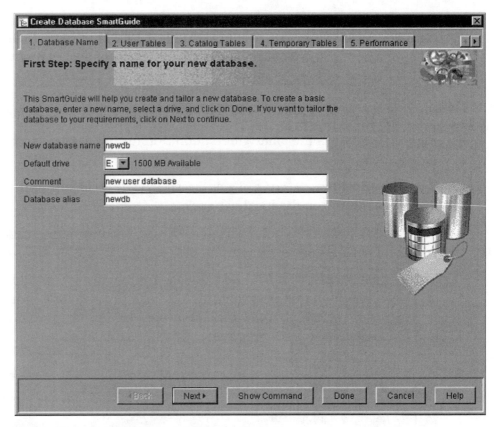

Figure 10.4 Creating a new database for the user.

create stored procedures and other database objects that work with that data.

As you can see, the interface from Control Center is the same regardless of the version of the database to which we are connected. One of the key differences is that you will not be able to access database objects such as stored procedures if they are not supported in the version of the database to which you connect. In Figure 10.5 we see the database contents of a remote production server.

This process is identical to adding a user to UDB 6.1. The next step is to use Control Center to pull across data from the remote server to our local development server, where we can create new objects that work with that data.

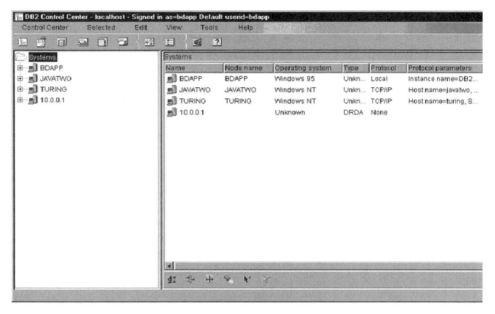

Figure 10.5 Connecting to a remote DB2 database.

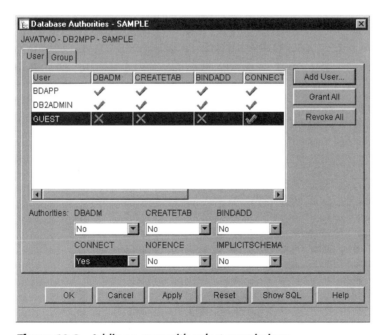

Figure 10.6 Adding a user with select permissions.

Especially in a database development environment there is a need to move objects such as data, scripts, stored procedures, triggers, and view definitions from a development server to a test environment and ultimately into production. The Control Center that ships with UDB 6.1 is an improvement on previous versions in that it not only can connect to multiple database versions, but allows interoperability within a multiserver environment.

In the same way that we saw the evolution of database application development move to *n*-tier, IBM is facilitating this with its Java offerings. Let's walk through an example of a developer using UDB in a multiserver setting.

In Figure 10.7 you can see how Control Center allows you to parse database objects (in this case tables), identify what they contain, and promote those for export. At some point it is always necessary to write some SQL, although the SQL SmartGuide provided with Control Center has come a long way toward making it unnecessary to keep huge reference texts of SQL commands around. Administration in particular, and increasingly the move to Java programming, means that you find yourself (speaking as a developer) working less with languages and dialects like SQL.

That doesn't mean that you give up SQL entirely. One of the key themes of this book is that you will continue to find uses for the technology and interfaces that you have already spent years learning to master. This applies to SQL as well.

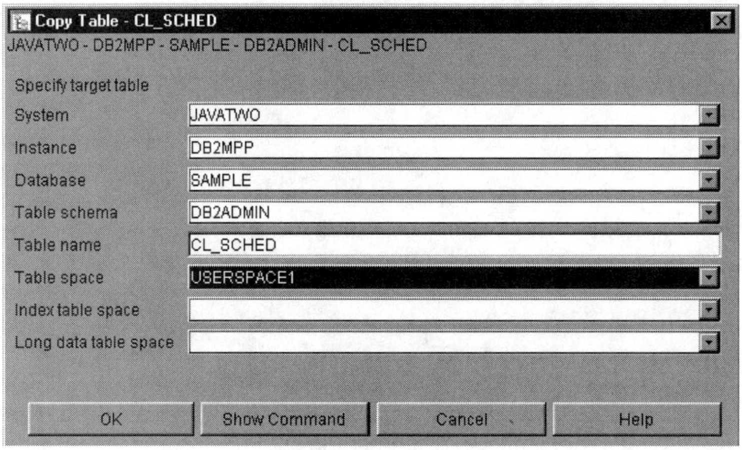

Figure 10.7 Copying and pasting database objects.

However, IBM has recognized that many developers are moving to Java and that soon it will be difficult for them to remember how to properly use the arcane syntax of Structured Query Language. (Okay, that's overstating the point, but it *is* an interesting idea!)

In any case, you can use Control Center to create SQL that pulls data from one database, where you have select permissions, and transfer it to your personal database, where you can do more interesting things with it.

In Figures 10.8 and 10.9 you see screen captures of how we accomplished moving the data over to our new database from the production Unix server.

The SmartGuide approach to pulling data out of DB2 is also walked through in the chapter on VisualAge for Java. Of course, you can always choose to write your own SQL and run it as a script from the Control Center, or you can let the wizard generate the basics and edit it prior to execution.

Not only have we created a developer's database on a Windows machine; we have moved data off a production server and into its new home for subsequent creation of database objects. All this and we didn't even have to get up from our chair!

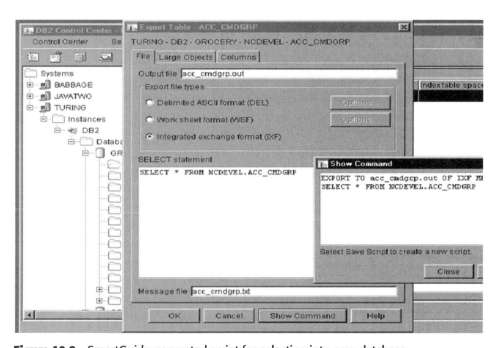

Figure 10.8 SmartGuide-generated script for selecting into new database.

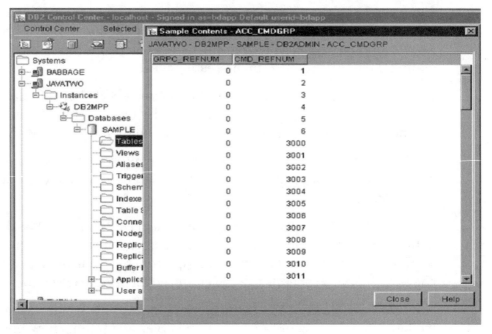

Figure 10.9 The data in its new home.

Creating Stored Procedures in UDB 6.1

As mentioned earlier in this chapter, as relational databases have evolved, two of the most valuable features to emerge have been stored procedures and triggers. By putting all of the logic required to manipulate the relational data in a single program, compiled and stored on the database server itself, you can realize several advantages. Stored procedures were introduced in DB2 V2.1 Common Server and in MVS in DB2 4.1, but the most powerful Java-related innovations are in Java stored procedures in the database. Before we go into that, however, it might be worthwhile to cover the basics of stored procedure characteristics and behavior.

Advantages of Stored Procedures

Stored procedures perform better. Because they are precompiled, you can ensure that the best indexes are used, and because they are stored and executed on the database server, network traffic is minimized to the procedure name and parameters.

Stored procedures mask complexity. It is not necessary to fully understand the data model or to know how to effectively link tables together. The stored procedure returns an entire set of results regardless of how much processing was required to arrive at that set.

DB2 handles stored procedures differently than other relational database implementations such as SQL Server. A calling application must exist on the client, and rows are not returned to the screen; instead they are bound to variables in the calling application, or they are written to a file.

The Command Center allows you to view stored procedures that are already in place on the server, or to write your own.

Creating SQL Stored Procedures

Triggers are like stored procedures except that they are not called; they are fired by operations that change the data. This includes insert, update, and delete actions taken on database objects where triggers have been defined. For our purposes here, we can treat triggers and stored procedures in much the same way. Practically speaking, you can take syntax used to create a stored procedure and turn it into a trigger with few modifications, or you can extract the SQL logic from a trigger and turn it into a stored procedure.

One of the key architectural advantages to using stored procedures is the same benefit to separating concerns and segregating developer capabilities in more general object development. It lets people focus on creating programs using tools and resources with which they are familiar, or enables them to focus on using the objects created by someone else because they understand the domain, the user interface, or some other major development function.

Stored procedures allow you to isolate operations that change the data to a single set of syntax that is easier to create and easier to maintain than distributing the logic throughout applications.

Figure 10.10 shows the stored procedure editing bench in the Command Center.

Stored procedures have their own control of flow logic, as well as means of declaring and working with variables. You can define parameters for input, output, or both. Moreover, stored procedures can return customized error messages.

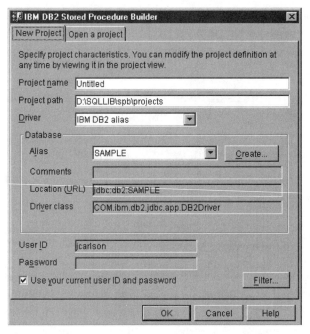

Figure 10.10 Creating a stored procedure using Control Center.

The two phases of stored procedure creation and execution are *client side* and *server side*. On the client side you must:

- Connect to the database.
- Declare, allocate, and initialize the SQLDA structure (alternately you can define the host variables).
- Allocate storage for the structure with the number of SQLVAR elements to be handled.
- Set the SQLN field to the allocated number of SQLVAR elements.
- Initialize each SQLVAR element.
- Set SQLTYPE to the datatype of variables to be returned.
- Set SQLLEN to the size of the column holding the variables.
- Allocate storage for SQLDATA in keeping with SQLTYPE and SQLLEN definitions.
- Allocate storage for SQLIND in keeping with SQLTYPE and SQLLEN definitions.
- Invoke SQL Call.

The stored procedure executes in the background, returning data back to the calling program or writing the data out to a file. The return value of the stored procedure is not returned to the calling application, so you may not use successful or failure execution as a case statement inside your program unless you explicitly pass back a database value to indicate the procedure completed (or not).

Connecting Java Applications to DB2

All of the things we established about stored procedures using SQL hold true for Java stored procedures as well. The difference is that you can create Java stored procedures using Java syntax for the control of flow, exception handling, and binding data to classes, instead of to the more traditional variables. However, there are a few specific steps that must be taken if you wish to use Java to create your DB2 stored procedures.

To use JDBC with your DB2 server you must:

- Install DB2 (client or server) on the same machine as your Web server.
- Use the tempjava.sql package instead of java.sql.
- Install the JDBC driver (ibm.sql.DB2Driver for applications and ibm.netsql.DB2Driver for applets).

You can test your setup by running the DB2Appl.java application that ships with DB2 Sample database and can be found in the sqllib\samples\ java subdirectory. Execute this by entering java DB2Appl at the command line.

The preceding steps give you Java-to-DB2 connectivity, which is not the same thing as creating Java stored procedures. We will now look at how you use Java as the language for creating stored procedures in DB2 6.1.

Creating Java Stored Procedures

The new support for the Java language does not take away your ability to create user-defined functions and stored procedures using other more traditional techniques. If you are used to using that syntax, by all means carry on. On the other hand, if you are new to DB2, then you might consider leveraging your newfound Java expertise into the creation of database objects such as UDFs and stored procedures with that syntax.

The functionality of these database objects is the same whether you write them in Java or not. However, when working with Java, they are treated simply as methods in Java classes. Once you create the procedure and register it, you must then place the classes in the correct location, where they can then be called from any program. DB2 runs them through a Java interpreter and they are treated as an application, allowing them to avoid applet security restrictions.

All Java classes implemented as stored procedures must be stored under the sqllib\function directory. To file the class bbj.samples.sample1 you would store the byte-code file in sqllib\function\samples.

Remember, you must register your Java stored procedure by updating the DB2CLI.Procedures table.

Let's take a look at a sample Java stored procedure DB2stp.java (sqllib\ samples\java).

DB2STP.JAVA Client-Side Java Stored Procedure

```
//   Source File Name: DB2SpCli.java %I%
//
//   Licensed Materials -- Property of IBM
//
//   (c) Copyright International Business Machines Corporation, 1996, 1997.
//       All Rights Reserved.
//
//   US Government Users Restricted Rights -
//   Use, duplication or disclosure restricted by
//   GSA ADP Schedule Contract with IBM Corp.
//   Sample Program - Client side of Java Stored Procedure Sample

//   Steps to run the sample:
//   (1) you must have the "sample" database catalogued on the client
//   (2) compile the stored procedure (javac DB2Stp.java) and copy it
//       to the sqllib/function sub-directory
//   (3) compile this java file (javac DB2SpCli.java)
//   (4) run the sample (java DB2SpCli [username password])

//   NOTES: (1) The CLASSPATH and shared library path environment variables
//              must be set, as for any JDBC application.
//          (2) Visit http://www.software.ibm.com/data/db2/java
//              for current DB2 Java information

//   Class DB2SpCli contains four methods:
//   (1) registerStoredProc: register the stored procedure
//   (2) callStoredProc: call the stored procedure
//   (3) main: application body (register and call the stored procedure)

import java.sql.*;              // JDBC classes
import java.math.*;             // BigDecimal
import COM.ibm.db2.jdbc.app.*;  // DB2 UDB JDBC classes

class DB2SpCli
{
```

```
  static
  {
    try
    {
      System.out.println ();
      System.out.println ("  Java Stored Procedure Sample");
      Class.forName ("COM.ibm.db2.jdbc.app.DB2Driver").newInstance ();
    }
  catch (Exception e)
    {
      System.out.println ("\n Error loading DB2 Driver...\n");
      e.printStackTrace ();
    }
}

// (1) register the stored procedure
public static void registerStoredProc (Connection con,
                                       String name,
                                       String classMethod,
                                       String mode) throws Exception

{
  try
    {
      // drop the stored procedure if it exists
      Statement dropStmt = con.createStatement ();
      dropStmt.executeUpdate ("DROP PROCEDURE " + name);
      dropStmt.close ();
    }
  catch (SQLException e)
    {
      // ignore this error
    }

    try
      {
        Statement stmt = con.createStatement ();

        // construct a parameter list for the stored procedure and
        // register it in the system catalogs
        String parameterList =
          "(in    table         varchar(20)," +
          " in    modifier       int," +
          " inout department    varchar(10)," +
          " out   payrollBefore double," +
          " out   payrollAfter  double," +
          " out   avgSalBefore  double," +
          " out   avgSalAfter   double," +
          " out   numOfUpdates  int," +
          " out   medianEmpName varchar(40))";

        System.out.println ("\n  Registering Java stored procedure " +
name +
```

```
                                    "\n      as " + classMethod +
                                    "\n      in " + mode + " mode");

        stmt.executeUpdate ("CREATE PROCEDURE " + name + parameterList +
                            " LANGUAGE JAVA " +
                            " PARAMETER STYLE DB2GENERAL " + mode +
                            " EXTERNAL NAME '" + classMethod + "'");
        stmt.close ();
      }
    catch (SQLException e)
      {
        System.out.println ("\n Error received registering stored
procedure");
        throw e;
      }
  }

// (2) call the requested stored procedure and display results
public static void callStoredProc (Connection con,
                                   String tableName,
                                   String name,
                                   int percentModification,
                                   String department) throws Exception
{
  // prepare the CALL statement
  CallableStatement stmt;
  String sql = "Call " + name + "(?,?,?,?,?,?,?,?,?) ";
  stmt = con.prepareCall (sql);

  // register the output parameters
  stmt.registerOutParameter (4, Types.DOUBLE);
  stmt.registerOutParameter (5, Types.DOUBLE);
  stmt.registerOutParameter (6, Types.DOUBLE);
  stmt.registerOutParameter (7, Types.DOUBLE);
  stmt.registerOutParameter (8, Types.INTEGER);
  stmt.registerOutParameter (9, Types.CHAR);
  // set all parameters (input and output)
  double totalPayrollBefore = 0.00;
  double totalPayrollAfter = 0.00;
  double averageSalaryBefore = 0.00;
  double averageSalaryAfter = 0.00;
  String medianEmployeeName = "This field is not defined yet";
  int numberOfUpdates = 0;
  stmt.setString (1, tableName);
  stmt.setInt (2, percentModification);
  stmt.setString (3, department);
  stmt.setDouble (4, totalPayrollBefore);
  stmt.setDouble (5, totalPayrollAfter);
  stmt.setDouble (6, averageSalaryBefore);
  stmt.setDouble (7, averageSalaryAfter);
  stmt.setInt (8, numberOfUpdates);
  stmt.setString (9, medianEmployeeName);
```

```
    // call the stored procedure
    System.out.println ("\n Calling stored procedure: " + name);
    stmt.execute ();
    System.out.println ("\n Returned from stored procedure: " + name);

    // retrieve output parameters
    BigDecimal totPayBefore = new BigDecimal (stmt.getDouble (4));
    BigDecimal totPayAfter = new BigDecimal (stmt.getDouble (5));
    BigDecimal avgSalBefore = new BigDecimal (stmt.getDouble (6));
    BigDecimal avgSalAfter = new BigDecimal (stmt.getDouble (7));
    numberOfUpdates = stmt.getInt (8);
      medianEmployeeName = stmt.getString (9);

      // display the information returned from the stored procedure
      System.out.println ();
      System.out.println ("              Percent modification:    " +
                          percentModification + "%");
      System.out.println ("        Department being modified:    " +
                          department);
      System.out.println ();
      System.out.println ("              Total payroll before: $ " +
                          totPayBefore.setScale (2,
    totPayBefore.ROUND_HALF_UP));
      System.out.println ("             Average salary before: $ " +
                          avgSalBefore.setScale (2,
    avgSalBefore.ROUND_HALF_UP));
      System.out.println ();
      System.out.println ("   Number of salary modifications:    " +
                          numberOfUpdates);
      System.out.println ();
      System.out.println ("               Total payroll after: $ " +
                          totPayAfter.setScale (2,
    totPayAfter.ROUND_HALF_UP));
      System.out.println ("              Average salary after: $ " +
                          avgSalAfter.setScale (2,
    avgSalAfter.ROUND_HALF_UP));
      System.out.println ();
      System.out.println ("               Median Employee Name:    " +
                          medianEmployeeName);
    stmt.close ();
}

// (3) main application: .connect to the database
//                       .register the stored procedure
//                       .call the stored procedure
public static void main (String argv[])
{
  Connection con = null;
  try
    {
      String url = "jdbc:db2:sample";
      String callName = "SAMPLESTOREDPROC";
```

```
      // you may specify the schema name
      // String callName = "MYSCHEMA.SAMPLESTOREDPROC";
      String storedProcName = "DB2Stp!salaryModification";
      String mode = "not fenced";
      String table = "EMPLOYEE";
      String department = "C01";
      int percentModification = 5;

      if (argv.length == 0) {
         // connect with default id/password
         con = DriverManager.getConnection(url);
         }
      else if (argv.length == 2) {
         String userid = argv[0];
         String passwd = argv[1];
           // connect with user-provided username and password
           con = DriverManager.getConnection(url, userid, passwd);
           }
        else {
           System.out.println("\nUsage: java DB2SpCli [username
password]\n");
           System.exit(0);
         }

        // register the stored procedure
        registerStoredProc (con, callName, storedProcName, mode);

        // call the stored procedure
        callStoredProc (con, table, callName, percentModification,
department);

        con.close ();
      }
    catch (Exception e)
      {
         try { con.close(); } catch (Exception x) { }
         e.printStackTrace ();
      }
     }
}
```

The other half of the equation is the server-side portion of the stored procedure, which has to be available for calling from the client application. The logic to supply the procedure defined in the preceding code is as follows:

DB2STP.java *Server Side portion of the Sample Stored Procedure*

```
//  Source File Name: DB2Stp.java  %I%
//
//  Licensed Materials -- Property of IBM
//
```

```
//  (c) Copyright International Business Machines Corporation, 1996, 1997.
//     All Rights Reserved.
//
//  US Government Users Restricted Rights -
//  Use, duplication or disclosure restricted by
//  GSA ADP Schedule Contract with IBM Corp.

//  Sample Program - Java Stored Procedure (called by DB2SpCli)

//  Steps to set up server side:
//  (1) create and populate the SAMPLE database (db2sampl)
//  (2) compile this java file (javac DB2Stp.java)
//  (3) copy the resultant DB2Stp.class file into sqllib/function

//  NOTES: (1) The jdk11_path database manager configuration parameter
//             must be set
//         (2) The CLASSPATH and shared library path environment variables
//             must be set, as for any JDBC application.
//         (3) Visit http://www.software.ibm.com/data/db2/java
//             for current DB2 Java information

// Class DB2Stp contains one method:
// (1) salaryModification: stored procedure body

import java.sql.*;              // JDBC classes
import java.math.*;             // BigDecimal
import COM.ibm.db2.jdbc.app.*;  // DB2 UDB JDBC classes
import COM.ibm.db2.app.*;       // StoredProc and associated classes

///////
// Java stored procedure is in this class
///////
class DB2Stp extends StoredProc
{
  // (1) stored procedure body - modify employee salaries as requested
  //     return:
  //        . the total payroll before the increase
  //        . the average salary before the increase
  //        . the median employee salary after the increase
  //        . the total payroll after the increase
  //        . the average salary after the increase
  public void salaryModification (String table,
                                  int percentModification,
                                  String department,
                                  double totalPayrollBefore,
                                  double totalPayrollAfter,
                                  double averageSalaryBefore,
                                  double averageSalaryAfter,
                                  int numberOfUpdates,
                                  String medianEmployeeName) throws
Exception
  {
    int counter = 0;
```

```java
double salary = 0.00;
double payrollBefore = 0;

// get caller's connection to the database; inherited from StoredProc
Connection con = getConnection ();

// calculate the total payroll and average salary before the increase
Statement stmt = con.createStatement ();
String sql = "Select * from " + table;
ResultSet rs = stmt.executeQuery (sql);

while (rs.next ())
  {
    salary = rs.getDouble (12);
    payrollBefore += salary;
    counter++;
  }
rs.close();

int median = counter / 2;
double averageBefore = payrollBefore / counter;
double realPercent = percentModification;
realPercent = 1.00 + (realPercent / 100.00);

// update the salaries for the requested department
int employeeUpdates = 0;
sql = "Update " + table + " set salary = salary * " + realPercent +
  " where workdept = '" + department + "'";
employeeUpdates = stmt.executeUpdate (sql);

// Calculate the total payroll and average salary after the increase
// and retrieve the median salary as well...
sql = "Select * from " + table + " order by salary ";
counter = 0;
double payrollAfter = 0.00;

rs = stmt.executeQuery (sql);
while (rs.next ())
  {
    salary = rs.getDouble (12);
    payrollAfter += salary;
    counter++;
    if (counter == median)
      {
        medianEmployeeName =
          rs.getString (2) + " " +
          rs.getString (3) + " " +
          rs.getString (4);
      }
  }
rs.close ();

double averageAfter = payrollAfter / counter;
```

```
    // set values for the output parameters
    set (4, payrollBefore);
    set (5, payrollAfter);
    set (6, averageBefore);
    set (7, averageAfter);
    set (8, employeeUpdates);
    set (9, medianEmployeeName);

    // close off everything before we leave
    stmt.close ();
    con.close ();
  }
}
```

These two portions of code work together to get the job done. Using the same techniques you can create Java-stored procedures that execute across the network with whatever functionality you need. The main point is that it isn't just SQL or C anymore. Even in DB2, your Java skills can be put to work.

Hand-coding the Java stored procedures is not what I recommend. You may be interested to know that you can use VisualAge for Java 3.0 to

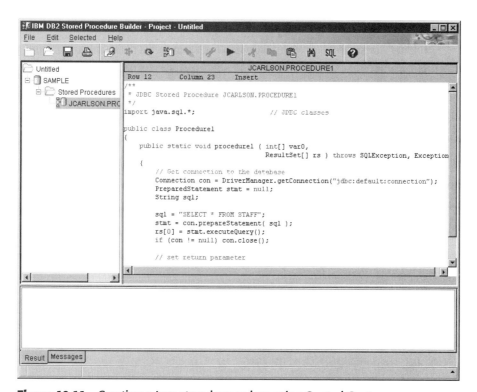

Figure 10.11   Creating a Java stored procedure using Control Center.

build stored procedures, or you can edit them through Control Center. (See Figure 10.11.)

Here you see where you create the Java stored procedure using Control Center. I *did* tell you this program meant you wouldn't have to get out of your chair!

Using VAJ 3.0 to Generate DB2 Stored Procedures

Since we're on the topic of creating stored procedures, this is probably the best place to walk through the new stored procedure builder available in VisualAge for Java 3.0. We are using the beta version here, so it may have improved a bit by the time you read this. Still, here is the base functionality you should expect for using VAJ to generate your stored procedures.

From looking at the Java code from the handcrafted Java stored procedures, you have to admit that it would be nice if there was a better way. From experience, we at WNS have seen that programmers who excel at C, PowerBuilder, or other languages do not always really understand or appreciate SQL.

Having to merge or embed SQL into the programs is an awkward process at best, and once again IBM has come up with a set of tools to assist in this process. Our first look at DB2 6.1 Stored Procedure Builder was very impressive, both to the new developers and the old SQL hands. This looks like a winner, folks.

That being said, you would no doubt prefer to make up your own minds, so let's walk through the process of using SPB for DB2 6.1 under Visual-Age for Java 3.0.

From the selected workspace tools menu option in VisualAge for Java 3.0 (beta), choose SQL Stored Procedure Builder. This will start up DB2 on the local machine (if not already running) and display the dialog box shown in Figure 10.12.

The stored procedure builder workbench is displayed in Figure 10.13. The workbench allows you to create stored procedure projects to load, edit, and save. Additionally, the workbench provides three work areas consisting of a tree view of your assets, the Java and SQL code on the right, and underneath the two a log of messages, errors, and exceptions.

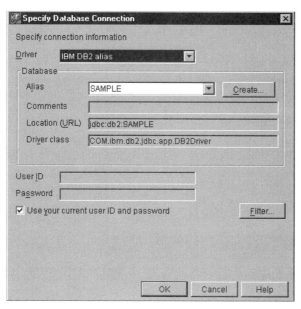

Figure 10.12   DB2 stored procedure builder wizard in VAJ 3.0.

We want to create a Java stored procedure. If you right-mouse-click on the database, the workbench brings up the options shown in Figure 10.14.

The wizard walks you through the stored procedure naming and creation process, as shown in the following dialogs.

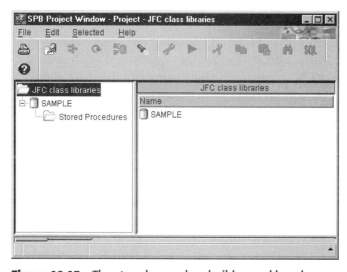

Figure 10.13   The stored procedure builder workbench.

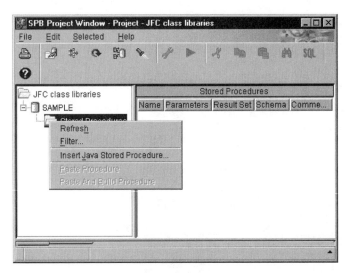

Figure 10.14 Stored procedure options.

We noticed that the default name included a period as a prefix, which we thought was kind of strange. Interestingly, the microhelp jumps out at you whenever you position the cursor on some aspect of the procedure builder. This is more informative than distracting, though I suspect that with more familiarity with the workbench you may be looking for ways to turn it off. In any case, one of the microhelp messages that we got when stepping through the proc builder for the first time was a note to the effect that all proc names had to start with an alphanumeric. Fine by me, but I wonder who came up with .Procedure1 as the default name? (See Figure 10.15.)

As shown in Figure 10.16, you step through the procedure assistant and it gathers more information. Evidently you can concatenate a bunch of existing stored procedures into a single new one by defining the pattern. Check the www.wns.com Web site under the technical area for more DB2-related findings and white papers.

In Figure 10.17 you see where you can define your own SQL if you have any idea what you are doing—or you can bring up the SQL Assistant. This is covered in the Data Access Builder section of Visual-Age for Java (Chapter 4). Just a quick note if you haven't been exposed to the SQL Assistant yet. This thing is pretty impressive. For those who are unfamiliar with SQL, it could be a lifesaver. In our shop we typically have a SQL guru craft out some utility views for the developers to work with or power users to include as the basis for their bean building.

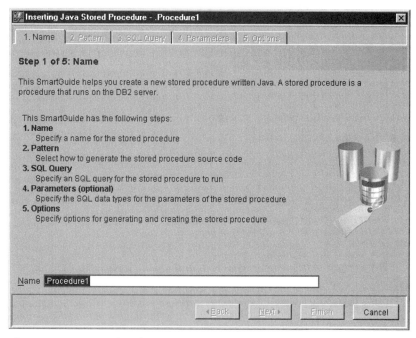

Figure 10.15   Naming the procedure to be built.

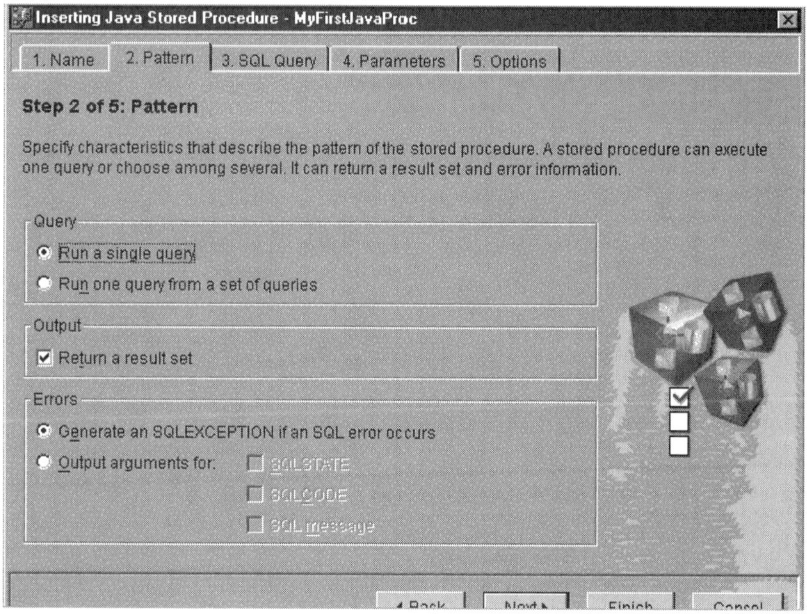

Figure 10.16   Step two of the procedure builder.

For those of you who are used to writing stored procedures and have some idea of where you would use input and output parameters, Figure 10.17 shows how the SmartGuide allows you to define those. Input parameters gather data like name, while output parameters are used for making up the result set.

Usually you do not want to query on a column that you do not want returned, so most frequently you would use input/output, but the flexibility to choose is build into the wizard. Figure 10.18 shows where you choose this option.

Having opted for parameter definition, Figure 10.19 shows the dialog box for further definition of each parameter desired whether input, output, or both.

After clicking Finish, as shown in Figure 10.20, the stored procedure is parsed and compiled. The end result is to return you to the workbench with the open stored procedure for your review. This is shown in Figure 10.21.

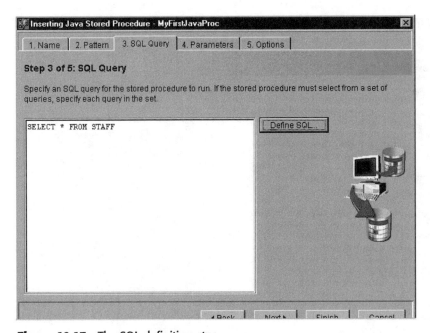

Figure 10.17 The SQL definition step.

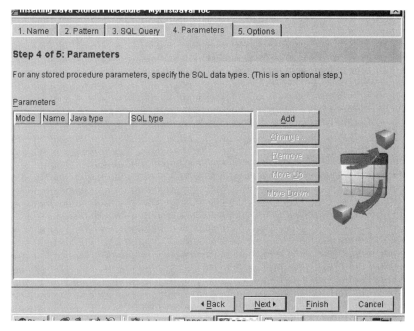

Figure 10.18 Defining procedure parameters in and out.

At this point you can edit or just view the Java stored procedure. The actual text of the very simple example we created with this wizard is shown in the following code. You should compare it for complexity with the client- and server-side procedure definitions to see how much more cogent the code generated is, compared to the older approach.

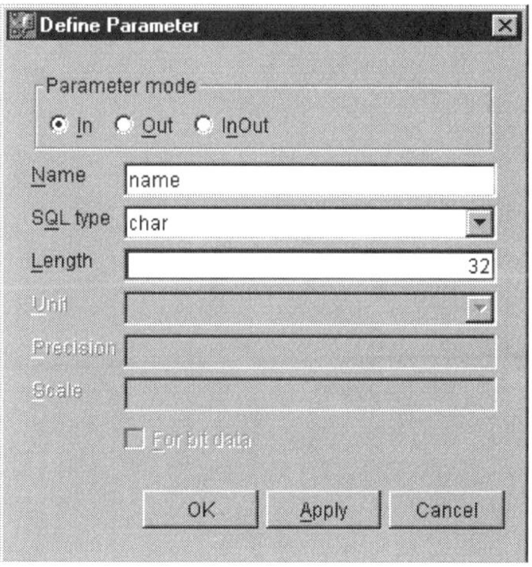

Figure 10.19 The parameter definition dialog.

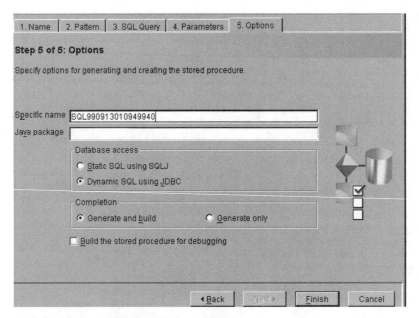

Figure 10.20 Finished procedure definitions.

Java Stored Procedure Code

```
/**
 * JDBC Stored Procedure MYSECONDPROC
 */
import java.sql.*;                      // JDBC classes

public class MysecondProc
{
    public static void mysecondProc ( String[] lname2,
                                      ResultSet[] rs ) throws
SQLException, Exception
    {
        // Get connection to the database
        Connection con =
DriverManager.getConnection("jdbc:default:connection");
        PreparedStatement stmt = null;
        String sql;

        sql = "SELECT name FROM STAFF";
        stmt = con.prepareStatement( sql );
        rs[0] = stmt.executeQuery();
        if (con != null) con.close();

        // set return parameter
        lname2[0] = lname2[0];
    }
}
```

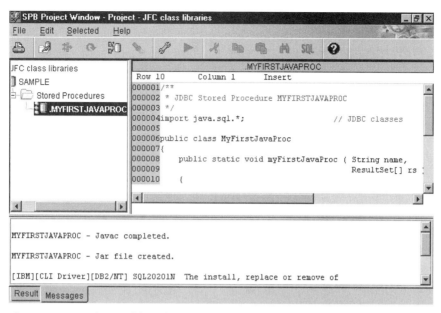

Figure 10.21 The workbench view of the completed procedure.

Now I ask you, is that clean or what?

Other HouseKeeping Tasks

I didn't want to turn this chapter into too much of a tutorial on Control Center, since many of you have already been exposed to the product on other releases. However, given the Java-based nature of the application, it is interesting to see that all of the functions that were found in previous versions of the product (based on more traditional languages) can still be found ready to go in a Java application.

Also, it might be useful as a comment on DB2 to make a quick note of some of the most common database administration tasks and how they are supported with this visual tool.

In Figure 10.22 you can see the size of the transaction log, as well as the freespace available. In the event that you needed to allocate more space to the device, this can also be accommodated using Control Center. The device management screen is shown in Figure 10.23.

Developers, especially, seem to run out of log space more frequently than any other group with whom I have worked. Personally, I suspect this is a consequence of the focus on test transactions, which often com-

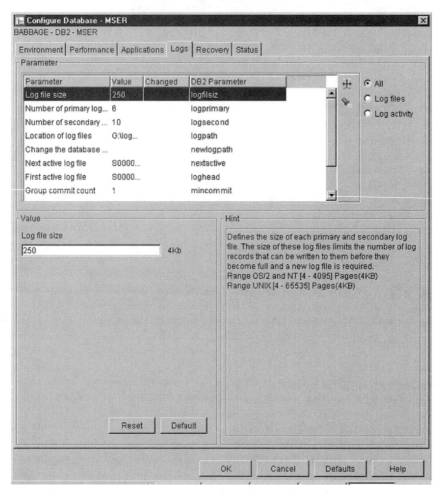

Figure 10.22 Checking the transaction log size for a UDB database.

plete successfully, allowing the developer to move to the next part of application development while forgetting that some housekeeping will eventually be in order.

Part of the development effort in a Big Blue Java shop is to pull together data resources from many sources. Unfortunately or otherwise, the days of one server–one client seem to be gone for good (or have moved to Redmond). That does, however, open up a world of opportunity for those of us who would like to be able to develop complex and sophisticated applications.

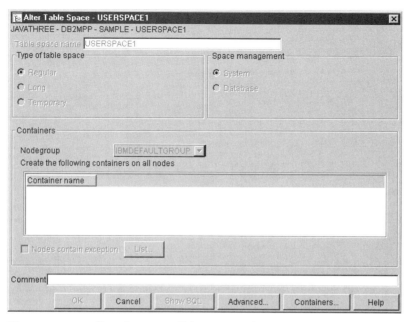

Figure 10.23 Allocating more disk space to the transaction.

Summary

There will, naturally, be entire books devoted to DB2 UDB 6.1 and how you can incorporate its features into a Java development environment. This chapter should have given you some insight into the commitment that IBM has made to UDB. As well, it is clear that the company is putting a great deal of work into making the product Java-enabled.

Object orientation holds a tremendous amount of promise (and complexity) for the applications that we will be developing over the next decade. However, the strides made in the past decade to move databases into a relational environment are not going to be rendered obsolete—or at least that is the view we are taking at WNS. Instead, once again we see that the real value of computers is their ability to link and integrate.

IBM is fully supporting Java in the database, and has as well opened up DB2 as a datastore available for all Big Blue Java development environments from NetObjects Fusion, to WebSphere Studio, SanFrancisco, and WebSphere application servers. In this way, we are given access to all the power of the older technology while being able to build on the promise of the new ones.

CHAPTER 11

Big Blue Hardware

Those of you who know anything about Thomas Watson Sr. know that this future IBM CEO started out selling sewing machines and ultimately became right-hand man to John Patterson, CEO and resident tyrant of National Cash Register. According to legend, he got fired. When the young (and no doubt brash) Watson subsequently ventured out in the marketplace, he was selling hardware. IBM has successfully navigated some of the most dramatic changes in the business world of the twentieth century. This would look good on anybody's resume, I should think.

IBM's record of moving from tabulating machines to computers, and from cash registers (though it still sells a very solid point-of-sale system, including cash registers) to laptop computers and mainframes, while becoming a $100 billion per year company, has added up to an impressive performance on the whole.

My point is not to sing IBM's praises but to note that the company has a long-standing tradition of making money selling hardware to business. It's as if Business was its middle name. Hey, wait a second, Business *is* its middle name! And that means that its last name is Machines. Which brings me back to hardware.

I would be the last person to say that IBM is just a hardware company. But to be candid, I really like its hardware. I have a WorkPad, and I had a ThinkPad until it was stolen. When the insurance company gets around to fulfilling its commitment, I will once again be an enthusiastic Thinkpad user. Our Java development group uses Intellistations at the office. I recommend Netfinity servers to my customers for NT and Linux, and we support some very large databases on RS-6000s. Not to mention the DL2 integration work we do with AS/400 customers. All in all, it's been great stuff to work with.

Inarguably, IBM is more than just a hardware company. It provides services and software in significant numbers. But when it saw that somebody (Sun) had placed Java out in the public domain (more or less) and that Java could revolutionize its hardware offerings, it jumped at the opportunity.

To me, that's impressive.

So IBM will sell you hardware for your NT operating system, and for your Novell LAN, or if you want to wear the Red Hat, Linux is available. Other people's software is no longer a bad thing. Just so long as your hardware is Blue.

This seems fair enough to me. As a Canadian, I have worked a lot with clone machines. For some reason (probably innate frugality) Canada has a much higher percentage per capita of no-name machines installed in businesses and homes than does the United States.

As a system professional whose company has had to support those machines, I have to tell you that I hate them.

It's not that they don't work. It's that they *almost* work. Or they *sometimes* work. They may work on consecutive days, even. But they don't have sufficient manufacturer's support, and they aren't well-engineered business machines. They may be fine for my kids, but I wouldn't bet my business on them.

With the percentage of cost allocated to support time over the initial cost outlay on the hardware itself, it makes sense to value support. Even if this does mean the price tag on the purchase order is higher.

Well, enough ranting and raving. Let's look at the range of hardware that IBM has available and what the company's Java strategy is for each particular piece of gear.

The IBM WorkPad

This is actually a 3 Com Palm Pilot in a cooler black-leather jacket (see Figure 11.1). I picked mine up at the Solutions '99 Conference to replace the Pilot professional, and I have to admit, this thing is great.

Apparently if you drop a WorkPad from a great height onto a hard surface, the case will shatter, but I have avoided performing that particular test. Most of the time, I just use it to plan my day. There are two particularly interesting new developments for the WorkPad that make it worthy of note.

DB2 Anywhere

Sales force automation is all the rage in some of the circles I frequent, so yes, I had heard about downloading database files and using synchronization to move changes from the WorkPad up to a corporate database. I was, however, a bit surprised at how easy it was.

If you work in an office and juggle to-do lists, calendars, and addresses, *and* you haven't yet looked at a WorkPad, put it on your wish list for someone who wants to make you happy.

Intellisync

The WorkPad's ability to integrate my to-do list, address list, and short memos with my personal productivity software (their name for it, not mine!) is one of the greatest features of working with this tool. You can link between the Palm Desktop or any of a number of third-party tools such as Lotus Organizer and Microsoft Outlook, as well as contact managers such as Act! and Maximizer.

Figure 11.1   The IBM WorkPad C3.

One-button synchronization, as well as the ability to refresh the desktop after a rebuild (or—as has happened once—to refresh the WorkPad after it lost its mind) are great features. See Figure 11.2.

One of the little gotchas to watch out for here is overwriting your Work-Pad mail with your inbox from your personal computer. Generally this fills up the memory on the PDA and it takes a while to delete everything you picked up.

Many of my favorite games are actually Java applications which have been translated into .prc format, which is the executable format for the Palm Pilot and WorkPad devices.

The upshot of this is simply that the WorkPad is the smallest member to date of the Big Blue Java hardware family. You can not only use Java to write applications for it; you can deploy data on it. Last, some folks have been busy converting the infrared scanner into a data acquisition device. At Solutions '99, the SanFrancisco folks were demonstrating how the WorkPad could be used as a way of collecting data to be fed up into SF objects.

The move to wireless messaging and internet based synchronization is also fueling the move to personal digital assistants. My first exposure to the WorkPad came from a seatmate on a flight from Nashville to Toronto. He spent forty-five minutes extolling the virtues of the technology. I have never met anyone who bought one and didn't like it. That pretty much says it all.

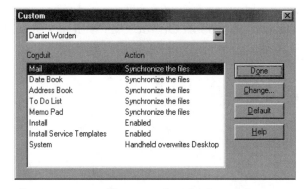

Figure 11.2   Intellisync synchronization options.

ThinkPad Notebooks

As a very frequent flier I moved over to the notebook as a desktop replacement system several years ago. The biggest issue at that time was monitor size and resolution. This necessitated a docking station, extra monitor, keyboard, and mouse. When the lease expired on my old notebook, I looked around and decided to go with the ThinkPad 390e (see Figure 11.3).

Perhaps the single coolest thing about this device was the optional DVD player, which of course I just had to have. This thing coverts the notebook into a very usable entertainment device, and when you output to a projector through the S-Video cable, it is simply amazing. It makes a wonderful combination of business power and entertainment capabilities. The relationship this has with Java may not be readily apparent at first (okay, at all), but it is worth noting.

As part of the research for this book, I loaded NetObjects Fusion, WebSphere Studio, and VisualAge for Java onto the notebook. It performed just fine. The only area where a notebook generally scrimps and is difficult to upgrade is on memory. If you are planning to do any kind of Java development on a notebook, make sure it has 128 megabytes of RAM.

IntelliStations

We bought the Pentium III 500 Mhz Intellistation Mpro series in May 1999 for our SanFrancisco development stations. We configured them with lots of SCSI disk and 512 megabytes of RAM. Guess what. They're not fast enough.

The bottom line is that if you are going to create Java applications using VisualAge for Java, WebSphere, and SanFrancisco, you are going to

Figure 11.3 My stolen ThinkPad—reward if found!

want to get as much hardware under the development environment as you can get.

Our biggest problem was in the amount of time it took to restart the development tools. Consistently, the CPU utilization would hit 100 percent and stay there.

Congratulating ourselves on having had the foresight to buy dual CPU-capable workstations, we cannibalized one to determine whether the extra CPU would help. As you can see in Figure 11.4, it certainly did when working with SanFrancisco. However, the restart time for VisualAge for Java was unaffected.

Essentially, we found that we never used more than 384 megs of RAM, even if we were using SanFrancisco server and VisualAge for Java together. Just using the SF client development environment running against a different server used a little less RAM. While 512 megabytes might seem like a lot, don't forget it wasn't long ago that we were talking about 512k for RAM! Figure 11.5 shows that starting up SanFrancisco places a heavy demand on the processor.

Another point to keep in mind is your network speed. We found a big benefit in upgrading to 10/100 from a standard 10 megabytes per second. Not only were file transfers obviously faster, but it took less than half the time to pull from the VisualAge for Java repository when a developer started up under the new network.

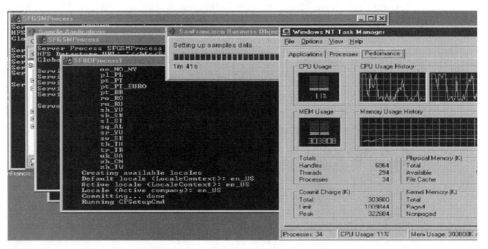

Figure 11.4 CPU utilization on SanFrancisco startup.

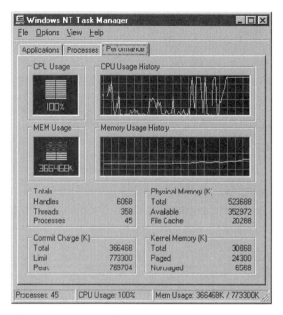

Figure 11.5 Developer's workstation CPU utilization.

The bottom-line requirement for developer stations is lots of RAM and go with dual processors. It might seem like a Cadillac, but the faster the machines, the less wait-time the developers have to invest. Our standard developers workstation is shown in Figure 11.6.

NetFinity Servers

We have been working with the 5500 servers since 1998, and they are pretty robust beasties. One of the things we found out about them is that they have a first-rate extended warranty package, which is among other things, on-site and transferable in the event the box is sold to a new owner.

For one of our customers, we opted for the 5500 M20 with full RAID 5 of six 9.1 GB SCSI drives with dual 500 Mhz processors (see Figure 11.7).

Figure 11.6 The Intellistation M-Pro.

Figure 11.7 NetFinity 5500 M20.

It took us a while to uncover why it seemed slower than even a single processor AMD clone when running SanFrancisco and WebSphere services.

The NetFinity has a configuration utility that lets a qualified, read-trained, NetFinity technician optimize the performance of the box. Just a word to the wise for anyone looking to run their Big Blue Java applications on a NetFinity—be prepared to do some tuning to get the right performance.

However, the trade-off in reliability means that the juice is worth the squeeze. We recommend the NetFinity servers, but we've learned that there is more to them than meets the eye when it comes to configuration and installation.

The 5500 is the kind of box that makes you feel like you're getting some hardware for your money.

It's interesting to note that you can now order your NetFinity with Linux preinstalled if you so choose, right from IBM.

AS/400

The AS/400 has one of the most loyal customers of any computing platform anywhere. I am told that the reliability and performance characteristics of this box really appeal to business systems people who have to support distributed operations.

As I mentioned in the discussion on IBM's Java strategy, a good deal of thought has gone into how the AS/400 community can leverage the new direction, especially as a deployment environment for Big Blue Java applications.

Apparently, there is a move afoot to build the Java Virtual Machine right onto the motherboard of the AS/400 to ensure that it is the fastest box you could choose to run Java applications. At WNS our own approach has been to integrate the DB2-400 data stores with SanFrancisco running on other platforms. This allows us to play with the object servers without possibly running afoul of production systems on the AS/400.

If I'm not mistaken, the AS/400 was the first of the black servers from IBM. It certainly has had an impact on the other kids! An example of a big AS/400 is shown in Figure 11.8.

RS6000 and AIX

Most IT people know that the RS6000 Unix server (see Figure 11.9) was the platform for Deep Blue, the computer that defeated Gary Kasparov and went on to make chess and computing history. A less known fact is that the system was running a vanilla-flavored DB2 database that had not been optimized from a physical data modeling standpoint. Not only did the RS6000 win, but it did so without having to be souped up!

There are configurations of RS6000 and AIX for virtually any size of operation. In fact, you could say that IBM can live up to its scalability claims with just the one product line. From a small back-office Web server to an SP cluster powerful enough to support the Nogano Olympic site, there is an RS6000 to fit.

Personally, I find the 64-bit version of AIX to be one of the most interesting aspects of this platform. Version 4.3 of AIX takes full advantage of the 64-bit capabilities of the PowerPC chipset on which it is based. Keep in mind that this has been out for a couple of years now, so the growing pains are past—quite unlike the other 64-bit versions which are just coming out now.

When combined with high-speed disk subsystems like SSA, the RS6000 makes a highly effective Web application server. That it supports WebSphere, SanFrancisco, and HTTP server doesn't hurt either.

Figure 11.8 Form factor of the AS/400e–730.

Figure 11.9   The RS6000—reigning king of chess.

Numa-Q

IBM acquired Sequent in 1999, and with it a fascinating hardware product for instantly creating highly scalable Web servers. NUMA stands for Non-Uniform Memory Access, which to my way of thinking is almost as arcane as PCMCIA for an acronym/name. In any case, the purpose of NUMA is to extend the bus speed available to multiple processors within a single system. Without faster bus speeds to support the processors, the ability to move data between processors and controllers becomes a bottleneck. This limits the scalability of the platform to the constraints of the lowest common denominator.

Sequent was highly regarded for its work in high-speed backplanes. This expertise has been brought to the fore with NUMA. The Numa-Q incorporates Intel Pentium III Xeon processors and is designed to allow scalability past the limits of traditional PC bus architectures for both Unix and Windows NT implementations.

The Numa-Q is shown in Figure 11.10.

Figure 11.10   Become an instant ASP with Numa-Q.

Numa-Q will appeal to those organizations whose Web sites and application servers need more than the four processors maximum available to the NetFinity.

S390

The S390 (the mainframe, Big Iron, Glass House Machine, or whatever you want to call it) is the heavyweight of computing power. And its proponents will tell you that tales of its demise at the hands of client/server systems have been greatly exaggerated.

As a Java developer, the S390 has one overwhelmingly appealing characteristic. It is the biggest JVM in the world (see Figure 11.11). You just can't put more hardware under your Java applet. So, if you still have performance problems after that, you had better take another look at the programs architecture!

The S390 has been certified to run Java, and at the time of this writing the Big Blue Box supported JDK 1.1, WebSphere Advanced, and Enterprise, as well as SanFrancisco and HTTP server. In short, IBM has already made good on its strategy to bring a unified playing field for applications to run on its gear.

Figure 11.11 The biggest JVM—the S390 mainframe.

Summary

IBM has been a hardware supplier since times of old. And it doesn't seem to be in any hurry to give that up. Across the board, IBM either makes or resells any piece of gear that an e-business customer would want. It has also made sure that this gear conforms to its Java strategy.

The way to application development in the future is clear. Existing applications must be supported and integrated with new ones. Those new ones will run on the same platforms that we already have installed, as well as being supported by the trained and experienced technologists who already look after their care and feeding.

A new software architecture no longer means an automatic replacement of the old systems. By leveraging Java across all of its hardware, IBM has found that the politics of inclusion are the best way to preserve existing customer investments while gaining the lion's share of the market for new systems.

CHAPTER 12

Building a Java Applet

I n this chapter we look at Java applet development considerations using the Model-View-Controller paradigm.

Of course, anyone can develop a single system or two-tier client/server application using Java. It may even turn out that this will be technically challenging. However, the real key to working with Big Blue Java is to focus on understanding and working with the overhead implicit in some of the more complicated (and powerful) offerings such as SanFrancisco and WebSphere.

To ease into this technology, let's look at the way we would use applet technology to create our comic book application, using the model-view-controller paradigm that IBM has chosen to build its development tools.

By the way, there are many arguments regarding the soundness of the model-view-controller development approach. To those of you who want to have such an argument, I say go ahead. Just leave me out of it. We are not in the business of creating frameworks or inventing development paradigms. We're in the business of writing software using tools that solve real business problems. I hope this theme has come across in the book so far and that this is not the first you've heard of it.

The ComicBook Applet

By now we all know what we are trying to accomplish with the comic book application. Here we are going to use VisualAge for Java to create it, using the model-view-controller approach. You might think that first we use the VCE to create a view of the application, then define the logic—but actually we want to define the logic through the definition of a bean. This includes:

- Add
- Delete
- Get
- Save

These functions work on a list of comic books. As we go through this chapter you should be able to see how Java and object orientation combine to make working on a list quite a different experience from what you may have been exposed to in the past. This is especially true if you are intimate with the differences between VSAM and ISAM, or if you've been steeped in relational rhetoric, as I have for the past 15 years.

This functionality is handled primarily by the controller. The controller defines the activities that can be taken on the entity comic book. Of course, we also need something to contain the specifics of a comic book, and this is a bean or an object, and they are treated as the model in terms of M-V-C development. Last, we will abstract the requirements for a visual front end to display what we know about comic books as well as showing actions to be taken by the controller as directed by the user.

The comic book class is defined in the Java code shown here:

```
package ComicBookCollectionApplet;

/**
 * This type was created in VisualAge.
 */
public class ComicBook extends java.lang.Object {
    private String fieldTitle = new String();
    private String fieldCondition = new String();
/**
 * This method was created in VisualAge.
 * @param title java.lang.String
 * @param condition java.lang.String
 * @param publicationDate java.lang.String
```

```
 */
public ComicBook(String title, String condition) {
    setTitle(title);
    setCondition(condition);
}
/**
 * Gets the condition property (java.lang.String) value.
 * @return The condition property value.
 * @see #setCondition
 */
public String getCondition() {
    return fieldCondition;
}
/**
 * Gets the title property (java.lang.String) value.
 * @return The title property value.
 * @see #setTitle
 */
public String getTitle() {
    return fieldTitle;
}
/**
 * Sets the condition property (java.lang.String) value.
 * @param condition The new value for the property.
 * @see #getCondition
 */
public void setCondition(String condition) {
    fieldCondition = condition;
}
/**
 * Sets the title property (java.lang.String) value.
 * @param title The new value for the property.
 * @see #getTitle
 */
public void setTitle(String title) {
    fieldTitle = title;
}
/**
 * This method was created in VisualAge.
 * @return java.lang.String
 */
public String toString() {
    return this.getTitle();
}
}
```

This bean contains accessor/mutator methods. This may sound like the Toxic Avenger was here, but it is only referring to the get/set methods we want to associate with our comic books. The beans must have these methods defined, whereas a class or an object may not have these methods. To allow someone to access an object's data without defining these accessor/mutator methods, you could simply define your variables as public.

There is a big maintenance benefit to this. If we decide to change a datatype from int to long, it is only necessary to change the accessor/mutator methods, rather than any parts of the client code that might use them, which must be done if the object is treated as a bean.

Within the class we have *set title*, *get title*, *set condition*, *get condition*. This is probably the most basic Java class imaginable, which explains why we're using it.

A class is, of course, a template for an object. An object must be instantiated, meaning there has to be a specific comic book object; otherwise, we have a class.

In the context of developing an application, we can now define what we wish to be able to do with this class (or, when the time comes, with these objects).

As we covered in the chapter on using VisualAge for Java (Chapter 4), the basic work panel for creating any sort of Java application is displayed in Figure 12.1. From here, we start to define the screen objects using Swing.

Of course, the first thing we have to do is include our resources, which in this case covers the nonvisible beans that we wrote using the code shown earlier in the chapter. The form for this is shown in Figure 12.2. Technically we wrote that code while using VisualAge for Java, not NotePad or SlickEdit, but this is where we use VAJ to pull the application together. I didn't want to confuse the issue by showing text editing inside VAJ—for that see the VisualAge for Java chapter.

Anyway, you can see in Figure 12.3 that at this point we are ready to drop our Swing widgets onto the screen and connect the nonvisible beans to them.

Using the Swing elements, JPanel, label, and text as well as the add/delete buttons, we create the user interface screen, which to be functional must be connected to the nonvisible control beans that we declared earlier.

The net result of all this effort is to create an application, which in our case is shown in Figure 12.4.

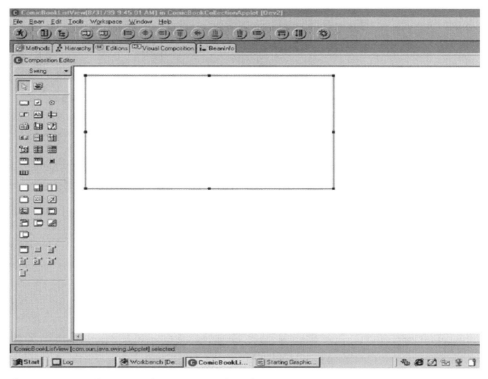

Figure 12.1 Using VAJ to lay out a user interface.

Isn't it interesting that that process would require the following code! In fact, this code was generated by VisualAge for Java after we developed the ComicBook applet.

```java
package ComicBookCollectionApplet;

import com.sun.java.swing.*;
import java.util.*;
import ComicBookCollectionApplet.ComicBook;
import java.io.*;


/**
 * This type was created in VisualAge.
 */
public class ComicBookListController extends java.lang.Object{

    private DefaultListModel fieldComicBookList = newDefaultListModel();
    private String SerializedComicBookFileName = "d:\\ComicBooks.ser";
/**
 * ComicBookListController constructor comment.
```

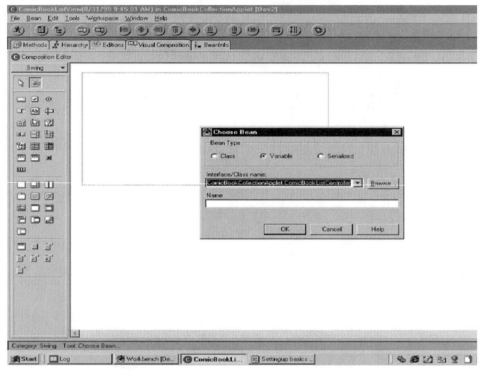

Figure 12.2 The user form.

```
 */
public ComicBookListController() {
     super();
}
/**
 * Perform the addEntry method.
 * @param title java.lang.String
 * @param condition java.lang.String
 */
public void addEntry(String title, String condition) {
     getComicBookList().addElement(new ComicBook(title, condition));
     return;
}
/**
 * Perform the deleteEntry method.
 * @param title java.lang.String
 * @param condition java.lang.String
 */
public void deleteEntry(String title, String condition) {
     Enumeration e = getComicBookList().elements();
     ComicBook c = null;
     while (e.hasMoreElements()){
```

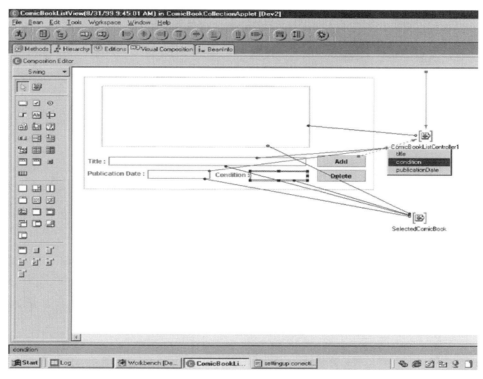

Figure 12.3 Connecting the components using VisualAge for Java.

```
        c=(ComicBook)e.nextElement();
        if (c.getTitle().equals(title) &&
c.getCondition().equals(condition)){
            getComicBookList().removeElement(c);
            return;
        }
    }
    return;
}
/**
 * Gets the comicBookList property (com.sun.java.swing.DefaultListModel)
 * value.
 * @return The comicBookList property value.
 * @see #setComicBookList
 */
public DefaultListModel getComicBookList() {
    return fieldComicBookList;
}
/**
 * Perform the init method.
 */
public void init() {
```

Figure 12.4 The applet running in test mode.

```
try {
    FileInputStream fIn = new
    FileInputStream(SerializedComicBookFileName);
    ObjectInputStream in = new ObjectInputStream(fIn);
    setComicBookList((DefaultListModel)in.readObject());
}
catch(FileNotFoundException e){
    setComicBookList(new DefaultListModel());
}
catch(Exception e){
System.out.println("Error loading file: " + e);


}
    return;
}
/**
 * Perform the saveList method.
 */
public synchronized void saveList() {
    try{
        FileOutputStream fOut = new FileOutputStream(
        SerializedComicBookFileName);
        ObjectOutputStream out = new ObjectOutputStream( fOut);
        out.writeObject( getComicBookList());
    }
    catch( IOException e){
        System.out.println("Error saving list: " + e);
    }
```

```
        return;
    }
/**
 * Sets the comicBookList property (com.sun.java.swing.DefaultListModel)
 * value.
 * @param comicBookList The new value for the property.
 * @see #getComicBookList
 */
public void setComicBookList(DefaultListModel comicBookList) {
    fieldComicBookList = comicBookList;
}
}
```

This controller essentially holds an array of objects in accordance with the abstract table model. The controller creates a model and adds objects to it as driven by the application.

In this case, we have implemented the functions add/delete/get, and saved the list that is pulled into the model.

Interestingly, the Save feature requires that we make the changed data persistent. It is important to note that the controller actually instructs the changed object ComicBook on how to change itself. The accessor/mutator methods inside the ComicBook object are the only ones that the controller can activate.

The view provides the user with a way to both interact with the controller and see the data held in the ComicBook object. But don't forget that the ComicBook object is not a database table; it is more like a database row—a row with associated methods for getting column contents. The controller works as the table and has associated methods for inserting, updating, and deleting entire rows. It must request that the ComicBook object perform Select, Update, or Insert operations on a particular column.

The code generated for these activities resulting in the creation of the view is shown here:

```
package ComicBookCollectionApplet;

/**
 * This type was created in VisualAge.
 */
public class ComicBookListView extends com.sun.java.swing.JApplet
implements com.sun.java.swing.event.ListSelectionListener,
java.awt.event.ActionListener, java.beans.PropertyChangeListener {
    private com.sun.java.swing.JList ivjComicBookList = null;
    private ComicBookListController ivjComicBookListController1 = null;
```

```java
    private com.sun.java.swing.JPanel ivjJAppletContentPane = null;
    private java.awt.BorderLayout ivjJAppletContentPaneBorderLayout =
null;
    private com.sun.java.swing.JButton ivjJButton1 = null;
    private com.sun.java.swing.JButton ivjJButton2 = null;
    private com.sun.java.swing.JLabel ivjJLabel1 = null;
    private com.sun.java.swing.JLabel ivjJLabel2 = null;
    private com.sun.java.swing.JPanel ivjJPanel1 = null;
    private com.sun.java.swing.JTextField ivjJTextField = null;
    private com.sun.java.swing.JTextField ivjJTextField1 = null;
    private boolean ivjConnPtoP2Aligning = false;
    private ComicBook ivjSelectedComicBook = null;
/**
 * ComicBookListView constructor comment.
 */
public ComicBookListView() {
    super();
}
/**
 * Method to handle events for the ActionListener interface.
 * @param e java.awt.event.ActionEvent
 */
/* WARNING: THIS METHOD WILL BE REGENERATED. */
public void actionPerformed(java.awt.event.ActionEvent e) {
    // user code begin {1}
    // user code end
    if ((e.getSource() == getJButton1()) ) {
        connEtoM2(e);
    }
    if ((e.getSource() == getJButton2()) ) {
        connEtoM3(e);
    }
    // user code begin {2}
    // user code end
}
/**
 * connEtoM1: (ComicBookListView.init() -->
 * ComicBookListController1.init())V)
 */
/* WARNING: THIS METHOD WILL BE REGENERATED. */
private void connEtoM1() {
    try {
        // user code begin {1}
        // user code end
        getComicBookListController1().init();
        // user code begin {2}
        // user code end
    } catch (java.lang.Throwable ivjExc) {
        // user code begin {3}
        // user code end
        handleException(ivjExc);
```

```
        }
}
/**
 * connEtoM2:
(JButton1.action.actionPerformed(java.awt.event.ActionEvent) -->
ComicBookListController1.addEntry(Ljava.lang.String;Ljava.lang.String;)V)
 * @param arg1 java.awt.event.ActionEvent
 */
/* WARNING: THIS METHOD WILL BE REGENERATED. */
private void connEtoM2(java.awt.event.ActionEvent arg1) {
    try {
        // user code begin {1}
        // user code end
    getComicBookListController1().addEntry(getJTextField1().getText(),
getJTextField().getText());
        // user code begin {2}
        // user code end
    } catch (java.lang.Throwable ivjExc) {
        // user code begin {3}
        // user code end
        handleException(ivjExc);
    }
}
/**
 * connEtoM3:
(JButton2.action.actionPerformed(java.awt.event.ActionEvent) -->
ComicBookListController1.deleteEntry(Ljava.lang.String;Ljava.lang.String;)
V)
 * @param arg1 java.awt.event.ActionEvent
 */
/* WARNING: THIS METHOD WILL BE REGENERATED. */
private void connEtoM3(java.awt.event.ActionEvent arg1) {
    try {
        // user code begin {1}
        // user code end


    getComicBookListController1().deleteEntry(getJTextField1().getText()
, getJTextField().getText());
        // user code begin {2}
        // user code end
    } catch (java.lang.Throwable ivjExc) {
        // user code begin {3}
        // user code end
        handleException(ivjExc);
    }
}
/**
 * connPtoP1SetSource: (ComicBookListController1.comicBookList <-->
ComicBookList.model)
 */
```

```java
/* WARNING: THIS METHOD WILL BE REGENERATED. */
private void connPtoP1SetSource() {
    /* Set the source from the target */
    try {

    getComicBookListController1().setComicBookList((com.sun.java.swing
.DefaultListModel)getComicBookList().getModel());
        // user code begin {1}
        // user code end
    } catch (java.lang.Throwable ivjExc) {
        // user code begin {3}
        // user code end
        handleException(ivjExc);
    }
}
/**
 * connPtoP1SetTarget: (ComicBookList.model <-->
 * ComicBookListController1.comicBookList)
 */
/* WARNING: THIS METHOD WILL BE REGENERATED. */
private void connPtoP1SetTarget() {
    /* Set the target from the source */
    try {

    getComicBookList().setModel(getComicBookListController1()
.getComicBookList());
        // user code begin {1}
        // user code end
    } catch (java.lang.Throwable ivjExc) {
        // user code begin {3}
        // user code end
        handleException(ivjExc);
    }
}
/**
 * connPtoP2SetTarget:  (ComicBookList.selectedValue <--> ComicBook1.this)
 */
/* WARNING: THIS METHOD WILL BE REGENERATED. */
private void connPtoP2SetTarget() {
    /* Set the target from the source */
    try {
        if (ivjConnPtoP2Aligning == false) {
            // user code begin {1}
            // user code end
            ivjConnPtoP2Aligning = true;

    setSelectedComicBook((ComicBookCollectionApplet.ComicBook)
getComicBookList().getSelectedValue());
            // user code begin {2}
            // user code end
            ivjConnPtoP2Aligning = false;
```

```
        }
    } catch (java.lang.Throwable ivjExc) {
        ivjConnPtoP2Aligning = false;
        // user code begin {3}
        // user code end
        handleException(ivjExc);
    }
}
/**
 * connPtoP3SetTarget:  (ComicBook1.title <--> JTextField1.text)
 */
/* WARNING: THIS METHOD WILL BE REGENERATED. */
private void connPtoP3SetTarget() {
    /* Set the target from the source */
    try {
        getJTextField1().setText(getSelectedComicBook().getTitle());
        // user code begin {1}
        // user code end
    } catch (java.lang.Throwable ivjExc) {
        // user code begin {3}
        // user code end
        handleException(ivjExc);
    }
}
/**
 * connPtoP4SetTarget:  (ComicBook1.condition <--> JTextField.text)
 */
/* WARNING: THIS METHOD WILL BE REGENERATED. */
private void connPtoP4SetTarget() {
    /* Set the target from the source */
    try {
        getJTextField().setText(getSelectedComicBook().getCondition());
        // user code begin {1}
        // user code end
    } catch (java.lang.Throwable ivjExc) {
        // user code begin {3}
        // user code end
        handleException(ivjExc);
    }
}
/**
 * This method was created in VisualAge.
 */
public void destroy() {
    ivjComicBookListController1.saveList();

}
/**
 * Gets the applet information.
 * @return java.lang.String
 */
```

```java
public String getAppletInfo() {
    return "ComicBookCollectionApplet.ComicBookListView created using
VisualAge for Java.";
}
/**
 * Return the ComicBookList property value.
 * @return com.sun.java.swing.JList
 */
/* WARNING: THIS METHOD WILL BE REGENERATED. */
private com.sun.java.swing.JList getComicBookList() {
    if (ivjComicBookList == null) {
        try {
            ivjComicBookList = new com.sun.java.swing.JList();
            ivjComicBookList.setName("ComicBookList");
        ivjComicBookList.setSelectionMode(com.sun.java.swing
.ListSelectionModel.SINGLE_SELECTION);
            // user code begin {1}
            // user code end
        } catch (java.lang.Throwable ivjExc) {
            // user code begin {2}
            // user code end
            handleException(ivjExc);
        }
    };
    return ivjComicBookList;
}
/**
 * Return the ComicBookListController1 property value.
 * @return ComicBookCollectionApplet.ComicBookListController
 */
/* WARNING: THIS METHOD WILL BE REGENERATED. */
private ComicBookListController get ComicBookListController1() {
    if (ivjComicBookListController1 == null) {
        try {
            ivjComicBookListController1 = new
ComicBookCollectionApplet.ComicBookListController();
            // user code begin {1}
            // user code end
        } catch (java.lang.Throwable ivjExc) {
            // user code begin {2}
            // user code end
            handleException(ivjExc);
        }
    };
    return ivjComicBookListController1;
}
/**
 * Return the JAppletContentPane property value.
 * @return com.sun.java.swing.JPanel
 */
/* WARNING: THIS METHOD WILL BE REGENERATED. */
```

```
private com.sun.java.swing.JPanel getJAppletContentPane() {
     if (ivjJAppletContentPane == null) {
          try {
               ivjJAppletContentPane = new com.sun.java.swing.JPanel();
               ivjJAppletContentPane.setName("JAppletContentPane");
     ivjJAppletContentPane.setLayout(getJAppletContentPaneBorderLayout());

ivjJAppletContentPane.setBackground(java.awt.Color.white);
               getJAppletContentPane().add(getJPanel1(), "South");
               getJAppletContentPane().add(getComicBookList(),
"Center");
               // user code begin {1}
               // user code end
          } catch (java.lang.Throwable ivjExc) {
               // user code begin {2}
               // user code end
               handleException(ivjExc);
          }
     };
     return ivjJAppletContentPane;
}
/**
 * Return the JAppletContentPaneBorderLayout property value.
 * @return java.awt.BorderLayout
 */
/* WARNING: THIS METHOD WILL BE REGENERATED. */
private java.awt.BorderLayout getJAppletContentPaneBorderLayout() {
     java.awt.BorderLayout ivjJAppletContentPaneBorderLayout = null;
     try {
          /* Create part */
          ivjJAppletContentPaneBorderLayout = new
java.awt.BorderLayout();
          ivjJAppletContentPaneBorderLayout.setVgap(15);
          ivjJAppletContentPaneBorderLayout.setHgap(15);
     } catch (java.lang.Throwable ivjExc) {
          handleException(ivjExc);
     };
     return ivjJAppletContentPaneBorderLayout;
}
/**
 * Return the JButton1 property value.
 * @return com.sun.java.swing.JButton
 */
/* WARNING: THIS METHOD WILL BE REGENERATED. */
private com.sun.java.swing.JButton getJButton1() {
     if (ivjJButton1 == null) {
          try {
               ivjJButton1 = new com.sun.java.swing.JButton();
               ivjJButton1.setName("JButton1");
               ivjJButton1.setText("Add");
               // user code begin {1}
```

```
                        // user code end
                } catch (java.lang.Throwable ivjExc) {
                        // user code begin {2}
                        // user code end
                        handleException(ivjExc);
                }
        };
        return ivjJButton1;
}
/**
 * Return the JButton2 property value.
 * @return com.sun.java.swing.JButton
 */
/* WARNING: THIS METHOD WILL BE REGENERATED. */
private com.sun.java.swing.JButton getJButton2() {
        if (ivjJButton2 == null) {
                try {
                        ivjJButton2 = new com.sun.java.swing.JButton();
                        ivjJButton2.setName("JButton2");
                        ivjJButton2.setText("Delete");
                        // user code begin {1}
                        // user code end
                } catch (java.lang.Throwable ivjExc) {
                        // user code begin {2}
                        // user code end
                        handleException(ivjExc);
                }
        };
        return ivjJButton2;
}
/**
 * Return the JLabel1 property value.
 * @return com.sun.java.swing.JLabel
 */
/* WARNING: THIS METHOD WILL BE REGENERATED. */
private com.sun.java.swing.JLabel getJLabel1() {
        if (ivjJLabel1 == null) {
                try {
                        ivjJLabel1 = new com.sun.java.swing.JLabel();
                        ivjJLabel1.setName("JLabel1");
                        ivjJLabel1.setText("Title");
                        // user code begin {1}
                        // user code end
                } catch (java.lang.Throwable ivjExc) {
                        // user code begin {2}
                        // user code end
                        handleException(ivjExc);
                }
        };
        return ivjJLabel1;
```

```
}
/**
 * Return the JLabel2 property value.
 * @return com.sun.java.swing.JLabel
 */
/* WARNING: THIS METHOD WILL BE REGENERATED. */
private com.sun.java.swing.JLabel getJLabel2() {
    if (ivjJLabel2 == null) {
        try {
            ivjJLabel2 = new com.sun.java.swing.JLabel();
            ivjJLabel2.setName("JLabel2");
            ivjJLabel2.setText("Condition");
            // user code begin {1}
            // user code end
        } catch (java.lang.Throwable ivjExc) {
            // user code begin {2}
            // user code end
            handleException(ivjExc);
        }
    };
    return ivjJLabel2;
}
/**
 * Return the JPanel1 property value.
 * @return com.sun.java.swing.JPanel
 */
/* WARNING: THIS METHOD WILL BE REGENERATED. */
private com.sun.java.swing.JPanel getJPanel1() {
    java.awt.GridBagConstraints constraintsJLabel1 = new
java.awt.GridBagConstraints();
    java.awt.GridBagConstraints constraintsJLabel2 = new
java.awt.GridBagConstraints();
    java.awt.GridBagConstraints constraintsJTextField1 = new
java.awt.GridBagConstraints();
    java.awt.GridBagConstraints constraintsJTextField = new
java.awt.GridBagConstraints();
    java.awt.GridBagConstraints constraintsJButton1 = new
java.awt.GridBagConstraints();
    java.awt.GridBagConstraints constraintsJButton2 = new
java.awt.GridBagConstraints();
    if (ivjJPanel1 == null) {
        try {
            ivjJPanel1 = new com.sun.java.swing.JPanel();
            ivjJPanel1.setName("JPanel1");
            ivjJPanel1.setLayout(new java.awt.GridBagLayout());
            ivjJPanel1.setBackground(java.awt.Color.white);

            constraintsJLabel1.gridx = 0; constraintsJLabel1.gridy =
0;
            constraintsJLabel1.gridwidth = 1;
```

```
constraintsJLabel1.gridheight = 1;
            constraintsJLabel1.anchor =
java.awt.GridBagConstraints.CENTER;
            constraintsJLabel1.weightx = 0.0;
            constraintsJLabel1.weighty = 0.0;
            getJPanel1().add(getJLabel1(), constraintsJLabel1);

            constraintsJLabel2.gridx = 0; constraintsJLabel2.gridy =
1;
            constraintsJLabel2.gridwidth = 1;
constraintsJLabel2.gridheight = 1;
            constraintsJLabel2.anchor =
java.awt.GridBagConstraints.CENTER;
            constraintsJLabel2.weightx = 0.0;
            constraintsJLabel2.weighty = 0.0;
            getJPanel1().add(getJLabel2(), constraintsJLabel2);

            constraintsJTextField1.gridx = 1;
constraintsJTextField1.gridy = 0;
            constraintsJTextField1.gridwidth = 2;
constraintsJTextField1.gridheight = 1;
            constraintsJTextField1.fill =
java.awt.GridBagConstraints.HORIZONTAL;
            constraintsJTextField1.anchor =
java.awt.GridBagConstraints.CENTER;
            constraintsJTextField1.weightx = 1.0;
            constraintsJTextField1.weighty = 0.0;
            getJPanel1().add(getJTextField1(),
constraintsJTextField1);

            constraintsJTextField.gridx = 2;
constraintsJTextField.gridy = 1;
            constraintsJTextField.gridwidth = 2;
constraintsJTextField.gridheight = 1;
            constraintsJTextField.fill =
java.awt.GridBagConstraints.HORIZONTAL;
            constraintsJTextField.anchor =
java.awt.GridBagConstraints.CENTER;
            constraintsJTextField.weightx = 1.0;
            constraintsJTextField.weighty = 0.0;
            getJPanel1().add(getJTextField(), constraintsJTextField);

            constraintsJButton1.gridx = 4; constraintsJButton1.gridy
= 0;
            constraintsJButton1.gridwidth = 1;
constraintsJButton1.gridheight = 1;
            constraintsJButton1.fill =
java.awt.GridBagConstraints.HORIZONTAL;
            constraintsJButton1.anchor =
java.awt.GridBagConstraints.CENTER;
            constraintsJButton1.weightx = 0.0;
            constraintsJButton1.weighty = 0.0;
            getJPanel1().add(getJButton1(), constraintsJButton1);
```

```
                constraintsJButton2.gridx = 4; constraintsJButton2.gridy
= 1;
                constraintsJButton2.gridwidth = 1;
constraintsJButton2.gridheight = 1;
                constraintsJButton2.fill =
java.awt.GridBagConstraints.HORIZONTAL;
                constraintsJButton2.anchor =
java.awt.GridBagConstraints.CENTER;
                constraintsJButton2.weightx = 0.0;
                constraintsJButton2.weighty = 0.0;
                getJPanel1().add(getJButton2(), constraintsJButton2);
                // user code begin {1}
                // user code end
            } catch (java.lang.Throwable ivjExc) {
                // user code begin {2}
                // user code end
                handleException(ivjExc);
            }
        };
        return ivjJPanel1;
}
/**
 * Return the JTextField property value.
 * @return com.sun.java.swing.JTextField
 */
/* WARNING: THIS METHOD WILL BE REGENERATED. */
private com.sun.java.swing.JTextField getJTextField() {
        if (ivjJTextField == null) {
            try {
                ivjJTextField = new com.sun.java.swing.JTextField();
                ivjJTextField.setName("JTextField");
                // user code begin {1}
                // user code end
            } catch (java.lang.Throwable ivjExc) {
                // user code begin {2}
                // user code end
                handleException(ivjExc);
            }
        };
        return ivjJTextField;
}
/**
 * Return the JTextField1 property value.
 * @return com.sun.java.swing.JTextField
 */
/* WARNING: THIS METHOD WILL BE REGENERATED. */
private com.sun.java.swing.JTextField getJTextField() {
        if (ivjJTextField1 == null) {
            try {
                ivjJTextField1 = new com.sun.java.swing.JTextField();
                ivjJTextField1.setName("JTextField1");
```

```
                    // user code begin {1}
                    // user code end
            } catch (java.lang.Throwable ivjExc) {
                    // user code begin {2}
                    // user code end
                    handleException(ivjExc);
            }
        };
        return ivjJTextField1;
}
/**
 * Return the ComicBook1 property value.
 * @return ComicBookCollectionApplet.ComicBook
 */
/* WARNING: THIS METHOD WILL BE REGENERATED. */
private ComicBook getSelectedComicBook() {
        // user code begin {1}
        // user code end
        return ivjSelectedComicBook;
}
/**
 * Called whenever the part throws an exception.
 * @param exception java.lang.Throwable
 */
private void handleException(Throwable exception) {

        /* Uncomment the following lines to print uncaught exceptions to
stdout */
        // System.out.println("--------- UNCAUGHT EXCEPTION ---------");
        // exception.printStackTrace(System.out);
}
/**
 * Handle the Applet init method.
 */
/* WARNING: THIS METHOD WILL BE REGENERATED. */
public void init() {
        try {
                setName("ComicBookListView");
                setSize(500, 400);
                setContentPane(getJAppletContentPane());
                initConnections();
                connEtoM1();
                // user code begin {1}
                // user code end
        } catch (java.lang.Throwable ivjExc) {
                // user code begin {2}
                // user code end
                handleException(ivjExc);
        }
}
/**
```

```
 * Initializes connections
 */
/* WARNING: THIS METHOD WILL BE REGENERATED. */
private void initConnections() {
    // user code begin {1}
    // user code end
    getComicBookList().addPropertyChangeListener(this);
    getComicBookList().addListSelectionListener(this);
    getJButton1().addActionListener(this);
    getJButton2().addActionListener(this);
    connPtoP1SetTarget();
    connPtoP2SetTarget();
    connPtoP3SetTarget();
    connPtoP4SetTarget();
}
/**
 * main entrypoint - starts the part when it is run as an application
 * @param args java.lang.String[]
 */
public static void main(java.lang.String[] args) {
    try {
        java.awt.Frame frame;
        try {
            Class aFrameClass =
Class.forName("com.ibm.uvm.abt.edit.TestFrame");
            frame = (java.awt.Frame)aFrameClass.newInstance();
        } catch (java.lang.Throwable ivjExc) {
            frame = new java.awt.Frame();
        }
        ComicBookListView aComicBookListView;
        Class iiCls =
Class.forName("ComicBookCollectionApplet.ComicBookListView");
        ClassLoader iiClsLoader = iiCls.getClassLoader();
        aComicBookListView =
(ComicBookListView)java.beans.Beans.instantiate(iiClsLoader,"ComicBookColl
ectionApplet.ComicBookListView");
        frame.add("Center", aComicBookListView);
        frame.setSize(aComicBookListView.getSize());
        frame.setVisible(true);
    } catch (Throwable exception) {
        System.err.println("Exception occurred in main() of
com.sun.java.swing.JApplet");
        exception.printStackTrace(System.out);
    }
}
/**
 * Method to handle events for the PropertyChangeListener interface.
 * @param evt java.beans.PropertyChangeEvent
 */
/* WARNING: THIS METHOD WILL BE REGENERATED. */
public void propertyChange(java.beans.PropertyChangeEvent evt) {
```

```
        // user code begin {1}
        // user code end
        if ((evt.getSource() == getComicBookList()) &&
(evt.getPropertyName().equals("model"))) {
            connPtoP1SetSource();
        }
        // user code begin {2}
        // user code end
}
/**
 * Set the SelectedComicBook to a new value.
 * @param newValue ComicBookCollectionApplet.ComicBook
 */
/* WARNING: THIS METHOD WILL BE REGENERATED. */
private void setSelectedComicBook(ComicBook newValue) {
    if (ivjSelectedComicBook != newValue) {
        try {
            ivjSelectedComicBook = newValue;
            connPtoP3SetTarget();
            connPtoP4SetTarget();
            // user code begin {1}
            // user code end
        } catch (java.lang.Throwable ivjExc) {
            // user code begin {2}
            // user code end
            handleException(ivjExc);
        }
    };
}
/**
 * Method to handle events for the ListSelectionListener interface.
 * @param e com.sun.java.swing.event.ListSelectionEvent
 */
/* WARNING: THIS METHOD WILL BE REGENERATED. */
public void valueChanged(com.sun.java.swing.event.ListSelectionEvent e) {
    // user code begin {1}
    // user code end
    if ((e.getSource() == getComicBookList()) ) {
        connPtoP2SetTarget();
    }
    // user code begin {2}
    // user code end
}
}
```

Luckily for us, this code did not have to be written by hand. Of course if you have an excellent imagination, memory, and visualization capacity, go to it. For the rest of us, VisualAge for Java manages the creation, interrelationship, and definition of properties for the application.

Tongue-in-cheek aside, you should be able to clearly see how Java is folded into the object-oriented Model-View-Controller development model. Granted, for simple applications this might seem like overkill. But the Big Blue Java solution is effective not only if you want to create applications for selling comic books, but for globally distributed operations that sell collectibles internationally. Our purpose is to explore how we can support that wide range of requirements with one set of technology and a single approach.

CHAPTER 13

Building Demo Applications with VisualAge for Java and Swing

O ne of the very practical requirements we asked of our new Java application development group was the creation of some demo applications that showed what it could do with the technology. These are actually much more valuable than they might seem at first glance. Such demo applications help the developers understand the tools they will be using for the creation of new applications; they give you (or management) something to see from the process; and since they are also a little less demanding than production applications, they can be developed faster.

A Demo Screen

As the management and life-skills guru Steven Covey would say, "Let us begin with the end in mind." In the first diagram (Figure 13.1), you see a view of the finished applet from within the applet viewer of VisualAge for Java.

This was ultimately what we took to our prospective customers to show them that we understood their business requirements and that we had customizable software that would help them apply technology to benefit their businesses.

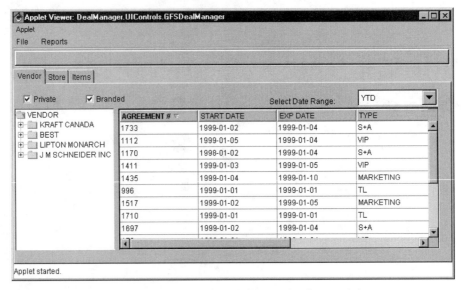

Figure 13.1 The finished Deal Manager applet running in a Web browser.

In this chapter we will evaluate the elements of building a browser-based demo application possessing all of the functionality that users have come to expect regardless of the operating environment they have to use. We will cover:

- The widgets included in the applet
- The classes and methods that make up the widget
- An explanation of the code for the classes and methods

Widgets

The following screens (Figures 13.2 to 13.10) provide a graphical representation of the widgets that we used to build the Deal Manager demo applet at WNS. You can choose to use the Visual Composition Editor or you can hand-code the widgets; there is no difference in the result, although at WNS we have standardized our development policy to force use of the visual programming model whenever applicable (and sometimes even when not applicable).

A blank content pane (JContentPane) is required to add widgets to an applet. This is the base of any applet.

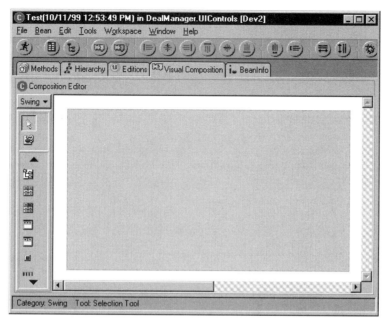

Figure 13.2 The basic startup frame for applet development with VisualAge for Java.

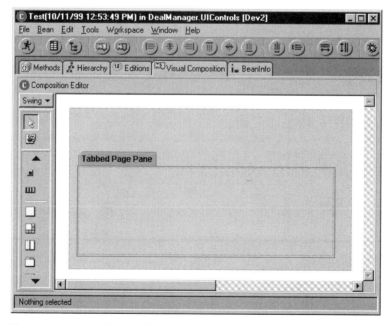

Figure 13.3 Starting application development by adding a split pane.

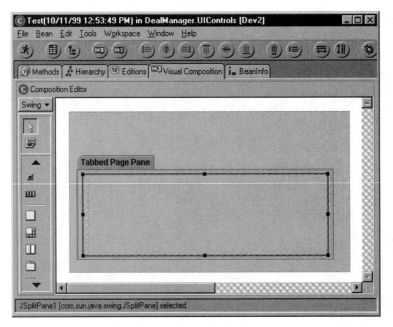

Figure 13.4 Increasing screen functionality by adding Swing objects.

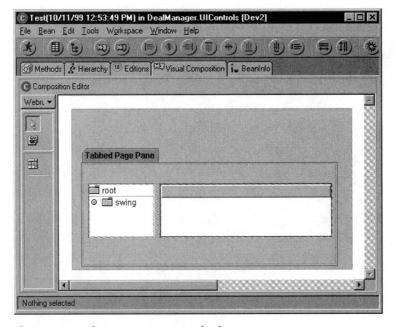

Figure 13.5 The screen starts to take form.

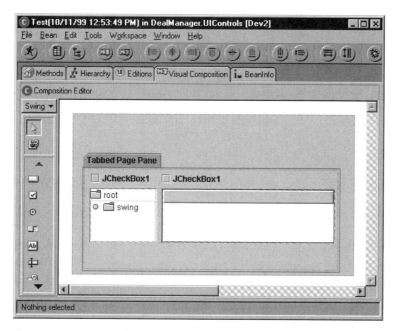

Figure 13.6 A JLabel and JCombobox are added to the applet for the date range.

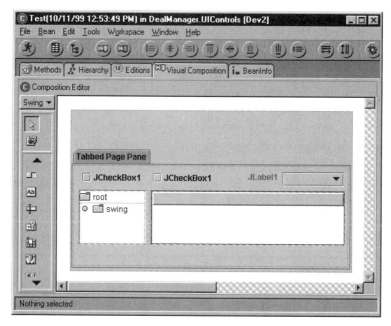

Figure 13.7 Another JLabel and a JTextbox are added to the applet for total.

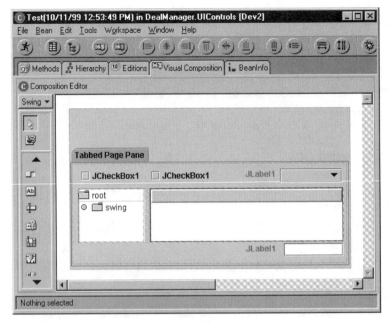

Figure 13.8 Adding user input widgets.

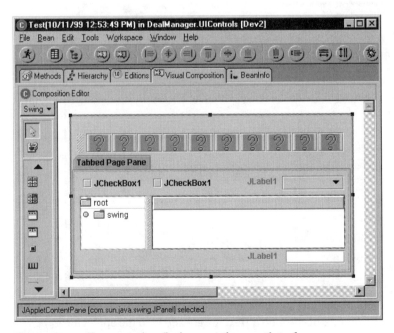

Figure 13.9 The menu bar fleshes out the user interface.

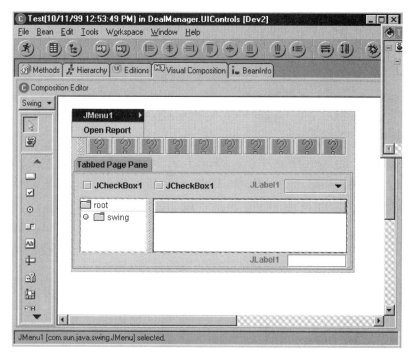

Figure 13.10 The finished screen prior to running in the applet viewer.

Once you have defined your project and resources as defined in the chapter on VisualAge for Java, and you have created a new window with a content pane, you can begin to build your screen form. A tabbed pane (JTabbedPane) is added to our applet to give us the ability of tab selection, which was defined as part of the systems specification by the business systems analyst and the user interface designer.

Each of the tabs within the application is expected to support at least a master detail level of data representation. Like any good graphical application, Deal Manager was designed to have a consistent look and feel from a user perspective. A split pane (JSplitPane) is added to each tabbed page pane. This will allow us to put a MultiColumnListbox and a JTree on one pane.

A JTree is added to the left side of the split pane, and a MultiColumnListbox is added to the right side of the split pane. The Jtree will give us a Windows Explorer–like look and feel. Selections within the tree will alter the data in the MCLB, which is basically a flexible table.

JCheckboxes are added to the applet for private and branded. The Jcheckboxes will have listeners added to catch any state changes and later the data in the MCLB accordingly.

Unlike Jcheckbox, Jcombobox does not come with its own label. So we add Jlabel to identify the combobox. The combobox offers selections and implements a listener that will alter data in the MCLB as it is changed.

The Jlabel is an identifier for the total box that will reflect the change of data within the multicolumn list box. The Jtestbox displays the total.

A JToolBar is added to the applet. The toolbars will support user interface buttons such as file, edit, view, print, and report. It also offers an alternative means of navigation to right-mouse-button support or pop-up menus.

A JMenu will be added to the applet, and JMenuItem(s) will be added to the JMenu. Like the toolbar, the primary purpose of this interface option is to provide the end user with additional means of working with the program. The functionality may already be supported, but people have different preferences such as keyboard shortcuts. These are implemented as part of the menu bar items.

From a developer's perspective, this is the finished applet. Since this is the Deal Manager demonstration, it is not tied to a database. The options for how to accomplish this are discussed as part of other chapters in the book. The key point here is to simply describe the process of creating a functional applet using the visual programming model and VisualAge for Java.

The Classes and Method Involved

Some of these classes and methods may change as the applet develops and as data changes. Notation will be as follows:

Class

Method( )

- DMMenuBar: Class file takes care of imports and instance variables
- DMMenuBar( ): Constructor creates the menu bar

- DMToolBar: Class file
- DMToolBar( ): Constructor that creates the toolbar
- VendorPopupMenu: Class file
- VendorPopupMenu( ): Constructor that creates (you guessed it) the pop-up menu
- mouseClicked(MouseEvent): Not used in Deal Manager
- mouseEntered(MouseEvent): Not used in DM
- mouseExited(MouseEvent): Not used in DM
- mousePresses(MouseEvent): Creates new pop-up by calling the constructor
- mouseReleased(MouseEvent): Creates new pop-up by calling constructors (used for Unix)
- VendorPopupMenuSelections: Class
- VendorPopupMenuSelections( ): Constructor
- actionPreformed(ActionEvent): Gets command from pop-up
- Foo_MCLB: Class file
- Foo_MCLB: Constructor for creating a new MLCB
- foo_refreshRows(String): Refreshes multicolumn list box when DataRangeComboBox changes
- foo_refreshRows(String, int): Refreshes MCLB when Jtree changes
- foo_refreshRows(boolean, boolean): Refreshes rows when check-boxes change
- foo_Rows( ): Creates and adds all rows to object and MCLB
- rowDeselected(ListboxEvent): Not used in DM
- rowSelected(ListboxEvent): Sets an object equal to selected row
- DealManager: Our applet
- actionPreformed(ActionEvent): Listens for checkboxes and calls to refresh rows
- getCategoryJTree( ): Builds Jtree for category pane
- getCategoryMCLB( ): Creates new foo_mclb for category pane
- getCategoryPane( ): Creates pane and adds elements to it
- getCustomerJTree( ): Creates Jtree and adds element to it

- getCustomerMCLB( ): Creates MCLB and adds elements to it

- getCustomerPane( ): Creates pane and adds elements to customer pane

- getDateRangeCombobox( ): Adds listener, creates new combo, and adds elements

- getDateRangeLabel( ): Creates labels

- getVendorBrandedCheckbox( ): Creates and sets checkbox

- getVendorPrivateCheckbox( ): Creates and sets checkbox

- getVendorJTree( )

- getVendorMCLB( )

- getVendorPane( )

- init( ): Initializes the DM applet. This happens first. Init sets the default look and feel; gets a content pane; and adds a tabbed pane, menubar, and tool bar in the same order as when we built the application (happens a bit faster, though).

- itemStateChanged(ItemEvent): Listener for combobox. Resets checkboxes and calls foo_refreshrows

- valueChanged(TreeSelectionEvent): Listener for trees (anybody remember the Smothers brothers?) Gets treepath, calls foo_refreshrows.

Explanation of Code Comprising Classes and Methods

This section will focus on the applet (DealManager) itself and make reference to other classes when necessary. Descriptions of what the code does will be found after // in the code. Each widget will only be explained once. For example, only one JTree will be explained, as the coding for all is nearly the same. We'll start with the WNSDealManager class:

```
Class
DealManager

//  Import all of the outside class files that are required to make the
//  applet run

import com.sun.java.swing.*;
import java.awt.*;
import com.sun.java.swing.tree.*;
import java.awt.*;
import GFSDABeans.*;
import java.sql.*;
```

```
import com.sun.java.swing.event.*;
import com.sun.java.swing.event.TreeSelectionListener;
import java.awt.event.*;
import java.util.*;
import com.ibm.webrunner.smclb.*;
import com.ibm.webrunner.smclb.event.ListboxEvent;
import com.ibm.webrunner.smclb.event.ListboxListener;
import com.ibm.webrunner.smclb.util.*;
import java.lang.*;
import DealManager.UIControls.*;
/**
 * This Class was created by James Carlson and revised by Bill Simpson for
 * WNS, Inc.
 * This is the sole property of Wordn Systems Inc. Do Not redistribute.
 */
public class GFSDealManager extends JApplet implements
                ItemListener,

    TreeSelectionListener,

                                            ActionListener{
// Create instance variables

    private JComboBox myComboBox = null;
    private Foo_MCLB myVendorMCLB = null;
    private Foo_MCLB myCategoryMCLB = null;
    private Foo_MCLB myCustomerMCLB = null;
    private JCheckBox myVendorBrandedCheckBox = null;
    private JCheckBox myVendorPrivateCheckBox = null;
    public static Object [] currentRowObject;
    public static Object [][] visibleRows;
    public static Object [][] visibleRowsAfterCheck = null;
    public static Object [][] visibleRowsDateChange = null;

}// End of class - Begin methods for WNSDealManager
```

actionPreformed(ActionEvent)
```
public void actionPerformed(ActionEvent evt) {

    //Create a boolean variable for private and checked Checkboxes
    boolean brandedChecked;
    boolean privateChecked;

    // Set true or false based on state of Checkbox
    privateChecked = myVendorPrivateCheckBox.isSelected();
    brandedChecked = myVendorBrandedCheckBox.isSelected();

    // Call foo_refreshRows method
    myVendorMCLB.foo_refreshRows(privateChecked, brandedChecked);
}
```

getCategoryJTree()
```
private JTree getCategoryJTree() {
    TreeSelectionModel selModel;

    // create root node
```

```
        DefaultMutableTreeNode vendor = new
DefaultMutableTreeNode("CATEGORY");

            // create sub nodes and add them to the root node
            DefaultMutableTreeNode bVendor = new
DefaultMutableTreeNode("BEVERAGE SYSTEMS");
            vendor.add(bVendor);
            // Repeat procedure for more nodes

        // add new JTree with root node tree node as model
        JTree myJTree = new JTree(vendor);

        // add a selection listener to this tree
        myJTree.addTreeSelectionListener(this);

        // make selection single selection only
        selModel = myJTree.getSelectionModel();
        selModel.setSelectionMode(TreeSelectionModel.SINGLE_TREE_SELECTION);

        return myJTree;
}
```

getCategoryMCLB()

```
private MultiColumnListbox getCategoryMCLB() {
    // get new MCLB
    Foo_MCLB myMCLB = new Foo_MCLB();
    myCategoryMCLB = myMCLB;

    // add all rows to MCLB
    myCategoryMCLB.foo_Rows();
    return myCategoryMCLB;
}
```

getCategoryPane()

```
private JPanel getCategoryPane() {
    // create new JPanel
    // this will be a tabbed page pane

    JPanel myPanel = new JPanel();

    // set properties
    myPanel.setBackground(Color.lightGray);
    myPanel.setLayout(null);

    // Add a JSplitPane to the JPanel
    JSplitPane mySplitPanel = new
JSplitPane(JSplitPane.HORIZONTAL_SPLIT);

    // Set JSplitPane properties
    mySplitPanel.setDividerSize(8);
    mySplitPanel.setPreferredSize(new java.awt.Dimension(700, 250));
    mySplitPanel.setLastDividerLocation(175);
    mySplitPanel.setBounds(1, 39, 690, 226);
    mySplitPanel.setDividerLocation(175);

    // Add JTree and MCLB to pane
    mySplitPanel.add(this.getCategoryJTree(), "left");
```

```java
        mySplitPanel.add(this.getCategoryMCLB(), "right");

        // Add mySplitPane to Applet
        myPanel.add(mySplitPanel);
        return myPanel;
}
```

getDateRangeComboBox()

```java
private JComboBox getDateRangeComboBox() {
        // create new JCombobox
        myComboBox = new JComboBox();

        // Set Properties
        myComboBox.setName("cmb_YTD");
        myComboBox.setBounds(559, 10, 130, 27);

        // Create and add objects
        Object YTD = " YTD";
        Object LYTD = " QYTD";
        Object QYTD = " LYTD";
        myComboBox.addItem(YTD);
        myComboBox.addItem(LYTD);
        myComboBox.addItem(QYTD);

        // add and ItemListener to this
        myComboBox.addItemListener(this);
        return myComboBox;
}
```

getDateRangeLabel()

```java
private JLabel getDateRangeLabel() {
        // create new JLabel
        JLabel myLabel = new JLabel();
        // Set Properties
        myLabel.setName("DealManger DateRange");
        myLabel.setText("Select Date Range: ");
        myLabel.setBounds(417, 21, 137, 15);
        return myLabel;
}
```

getVendorBrandedCheckBox()

```java
private JCheckBox getVendorBrandedCheckBox() {

        // create new JCheckbox
        myVendorBrandedCheckBox = new JCheckBox();
        // set properties
        myVendorBrandedCheckBox.setText("Branded");
        myVendorBrandedCheckBox.setBounds(118, 11, 99, 25);
        myVendorBrandedCheckBox.setSelected(true);
        // add an ActionListener to this
        myVendorBrandedCheckBox.addActionListener(this);
        return myVendorBrandedCheckBox;
}
```

init()

```java
public void init() {
    try {
            // Create a "Windows" look and feel

    UIManager.setLookAndFeel("com.sun.java.swing.plaf.windows
.WindowsLookAndFeel");
            // Set the name of the Applet
            setName("WNS - DealManager version 1.1");
            setSize(700, 350);

            //Setting up the Menu Bar
            setJMenuBar(new DMMenuBar());
            getContentPane().add(new DMToolBar(),"North");

            //Now I add the tabbed control panes
            JTabbedPane myTabbedPane = new JTabbedPane();
            myTabbedPane.insertTab("Vendor", null, getVendorPane(), null,
0);
            myTabbedPane.insertTab("Store", null, getCustomerPane(), null,
1);
            myTabbedPane.insertTab("Items", null, getCategoryPane(), null,
2);
            getContentPane().add(myTabbedPane);

            } catch (Exception e) { //java.lang.Throwable ivjExc

                e.printStackTrace();

            }
}
```

itemStateChanged(ItemEvent evt)
```java
public void itemStateChanged(ItemEvent evt) {
    // create an object to hold the value of a selected item form the
    // combo box
    Object value = myComboBox.getSelectedItem();
    String selected = value.toString();

    // reset the check boxes to 'selected'
    myVendorPrivateCheckBox.setSelected(true);
    myVendorBrandedCheckBox.setSelected(true);

    // call the foo_refreshRows method
    myVendorMCLB.foo_refreshRows(selected);
}
```

valueChanged(TreeSelectionEvent e)
```java
public void valueChanged(TreeSelectionEvent e) {

            // get the full selection path from the tree
            TreePath path = e.getPath();

            // create an object for this path and set up other variables
            Object pathObj[] = path.getPath();
            int i,max;
```

```java
        String formattedPath = "";
        String lastPath = "";
        String startPath ="";
        max = pathObj.length;

        // reset check boxes
        if (myVendorBrandedCheckBox.isSelected()==false &&
myVendorPrivateCheckBox.isSelected()==false ||
                myVendorBrandedCheckBox.isSelected()==true &&
myVendorPrivateCheckBox.isSelected()==false ||
                myVendorBrandedCheckBox.isSelected()==false &&
myVendorPrivateCheckBox.isSelected()==true ){
            myVendorBrandedCheckBox.setSelected(true);
            myVendorPrivateCheckBox.setSelected(true);
        }

        // reset combo box to YTD
        myComboBox.setSelectedIndex(0);

        // get the start path ie. VENDOR or CATEGORY
        startPath = pathObj[0].toString();

        // FOR Testing create the full path to selected object
        for(i=0;i<max;i++)
        {
            formattedPath+="/";
            formattedPath+=pathObj[i].toString();
            lastPath = pathObj[i].toString();
        }

        // get the last object in path
        lastPath = lastPath.trim();

        // Testing system outs
        System.out.println (formattedPath);
        System.out.println(startPath+"'");
        System.out.println(lastPath+"'");
        System.out.println("Tree Position = " +i);

        // IF vendor tree was tree that had a selection...
        if (startPath == "VENDOR" ){
            if (i==1){
                // if root clicked fill MCLB will all rows
                myVendorMCLB.foo_Rows();
            }
            if (i == 2 || i == 3){
                // if sub node clicked fill with specific rows
                myVendorMCLB.removeAllRows();
                myVendorMCLB.foo_refreshRows(lastPath, i);
            }
        }
        // create new if statements etc for other trees
}
```

Now I will look at other methods in other classes that are important for building the application:

Class
Foo_MCLB

```java
import com.sun.java.swing.*;
import java.awt.*;
import com.sun.java.swing.tree.*;
import java.awt.*;
import GFSDABeans.*;
import java.sql.*;
import com.sun.java.swing.event.*;
import com.sun.java.swing.event.TreeSelectionListener;
import java.awt.event.*;
import java.util.*;
import com.ibm.webrunner.smclb.*;
import com.ibm.webrunner.smclb.event.ListboxEvent;
import com.ibm.webrunner.smclb.event.ListboxListener;
import com.ibm.webrunner.smclb.util.*;
import java.lang.*;

public class Foo_MCLB extends com.ibm.webrunner.smclb.MultiColumnListbox
implements ListboxListener{

//  Create objects for all rows and a selected row
public static Object [][] fooRows;
private Object [] rowObject = null;
}
```

Foo_MCLB()

```java
public Foo_MCLB() {
// This is a constructor
      super();
      addListboxListener(this);
      // Now I setup the default behaviour for the MCLB
      setSelectable(true);
      //this.setSelectionForeground(Color.black);
      setBounds(50,30,120,57);

      // Now I will add some columns
      Object [] columns = {
          "AGREEMENT #",
          "START DATE",
          "EXP DATE",
          "TYPE",
          "AMOUNT PER CASE",
          "TOTAL CASES",
          "EARNED REVENUE"
      };
      addColumns(columns);

      // Set the width for all columns
```

```java
     for (int i = 0;  i<7;  i++){
          ListboxColumn column = getColumnInfo(i);
          column.setWidth(128);
     }

     // This will make all columns sortable (asc + dsc)
     for (int sub = 0; sub < columns.length; sub++){
       ListboxColumn column = getColumnInfo(sub);
       column.setSorter(new SelectionSorter());
     }
     // add a mouse listener to the MCLB
     addMouseListener(new VendorPopupMenu());

}
```

foo_refreshRows(String vendor, int pos)
the other foo_refreshRows work much the same

```java
public void foo_refreshRows(String vendor, int pos) {
     //remove all row from the MCLB
  removeAllRows();

  // Testing Code
     System.out.println("From foo_refreshRows - vendor " +vendor);
     System.out.println("From foo_refreshRows - position " +pos);

     int sub = 0;
     int elementPos = 0;

     //NOTE: Hard coded lengths for Object arrays will be replaced by
     //dynamically appendable vectors
     Object [][] elements = new Object [35][];

     // IF tree position clicked was a 2or 3 (ie. a vendor or subvendor)
     // loop through object to get matching data
     if (pos == 2 || pos == 3){
          // Loop through all rows
          while (sub < fooRows.length){
               rowObject = fooRows[sub];
               // If a match add a row
               if (pos == 2 && (String)rowObject[7] == vendor){
                    addRow(rowObject);
                    //elements[elementPos] = sub;

                    // add row to new object for current rows
                    elements[elementPos] = rowObject;
                    elementPos ++;
                    System.out.println("FooRows" +sub+   "added to
elements[" +elementPos+ "]");
               }
               else if (pos == 3 && (String)rowObject[8] == vendor){
                    addRow(rowObject);
                    //elements[elementPos] = sub;
                    elements[elementPos] = rowObject;
                    elementPos ++;
```

```
                    System.out.println("FooRows" +sub+ "added to
elements[" +elementPos+ "]");
                }
                sub ++;
            }
            // Make the rest of the new object nulls
            // this will be depricated when we change to vectors
            try{
                for(int i = elementPos+1; i<=elements.length;i++){
                    //elements[i] = -1;
                    elements[i] = null;
                    System.out.println("elements[] " +i+ "made null");
                }
            // catch all exceptions
            }catch(Exception e){
                System.out.println("End of Array");
            }
        }
        // repaint MCLB and make visible rows = all current rows in MCLB
        repaint();
        GFSDealManager.visibleRows = elements;
}
```

rowSelected(ListboxEvent evt)

```
public void rowSelected(ListboxEvent evt) {
    System.out.println("Row Selected");

    //get the integer value of the row selected
    int rowSelected = evt.getRow();

    // create object to hold row
    Object[] myObject;
    myObject = getRow(rowSelected);

    // make public static variable = row selected
    GFSDealManager.currentRowObject = myObject;
    System.out.println("current row object "
+(String)WNSDealManager.currentRowObject[0]);
}
```

Class
DMMenuBar

```
public DMMenuBar() {
// this is the constructor
    super();
    // Create and add items to menu bar

    JMenu myMenu = new JMenu("File");
    JMenuItem myMenuItem = new JMenuItem("New Report");
    myMenu.add(myMenuItem);

    myMenuItem = new JMenuItem("Open Reports");
    myMenu.add(myMenuItem);
```

```
        myMenuItem = new JMenuItem("Close Reports");
        myMenu.add(myMenuItem);

        myMenu.addSeparator();

        myMenuItem = new JMenuItem("Log-Off:jcarlson");
        myMenu.add(myMenuItem);

        add(myMenu);

        myMenu = new JMenu("Reports");

        myMenuItem = new JMenuItem("Open Reports");
        myMenu.add(myMenuItem);

        myMenuItem = new JMenuItem("Close Reports");
        myMenu.add(myMenuItem);

        add(myMenu);

}
```

Class
DMToolBar

```
public DMToolBar() {
// This is the constructor
        super();

        // Lets set up some of the apperances
        setBorderPainted(false);
        // Create and add buttons to tool bar
        JToolBar myToolBar = new JToolBar();

        myToolBar.add(new Button());

        add(myToolBar);
}
```

Class
VendorPopupMenu

```
public VendorPopupMenu() {
// This is the constructor
        super();

        setLightWeightPopupEnabled(false);
        JMenuItem aMenuItem;

        // a Menu item that will be displayed at the top of the menu
        aMenuItem = new JMenuItem("Cut");
        // add a ActionListener to the MenuItem for a new
        // VendorPopupMenuSelections
        aMenuItem.addActionListener(new VendorPopupMenuSelections());
        aMenuItem.setActionCommand("Cut");
        add(aMenuItem);
}
```

mousePressed(MouseEvent e)

```
public void mousePressed(MouseEvent e) {
```

```
                    //create new popup if right click

                    if (e.isPopupTrigger()){
                    JPopupMenu myPopUpMenu = new VendorPopupMenu();
                    myPopUpMenu.show(e.getComponent(),e.getX(),e.getY());
               }
          }
     }
```

Class
VendorPopupMenuSelections
actionPerformed(ActionEvent e)

```
public void actionPerformed(ActionEvent e) {
     // get selection
     String command = e.getActionCommand();

     // get selected row object
     Object [] row = WNSDealManager.currentRowObject;
     System.out.println((String)row[0]);

     // create if's for all possible selections
     if (command.equals("Cut")) {
          setSize(new Dimension(300,300));
          System.out.println(command.toString());
          //getContentPane().add(new JLabel("Data from row selected"));
          getContentPane().add(new JLabel("Data from row selected = " +
(String)row[0]));
          setVisible(true);
          return;
     }
```

CHAPTER 14

Database Connectivity with WebSphere Wizards

Y ou may not be able to view your SQL results if you do not have the WAS and HTTP servers configured properly. You must also have the ODBC drivers set up properly and available for administration through the control panel on the client workstation. One of the things we want to accomplish with this book is to have an end-to-end reference for those of you who are just getting into the Big Blue Java world. While you can get help on MS Windows from various places, we want to be sure that we have documented all of the steps involved in getting any of these tools and servers running. For that reason, we are starting off with some of the very basic Windows communications setup.

Bear with us if this seems a bit basic. If it's helpful to you, feel free to drop us an e-mail!

Before we begin with the WSS wizards we will ensure that you are set up correctly. First, select ODBC32 from the control panel. After double-clicking, you can get down to business with the following screen (Figure 14.1).

Select the System DSN tab. This is shown in Figure 14.2. The *system DSN* means that the connection will be available to anyone, regardless of

Figure 14.1 ODBC administration in Windows.

the login name or account used. *User DSNs*, in comparison, are specific to each login account.

If the driver you want does not appear in the list, click Add. You will see the following screen (Figure 14.3).

To get connected to DB2, select IBM ODBC DRIVER and click Finish. The screen shown in Figure 14.4 will appear. Click on the Add Database option.

This brings up the DB2 ODBC SmartGuide, which will step you through the process of creating an ODBC system DSN to use. The first SmartGuide panel is shown in Figure 14.5. You go through this process to connect Net-

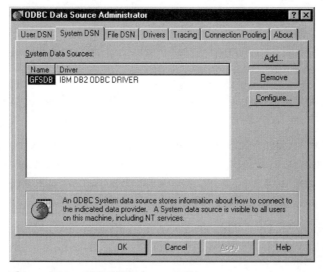

Figure 14.2 ODBC Windows settings.

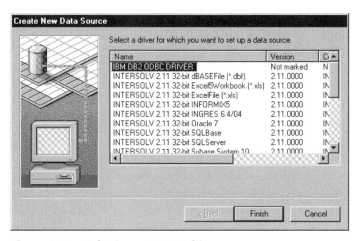

Figure 14.3 Selecting an ODBC driver.

Objects Fusion, DB2 Control Panel, Net.Commerce, WebSphere Studio, or any other application that expects to connect a Microsoft Windows–based client to a DB2 server.

Ensure that you select Search the Network, and click Next. This will let SmartGuide query through the network neighborhood to identify any DB2 servers on the network. As you can see, the results returned are the name of the host server and the database instance on that server. You must know to which server you want to connect as well as having a valid user ID and password. You will probably agree that these are not unreasonable requirements.

Speaking of user IDs and passwords, it is at this stage that you define what user account you want the ODBC link to use as shown in Figure 14.6. This can be seen as a potential security concern, since the ODBC link will not prompt for a password when invoked by a client application. On the other hand, it does make database access much more seam-

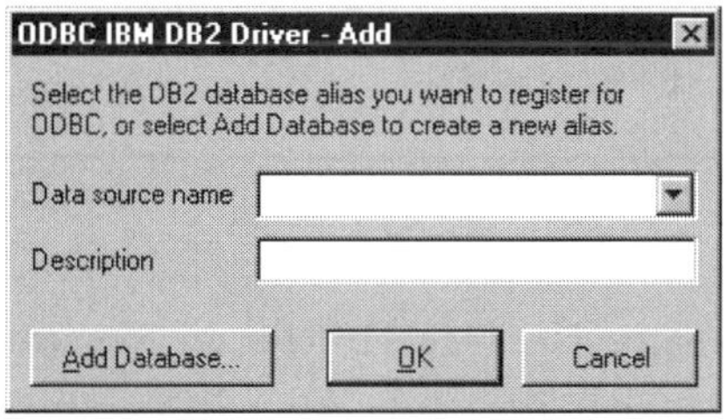

Figure 14.4 Choosing a DB2 database.

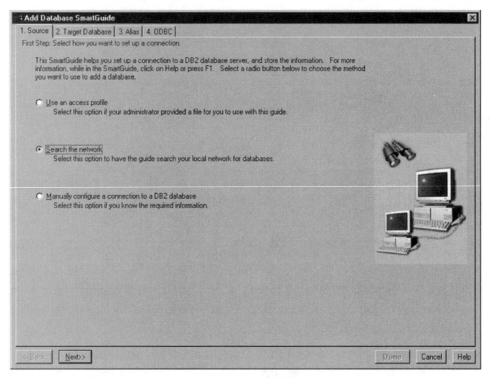

Figure 14.5 Add database SmartGuide.

less. Once again we see that ease of use has offsetting considerations. Limited security is one, and degraded performance is another.

If your workstation can see the GFSDB under JAVATWO, it will either show up in Known Systems or in Other Systems. If it shows up in the Known Systems section, you will want to cancel this operation (shown in Figure 14.7) then move on to the SQL wizard section of this document. If it is in Other Systems, select GFSDB and click Done. You can now test your connection (Figure 14.8).

By clicking the Test Connection button, you will see that the database alias is not GROCERY, but instead identifies GFSDB. Each ODBC connection defined is database- and user-specific.

Now your ODBC32–System DSN screen should look like Figure 14.9 for GFSDB.

Please note that you must make sure that the HTTP server and WebSphere servlet server are both up and running. With that we are now

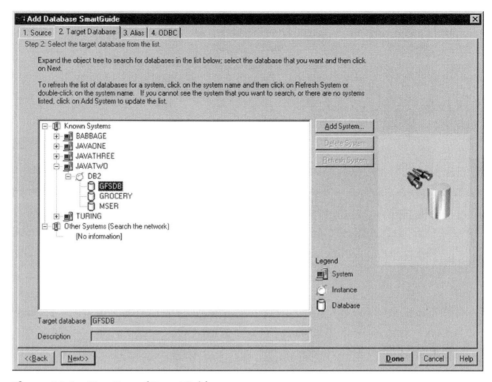

Figure 14.6 Step Two of SmartGuide.

ready to work on JDBC/WSS connectivity. As shown in Figure 14.10, select SQL WIZARD from the toolbar or Tools menu item.

This is the primary screen for the SQL wizard where you define the name of your SQL statement. The SQL wizard for WebSphere Studio (Figure 14.11) is a bit different from the SQL Assistant in DB2 or VisualAge for Java. Which one you decide you want to use may be a matter of preference, or a matter of convenience. If you have a SQL generation tool that you like, you will probably use it to generate the code that you include in other applications.

Like the ODBC connection, we have to add the database connection as depicted here with:

userid: db2admin

pass: password

After that, for DB2 you have to specify the schema on which you wish to build your select.

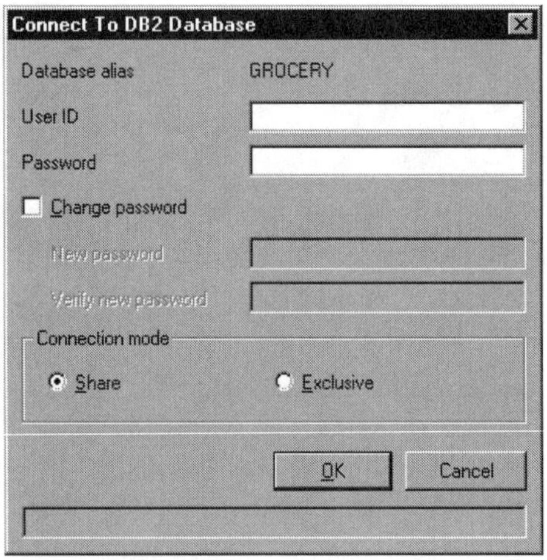

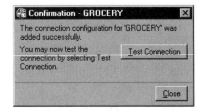

Figure 14.7 Setting user account information.

Figure 14.8 Testing your ODBC connection.

Once you have identified the particular schema you want to work with, you can select the table(s) for your SQL statement to manipulate (Figure 14.13).

You may decide at this point that you are going to retrieve results from more than one table. These can be clicked at the same time to allow you to enter the join logic desired. You can see how this is accomplished in Figure 14.14.

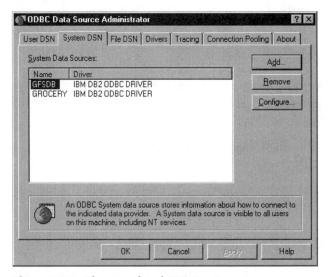

Figure 14.9 The completed ODBC entry.

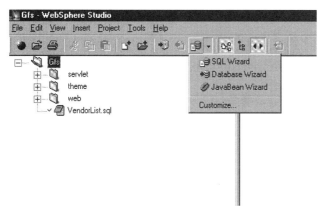

Figure 14.10 Accessing WSS wizards.

Select any columns in either table that you wish to base your JOIN on and then click Join. Note that the comment area shows that these will be linked as an inner join as opposed to an outer join. Options allows you to define more sophisticated table-handling characteristics.

Select the Columns tab in order to get listings of the column names for each table. Click on the Add button to add them to the list. The ones that you include will be displayed by the Select statement.

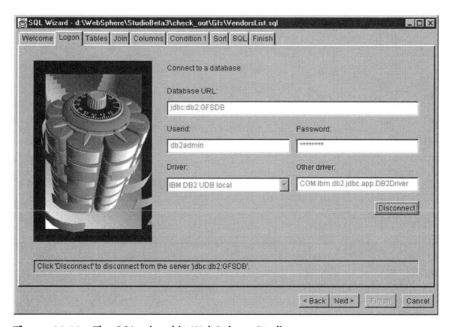

Figure 14.11 The SQL wizard in WebSphere Studio.

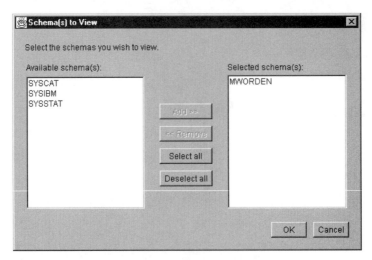

Figure 14.12 Collecting the connection details.

At this point you can add conditions for any of the columns in any of the tables that were selected, as shown in Figure 14.15.

Once you know exactly which tables you want to work with, understand the key relationships between the tables, and have specified the columns that hold that data, you can define how the results are to be ordered through the screens shown in Figures 14.16 and 14.17.

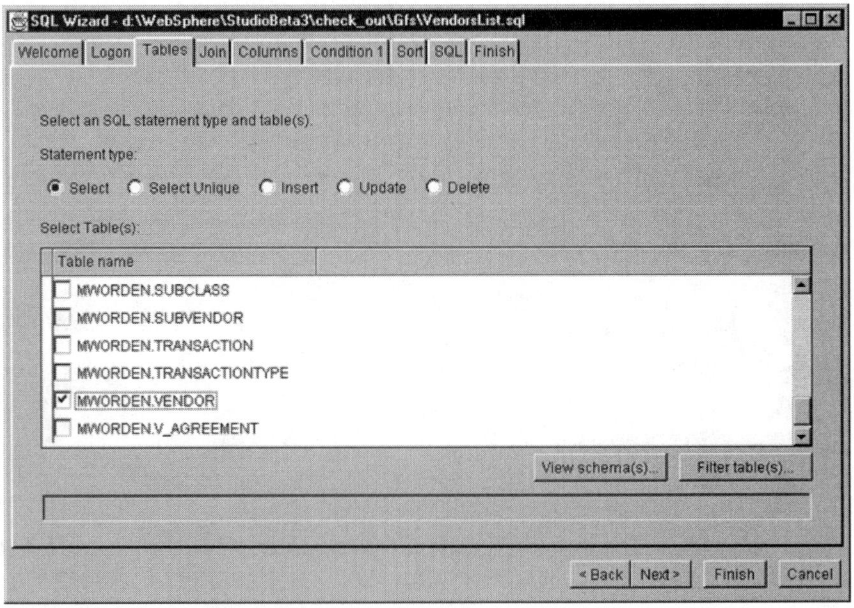

Figure 14.13 Selecting tables.

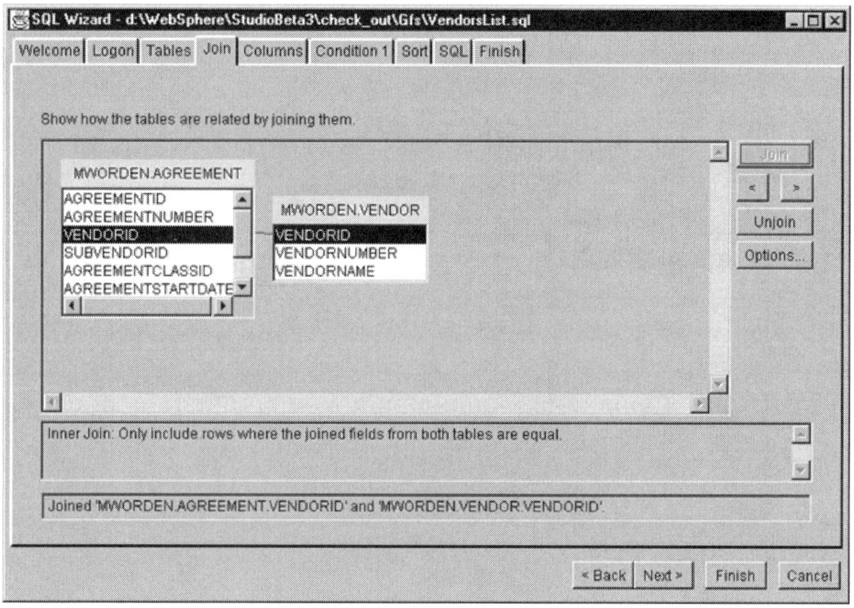

Figure 14.14 Linking multiple tables with SQL wizard.

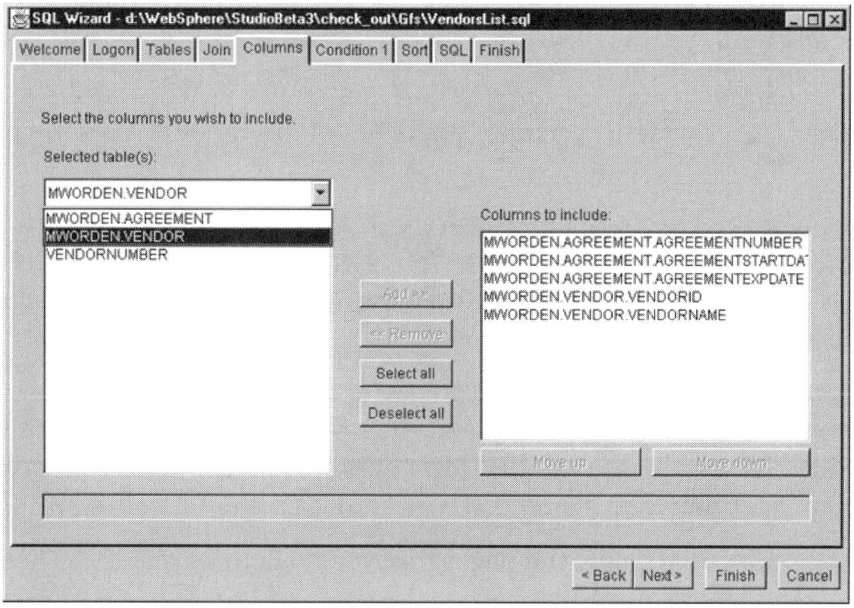

Figure 14.15 Including table columns.

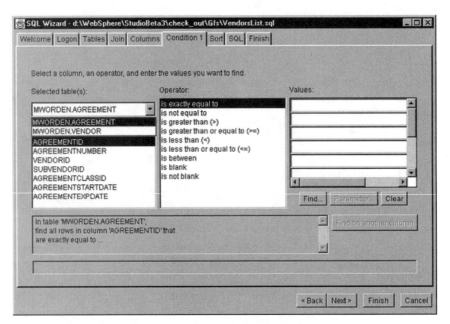

Figure 14.16 Filtering columns with predefined criteria.

You can now review your SQL statement, and even test it. This means the SQL wizard is a pretty complete SQL script builder. If you don't work with SQL syntax every day, it could be a lifesaver—not to mention a handy productivity tool. Click the Finish button to finish your SQL statement.

You can see the script for your SQL statement in WSS, as shown in Figure 14.18. To view it, simply double-click on the icon as shown in Figure 14.19.

Now we can begin to build with the *database wizard* so that we can add database connectivity to our Web pages. Select it from the toolbar or the Tools menu item. You will see the WSS workspace as shown in Figure 14.20.

After you fire up the database wizard, the first screen you see will ask you to select the SQL statement that you want to use for building the JSPs, classes, beans, and HTML pages. Select the one we just finished making. Click Next when you see the screen shown in Figure 14.21.

Then you must select the pages that you wish to be created. The options are shown in Figure 14.22.

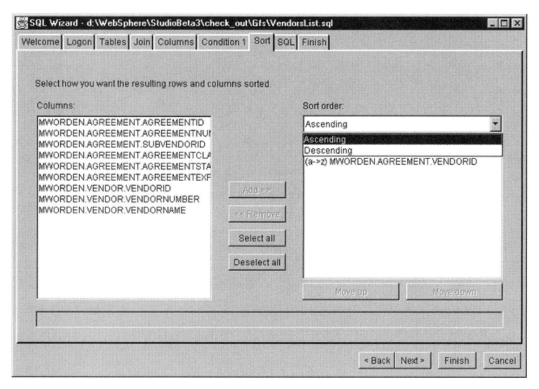

Figure 14.17   Specifying the sort order of returned data.

You can create an input page that will request specific information from the client. This *may* be able to be used for user validation. Click Next to see the specifics for the in/out page. This is shown in Figure 14.23.

To move forward, click Next. You will now be able to define the format for output and the columns that you want to be output. These are displayed in Figure 14.24.

This wizard can also be used to create error pages, or you can define a specific one for WSS to use. The error-handling options are shown in Figure 14.25.

A page can also be created if no data is returned from the SQL statement. (See Figure 14.26.) You would not want to handle this as an error, and you may be able to provide tips to the user—such as reducing the number of criteria.

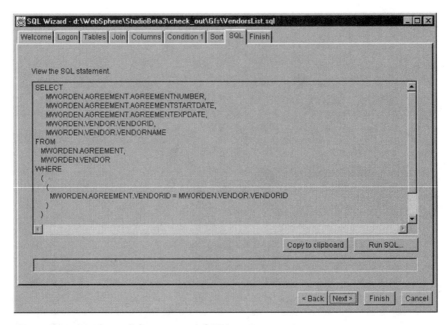

Figure 14.18 View of the generated SQL.

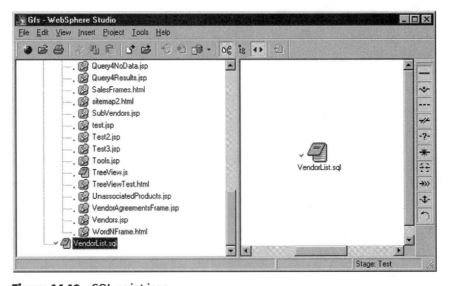

Figure 14.19 SQL script icon.

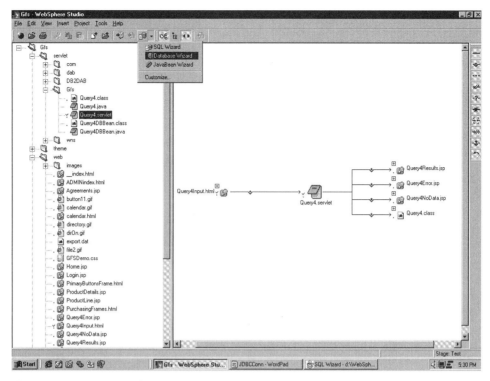

Figure 14.20   WSS workspace.

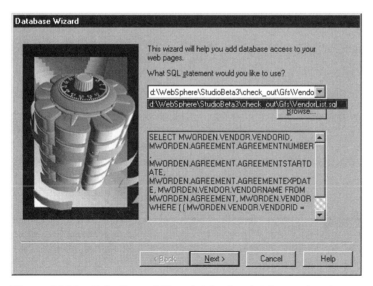

Figure 14.21   Selecting a SQL script for the database wizard.

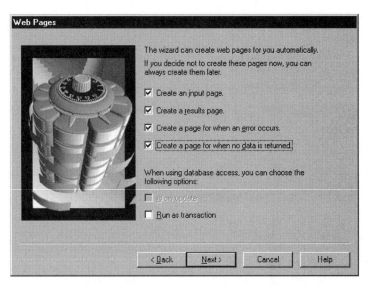

Figure 14.22 Web page options.

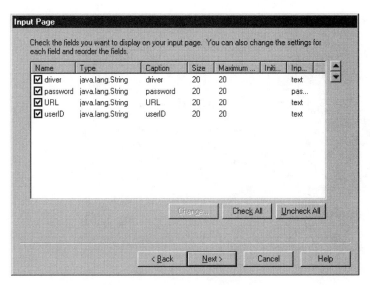

Figure 14.23 Specifying input/output options.

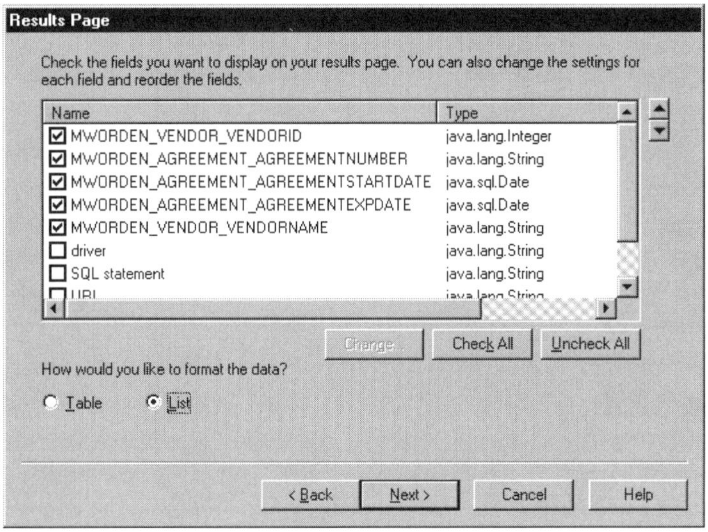

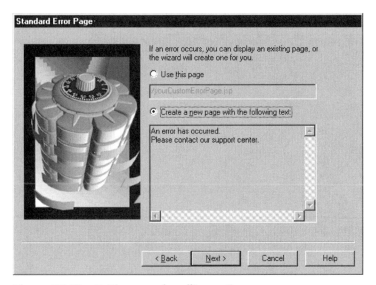

Figure 14.24 Setting output column types.

Figure 14.25 Setting error-handling options.

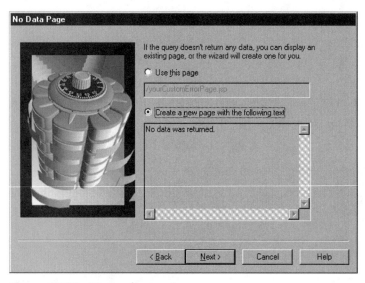

Figure 14.26 No-results warnings.

Next, select the methods that you want the server to run. As shown in Figure 14.27, only one exists. That makes it easy for us to decide which one to select.

A great feature of this WSS wizard is that it will allow you to save the query in the project as a bean. If this sounds good, select Yes and name your bean when you see the screen shown in Figure 14.28.

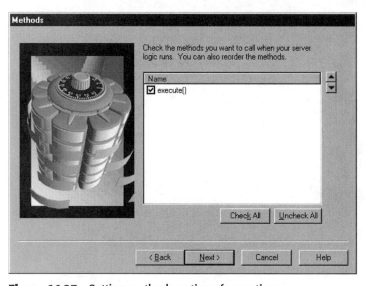

Figure 14.27 Setting methods options for runtime.

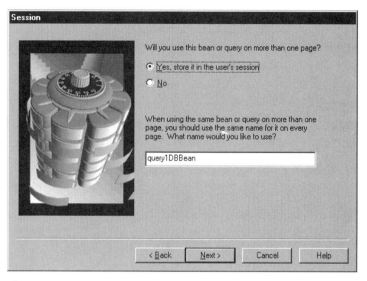

Figure 14.28 Naming your bean.

Click Next. Review your selections when you see the screen shown in Figure 14.29. Once everything is correct, click Finish.

All the pages and classes will be automatically generated and stored in your WSS project.

Figure 14.30 shows what it may look like in WSS once everything is created and run successfully. Note all of the requested pages and classes and beans.

Summary

There obviously is a great deal of power in working with JavaBeans and Java Server pages. When I worked with Excellerator and other application design tools that came with code generators in the late 1980s, the promise was that we would be able to completely generate an application without writing a line of code.

From the examples shown in this chapter, you should be able to appreciate how far code generation technology has come. IBM has provided a set of tools for generating data-enabled Web applications or Web-enabled database applications.

Figure 14.29 List of files automatically created.

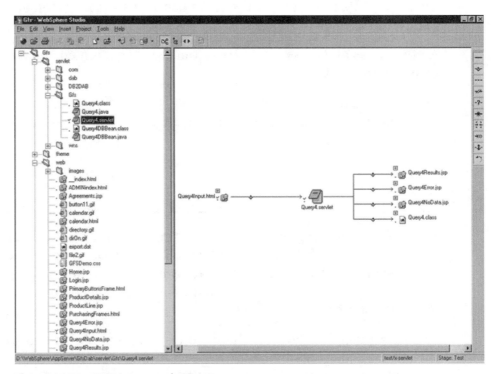

Figure 14.30 WSS-generated JSP resources.

The approach you choose in solving your e-business challenges is up to you. There is a tool in the box for everyone, regardless of their level or background.

It is interesting to me, as a systems analyst, that the common denominator is having deep domain knowledge and ensuring that you have modeled the process. Building applications, like writing code, are taking a backseat to relevance to the business.

If you understand the business problem to be solved, and you have access to the data you need to solve it, with WebSphere Studio and associated wizards you should be on the fast track to getting the job done.

CHAPTER 15

Model the Business First—
Not the Software

M y first foray into trying to document an approach to business systems analysis was in the little read *Developing Sybase Applications* (SAMs, 1995). In that particular work, I tried to bring together everything I had learned about determining requirements, diagramming a model of process flow, logical and physical data modeling, and introducing the notion of applying systems functions that use data to support business tasks. I called the technique *Integrated Task/Data Modeling methodology* (IT/DM).

You may be relieved to learn that I am not going to inflict that model on you here. Instead, I want to share with you an alternative technique that I hope you will find as useful as I have.

My work with business systems predates object orientation outside the classroom. As a result, I have developed a tremendous commitment to practicality and a confidence in the ability of sensible, intelligent people to be able to grasp concepts and put them to work in short order.

I met Jack Ladick, a business process expert, while flying home from a disastrous client engagement in Atlanta. I wasn't particularly in the mood to socialize, and it wasn't until we had both whipped out our laptops that we even said so much as hello. By the end of the conversation,

I was positive that Mr. Ladick and his partner Jane Roy held a very valuable key to developing working Big Blue Java applications. As ex-Digital Equipment Corporation strategic services (SS) senior consultants, they have both seen technology challenges and business changes like we all face today. Their specialty, however, turns out to be not technology, but process engineering.

Within a few hours of evaluating their tools and approach, I recognized that these folks had invested significantly more time and talent than I ever could into business process engineering. The tool works, and most important, it is now tightly coupled with the Big Blue Java approach of visual programming for Java application development.

What follows is the work Jack and Jane have put together to describe that all-important first step of understanding the business problem to be solved by an application.

If you follow through this chapter, I am positive that you will see a direct mapping to the Big Blue programming model that we discussed in Chapter 5.

The Challenge

Management of business operations and the effective deployment of resources and systems are challenging assignments. Business is a complex maze of interconnected processes, organizations, and information systems delivering a variety of product and service sets to meet ever-changing customer requirements. Effective managers view their business as a system of logical flows and interdependencies of work and information.

This understanding of the business as a system is necessary to effectively deploy and manage the business infrastructure, including organizational resources and information systems and technologies. To develop this level of understanding and to reduce the level of complexity, it is helpful or even necessary to represent the enterprise with *business models*.

What Is a Business Model?

A business model is a visual, abstract representation of some aspect or component of a business. Business models are used to convey the properties and attributes of complex business systems in an easy-to-understand format. By representing a business system as a visual or graphical model, the amount of information that can be assimilated and communicated is multiplied, and the complexity of business analysis and management is significantly reduced.

The models clearly convey business requirements and context for initiatives such as information technology deployment, organizational design, outsourcing, and performance measurement and management.

A business model may show characteristics such as:

- Process inputs, outputs, and their dependencies
- Process interdependencies
- Information requirements
- Organizational assignments
- Technology assignments
- Performance measures

Examples of business models include organization charts, activity flow charts, workflow drawings, and process models. Dynamic models may simulate business operations in a virtual real-time representation.

How Is a Business Model Structured?

Effective business models are built by the business community, not by technologists building technical solutions. Properly built, these models are an extremely valuable IT tool, but they must be useable, reusable, consistent, and understandable at all levels of the business. They must be business-friendly first, in order to be useful to the IT community.

Business models require the structure of architecture. Architecture defines the rules, standards, and principles through which the fundamental elements of the business system are defined. Once defined, these elements become the building blocks for models used to analyze or redesign the business systems in a given enterprise. They provide a consistent, structured foundation upon which analyses can be based. This foundation provides a common language to discuss the business.

A business architecture provides the ability to understand which tools and methods are required for particular areas of the business and to incorporate, manage, and measure their results within the business system as a whole.

Business architecture is essential when implementing comprehensive strategic applications. It is particularly valuable for measuring the effects that apparently minor changes in one part of the business will have on the entire enterprise. Once completed, the architecture can be applied to a variety of business programs.

To attain the maximum benefit, a completed architecture should be incorporated into the fundamental and strategic activities of a business. It should provide a basis for developing business plans, analyzing productivity, developing information systems, and organizing human resources. The resulting models can be continually analyzed and evolved without rebuilding the fundamental structure. A business architecture is, in essence, a blueprint of the business system.

TLN Business Consulting Ltd.'s Business Architecture Methodology (also known as BAM!) is a business modeling and analysis approach that is based on the principles of business architecture. It is effectively applied to enable such initiatives as process performance measurement and management, process improvement, organizational design, and information systems design and deployment. The Business Architecture Methodology delivers:

- Business process models that clearly describe the business objects, workflow, and the inter- and intradependencies among the objects
- Hand-off and process performance criteria and a measurement framework
- Business improvement opportunities and change recommendations
- Engaged employees with a shared view of the business

The BAM! approach emphasizes these key elements:

- Object orientation
- Functional modeling
- Event modeling
- Business system analysis

Object Orientation

When evaluating and building models of a business system, there is typically a large quantity of data available about its processes, organizations, and systems. It is easy to become overwhelmed by the volume and complexity of this data and thus be unable to construct logical, integrated assessments.

By narrowing the focus from the broad abstractions of processes, organizations, and systems to a limited number of concrete objects, an object-oriented business model manages the volume and complexity of the information without losing sight of the real-world business.

Object orientation is the application of a set of rule-based principles. When applied to a business architecture, the objects are the structural elements of the business.

TLN's Business Architecture Methodology defines five fundamental business objects:

1. **Business functions.** The activities fundamental to the defined enterprise

2. **Products.** The direct results of executing the business functions

3. **Resources.** The input required to build the products for business functions

4. **Customers.** The business function(s), which are by design the recipients of the products, both internal and external to the defined enterprise

5. **Suppliers.** The business function(s), which are "by design" the builders of the resources, both internal and external to the defined enterprise

By understanding these objects and their attributes and relationships, you can collect and evaluate a large volume of data about the business without becoming lost in its complexity.

This approach also facilitates rapid business requirement development in that it provides a structure within which all available data and information about the enterprise can be easily classified. Traditionally, either the amount of information collected is limited, or the scope of the effort is narrowed to facilitate meeting deadlines, or the model builder collects so much data that the task becomes insurmountable, causing missed deadlines and the potential to lose or overlook critical information.

Functional Modeling

Typically, in an effort to describe an enterprise, a business model is focused on an organization, a department, or a work group and its specific processes. Although it is extremely valuable to model and understand these views, it is much more effective to first describe and understand the business in terms of its functions.

In the Business Architecture Methodology, business models provide the ability to view and analyze the functional structure of an enterprise apart from the operations and processes assigned to people and organizations. Organizational assignments are not fundamental. Businesses often change them while continuing to execute the same functions. Functions are what you do, organizations are who does it, and processes are how it is done.

Solutions based solely on existing organizations and processes assume that the business knows what it is producing; that its employees are being utilized appropriately; and that its processes are efficient. These assumptions often lead to the implementation of short-term solutions at best and the implementation of inappropriate solutions at worst.

By removing the organizational and process biases, the focus remains on the fundamental objectives of the modeled business. The subsequent application of the organizational and operating aspects of the enterprise allow for assessing the ability to execute the business functions, given the current organization and processes.

Event Modeling

Most process models illustrate the detailed steps in a process or the activities involved in production. They focus on the vehicles for executing the individual process steps and generally ignore the goal or deliverables of the process. This traditional approach can drive the model builder to focus on the detailed activities, and to implement changes that "optimize the pieces and suboptimize the whole."

An event model focuses on the architectural elements of the business, illustrating the sequenced delivery of products and the consumption of resources in the order in which they occur. An event model clearly distinguishes the process steps from the sequence of events that deliver a quality product. It clearly differentiates between the core business processes (those which directly affect and deliver quality product to the customer) and support business processes (those which are the infrastructure that enable the core processes).

An event model can depict the execution of a particular function or set of functions and their relationships within an enterprise. By modeling the execution of an entire enterprise, you can clearly understand how the changes in one part of the business affect the entire enterprise. This provides the ability to truly improve efficiency and productivity throughout the enterprise.

Business System Analysis

Traditionally, business analysis is a term that is used to describe any general review of a business or segment of that business. These analyses are generally developed in a backroom environment and are usually performed after the fact. While valuable, most business analyses are used by a limited audience and are not easily understood by the general population—the people who do the work who have the most impact on the successful execution of the business system.

The BAM! approach to business analysis is business system modeling. It looks at the enterprise as a total business system that is designed to produce distinct, defined results. It understands that organization, process, and technology are applied to a business system to achieve defined results. BAM! first establishes what the enterprise does and then assesses how it is executed or should be executed.

BAM! facilitates two specific classes of business system analysis: *dynamic analysis* and *subsequent analysis*.

Dynamic Analysis

Dynamic analysis produces real-time results throughout model building. Inevitably, throughout the model development, information will be discovered that either contradicts the current understanding of how the business operates, or points out inefficiencies in the current system. These discoveries can often be resolved quickly, resulting in immediate benefit to the customer.

As these discoveries are made, the BAM! team assesses the impact, validates the conclusion, develops a change plan, and assigns accountability for managing the change.

Dynamic analysis is especially effective when the goal of the BAM! is to apply information technology to the business system. Often information technology is applied to an inefficient business system. Automating a broken or poorly performing business process does not solve the problem, and in fact it can exacerbate the problem.

Solutions resulting from dynamic analysis, however, are often mismanaged. Because these solutions are implemented before the architecture is completed, they are forgotten when analyzing the results of the implementation. Additionally, they are often implemented without a clear understanding of how to measure their impact on the business system. As with any solution, it is essential that they be managed and measured for their impact on the business system and that the employees be credited with the solutions.

Subsequent Analysis

Subsequent analysis is the most common type of managed analysis. When performed effectively, subsequent analysis is used to address and resolve particular issues within the business system. As previously discussed, the completed Business Architecture Model is reusable. This feature provides the analyst with the structure by which goals and issues can be addressed in a sequenced, prioritized, and controlled manner. It also enables concurrent analysis in that more than one analysis effort can be initiated using the same fundamental structure.

BAM! facilitates most types of subsequent analysis. Some of the more frequently used analyses are:

Redundancy analysis. Focuses on identifying duplicate functions, products, and resources to determine whether the duplication is by design or merely historical. It enables the enterprise to implement efforts to improve the cost and efficiency of the operation.

Connectivity analysis. Examines the relationships between suppliers and customers among business functions to determine who gets what from whom and why. It identifies dependencies and interdependencies and where breakdowns have occurred. It enables the enterprise to resolve supplier quality issues and hand-off issues, and facilitates the development of service level agreements both internal and external to the modeled business functions.

Process analysis. Examines how something gets done within the enterprise. It defines the goals and deliverables of the process and the process performance criteria. It enables the enterprise to clearly differentiate between process and product quality issues, to set and measure process performance targets, and to implement meaningful changes in productivity.

Organizational analysis. Examines the way that the enterprise has applied human resources and business structure. It illustrates how the enterprise has organized to execute the business functions and defines the responsibility and accountability for performance. It enables the enterprise to effectively allocate resources and expertise and to understand the implications of organizational change.

Technology analysis. Examines both the way that the existing information technology supports the business system and the potential application of information technology to enhance enterprise performance. It enables the enterprise to assess the effectiveness of currently implemented information technology, when and where new information technology can be effectively applied, and when and where information technology *cannot* be effectively applied.

The types of analyses you perform depend on the goals of your business initiative.

Important to the successful application of any consulting or management effort are the tools. TLN's Enterprise Modeling Tool (EMT!) is used in conjunction with the Business Architecture Methodology to develop business models and manage the large amount of associated data. EMT! can be used to interface to other modeling tools, including those associated with information systems and application development.

Building Business Models

The Business Architecture Methodology defines several fundamental modeling components:

- Functional diagram
- Functional model
- Operating model
- Connectivity model

- Event model
- Measurement model

These models are generally developed in the sequence indicated and are tightly integrated to maintain integrity during model evolution.

The Business Functions

A *business function* is a set of business activities performed in support of a strategy designed to accomplish the objectives of the business. It is important to understand that a business function is different from an organizational title. For example, an organizational title can be "Information Systems," while the business function may be defined as "Build Systems" or "Design Systems." A business function is also different from a process. A process is *how* the function is executed.

In a BAM! workshop setting, the business functions are defined by first brainstorming all activities (verb-noun pair) performed within the scope of the modeled enterprise, then grouping the activities by appropriate affinities, and finally assigning each group a name (meta-activity) along with a brief definition.

The function names and definitions are then entered into EMT! and form the foundational function tree. An acronym and a color assignment are automatically generated for later reference.

EMT! presents a Windows standard look and feel to the business manager or systems analyst who is the typical user of the software (Figure 15.1).

Building the Functional Diagram

Once the business activities have been classified, producing the high-level business functions (*what* the business does), we need to understand *how* the business operates. The functional diagram is the high-level business process model that establishes the context for further model development.

The functional diagram presents the defined core business functions as a critical path through the modeled enterprise, and a set of support functions that enable the core functions. The functional diagram is documented in EMT! An example of a specific function definition is shown in Figure 15.2.

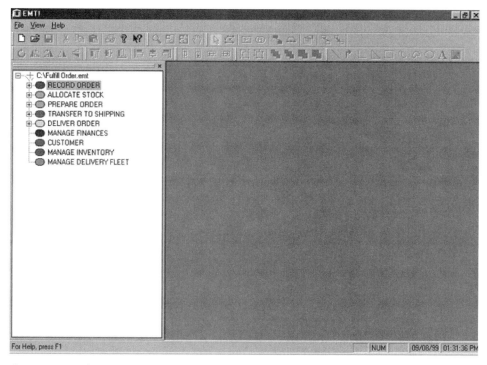

Figure 15.1   The Enterprise Modeling Tool interface.

In the workshop, the participants build one or more views of the sequence of functions, and then reconvene to negotiate and build one view.

The functional diagram establishes a context for the balance of the modeling effort. It will generally evolve as the remaining modeling activities bring additional information and understanding of the business.

Functional Model

The functional model builds upon the functional diagram by defining the products and resources for each business function.

A *product* is a deliverable or a result of a business function. For example, a product can be a plan, a trained employee, a system, or a report. A function must have at least one product. A function with no product would be operating with no planned result.

Working in teams, one function at a time, participants identify the products that are produced when performing the function. Participants write

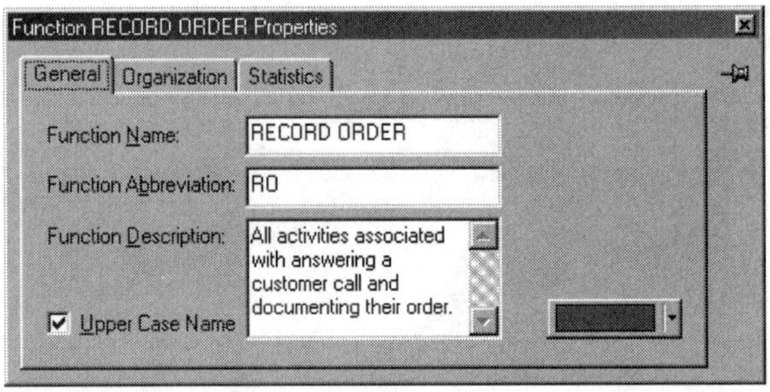

Figure 15.2 A business function defined.

a brief definition for each product, and then validate that for each activity there is at least one product identified.

When the products have been identified for all functions, this step is repeated for each function's resources. A *resource* is a deliverable required to execute the business function. A product of one function is generally the resource to another function. A function must have at least one resource. A function with no resource would be producing something from nothing.

As shown in Figure 15.3, as the products and resources for each function are identified and defined, they are entered into EMT!

The functional model and functional diagram are used by, and will evolve with, subsequent modeling efforts. The list of products and resources shown in Figure 15.4 was generated in a few minutes. A full listing for an enterprise will take considerably longer.

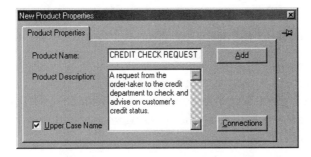

Figure 15.3 A product is produced by every function.

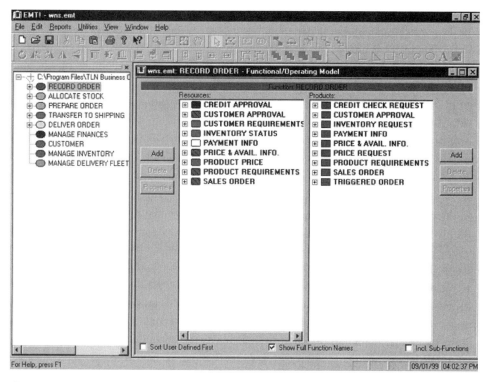

Figure 15.4 EMT! models the business by defining all functions and products.

Operating Model

There are types of cross-functional relationships that become key to determining business actions in the operations of the enterprise. The ability to clearly demonstrate and assess the connectivity within an enterprise provides a valuable view of the critical relationships in the enterprise. The operating model defines the connectivity of the business functions represented in the functional component.

To build the operating model you determine the customers for each product and the suppliers of each resource for each business function. Next, you connect the business functions based on these relationships. Every product must have at least one customer, and every resource must have at least one supplier.

A *customer* is a recipient of the product. The customer is another function internal or external to the modeled enterprise that has defined the specific product as a required resource, or that has been defined as a potential recipient of the product by the producing function. Every product produced within the modeled enterprise must have a customer (otherwise why is it produced?).

Each product has up to three destinations:

- It can be a resource to another business function within the enterprise.
- It can be a resource to the producing business function itself.
- It can be produced for consumption external to the modeled enterprise.

A product can simultaneously serve more than one customer from any of the three destinations.

Similarly, every resource in the enterprise must have a supplier. A *supplier* is the provider of the resource. The supplier is a function internal or external to the modeled enterprise that has defined the specific resource as a product to the requesting function or has been defined by the requesting function as a probable source. A resource to a business function without a supplier indicates a need with no supply.

As the customers and suppliers are identified for each function, they are entered into EMT!

Figure 15.5 shows customers and suppliers for a single process.

Connectivity Model

When a customer is defined for a particular product, there is an implication that the particular product is required as a resource by the customer. To ensure that the model is accurate, it is necessary to test that all of these implied products and resources are in fact valid. The EMT! software facilitates this validation by placing computer-generated products (and resources) in the implied supplier's (and customer's) functional model.

Figure 15.6 shows the entry screen to link products and resources to customers and suppliers.

If a computer-generated product (or resource) is a duplicate of a people-generated one, then they are combined and validated. If the computer-generated product (or resource) does not have a matching people-generated product (or resource), then one of the following scenarios exists:

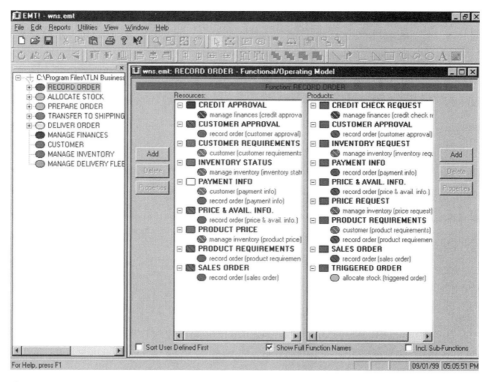

Figure 15.5 Customer and suppliers are captured in EMT!

- The product (or resource) is not actually produced (required).
- The product (or resource) is produced (required), but was just missed when creating the functional model.
- The product (or resource) is produced (required), and it already exists in the model, but the name is different.

To complete the model, these disconnects and discrepancies must be resolved through negotiation and modeling. When completed, the connectivity model is a validated and rationalized operating model.

In EMT!, the connectivity model is simply a completed and validated operating model.

Event Model

The event model (Figure 15.7) defines the high-level processes and events that are or should be executed to deliver the products that are

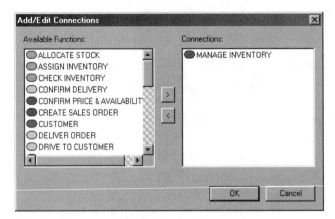

Figure 15.6 EMT! connects function customers and suppliers.

critical to the success of the enterprise. The event model establishes a framework to develop measurement criteria and measure process performance, assess opportunities for process improvement, assess the impact of new business scenarios, and design information systems and organizational structures.

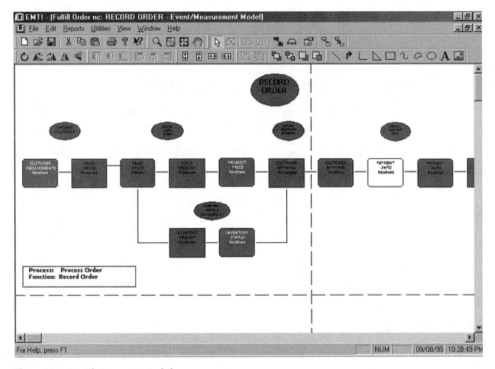

Figure 15.7 The event model.

The event component is developed by selecting one business function at a time and determining the most critical product/resource combination required for the function's success. You then determine the actual sequence of resource consumption and product production that occurs in the delivery of the critical product.

You build the event model (like the one shown in Figure 15.7) by sequencing the products and resources as they relate to each other and in the order that they occur. Conversions between products and resources illustrate the subfunctions of the business function. By using the products and resources defined in the functional component to build this model, the processes are based on the critical elements of your business.

Once you determine a high-level process view of each function, you integrate these views to create a high-level end-to-end process view of the modeled enterprise.

Measurement Model

The measurement model is an extremely effective tool for business performance management.

Once the event model has been completed, the measurement model is developed. Using the event model as a base, a set of process performance criteria is developed to enable the measurement of the execution of the business processes.

The performance criteria should address:

Cycle time. Elapsed time and actual time.

Volume. Units into the process, units out of the process.

People. Involved in the process, affected by the process.

Quality. Conformance to spec, consistency.

Cost. Operational cost, people cost.

What you collect will vary based on business requirements and initiative goals. At a minimum you should collect the cycle time measurement points from both internal and customer perspectives.

The measurement model can be integrated with any business measurement environment to provide a comprehensive dashboard of process and product performance and quality. The measurement model is also very effective as a foundation for service level management. A sample measurement model is shown in Figure 15.8.

Applying Business Models to IT Requirements

In a general sense, the primary role of information systems is to gather, store, move, and present accurate data in a timely, useable manner. The BAM! models we have built thus far are in effect an information catalogue and information workflow. These models are easily applied in any systems development environment and translated into the appropriate information system design models.

The attributes of the information objects and processes define the fundamental requirements of the information systems. These attributes are negotiated by the producer and consumer (supplier and customer), and added to the business models as shown in Figure 15.9.

By linking the technical models to the business models, changes in either environment can be assessed for impact and incorporated into all levels of modeling. Figure 15.10 shows a completed operating model.

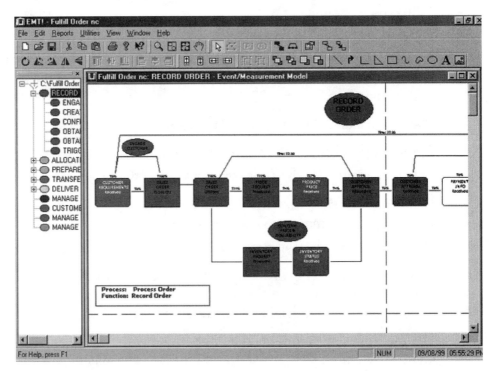

Figure 15.8 The event/measurement model.

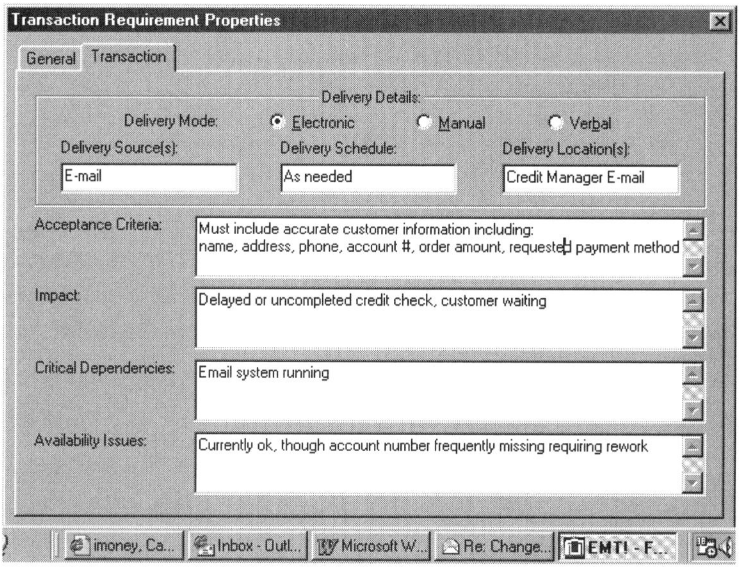

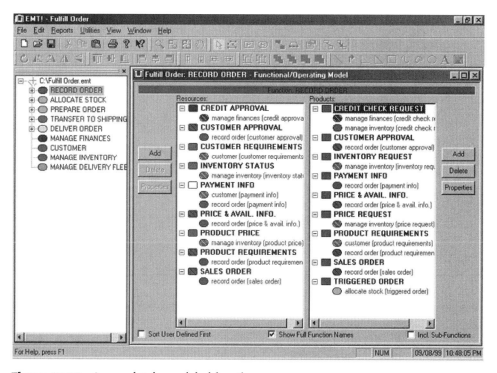

Figure 15.9 Defining specific functional requirements.

Figure 15.10 A completely modeled function.

Summary

The outcome of meeting with Jack and his partner Jane was that I became convinced that this tool and technique represents the clearest way to get input and buy-in from business managers that I have ever seen. Just in case I haven't been clear about this, Jane is the driving force behind EMT! as well as of its underlying methodology; and no, partner in this case isn't shorthand for anything, in this case partner means strictly business partner.

After evaluating EMT! I met with some folks at Metex systems in Toronto, home of the Blue Jays, the Raptors, and those beloved losers, the Maple Leafs. Regardless of the sports teams' performance, the software community there has been delivering solid Big Blue Java stuff in the form of VisualAge for Java and DB2 for some time now. Metex is an IBM and Rational Rose business partner that markets SF Bridge, an San-Francisco code generator that plugs into Rose.

From the business models generated in EMT!, you can create Rose models that in turn generate the SanFrancisco code you need to support the business with a Java application using that framework.

The central value of EMT! is that you can not only use it to validate your business requirements but can get the business manager to keep the updates in EMT! and roll these over to SanFrancisco and Rose, without having to rekey data or otherwise rely on manual synchronization techniques.

CHAPTER 16

SF Code Generation with SF Bridge

The SanFrancisco development community has been small, but growing and definitely capable. One of the first products on the market for San-Francisco was SF Bridge, a code generator that offered key advantages over the product that ships with SanFrancisco.

In my discussions with IBM and other SanFrancisco partners, I quickly saw that my friends at Metex, who are supporting SF Bridge, were offering a piece of software that could cut down redevelopment time. Since writing code is rewriting code, anything that makes managing migration easier is a must-have tool from my point of view.

After meeting with Jack Ladick, who offers the Enterprise Modeling Tool, we started talking with Metex about an integration process for taking business requirements, through the process model, and the subsequent translation to Rose models. As an established Rose partner, as well as offering SanFrancisco support, we will be able to tie EMT! into SF by way of Rose and the bridge code generator.

To give you a better idea of how this works, I asked Metex to chip in with a detailed description of its bridge product and how it works.

SF Bridge

The IBM SanFrancisco initiative has established a tools strategy to address the complexities of framework development. These complexities include repetitive coding tasks, the need for a consistent coding style, and an overall compliance with the framework implementation. To address these complexities, the principles of this strategy include an evolutionary approach to cross-tool and tool provider integration; the ability to address the needs of multiple development audiences, and the existence of multiple development scenarios. SF Bridge from Metex Systems Inc. implements the principles of this strategy with its integrated set of tools for SF application development. SF Bridge enables application and framework developers to extend the existing SF framework in conjunction with tools for visual modeling and Java development.

Composed of several tools, SF Bridge assists SanFrancisco developers with new development, or migration of existing IBM SF code generator–based models to Rose SF Bridge–based models. These tools include SF Code Generation Wizard, SF Modeling Wizard, and the SF Model Upgrade Tool.

The Rose SF Bridge is designed to work with the Rational Rose Visual Modeling Tool to increase effective development documentation, and to decrease development time for faster application deployment. Rational Rose, the industry's leading visual modeling tool, allows developers to define and communicate a software architecture, resulting in: accelerated development, by improved communication among various team members; improved quality, by mapping business processes to software architecture; and increased visibility and predictability, by making critical design decisions explicit visually. As well, SF Bridge currently offers developers support for both IBM's VisualAge for Java and Inprise's J-Builder. SF Bridge is currently available for SanFrancisco 1.2, 1.3, and 1.4, and Metex Systems will continue to deploy updates to the code generation rules of SF Bridge as the SanFrancisco project develops.

What Is Rose SF Bridge?

To be able to quickly understand and utilize the SanFrancisco framework, it is essential that a component-based visual modeling tool be used. Rose SF Bridge, the integrated tool kit for SanFrancisco development, intelligently bridges SanFrancisco's application framework with modeling and Java development tools by utilizing the industry standard Unified Modeling Language (UML).

Using the Rose SF Bridge greatly simplifies the SanFrancisco-based development process. The Rose SF Bridge assists the developer in overcoming the complexities of object-oriented development through a series of wizards, builders, and intelligent design and code generation rules aimed at simplifying SanFrancisco-based development.

How Does Rose SF Bridge Work?

To provide modeling, analysis, and design capabilities, the Rose SF Bridge is seamlessly integrated with Rational Rose via standard tool extensibility mechanisms, as well as with both IBM's VisualAge for Java and JBuilder, Inprise's RAD tool for building 100 percent pure Java applications. The Rose SF Bridge allows the developer to interact with a UML representation of the SanFrancisco framework and utilizes an internal rules engine that supports numerous design and code patterns specific to the SanFrancisco programming model. The Rose SF Bridge rules engine leverages these patterns to rapidly create and extend components that work within the SanFrancisco frameworks by generating implementation code based on a high-level design model.

SF Bridge enhances the features of the existing IBM SF code generator by providing a tighter integration to Rational Rose, improving the SF development workflow. In addition, the SF Bridge code generator is capable of performing merge-free code generation, which allows iterative development as design changes can be made in the Rose model and propagated to existing source code without loss of existing method bodies.

The SF Modeling Wizard

SF Bridge utilizes the visual modeling metaphor by using Rational Rose and the UML to capture semantic information about classes used and extended within the SanFrancisco framework. The modeling wizard component encourages SF-compliant design and automates the setting of Rose SF code generation properties used to customize code generation. In total, there are three workflows of the modeling wizard, including creating a new SF-compliant class, extending or modifying an existing class, and creating an aggregation (relationship) between two existing classes.

The dialogs of the wizard will vary, based on the chosen workflow. The result of stepping through the wizard dialogs is to create model elements with appropriate code generation property settings that are then used in the code generation activity. The modeling wizard provides an avenue to learn SF-compliant modeling techniques and automates the interaction a designer has with the visual modeling tool.

As an example, let's look at the new class creation workflow. In this case, the wizard is launched without an existing class selected in Rose. The class type selection screen is displayed in Figure 16.1.

You are then prompted to select one of the basic SanFrancisco object types from which to derive:

- Entity class
- Dependent class
- Command class
- Controller class

In this example, Create Entity Subclass is selected, and the Next button is pressed to advance to the class declaration screen. This is shown in Figure 16.2.

Here, properties common to all SanFrancisco object types are entered, including:

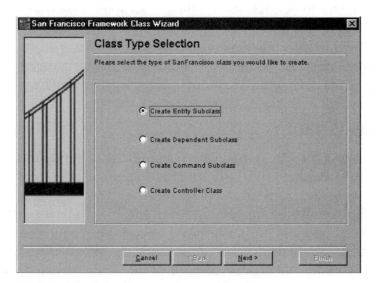

Figure 16.1   Creating a new class in SF Bridge.

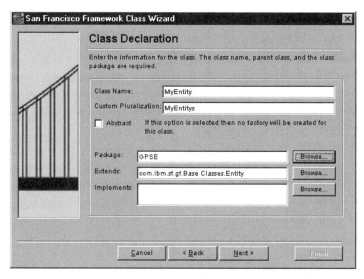

Figure 16.2 Each class is named with pluralization and package defined.

Class name. The name for the new class.

Custom pluralization. The custom pluralization for the class. The default plural form (class name + "s") will be filled in automatically. If the class has a nonstandard plural (e.g., company → companies), the plural can be entered here.

Package. The package to which the class will belong. The user can type in, or select a package via the Browse button.

Extends. The class that the new class extends. The property field will be automatically filled in with the name of the selected object type. Depending on the selected object type, the model browser—which can be used to browse for the class to be extended by selecting the Browse button—will be "fitted" with a filter to browse only classes that extend directly or indirectly from the selected object type. This allows the user to extend indirectly from the selected object type.

Implements. Any interfaces that will be implemented. The user can type in, or select via the Browse button, the interfaces that the class will implement.

Once these properties have been set, the Next button is pressed to proceed to the next screen (see Figure 16.3), which contains type-specific information. These type-specific properties vary, depending on the base SanFrancisco class originally chosen.

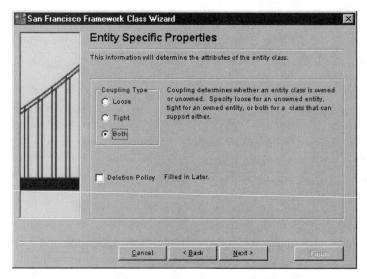

Figure 16.3 Properties specific to SF Entity classes.

Entity-Specific Properties:

- The coupling for the class (Tight, Loose, Both). The coupling determines whether an Entity class is owned or unowned. Specify Tight for owned, Loose for unowned, and Both for a class that will support either.
- The Deletion Policy flag

Dependent-Specific Properties

There are no type-specific properties associated with the Dependent class type. If the user is creating/modifying a class derived directly or indirectly from the Dependent class, there will be no type-specific screen presented in the wizard. Instead, the user will be immediately presented with the SanFrancisco documentation screen.

Command-Specific Properties

The user is prompted to set the Return Command flag for the class.

Controller-Specific Properties

The user is prompted to enter:

- The Owning Company
- The ControllerType (Simple, Aggregating)
- The IsDynamicIdentifier flag

Once these type-specific properties are set, the SanFrancisco documentation dialog is displayed as shown in Figure 16.4. Values are entered for:

- The version number
- Purpose
- Pre- and post-conditions
- Comments

After pressing Next, the wizard advances to the Summary screen (Figure 16.5), which shows all properties—generic and type-specific—for review prior to class creation.

After reviewing the summary, if you need to make changes to the classes, press the Back button, otherwise the Finish button completes creation of the class and returns you to the Rose model. As a result of the execution of the wizard a new class is created, and code generation properties are set as shown in Figure 16.6.

The Code Generation Wizard

SF Bridge code generation is based on the techniques of traditional language code generators; however, these techniques of mapping a

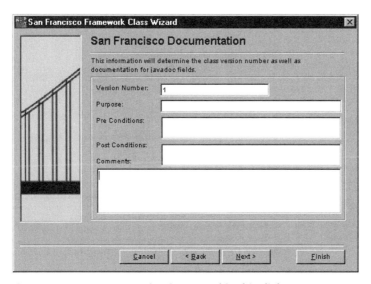

Figure 16.4 Documentation is entered in this dialog.

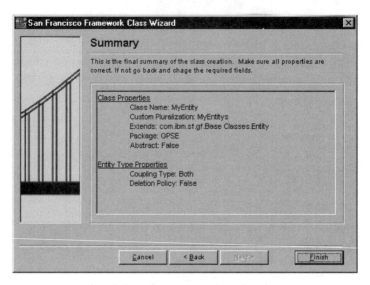

Figure 16.5 This dialog summarizes class details.

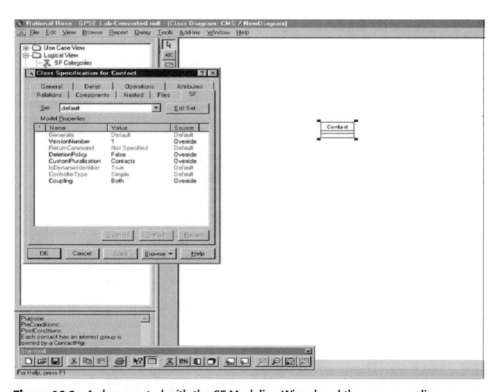

Figure 16.6 A class created with the SF Modeling Wizard and the corresponding properties in the class specification.

modeling notation to the object model of the target language have been enhanced to include flexible rule sets and well-known design patterns as present in the SF framework. Rational Rose and the UML are used to capture semantic information about classes used and extended within the SanFrancisco framework. Using this information, Rose SF Bridge executes a series of rules derived from the SanFrancisco programming model to generate implementation code specific to the foundation layer of the framework. This code generation shields the complexity of the framework and generates a significant amount of implementation code that allows the application to tie in to the foundation layer of the framework. Once a design has been prepared for code generation, through model structuring and the customizing of code generation properties, the Code Generation Wizard may then be invoked.

As an example, code for the DeliveryType class will be generated. As the DeliveryType class is an entity, the SanFrancisco programming model dictates that the Abstract Factory design pattern will be applied to the

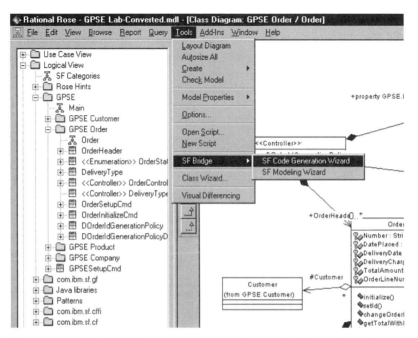

Figure 16.7 The SF Bridge code generator is launched from the tools menu of Rational Rose.

three classes in the implementation model. The following classes are the components of the Abstract Factory pattern:

Note: *Specification class* refers to the class to be generated from the specification model to the implementation model.

Interface class. Java interface retaining the name of the specification class and extending its superclass' Interface class.

Implementation class. Java class with the suffix "Impl" appended to the specification class name implementing the Interface class above and extending its superclass Implementation class.

The following mandatory operations are declared on the Implementation class:

- toString
- destroy
- internalizeFromStream
- externalizeToStream

Factory class. Java class with the suffix Factory appended to the BusinessObject Class name.

Next, creation and initialization logic is added to the Abstract Factory pattern classes above. One or more initialize methods on the Interface class and create methods on the Factory class are created for each initialize operation present on the specification class. The following is done to each of the created classes.

Interface Class

One or more initialize operations are created for each initialize operation present on the specification class. If Loose coupling is selected on the specification class, the parameters to the initialize method on the Interface class will match those found on the initialize or create method on the specification class. If the coupling property on the specification class is set to either Tight or Both, the first parameter on the specification initialize or create method is expected to be the owning class for the tight-coupling case. If the coupling property is set to Both, two initialize methods will be created on the Interface class for each initialize method present on the specification class.

Implementation Class

The following operations are declared:

- An empty constructor
- Uninitialize
- Update

Factory Class

If the Factory class exists, static create operations are declared for every initialize operation on the specification class. If Loose coupling is selected on the specification class, one static create operation is declared. If Tight coupling is selected, two static create operations are declared. If Both coupling is selected, all three static create operations are declared.

In addition, if tight coupling is selected, an abstract special factory operation is declared for every initialize operation on the specification class.

Figure 16.8 shows the code generation wizard with the Rose Model to Java Source configuration selected (red check mark) as active. Configurations are a way to group together execution pipelines of components within SF Bridge. For example, generating Java implementations to Java source code files requires a different set of target components then generating Java classes to the VisualAge for Java repository. Once a configuration has been set as active, the first step of code generation is to select the model elements to generate and click Apply in the tree view of the Master component in the Configure Components dialog.

Next, the target connection (i.e., base path directory) is set in the Connection tab as shown in Figure 16.9 and once again, Apply is pressed.

Now that the you have set the compulsory options, the Next button may be pressed to advance to the Step 2 dialog where the generation is executed and monitored.

As shown in Figure 16.10, the Master and Target models are set as the current Rose model selection and the Java Source Selection of C:\Source Code respectively. The Compare is now pressed to begin the process of exporting the Rose model selection, interprcting its code generation properties, applying SanFrancisco programming conventions, and exporting it to the Java source code format. Then, the existing source code (if any) is imported from the target directory, and a preliminary merge analysis takes place, from which a set of differences are identified and merge actions are proposed. Figure 16.11 shows this step of the code generation process.

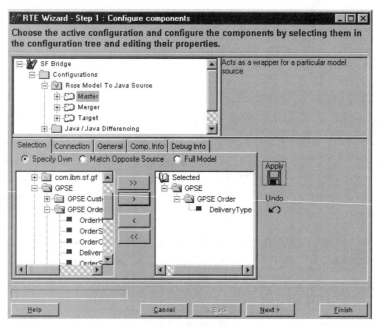

Figure 16.8 A class is selected for generation.

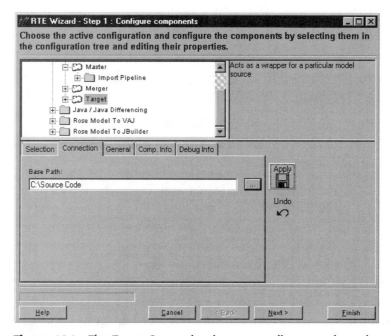

Figure 16.9 The Target Connection is set to a directory where the implementation source will reside.

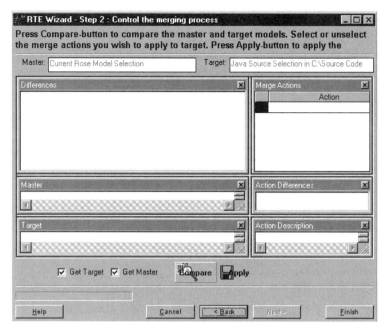

Figure 16.10 This dialog will compare the source and target models and report differences.

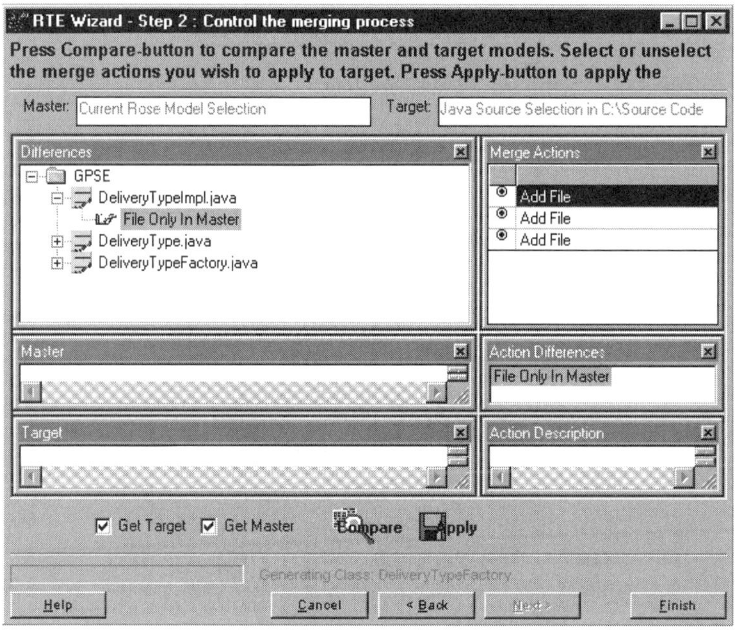

Figure 16.11 The differences are highlighted on the left and the proposed merge actions are displayed on the right.

Here we see that the generated files do not exist in the target model and hence the proposed merge actions are to Add the files. To complete these actions, Apply is pressed, resulting in the application of the merge actions as shown in Figure 16.12.

Following is a listing of the code that is generated from this activity. Notice that three classes have been generated: one for the interface, once for the implementation, and one for the creation called the *Factory*. Also, notice that actual method bodies are generated, and not just method signatures or skeletons. There is still some code required to complete details of business logic that extend the framework; however, a significant savings of implementation effort is achieved using the code generator.

Java source code listing for DeliveryType:

```
DeliveryType.java

package GPSE;

import com.ibm.sf.gf.*;
import com.ibm.sf.cf.*;
```

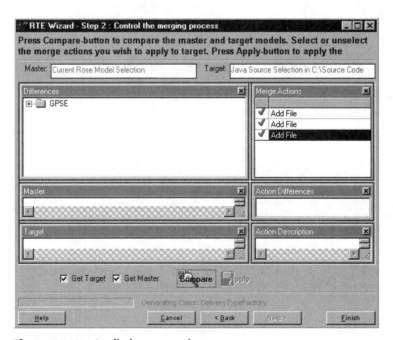

Figure 16.12 Applied merge actions.

```java
/**
 * <TT>
 * <BR><B>Purpose:</B>
 * <BR><B>Description:</B>
 * <BR><B>Note:</B>  This documentation has been automatically
 * generated.
 * </TT>
 * @version 1.3.4
 * @since JDK1.0
 */
public interface DeliveryType extends DescribableDynamicEntity {
    /**
     * The fully qualified name of this Interface class
     *
     * Note: This documentation has been automatically generated.
     */
    public static final String INTERFACE_NAME= "GPSE.DeliveryType";
    /**
     * Gets the attribute
     *
     * <BR><B>Assumptions:</B>
     * <BR><B>Note:</B>  This documentation has been automatically
     * generated.
     * @return DCurrencyValue
     * @exception com.ibm.sf.gf.SFException
     * <BR><B>Result:</B>
     * <BR><B>PreConditions:</B>
     * <BR><B>PostConditions:</B>
     */
    public DCurrencyValue getFlatRate() throws
com.ibm.sf.gf.SFException;
    /**
     * Sets the attribute
     *
     * <BR><B>Assumptions:</B>
     * <BR><B>Note:</B>  This documentation has been automatically
     * generated.
     * @param DCurrencyValue newFlatRate <I>(Mandatory)</I>
     * @return void
     * @exception com.ibm.sf.gf.SFException
     * <BR><B>Result:</B>
     * <BR><B>PreConditions:</B>
     * <BR><B>PostConditions:</B>
     */
    public void setFlatRate(DCurrencyValue newFlatRate) throws
com.ibm.sf.gf.SFException;
    /**
     * Gets the attribute directly
     *
     * <BR><B>Assumptions:</B>
     * <BR><B>Note:</B>  This documentation has been automatically
```

```
     * generated.
     * @return DCurrencyValue
     * @exception com.ibm.sf.gf.SFException
     * <BR><B>Result:</B>
     * <BR><B>PreConditions:</B>
     * <BR><B>PostConditions:</B>
     * <BR><B>RESTRICTED</B> : This method is NOT for client use
     */
    public DCurrencyValue getFlatRateForRestrictedUse() throws
com.ibm.sf.gf.SFException;
    /**
     * Gets the attribute
     *
     * <BR><B>Assumptions:</B>
     * <BR><B>Note:</B>  This documentation has been automatically
     * generated.
     * @return int
     * @exception com.ibm.sf.gf.SFException
     * <BR><B>Result:</B>
     * <BR><B>PreConditions:</B>
     * <BR><B>PostConditions:</B>
     */
    public int getNumberOfDays() throws com.ibm.sf.gf.SFException;
    /**
     * Sets the attribute
     *
     * <BR><B>Assumptions:</B>
     * <BR><B>Note:</B>  This documentation has been automatically
     * generated.
     * @param int newNumberOfDays <I>(Mandatory)</I>
     * @return void
     * @exception com.ibm.sf.gf.SFException
     * <BR><B>Result:</B>
     * <BR><B>PreConditions:</B>
     * <BR><B>PostConditions:</B>
     */
    public void setNumberOfDays(int newNumberOfDays) throws
com.ibm.sf.gf.SFException;
    /**
     * Gets the attribute
     *
     * <BR><B>Assumptions:</B>
     * <BR><B>Note:</B>  This documentation has been automatically
     * generated.
     * @return boolean
     * @exception com.ibm.sf.gf.SFException
     * <BR><B>Result:</B>
     * <BR><B>PreConditions:</B>
     * <BR><B>PostConditions:</B>
     */
    public boolean getExpedite() throws com.ibm.sf.gf.SFException;
```

```java
    /**
     * Sets the attribute
     *
     * <BR><B>Assumptions:</B>
     * <BR><B>Note:</B>  This documentation has been automatically
     * generated.
     * @param boolean newExpedite <I>(Mandatory)</I>
     * @return void
     * @exception com.ibm.sf.gf.SFException
     * <BR><B>Result:</B>
     * <BR><B>PreConditions:</B>
     * <BR><B>PostConditions:</B>
     */
    public void setExpedite(boolean newExpedite) throws
com.ibm.sf.gf.SFException;
    /**
     *
     * <BR><B>Assumptions:</B>
     * <BR><B>Note:</B>
     * @param DeliveryTypeController owner <I>(Mandatory)</I>
     * @param DescriptiveInformation description <I>(Mandatory)</I>
     * @param DCurrencyValue initFlatRate <I>(Mandatory)</I>
     * @param int initNumberOfDays <I>(Mandatory)</I>
     * @return void
     * @exception com.ibm.sf.gf.SFException
     * <BR><B>Result:</B>
     * <BR><B>PreConditions:</B>
     * <BR><B>PostConditions:</B>
     * <BR><B>RESTRICTED</B> : This method is NOT for client use
     */
    public void initialize(DeliveryTypeController owner,
DescriptiveInformation description, DCurrencyValue initFlatRate, int
initNumberOfDays) throws com.ibm.sf.gf.SFException;
    /**
     *
     * <BR><B>Assumptions:</B>
     * <BR><B>Note:</B>
     * @param DTime placeDate <I>(Mandatory)</I>
     * @return DTime
     * <BR><B>Result:</B>
     * <BR><B>PreConditions:</B>
     * <BR><B>PostConditions:</B>
     */
    public DTime calculateDeliveryDate(DTime placeDate);
}
DeliveryTypeImpl.java

package GPSE;
import com.ibm.sf.gf.*;
import com.ibm.sf.cf.*;

/**
```

```
 * <TT>
 * <BR><B>Purpose:</B>
 * <BR><B>Description:</B>
 * <BR><B>Note:</B>  This documentation has been automatically
 * generated.
 * </TT>
 * @version 1.3.4
 * @since JDK1.0
 */
public class DeliveryTypeImpl extends DescribableDynamicEntityImpl
implements DeliveryType, Distinguishable {
    /**
     * The version number of this class
     *
     * Note: This documentation has been automatically generated.
     */
    static final int versionNumber= 1;
    /**
     * The fully qualified name of this Implementation class
     *
     * Note: This documentation has been automatically generated.
     */
    public static final String IMPLEMENTATION_NAME=
"GPSE.DeliveryTypeImpl";
    protected DCurrencyValue ivFlatRate;
    protected int ivNumberOfDays;
    protected boolean ivExpedite;
    /**
     * Gets the attribute
     *
     * <BR><B>Assumptions:</B>
     * <BR><B>Note:</B>  This documentation has been automatically
     * generated.
     * @return DCurrencyValue
     * @exception com.ibm.sf.gf.SFException
     * <BR><B>Result:</B>
     * <BR><B>PreConditions:</B>
     * <BR><B>PostConditions:</B>
     */
    public DCurrencyValue getFlatRate() throws com.ibm.sf.gf.SFException{
        return (DCurrencyValue) Global.factory().copyDependent(null,
ivFlatRate);
    }
    /**
     * Sets the attribute
     *
     * <BR><B>Assumptions:</B>
     * <BR><B>Note:</B>  This documentation has been automatically
     * generated.
     * @param DCurrencyValue newFlatRate <I>(Mandatory)</I>
     * @return void
```

```
    * @exception com.ibm.sf.gf.SFException
    * <BR><B>Result:</B>
    * <BR><B>PreConditions:</B>
    * <BR><B>PostConditions:</B>
    */
   public void setFlatRate(DCurrencyValue newFlatRate) throws
com.ibm.sf.gf.SFException {
         setDirty();
         ivFlatRate = (DCurrencyValue)
Helper.setDependentToDependent(ivFlatRate, newFlatRate, this);
   }
   /**
    * Gets the attribute directly
    *
    * <BR><B>Assumptions:</B>
    * <BR><B>Note:</B>  This documentation has been automatically
    * generated.
    * @return DCurrencyValue
    * @exception com.ibm.sf.gf.SFException
    * <BR><B>Result:</B>
    * <BR><B>PreConditions:</B>
    * <BR><B>PostConditions:</B>
    * <BR><B>RESTRICTED</B> : This method is NOT for client use
    */
   public DCurrencyValue getFlatRateForRestrictedUse() throws
com.ibm.sf.gf.SFException {
         return (ivFlatRate);
   }
   /**
    * Gets the attribute
    *
    * <BR><B>Assumptions:</B>
    * <BR><B>Note:</B>  This documentation has been automatically
    * generated.
    * @return int
    * @exception com.ibm.sf.gf.SFException
    * <BR><B>Result:</B>
    * <BR><B>PreConditions:</B>
    * <BR><B>PostConditions:</B>
    */
   public int getNumberOfDays() throws com.ibm.sf.gf.SFException {
        return (ivNumberOfDays);
   }
   /**
    * Sets the attribute
    *
    * <BR><B>Assumptions:</B>
    * <BR><B>Note:</B>  This documentation has been automatically
    * generated.
    * @param int newNumberOfDays <I>(Mandatory)</I>
    * @return void
```

```
    * @exception com.ibm.sf.gf.SFException
    * <BR><B>Result:</B>
    * <BR><B>PreConditions:</B>
    * <BR><B>PostConditions:</B>
    */
   public void setNumberOfDays(int newNumberOfDays) throws
com.ibm.sf.gf.SFException {
        setDirty();
        ivNumberOfDays = newNumberOfDays;
   }
   /**
    * Gets the attribute
    *
    * <BR><B>Assumptions:</B>
    * <BR><B>Note:</B>  This documentation has been automatically
    * generated.
    * @return boolean
    * @exception com.ibm.sf.gf.SFException
    * <BR><B>Result:</B>
    * <BR><B>PreConditions:</B>
    * <BR><B>PostConditions:</B>
    */
   public boolean getExpedite() throws com.ibm.sf.gf.SFException {
        return (ivExpedite);
   }
   /**
    * Sets the attribute
    *
    * <BR><B>Assumptions:</B>
    * <BR><B>Note:</B>  This documentation has been automatically
    * generated.
    * @param boolean newExpedite <I>(Mandatory)</I>
    * @return void
    * @exception com.ibm.sf.gf.SFException
    * <BR><B>Result:</B>
    * <BR><B>PreConditions:</B>
    * <BR><B>PostConditions:</B>
    */
   public void setExpedite(boolean newExpedite) throws
com.ibm.sf.gf.SFException {
        setDirty();
        ivExpedite = newExpedite;
   }
   /**
    *
    * <BR><B>Assumptions:</B>
    * <BR><B>Note:</B>
    * @param DeliveryTypeController owner <I>(Mandatory)</I>
    * @param DescriptiveInformation description <I>(Mandatory)</I>
    * @param DCurrencyValue initFlatRate <I>(Mandatory)</I>
    * @param int initNumberOfDays <I>(Mandatory)</I>
```

```
      * @return void
      * @exception com.ibm.sf.gf.SFException
      * <BR><B>Result:</B>
      * <BR><B>PreConditions:</B>
      * <BR><B>PostConditions:</B>
      * <BR><B>RESTRICTED</B> : This method is NOT for client use
      */
     public void initialize(DeliveryTypeController owner,
DescriptiveInformation description, DCurrencyValue initFlatRate, int
initNumberOfDays) throws com.ibm.sf.gf.SFException {

          // NO MATCHING initialize METHOD
          // WAS FOUND IN THE PARENT CLASS
          // PLEASE UPDATE THE FOLLOWING
          // "super.initialize" CALL
          super.initialize(NO_MATCH_FOUND);

          BaseFactory factory = Global.factory();

          // Primitive types initialization
          ivNumberOfDays = initNumberOfDays;
          // No matching initialize parameter found for attribute
          // ivExpedite

          // Dependent initialization
          setFlatRate(initFlatRate);

          // No matching attribute was found for initialize parameter
          // owner
          // No matching attribute was found for initialize parameter
          // description
     }
     /**
      *
      * <BR><B>Assumptions:</B>
      * <BR><B>Note:</B>
      * @param DTime placeDate <I>(Mandatory)</I>
      * @return DTime
      * <BR><B>Result:</B>
      * <BR><B>PreConditions:</B>
      * <BR><B>PostConditions:</B>
      */
     public DTime calculateDeliveryDate(DTime placeDate) {
          // Please insert your code here
     }
     /**
      *
      * <BR><B>Assumptions:</B>
      * <BR><B>Note:</B>
      * @return String
      * <BR><B>Result:</B>  a String containing the Id of the
      * Distinguishable object
      *
```

```
 * #ValidationNotRequired
 * <BR><B>PreConditions:</B>  none
 * <BR><B>PostConditions:</B>  the object is not modified
 */
public String getId() {
    // Please insert your code here
}
/**
 * Retrieves the description of this object as a String
 * in a format/language determined by the locale that is currently
 * active in the environment this call was made in.
 *
 * <BR><B>Assumptions:</B>
 * <BR><B>Note:</B>
 * @return String
 * <BR><B>Result:</B>  language dependent description selected
 * using the active Locale. Returns "" if
 * this.getDescriptiveInformation()
 * == null or if a description cannot be found using the standard
 * lookup mechanism.
 * <BR><B>PreConditions:</B>
 * <BR><B>PostConditions:</B>  Object's state unmodified
 *
 * #index 1
 * #ValidationNotRequired
 */
public String getDescription() {
    // Please insert your code here
}
/**
 * Retrieves the description of this object as a String
 * in a format/language determined by the given Locale.
 *
 * <BR><B>Assumptions:</B>
 * <BR><B>Note:</B>
 * @param String locale determines which locale dependent
 * form of the description to retrieve <I>(Mandatory)</I>
 * @return String
 * <BR><B>Result:</B>  language dependent description of
 * object selected using the
 *                          given locale. Returns "" if
 * this.getDescriptiveInformation()
 * == null or if a description cannot be found using the standard
 * lookup mechanism.
 * <BR><B>PreConditions:</B>
 * <BR><B>PostConditions:</B>  Object's state unmodified
 *
 * #index 2
 * #ValidationNotRequired
 */
public String getDescription(String locale) {
```

```
            // Please insert your code here
    }
    /**
     * Retrieves the DescriptiveInformation object encapsulating
     * the locale sensitive description of this object.
     *
     * <BR><B>Assumptions:</B>
     * <BR><B>Note:</B>
     * @return DescriptiveInformation
     * <BR><B>Result:</B>  the DescriptiveInformation object
     * that represents the description of this Describable. Returns
     * null if this Describable has no DescriptiveInformation
     * attached to it.
     * <BR><B>PreConditions:</B>
     * <BR><B>PostConditions:</B>  Object's state unmodified
     *
     * #ValidationNotRequired
     */
    public DescriptiveInformation getDescriptiveInformation() {
          // Please insert your code here
    }
    /**
     * Returns a descriptive string for the object
     *
     * <BR><B>Assumptions:</B>
     * <BR><B>Note:</B>  This documentation has been automatically
     * generated.
     * @return String
     * @exception SFRuntimeException
     * <BR><B>Result:</B>
     * <BR><B>PreConditions:</B>
     * <BR><B>PostConditions:</B>
     */
    public String toString() throws SFRuntimeException {

          try {
                String retVal = super.toString();
                return (retVal);
          }
          catch (Exception ex) {
                throw (new SFRuntimeException(ex, new

     TextResource("MSG_RMTSFEXCEP_DEFAULT","com.ibm.sf.gf.resources
.SFExceptionResources",
                              (Object []) null, "Runtime Exception has
Occurred" )));
          }
    }
    /**
     * Constructor of this class
     *
     * <BR><B>Assumptions:</B>
```

```
       * <BR><B>Note:</B>  This documentation has been automatically
       * generated.
       * @return void
       * @exception com.ibm.sf.gf.SFException
       * <BR><B>Result:</B>
       * <BR><B>PreConditions:</B>
       * <BR><B>PostConditions:</B>
       */
      public void DeliveryTypeImpl() throws com.ibm.sf.gf.SFException {
           // Please insert your code here
      }
      /**
       * Reads the state of an object from a stream
       *
       * <BR><B>Assumptions:</B>
       * <BR><B>Note:</B>  This documentation has been automatically
       * generated.
       * @param BaseStream stream <I>(Mandatory)</I>
       * @return void
       * @exception java.io.IOException
       * <BR><B>Result:</B>
       * <BR><B>PreConditions:</B>
       * <BR><B>PostConditions:</B>
       */
      public void internalizeFromStream(BaseStream stream) throws
java.io.IOException {

              // Should we skip this internalization
              if (stream.skipThisClass(IMPLEMENTATION_NAME)) {
                   super.internalizeFromStream(stream);
                   return;
              }
              // internalize the version number
              int objectIntStreamVersion = stream.readInt();

              // read the primitive types
              ivNumberOfDays = stream.readInt();
              ivExpedite = stream.readBoolean();

              // read the DescribableDynamicEntityImpl's (parent of current
              // class) state
              super.internalizeFromStream(stream);

              // read the contained dependents
              ivFlatRate = (DCurrencyValue) stream.readDependent(this,
ivFlatRate);
      }
      /**
       * Writes the state of an object to a stream
       *
       * <BR><B>Assumptions:</B>
       * <BR><B>Note:</B>  This documentation has been automatically
```

```
      * generated.
      * @param BaseStream stream <I>(Mandatory)</I>
      * @return void
      * @exception java.io.IOException
      * <BR><B>Result:</B>
      * <BR><B>PreConditions:</B>
      * <BR><B>PostConditions:</B>
      */
     public void externalizeToStream(BaseStream stream) throws
java.io.IOException {

          // externalize the version number.
          stream.writeInt(versionNumber);

          // Write the primitive types.
          stream.writeInt(ivNumberOfDays);
          stream.writeBoolean(ivExpedite);

          // Write the DescribableDynamicEntityImpl's (parent of current
          // class) state
          super.externalizeToStream(stream);

          // Write the contained dependents
          stream.writeDependent(this, ivFlatRate);
     }
     /**
      * Destroys the state of an object
      *
      * <BR><B>Assumptions:</B>
      * <BR><B>Note:</B>  This documentation has been automatically
      * generated.
      * @return void
      * @exception com.ibm.sf.gf.SFException
      * <BR><B>Result:</B>
      * <BR><B>PreConditions:</B>
      * <BR><B>PostConditions:</B>
      */
     protected void destroy() throws com.ibm.sf.gf.SFException {
          BaseFactory factory = Global.factory();

          // Dependent destruction
          factory.deleteDependent(this, ivFlatRate);

          // call parent to destroy its contained objects
          super.destroy();
     }
}

DeliveryTypeFactory.java

package GPSE;

import com.ibm.sf.gf.*;
import com.ibm.sf.cf.*;
```

```
/**
 * <TT>
 * <BR><B>Purpose:</B>
 * <BR><B>Description:</B>
 * <BR><B>Note:</B>  This documentation has been automatically
 * generated.
 * </TT>
 * @version 1.3.4
 * @since JDK1.0
 */
public abstract class DeliveryTypeFactory extends DynamicEntityFactory {
    /**
     *
     * <BR><B>Assumptions:</B>
     * <BR><B>Note:</B>
     * @param DeliveryTypeController owner <I>(Mandatory)</I>
     * @param AccessMode access <I>(Mandatory)</I>
     * @param DescriptiveInformation description <I>(Mandatory)</I>
     * @param DCurrencyValue initFlatRate <I>(Mandatory)</I>
     * @param int initNumberOfDays <I>(Mandatory)</I>
     * @return DeliveryType
     * @exception com.ibm.sf.gf.SFException
     * <BR><B>Result:</B>
     * <BR><B>PreConditions:</B>
     * <BR><B>PostConditions:</B>
     */
    public static final DeliveryType
createDeliveryType(DeliveryTypeController owner, AccessMode access,
DescriptiveInformation description, DCurrencyValue initFlatRate, int
initNumberOfDays) throws com.ibm.sf.gf.SFException {
    }
    /**
     *
     * <BR><B>Assumptions:</B>
     * <BR><B>Note:</B>
     * @param DeliveryTypeController owner <I>(Mandatory)</I>
     * @param AccessMode access <I>(Mandatory)</I>
     * @param Handle locationHandle <I>(Optional)</I>
     * @param DescriptiveInformation description <I>(Mandatory)</I>
     * @param DCurrencyValue initFlatRate <I>(Mandatory)</I>
     * @param int initNumberOfDays <I>(Mandatory)</I>
     * @return DeliveryType
     * @exception com.ibm.sf.gf.SFException
     * <BR><B>Result:</B>
     * <BR><B>PreConditions:</B>
     * <BR><B>PostConditions:</B>
     */
    public static final DeliveryType
createDeliveryType(DeliveryTypeController owner, AccessMode access, Handle
locationHandle, DescriptiveInformation description, DCurrencyValue
```

```
initFlatRate, int initNumberOfDays) throws com.ibm.sf.gf.SFException {
    }
    /**
     *
     * <BR><B>Assumptions:</B>
     * <BR><B>Note:</B>
     * @param DeliveryTypeController owner <I>(Mandatory)</I>
     * @param AccessMode access <I>(Mandatory)</I>
     * @param Handle locationHandle <I>(Optional)</I>
     * @param DescriptiveInformation description <I>(Mandatory)</I>
     * @param DCurrencyValue initFlatRate <I>(Mandatory)</I>
     * @param int initNumberOfDays <I>(Mandatory)</I>
     * @return DeliveryType
     * @exception com.ibm.sf.gf.SFException
     * <BR><B>Result:</B>
     * <BR><B>PreConditions:</B>
     * <BR><B>PostConditions:</B>
     */
    public abstract DeliveryType create(DeliveryTypeController owner,
AccessMode access, Handle locationHandle, DescriptiveInformation
description, DCurrencyValue initFlatRate, int initNumberOfDays) throws
com.ibm.sf.gf.SFException;
```

Now that source code exists in the directory specified by the target model, for subsequent generation, as the design evolves, there may be more complex merge actions. Figure 16.13 shows the generation process once an additional attribute has been added for the Delivery-Type class. Notice that the merge actions are more complex than just adding an attribute, as this attribute is referenced in a number of locations within the target implementation; in particular the internaliz-FromStream method difference is highlighted. Once again, the value of the code generator is obvious, and the power of incremental generation is evident, as the alternative would be for a developer to manually search source code listings to ensure that the full impact of the additional attribute is realized.

VisualAge for Java Integration

In the previous section the Rose model to Java source configuration was examined. As an alternative, a Rose model may be translated to the VisualAge for Java repository. For consistency and ease of use, the steps for generation to VisualAge for Java are very similar to generation to Java source files, with the exception of the target connection. Figure 16.14 shows this connection setting.

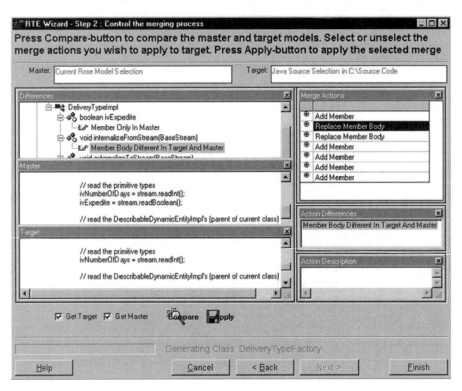

Figure 16.13 Master and target differences and the proposed merge actions.

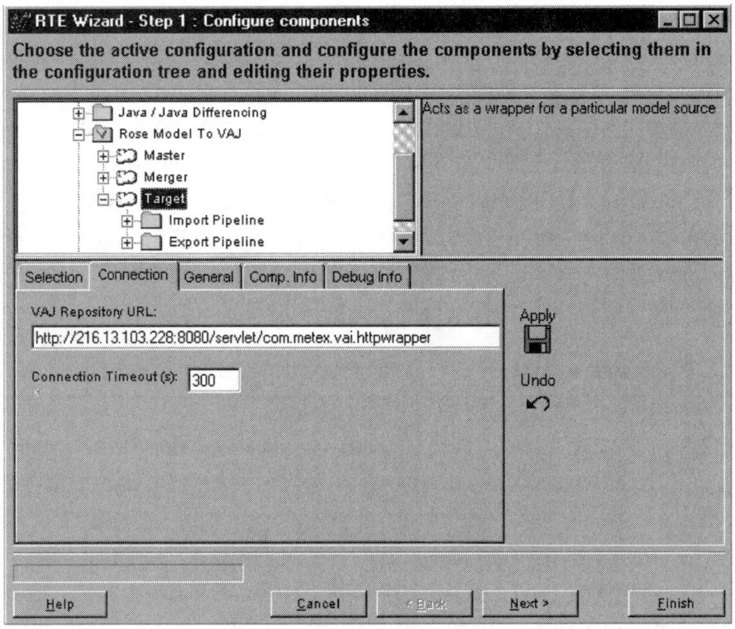

Figure 16.14 Setting the target connection for the VAJ repository.

In this case, the target is a http address that identifies the Java servlet that brokers communication between SF Bridge and the VisualAge for Java repository. The launch of this broker is shown in Figure 16.15, which displays VisualAge and the menu option to run the HTTP VA Integrator.

The Model Upgrade Tool

As some developers may have an existing investment in the original IBM SF code generator, Metex has worked with IBM to provide a tool to allow those developers the opportunity to switch from a somewhat unconventional code generation process to one more integrated with both the Rose visual modeling tool and the VisualAge for Java development environment. The SanFrancisco Model Upgrade Tool performs the conversion necessary to allow models originally designed for the IBM SanFrancisco Code Generator (SFCG) to be processed by Metex's SF Bridge. The intent is to ease the transition of existing SanFrancisco developers using the SFCG to Rose SF Bridge by automating as much of the conversion process as possible.

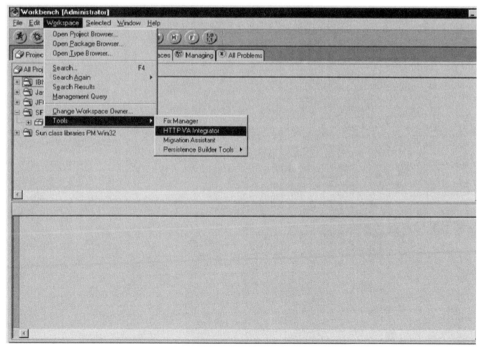

Figure 16.15 VisualAge for Java—enabling the HTTP VA Integrator.

The upgrade is performed in three steps:

1. Processing #directives included in the documentation field of the model elements.
2. Analyzing and converting create and initialize operations found in classes.
3. If desired, removal of #directives mentioned in Step 1.

Summary

As framework developers and users have no doubt observed, the ability to quickly understand and develop with a framework is critical, and hence it is essential that a component-based visual modeling tool be used. Rose SF Bridge, the integrated toolkit for SanFrancisco development, intelligently bridges SanFrancisco' application framework with modeling and Java development tools by utilizing the industry standard Unified Modeling Language (UML). SF Bridge assists the developer in overcoming the complexities of object-oriented development through a series of wizards, builders, and intelligent design and code generation rules aimed at simplifying SanFrancisco-based development.

Introduction to SanFrancisco

Even an introduction to SanFrancisco application components for business is complicated. Part of this is due to the different concerns of the audiences affected by the framework. Like the Indian proverb about the blind men and the elephant, SanFrancisco seems like very different things to different people.

Still, I would like to make sure that anyone reading through this description of the product has a solid grasp on generally what SanFrancisco is, what it does, and where it could be used.

You might be interested to know that originally this book, *Big Blue Java*, started out as a SanFrancisco-only technical book. But after working with the technology and gaining more experience with developing solutions with SanFrancisco, I realized that it is very difficult to grasp SF without a solid background in object-oriented programming generally, and WebSphere, VisualAge for Java, and modeling tools specifically. In some ways, the subject matter covered in the book to this point forms the prerequisites to being able to take on SanFrancisco as a product.

Three major groups of people are deeply involved in using SanFrancisco from the outset: domain experts, programmers (naturally), and administrators. The purpose of this chapter is to touch on the aspects of the program relevant to all; and then in subsequent chapters to break out the treatment of the material to be more deeply applicable to one group or the other.

Goals of SanFrancisco

IBM started working on SanFrancisco in 1995, and the underlying technology chosen for the project was C/C++. At that time, the major goals for the product were:

- Create a reusable framework for application development
- Lower application maintenance costs
- Support portability of applications across platforms

The problem was, the technology just couldn't support the project. In 1996 a decision was taken to migrate the whole thing over to Java. Within months, SF development manager Chris Jones and his team were officially recognized by chairman Lou Gerstner for having done the impossible. The project went from off the rails to a working version using Java in unheard-of time.

SanFrancisco Drivers

It is interesting to keep in mind that from the beginning, the SanFrancisco project was championed, and tightly integrated with, some of the larger IBM business partners. The partners, most based in Europe, were facing huge coding challenges related to migrating their software applications to support the EC and the (then) coming Eurodollar.

Like most organizations addressing the challenge of a major rewrite of existing applications, by the late 1990s people started asking for a better way to write software. IBM was rightly seen as an organization with the resources and abilities to sponsor this effort. Because the process turned out to be just too difficult to accomplish using a more traditional language like C, and given the success of the Java language, as 1997 rolled on people within IBM began to take notice of SanFrancisco. Ultimately, Java has become the key technology theme within the IBM organization. I think it is fair to say this is in no small part due to the people who worked so hard on proving that SanFrancisco could deliver the goods, thereby proving the capabilities of Java in a real-world test.

As we explore SanFrancisco and Java business components, you should find this background information useful. SanFrancisco was intended to be a leg up for organizations facing massive rewrites of their applications. It is most definitely an aid to development with the emphasis on transitioning to a new development architecture where reusability is paramount and components are king.

SanFrancisco Defined

SanFrancisco is a *development framework* for creating commercial applications that includes a set of prebuilt, pretested components. A development framework is analogous to a *class library*, but with important differences.

Both class libraries and frameworks include reusable design and application code. Frameworks extend that to include a defined process, architecture, and implementation. A class library must be turned into an application, whereas a framework is an existing application that can be extended and modified.

SanFrancisco is a set of application components that includes the defined relationships, process flow, and design, all implemented in a working application, albeit without a user interface.

SanFrancisco Domain Area

In the goals for SF we saw that from the outset the application framework was intended to be used to develop commercial systems. IBM recognized that a great deal of coding effort was consistently being wasted in re-creating the wheel, as it were.

For example, General Ledger functionality is highly similar from one organization to the next. I remember a vice president of finance telling me in the late 1980s that the world doesn't need another General Ledger program. This was before the rise of SAP and ERP systems, not to mention Web-based interfaces, but his point was a good one. The functional problems (the business logic) had already been completely worked out for a General Ledger application.

Unfortunately, perhaps, there are other drivers for applications, new interfaces like the Web, and new languages such as Java that provide compelling reasons for rearchitecting a product. This is precisely where the value of SanFrancisco for my organization came into play.

IBM has not only provided the underlying technical infrastructure foundation for a Java-based set of business components, but has implemented a tremendous amount of reusable logic for General Ledger, Accounts Receivable, Accounts Payable, Warehouse, and Inventory. Last, they have done this using a design and development methodology that promotes object-oriented integration, extensibility, customization, and reuse.

In short, SanFrancisco is a complete set of tools for constructing business applications that address distribution and finance. These tools include models, components, and an architectural framework for pulling it all together. Last, the deployment model for SF supports rollout of applications that run on:

- AIX
- AS/400
- HP-UX
- Siemens-Nixdorf Reliant UNIX
- Solaris
- Windows NT

With SanFrancisco Application Business Components for Java, the development team met their longstanding objective of cross-platform portability of applications.

Scope of the Application Area

The reason for mentioning European business partners is that this provides a quick way to relate to the scope of the challenge SF has been positioned to address. When we say that SF components can be used to build distribution systems, we are talking about distribution across multiple countries, with different tax regimes and languages. Very large scale business systems are supported.

Multiple organizations, different reporting requirements, and consolidation of subsidiaries are all accounted for as part of SanFrancisco components as delivered.

The key to where IBM wants independent software vendors to use SanFrancisco is in creating applications with unique selling features and true value added coded on top of the 40 to 60 percent of a complete application right out of the box.

At WNS, we first used SanFrancisco in 1998 to create an application dedicated to helping manage sales and promotion costs for the food industry. The value added is focused primarily in our understanding of the domain, the way the customers use the data—and that is implemented in the ways we have extended SanFrancisco base objects.

What SanFrancisco Gives You

From the brief overview so far, you should be able to see how SanFrancisco is positioned to provide a base for developing Java applications using object-oriented techniques. The approach gives you reuse, portability, and masking of complexity, so that developers can focus on business logic and value added, rather than having to wrestle with the implementation of a distributed system.

From an administrator's perspective, SanFrancisco is an application server that expects to work inside an Enterprise JavaBeans architecture. The underlying infrastructure is managed by WebSphere, as is the integration to other beans and services such as legacy data access.

As we move into more detail about SanFrancisco, administrators will see how the SF servers are tied to WebSphere, where developers will want to focus on the design patterns that are shipped with the product.

At this point, to give you a high-level overview of what you get when you use SF, I should describe the layers of functionality that SanFrancisco provides.

SanFrancisco is defined as three separate (but equally important) layers:

- Foundation
- Common business objects (CBOs)
- Core business processes (CBPs)

Originally, the SanFrancisco foundation layer had to look after naming services and registration of object names, and so on. But as SF has emerged into the mainstream of IBM Java solutions, these services have increasingly moved off to other more generic servers such as WebSphere. Version 2.0 of SanFrancisco is an Enterprise JavaBeans implementation and, as such, the foundation layer is managed in keeping with the EJB architecture. SanFrancisco does not depart from it. The base layer defines a set of classes that help programmers to implement basic business objects and processes, and to make them persistent. It also defines a rigid set of programming guidelines used to take advantage of SanFrancisco facilities.

Foundation

The foundation layer provides the object naming and container management features needed to let SanFrancisco run. This is most easily seen as the Logical SanFrancisco Network, which is a process that has to be up and running before you can work with SF.

When IBM first began working on the framework, it discovered that a great deal of infrastructure programming had to be done in order to get an object-oriented framework to go. This work first became the foundation layer of SanFrancisco and has ultimately led to the involvement of IBM in helping to define the Enterprise JavaBean specification. This will be managing the foundation layer of SanFrancisco in release 2.0 and later.

For the meantime, when you install SanFrancisco, it provides its own network listeners and other foundation services to ensure that the applications using SF objects will be able to perform properly.

The foundation layer includes the base object model and utilities.

Common Business Objects

The common business objects layer includes objects used by multiple applications. This layer also introduces many object-oriented patterns that are used throughout the vertical domains (such as controllers, key/keyables, and others).

This layer provides the objects most often needed in any enterprise application. For example:

Business partner. Customer or supplier with their associated properties; contact information, financial profiles, and so on.

Company. Descriptions of company structure and relationships.

Financial. All properties associated with the financial details of commercial transactions—who paid what to whom, when, for what and how.

Currency. Default currency to be used by a company, exchange rates, other currencies to be handled.

Calendar. Fiscal year, period reporting and natural calendars.

Core Business Processes

The core business processes layer provides business domain–specific classes that are implemented using the patterns and programming model defined in the base layer. Classes in the core business processes layer can be used directly to implement business processes such as accounting, sales order processing, inventory management, and product distribution. More often, though, these classes will be used as a base, and extended to apply more directly to specific domains and applications.

SanFrancisco Beans

With the release of SanFrancisco 1.4, you get JavaBeans, which allow you to create applications using VisualAge for Java much quicker and cheaper than ever before.

Advantages of Using SanFrancisco Beans

Using SanFrancisco Beans offers the programmer distinct advantages:

- Simplifies the SanFrancisco programming model because many SanFrancisco concepts are automatically built in.
- Offers a shorter learning curve than traditional SanFrancisco class and framework development.
- Supports the rapid development of simple applications. SanFrancisco Beans are, in fact, targeted at developing static maintenance applications (such as updating, adding, and removing instances of objects) and more dynamic simple operational applications.
- Leverages existing visual programming tools, allowing you to integrate SanFrancisco with various integrated development environments (IDEs) that support JavaBeans.
- Follows the Sun JavaBean industry standard component architecture.
- Allows quick assembly of some applications using the set of prebuilt beans that ship with SanFrancisco. These prebuilt beans serve as concrete examples of SanFrancisco Bean concepts, with each bean representing one SanFrancisco business object interface. Listed below are some of the prebuilt beans:
  - AddressBean
  - BusinessPartnerBean

- CountryBean
- CurrencyBean
- ExchangeRatePeriodBasedBean
- FiscalCalendarBean
- UnitOfMeasureBean
- Includes the SanFrancisco bean wizard that helps you to build your own SanFrancisco Beans for SanFrancisco classes or your own classes.

SanFrancisco Environment Settings

One of the most consistent problems we found in getting the SanFrancisco logical network (LSFN) up and running on any given machine was achieving the correct settings of environment variables. Eventually we came up with a checklist that allowed us to see whether installation of another Java program stepped on our settings, or alerted us to any of the other myriad ways they could become undone.

SF Environment Variables

```
SanFrancisco Run-Time Environment From JavaThree
Path = e:\SF\SF140\com\ibm\sf\bin;
CLASSPATH = .;
e:\SF\SF140;
D:\IBMVJava\eab\runtime20;
D:\IBMVJava\eab\runtime;
D:\IBMVJava\eab\runtime20\jdebug.jar;
D:\IBM\Connectors\Encina\Classes;
D:\WebSphere\AppServer\classes;
D:\WebSphere\AppServer\web\classes;
d:\SQLLIB\java\db2java.zip;
d:\SQLLIB\java\runtime.zip;
D:\swing-1.0.3\swingall.jar;
```

The path statement must point to the SF bin subdirectory for SanFrancisco to find necessary executables and resources. In addition the classpath must be set and the Swing directory must be in the classpath.

SF Components

IBM's SanFrancisco (SF) software consists of pretested business objects and processes written in Java. Using Java's Remote Method Invocation

(RMI) and CORBA IIOP packages to support a distributed computing environment, SanFrancisco can scale up to multiple servers using different operating systems. The basic transport and communication mechanisms are supported in SanFrancisco by using three main objects:

- *Entities.* Entities are persistent objects that can be mapped to a relational database such as DB2, Oracle, and SQL Server or stored in a flat file in Posix form.

- *Dependent.* Dependent objects differ from entities in that they are not shared; transient dependent objects can stand alone, but persistent dependent objects must be held contained in an entity.

- *Commands.* Command subclasses are a specialized type of dependent object that represents business tasks, calculations, and other actions that control or modify business objects. They provide the ability to optimize performance and secure transactions in a distributed environment.

SanFrancisco Objects

The distributed nature of the SF environment requires the use of non-standard Java objects, namely entity, command, and dependent objects. These objects are not standard today, but they are so useful we expect them to be incorporated into the standard EJB specification.

Entities

Entities are distributed objects that can map their encapsulated information to a database table through the default or extended schema mapper utility. The default schema mapper (DSM) streams an object's data to a database table in hexadecimal form, thus rendering the information indecipherable to legacy applications. In contrast, an application architect can map an object's data to legacy database tables using the extended schema mapper (XSM). The ability of the XSM to map legacy data allows for migration from legacy applications to a distributed object environment.

Entity Creation Example

To illustrate the basics of creating a SF entity object, Figure 17.1, created with the Enterprise Modeling Tool (EMT), illustrates the sequence of object creation required to create a simple SF entity, BusinessPartner.

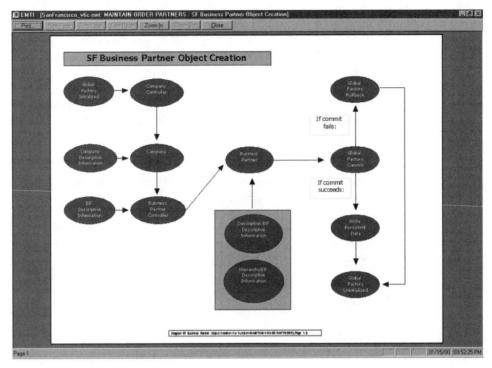

Figure 17.1 An EMT model shows the SF objects called to create BusinessPartner.

Figure 17.1 shows the order of object creation/retrieval is Global Factory, Company Controller BusinessPartnerController, and finally BusinessPartner. DescriptiveInformation objects are used throughout the process to add information specific to an entity. The code that produces the BusinessPartner just described is as follows:

```
/**
 * This Class was created by James Carlson for WNS Canada Inc.
 * This is the sole property of WNS Canada Inc. Do Not redistribute.
 * If you have any questions call the Java Development Group
 * at 1-800-343-3579
 *
 *
 * @param args java.lang.String[]
 */
public static void main(String args[]) {
  try {
    Global.initialize();
    Global.factory().begin();
    System.out.print("Creating Company ... ");
    AccessMode accessMode = AccessMode.createPlusWrite();
    CompanyController controller = (CompanyController)
CompanyContext.getCompanyController();
```

```
    Company enterprise = EnterpriseFactory.createEnterprise(controller,
accessMode, "1","WNS US Inc.", "WNS US Inc",Product, "EN_US",
(DescriptiveInformation)null);

    CompanyContext.setProcessDefaultActiveCompany(enterprise);
    System.out.println("done!");
    System.out.print("Rolling Back ... ");
    Global.factory().rollback();
    Global.uninitialize();
    System.out.println(" done!");
  } catch (GFException gfe) {
    System.out.println("WNSOrderPartnerDemo :: main() - Excpetion :" +
gfe.getClass());
    System.out.println("WNSOrderPartnerDemo :: main() - Message :" +
gfe.getMessage());
    gfe.printStackTrace();
  } catch (SFException sfe) {
    System.out.println("WNSOrderPartnerDemo :: main() - Excpetion :" +
sfe.getClass());
    System.out.println("WNSOrderPartnerDemo :: main() - Message :" +
sfe.getMessage());
    sfe.printStackTrace();
  }
  System.exit(0);
}
```

For the sake of brevity, the code that creates the DescriptiveInformation object has been omitted, but the preceding code sample effectively demonstrates a SF transaction and the creation of a standard SF entity.

Commands

Commands are Java objects that can be extended for customization purposes, can increase performance, and are commonly used to retrieve information from the SF object framework. For example, one may wish to access a specific widget held by a BusinessPartner. Commands also have the inherent ability to be assigned security levels. In some cases, BusinessPartner members may be considered confidential; limiting the ability to run the command to only those commands registered with a sufficiently high security level can restrict access to these members. This further enhances the ability to divide work between framework builders, bean builders, and bean assemblers.

Command Example

The EMT model in Figure 17.2 depicts the creation of a command. This command provides the ability to setup CurrencyControllers and various controllers for our DealManager SanFrancisco Product.

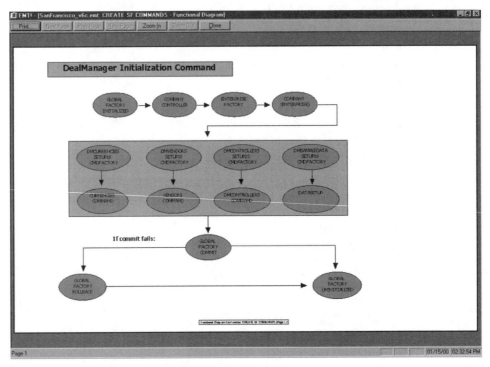

Figure 17.2 An EMT model showing a SF command.

Figure 17.2 shows the functionality as implemented by the command. The source code that creates the command creation follows.

```
/**************************************************
**
** <br><strong>Object Changed:</strong> Resource
**
** @exception com.ibm.sf.gf.SFException
**
**************************************************/

protected void handleDo() throws com.ibm.sf.gf.SFException {
        if (getTargetHdl() == null ) {
        System.out.println("DealManagerSetupCmd target is null");
        System.exit(0);
    }

    System.out.print("DealManagerSetupCmd :: main () : setting up the
DealManager Enterprise Company - ABC Company ... ");

    AccessMode accessMode = AccessMode.createNormal();
    CompanyController controller =
(CompanyController)(getObjectFromHandle(ivTargetHdl,
AccessMode.createPlusWrite())));
```

```
        //check if Enterprise already exists, if not create one
        Enterprise enterprise = CompanyContext.getEnterprise();

        if (enterprise == null) {
            enterprise = EnterpriseFactory.createEnterprise(
                    controller,
                    accessMode,
                    "1",
                    "WNS Canada Inc.",
                    "WNS Canada Incorporated",
                    Product,
                    "EN_US",
                    (DescriptiveInformation)null);
        }   else {
            System.out.println("Enterprise : " + enterprise.getLegalName()
+ " already exists");
        }
        setCompany(enterprise);
        CompanyContext.setProcessDefaultActiveCompany(enterprise);
        System.out.println("done!");

    // Create and run setup command for Currencies.
    DMCurrenciesSetup10Cmd currenciesCmd =
DMCurrenciesSetup10CmdFactory.createDMCurrenciesSetup10Cmd(enterprise);
    currenciesCmd.doAll();

     // Create and run setup command for Vendors.
    DMVendorsSetup10Cmd vendorsCmd =
DMVendorsSetup10CmdFactory.createDMVendorsSetup10Cmd(enterprise);
    vendorsCmd.doAll();

   // Create and run setup command for controllers
  DMControllersSetup10Cmd DMControlllersCmd =
DMControllersSetup10CmdFactory.createDMControllersSetup10Cmd(enterprise);
    DMControlllersCmd.doAll();

    // Create and run setup command for sample data
    DMSampleDataSetupCmd dataSetup =
DMSampleDataSetupCmdFactory.createDMSampleDataSetupCmd(enterprise);
    dataSetup.doAll();
        }
```

Because commands hide the information retrieval mechanism through encapsulation, framework builders can optimize the commands and rework the framework with minimal impact on the bean builders or bean assemblers.

Dependents

Dependents, transient by nature, are required to support an Entity's distributed nature. Entities are truly unique objects and require special attention to the objects that they contain; Entities can only contain other Entities, Dependents, or Strings. The default dependents that contain

Java primitives are DBoolean, DCharacter, DDouble, DFloat, DInterger, DLong, and DShort.

Dependent Example

The following EMT model (see Figure 17.3) depicts the creation of the dependent object, MyDependentDemo.

The corresponding source code is shown here.

```
 * @param args an array of command-line arguments
 */
public static void main(java.lang.String[] args) {
      try {
            Global.initialize();
            Global.factory().begin();
            // creates a Dependent indepdently of a Entity.
            // the DSFDependentDemo also supports the creation of the
            // Dependent in an entity!
            DSFDependentDemo myDependentDemo =
DSFDependentDemoFactory.createDSFDependentDemo(Product); // the parameter
```

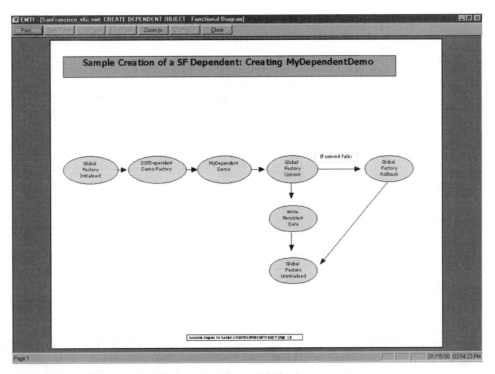

Figure 17.3 The dependent's functionality and behavior.

```
// is simply an example of data that the dependent encapsulates

    } catch (GFException gfe) {
        System.out.println("SFDependentDemo::main() - Unexpected
error:"+gfe.getMessage());
        gfe.printStackTrace();
    } catch (SFException sfe) {
        System.out.println("SFDependentDemo::main() - Unexpected
error:"+sfe.getMessage());
        sfe.printStackTrace();
    }
}
```

SF Transactions

One of the key benefits to the SF architecture is that access to all SF objects is transactional. This allows for the deployment of transaction-based applications that can scale up to a large number of users. Transactions are initiated by calling the static method on the Global.Factory() object. The static nature of this object allows one to call the method without having to instantiate the object. Objects can be accessed in a transaction with the following access modes:

- setNoLock
- setNormal
- setPlusWrite
- setCritical
- createNoLock
- createPlusWrite
- createCritical

Although these modes are configured with locking parameters, they are customizable. The locking mechanism that SanFrancisco employs is extremely robust, and works well with the XSM. The locking parameters that SF supports are

- No_Lock
- Optimistic
- Optimistic_clean
- Read
- Write

A conflict occurs whenever one application attempts to gain a lock when another transaction holds a concurrent pessimistic lock, be it read or write. As clearly shown by the inherent transactional control in San-Francisco, applications can be quickly built to support a great number of users. This functionality is very important when one considers a Web-sphere application that must deal with a large number of users.

In summary, SanFrancisco provides application designers with a ready-made transaction and distributed framework, which is both robust and fully customizable.

SF Collections

Data organizing in SanFrancisco relies on collections, objects that provide the ability to hierarchically organize data. SanFrancisco collections can be organized so that a child inherits the objects in the parent. There are six basic collections:

- List
- Map
- Set
- EntityOwningMap
- EntityOwningList
- EntityOwningSet

These collections provide sorting, error checking, and SQL-like query statements. There are many collections in Java; however the ability to issue SQL-like statements on objects within the collections provides a level of sophistication that would be difficult to achieve without the framework.

SanFrancisco Security

As is typical of an IBM product, SanFrancisco incorporates a built-in, advanced, and robust security model. And as would be expected with a distributed application, security of enterprise objects is one of SanFrancisco's strengths. Commands are central to the security model.

As previously mentioned, commands are created by extending the SF Command object. New commands can be registered with a specific security level such that only users with the same or higher level can execute the command.

SanFrancisco Application Development

The SanFrancisco RoadMap documents the recommended SanFrancisco development approach. This provides a set of standard templates and links to specific examples for creating portions of a GL application. SanFrancisco development consists of four standard activities.

1. Collect and document the requirements.
2. Analyze the requirements.
3. Design the code.
4. Generate and test the code.

The integration of SanFrancisco into a customized application will be greatly aided if the solution provider provides requirements in defined processes. This is where an application like Enterprise Modeling Tool can be used not only by the businesspeople for definition of what the application needs to support, but by the development staff to ensure it has mapped the object model correctly to the real-world requirements.

When the analysis of business process is complete, the *mapping* to San-Francisco will provide a detailed utilization of SF functionality. Mapping is the activity of relating your application processes, tasks, and scenarios to the SF model. The best approach is to map the SF applications scenarios (which detail the activities performed for a particular task within a process) to the application to be developed.

SF is an object-oriented framework that provides the basis for general applications in the areas of Accounts Payable/Receivable, Warehouse Management, Order Management, and General Ledger. Many companies are seeking to invest in technology that is scalable, customizable, robust, and stable over the long run. IBM's SF addresses these issues by employing logical SF networks that provide an object-oriented framework. The framework is implemented in Java, allowing for reusable OO code and the ability to customize any component. However, despite the ability to customize OO Code, the SF framework has proven to be exceptionally challenging to customize.

SF runs on a logical network that is run inside of a Java Virtual Machine. This provides the framework with the platform independence required by many companies, as these networks are built from almost 100 percent pure Java.

You can implement many LSFNs on heterogeneous platforms all communicating with each other. The framework manages distributed objects and the creation and destruction of the objects. This enhances the scalability of the LSFNs across multiple platforms, as object creation can be load-balanced.

Let me make a note on the framework. The framework employs a layered architecture that allows application developers to use components of the framework. The framework is divided into three parts: the foundation, the common business objects and processes, and applications. This is depicted in Figure 17.4, developed by IBM to show how SF elements fit together.

The foundation manages object deployment and destruction, security, and configuration. This is the component that removes the implementation details of distributed computing, platform dependency, interactions among distributed objects, and transactional integrity. The foundation also manages persistence. (As a matter of fact, SF objects have no

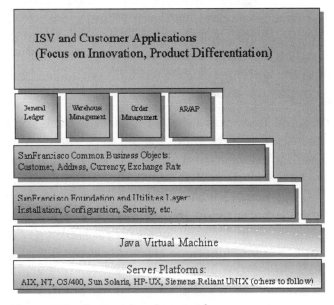

Figure 17.4 SanFrancisco framework.

knowledge of the data storage technology used for persistence; SF's persistence is fully managed by the foundation layer.)

The common business objects and processes layer contains classes which produce objects necessary to support general business functions. A good example of a low-level common business object (CBO) is the currency object. A controller (similar to the MVC of the comic book examples) is owned by a company that holds this object. The company then has access to information regarding exchange rates from its currency collection. This will be discussed in greater detail in this chapter.

Applications are generic functions that are required by almost every business. These functions are showcased in the samples associated with SF1.4.0. The warehouse sample application is shown in Figure 17.5 and the following text.

A series of applications support the warehouse function in Figure 17.5. These sample applications are based on the sample data and thus the sample CBO provided with SF. As you can see from the framework fig-

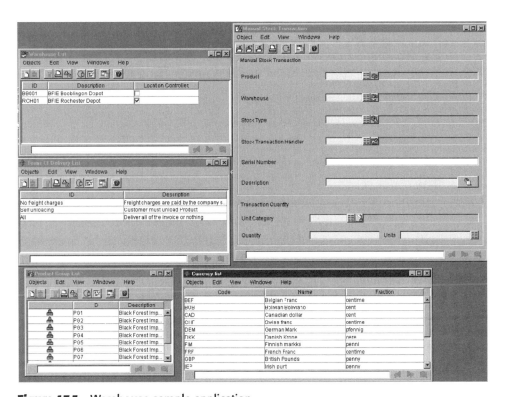

Figure 17.5 Warehouse sample application.

ure, an additional layer is added by the application programmer. This layer is built by extending the framework from natural extension points and using the ability to modify and create your own CBO.

The SF logical networks run on Java Virtual Machines on many platforms including Windows NT, OS/400, AIX, Solaris, HP-UX, and Reliant UNIX. The nature of Java is such that OO code is reusable across different heterogeneous operating systems. Due to the ability to create a distributed computing environment across multiple heterogeneous platforms, one can easily scale the production environment with existing equipment and new platforms that may develop.

SF Sample Applications

There are several important things to keep in mind about the sample applications. First and foremost, these are not toy applications. They are real, working examples of what the framework does using the default (unextended) behavior of the objects.

The samples are probably the best way to start to familiarize yourself with what functionality is in the framework. At WNS, we decided to look for real-world applications that would use the default behavior of the framework, rather than focusing on extending it.

One of the key reasons for this was that in writing applications that interfaced to the business objects in the Towers (like Order Management, Warehouse, or General Ledger) we would be protected when the next release of SanFrancisco was available.

The other reason was speed of development. At various times when we tried to extend the framework we found that our delivery dates were consistently being pushed back. We didn't have enough experience with the process of dancing with SanFrancisco to be able to estimate properly. As a result we had the usual problems associated with delivering late.

To avoid this, as well as to protect against getting deprecated or obsoleted in future releases, we focused on developing SF applications through the beans provided. The samples were our first clue regarding how much power actually resided in the SF framework as delivered. To my way of thinking, it's worth going through that process if only to satisfy yourself that SF is or is not something you want to use.

Running Sample SanFrancisco Applications

As you will see in Figure 17.6, the SanFrancisco sample applications all start up their own SanFrancisco servers. This means that even running the samples requires some healthy hardware underneath. You may want to start and stop each server as you walk through the samples.

In the SanFrancisco program groups you will find a command to launch the samples. Click on this and you will fire up the sample servers.

Of course the servers aren't really all that interesting from a demonstrated functionality standpoint. What you really want to see is what applications are available to run under the servers. To do this, you want to run the samples, which results in a screen like the one shown in Figure 17.7.

There is a bunch of functionality that is demonstrated in the sample applications.

Creating a SanFrancisco Bean-Based Application

While there are wizards we use to create SanFrancisco Beans, there are also a number of beans that are provided as part of the installation of 1.4.

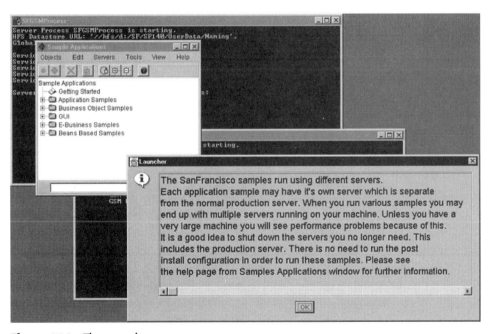

Figure 17.6 The sample servers.

The samples shown earlier should clearly demonstrate the amount of programming functionality provided as part of SanFrancisco. What we are going to do here is use VisualAge for Java to create an applet that uses a SanFrancisco Bean. (See Figure 17.8).

The bean wizard generates the stubs and skeletons that we need in order to be able to extend our own applications. There are three kinds of applications that can be created using the wizard: *entities*, *dependents*, and *commands*. (See Figures 17.9 through 17.14.)

Since I just want to create a stand-alone applet that doesn't do a whole lot (but I do want it to have persistence), I select Entity. Dependents are not persistent, while commands perform actions on persistent entities.

To move to the next dialog, you must define the project and package where you want the class to reside. Generally speaking, this isn't much different from setting up a new applet in VisualAge for Java.

Since I want to work with the company beans, I have to define this.

As a matter of getting around, you can type the first few characters of the class you want and SanFrancisco will take you down the list to the desired spot. The name of the package is provided automatically at that point. You can then click OK to add the class.

Using the BeanControllers, we started playing around with the pallets. Some of the widgets available include this databeancontroller. Clicking on the About this Bean property value provides the following help.

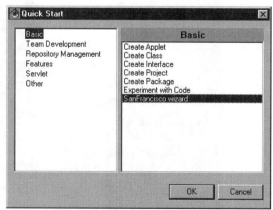

Figure 17.7 The sample applications.

Figure 17.8 Starting the bean wizard in VisualAge for Java.

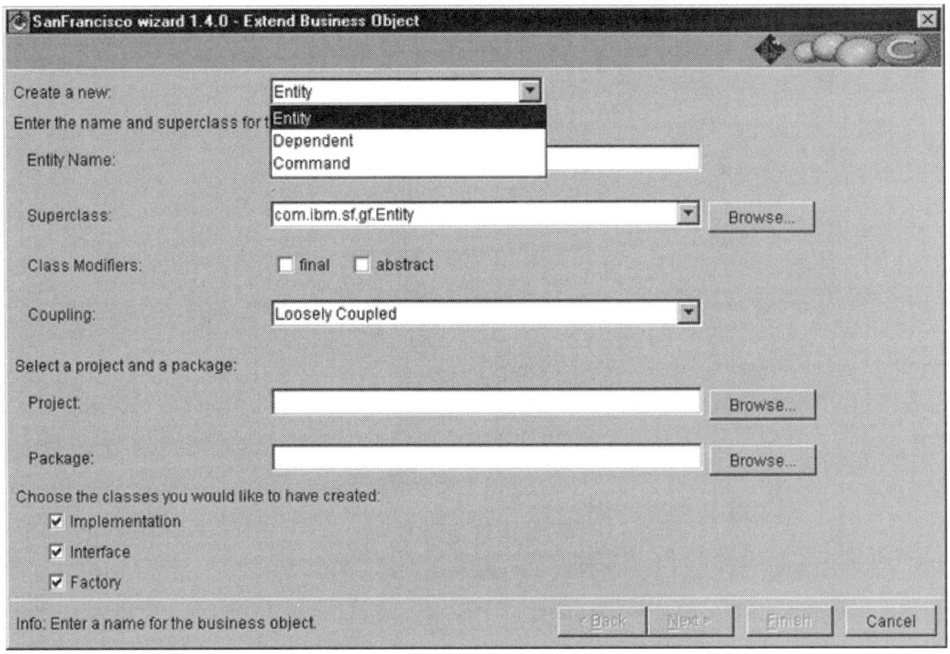

Figure 17.9 The SF Bean dialog box.

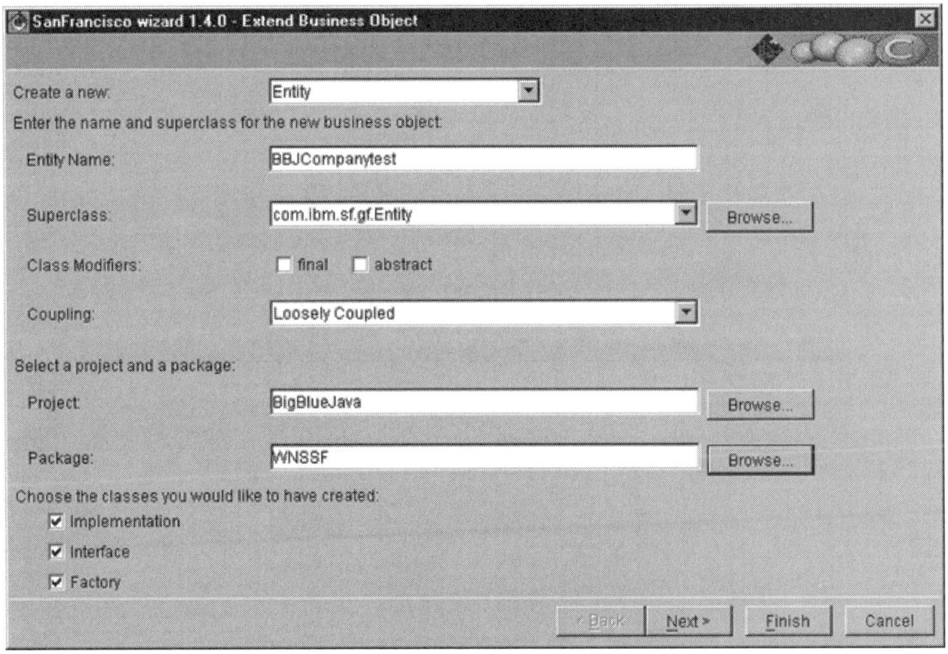

Figure 17.10 Step two of the bean wizard.

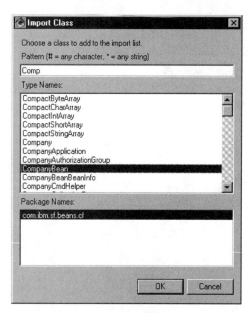

Figure 17.11   SF class listings.

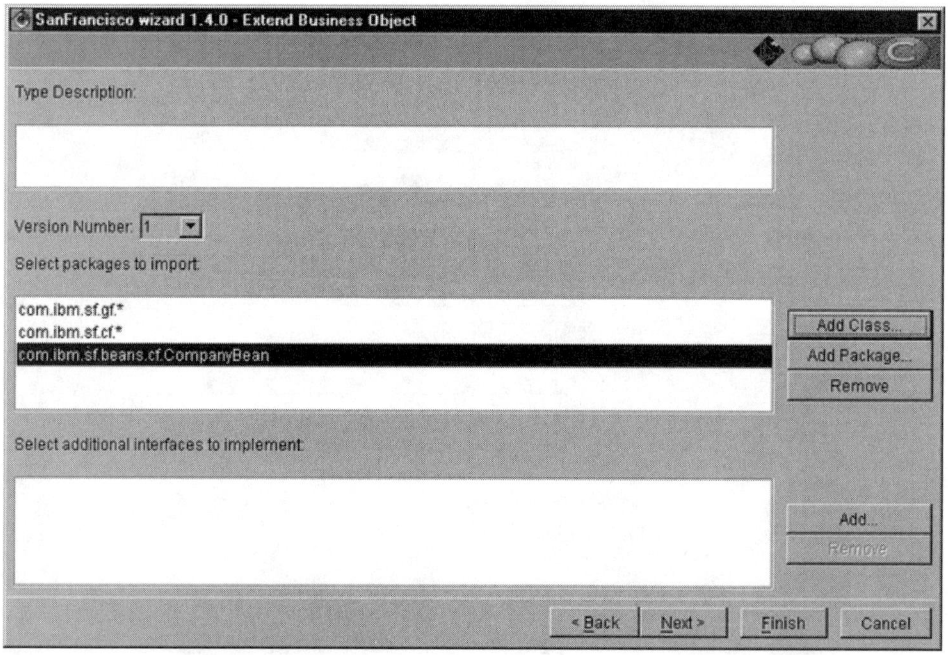

Figure 17.12   Selecting a controller.

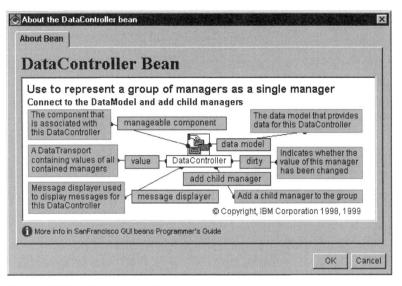

Figure 17.13   Bean properties.

The property box is the same for SF Beans as for any other Java component, with the exception of having some SanFrancisco awareness built in.

The wiring diagrams show you how to connect the beans to other components such as UIPanel, to help you get used to the way SF Beans are used. This is an extremely helpful feature, and after working with it for a

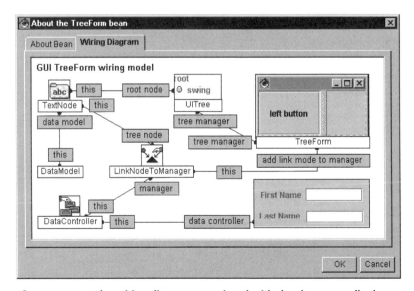

Figure 17.14   The wiring diagram associated with the data controller bean.

couple of days you start to look for the same kind of help from all of the other components. (Unfortunately they haven't been written yet.)

The About this Bean properties provided as part of the SF Beans comprise a very helpful feature. To quickly create an SF application, I am including them for the top 10 that we have used. By walking through this process you should be able to gain a sense of applicability of this technology to your requirements. At that point you might be more interested in the investment of time and effort necessary to get even an initial SF environment up and running. Of course, then you can check these properties out for yourself, but in the meantime, I suspect this will provide an excellent quick reference on how to use SF components as a bean assembler.

The UI tree bean (see Figures 17.15 and 17.16) is essentially a swing Jtree with more functionality built in.

The wiring diagrams provide a really important shortcut to being able to quickly assemble applications using SF components under VisualAge for Java.

The UIPanel itself takes the place of the JPanel. Like the other SF components, this provides additional SF functionality, including means of integrating with data controls. The properties for this bean are shown in Figure 17.17.

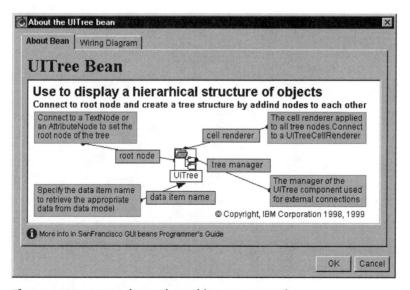

Figure 17.15   UI tree bean About this Bean properties.

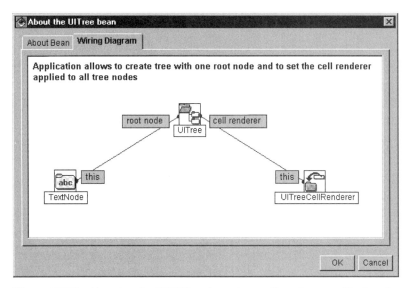

Figure 17.16 How to wire SF UI Tree bean to a cell renderer and text node.

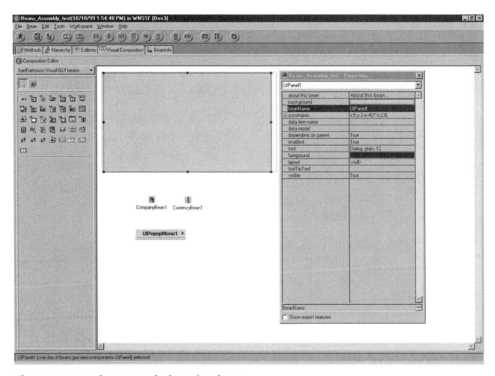

Figure 17.17 The UIPanel of SF Visual Beans.

You can see in Figure 17.17 the collection of SanFrancisco Visual GIU beans in the drop-down pallet on the left-hand-side of the screen. The UIPanel itself is drawn in the center and would represent the entire visible area of the application when run.

Figure 17.18 shows the About this Bean properties of the SF UIPanel.

Once you understand where to use the UIPanel, which is really the same place you would use a Jpanel, you can then wire up the connectable features to a data controller. Don't forget, every aspect of the SF Beans has been crafted to closely follow the Model-View-Controller paradigm for application development. The thing we loved about the wiring diagrams (Figure 17.19) was the way they took the guesswork out of how to connect the objects using VisualAge for Java.

The main point of this exercise is to enable you to see how you can start using visual SanFrancisco objects through VisualAge for Java to begin to create applications right away.

The need for a solid understanding of object-oriented approaches, a proper model, and software design is in no way eliminated, but at least you can get started with SF and see what it can do for you. We found this to be a tremendous boost on the learning curve—and I hope that you will, too.

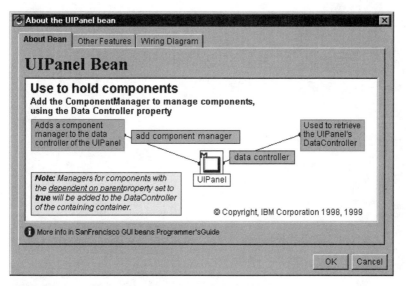

Figure 17.18 About the UIPanel.

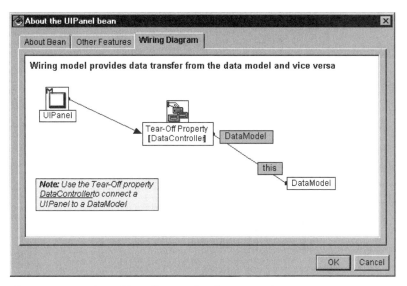

Figure 17.19 The wiring diagram for the UIPanel.

An SF Route Map

One of the things that most developers who face SanFrancisco for the first time immediately see is that the sheer size of the framework is daunting. Since we have been using the analogy of a framework as transit system, here I'd like to provide you with a route map. Since Rose is the object model tool recommended by IBM, on the following pages I will show you the Rose models for each of the SF pages and how they relate to each other. I should note that a lot of this is available from IBM as part of its SanFrancisco documentation, but it took us forever to uncover it.

Given how useful the high-level description of the overall SanFrancisco package collections and their interfaces is, I thought it would be valuable to cover it here.

Figure 17.20 depicts a package diagram indicating the dependencies between the main SanFrancisco packages. The packages are maintained in a hierarchy where the base layer contains:

- Util
- Gf

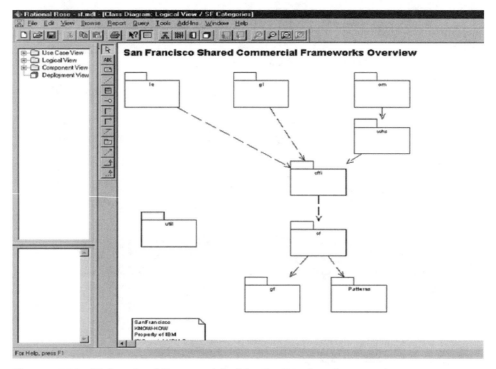

Figure 17.20   Highest-level Rose model of the SanFrancisco framework.

- Cf
- Pattern packages

The common business process layer includes:

- Cffi
- Whs
- Om
- Gl
- Le

Brief Description of the SF Packages

Each of the packages contains classes that provide the functionality of the SF framework as delivered. In the interest of helping you get your arms around SanFrancisco, we will summarize each of the packages shown in Figure 17.20 and briefly describe its contents and functionality.

The Core Business Processes Layer

The following sections introduce the core business processes that IBM currently ships with SanFrancisco 1.4. The impending move to EJB should not change the way the framework is structured so much as implements the classes internally in a manner compliant with the EJB specification.

- SanFrancisco General Ledger
- SanFrancisco Accounts Receivable/Accounts Payable
- SanFrancisco Warehouse Management
- SanFrancisco Order Management

Let's look at a high level that is provided by that core business process.

The main purpose of the General Ledger (Figure 17.21) is to report the flow of money for your company. This is required for legal reasons and for managing your business. A standard approach for this accounting

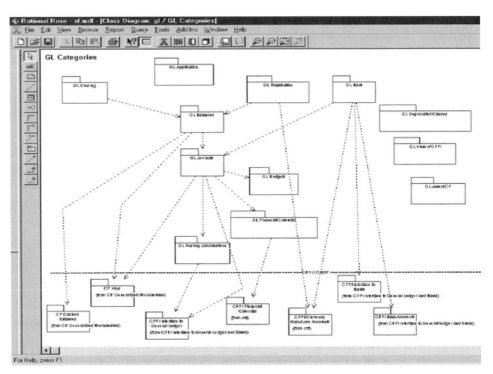

Figure 17.21 General Ledger (GL Bank Package).

process has been developed. This can be illustrated in the accounting cycle. This cycle consists of three main steps:

1. Setting up the structure
2. Day-to-Day activities
3. Periodic activities

General Ledger Framework Categories

As with other layers of SanFrancisco, the General Ledger is divided into categories. These categories group related processes and their associated classes together. This section provides an overview of each of the categories in the General Ledger.

Posting Combinations

This category provides the processes and business objects for defining and working with the chart of accounts. Posting combinations include the definition of the account, account validation criteria, and the type of account.

Journal

This category provides the processes and business objects for creating, maintaining, and finalizing transactions in the General Ledger. Journal includes support for both value and quantities, support for transactions in a currency other than your General Ledger's currency, and support to define what makes a valid transaction.

Balances

This category provides the basis for creating reports and balance inquires. It provides the processes and business objects to flexibly define criteria for which balances are needed. The criteria can include the fiscal period, the type of account, and the prime currency. Balances includes support to extend the criteria and to store and maintain balances for specific criteria for fast access.

Budgets

Budgets provide the ability to include budgets in the General Ledger. The SanFrancisco General Ledger keeps the budgets in the same ledger, which allows all of the same functions to be applied. Although the two types of journals are combined within the framework, the application could decide to make it appear as if two separate ledgers are used.

GL Financial Calendar

This category uses the Financial Calendar from the common business objects to add information about the fiscal periods with respect to the General Ledger. In particular, it specifies whether the fiscal period is open or closed, and identifies the current (or default) period.

Closing

Closing provides the processes and business objects to support year-end processing. The framework provides a simple example of closing, because this process varies dramatically between businesses.

Banks

This category supports the processes and business objects for dealing with the bank. This includes tracking transactions within the bank, managing bank statements, and reconciling the bank statement with the bank transactions.

Revaluation

This category provides the processes and business objects to support the revaluation of currencies. A currency is revalued when you have a bank account in a currency other than your General Ledger's currency (base currency) and when the exchange rate changes over time. When this occurs, the original value in your base currency may no longer reflect the correct value, so a revaluation is done using a more current exchange rate. This category supports both realized and unrealized gain and losses.

Accounts Receivable/Accounts Payable (AR/AP) is used to accurately record the level and age of indebtedness between a company and its individual customers and suppliers. Each transaction (called an *item* in the AR/AP core business process) that occurs between a company and its business partners is recorded. Accounts Receivable/Accounts Payable has been designed so that it is not restricted to use only with customers and suppliers but also can be used to keep track of other types of open-item accounts. This is handled by using the concept of an account that is not restricted to being either a customer or supplier. You can then specify a ledger type that is definable by an application built on top of this core business process. (See Figure 17.22.)

AR/AP items can be either *ledger items* or *log items*. Ledger items are items that have been approved and accepted by the company. Log items

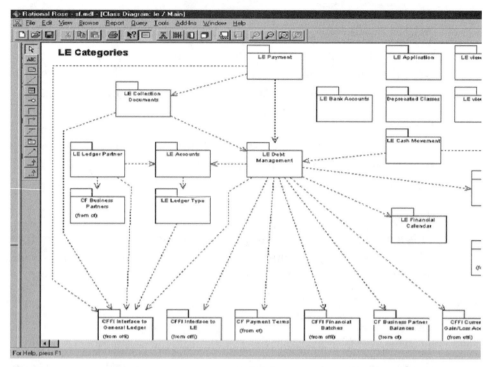

Figure 17.22   SanFrancisco Accounts Receivable/Accounts Payable (LE Collections Package).

are the unapproved items that the company has knowledge of that are pending approval. For example, an invoice from a supplier may have to be approved by the relevant purchasing manager before it can be accepted onto the ledger. In this case, the item may be recorded on the log as a record of receipt. After a log item has been approved, it can be transferred to the ledger and therefore becomes a ledger item. At that time, ledger items become associated with generic dissections in the General Ledger for the income or expense (for example) and to the relevant control account. A log item may optionally have generic dissections in the General Ledger. The use of log items is optional; items can be created directly as ledger items.

Accounts Receivable/Accounts Payable Framework Categories

As with other layers of SanFrancisco, the Accounts Receivable/Accounts Payable (AR/AP) framework is divided into categories. These categories bring together related processes and associated classes. This section provides an overview of each of the categories in Accounts Receivable/ Accounts Payable.

Ledger Types

This category provides the basis for classifying accounts and holding default information specific to an account type. Normally, the application would provide instances of this class for Accounts Receivable (AR) and Accounts Payable (AP). AR/AP is easily extendable for introducing additional types of accounts, however. For example, you could define an account type that represents an employee.

LE Accounts

This category provides the business object that represents a specific account within AR/AP. These accounts normally represent a third party in a financial transaction (for example, a customer or supplier). You may attach default values to the LE account that may be used during the processing of financial transactions that relate to this account.

Ledger Partner

This category is the framework-provided implementation of an LE account. It is the AR/AP representation of a business partner. You can use the ledger type to specify the role of the business partner, which is typically a customer or supplier. AR/AP supports a specific business partner acting in both of these roles—or even more, if you specify additional ledger types.

LE Bank Accounts

This category extends the internal bank accounts that were introduced in the CBO layer to provide details specific to processing financial transactions within AR/AP.

LE Payment Method

This category extends the base payment methods business objects that were introduced in the CBO layer. They provide information needed for processing payments and collection documents.

LE Financial Calendar

This category uses the financial calendar from the CBO layer to add information about the fiscal periods with respect to AR/AP. In particular, this information specifies whether the fiscal period is open or closed, as well as the current or default period.

Core Categories

This provides the processes and business objects that you use to create and manage financial transactions that will appear in AR/AP, such as the following:

- Invoices
- Credit notes
- Payments
- Adjustments
- Currency gains or losses
- Allocations

Log Item

This category provides the business object used to represent a financial transaction that is awaiting approval. These financial transactions are usually invoices, credit notes, or payments. The log item holds the necessary information about the transaction that allows the transaction to be reflected accurately in the General Ledger. Actually updating the General Ledger for these unapproved items, however, is optional. After the log item has been approved, this category provides support for transforming the approved log item into a ledger item. Use of log items is entirely optional.

Ledger Item

This category provides the business objects used to represent an approved financial transaction. You can either create ledger items directly or they may start out as log items (before approval) and become transformed into ledger items (after approval). Ledger items contain all of the information necessary to reflect their associated financial transactions in the General Ledger and to match these financial transactions with their corresponding opposites. For example, a ledger item could be a payment against an invoice.

Installment

This category provides the business objects that allow the value of a log item or ledger item to be split into multiple parts. Each of these parts can have its own due dates and settlement discounts. Each part will be reflected in the General Ledger with specific postings as necessary. If multiple currencies are involved, then the value on the installment may be revalued as necessary due to currency fluctuations.

Allocation

This category represents business objects that support matching financial transactions that in turn represent debits and credits. This matching is performed at the installment level and supports both full and partial satisfaction of the amount that the installment represents. Usually allocation is performed by allocating either payments or credit notes against invoices. AR/AP also supports allocating customer invoices against supplier invoices. The allocation processing can handle making the appropriate postings to the General Ledger to reflect gains or losses that result from the following situations:

- Reflecting gains or losses that result from currency fluctuations
- Matching installments that have differing General Ledger control accounts
- Matching installments that are associated with different LE accounts (for example, a parent company paying the invoices of a subsidiary)

Optional Support Categories

These categories provide support for various financial processing within AR/AP. Their use is optional and other aspects of the framework do not depend on their use.

Collection Documents

This category provides the business objects that represent the movement of payments through the AR/AP system. It includes support for tracking cash (for example, cash, checks, and so on) from the time it was originally received to the time when it is actually assigned to a ledger partner and eventually represented by a posted ledger item. Support is also provided for the more complex type of payment called a *collection document* (also known as a *bill of exchange*).

Payments

This category provides business objects for the payment of installments that have resulted due to invoices that you have received. It processes the installments to be paid and creates the necessary ledger items and bank movements to represent these payments.

LE Financial Batches

The financial batch support introduced in the CBO layer is extended to allow the inclusion of log items, ledger items, and allocations within the same financial batch that already contains General Ledger journals.

Warehouse management (Figure 17.23) provides the core business objects and processes that are required by applications that work with goods that are in stock (e.g., distribution or manufacturing). A key aspect of warehouse management is the definition of products and warehouses. These are the main business objects for containing persistent warehousing information. Additional functions, such as inventory, stock transactions, and other product-based and warehouse-based capabilities are associated with these definitions. Most of these additional functions are accessed through the interfaces of the product and warehouse classes.

On top of these core business object definitions, warehouse management defines a set of domain processes that can be used to work with the core business objects of the framework. These processes are incomplete implementations that are meant to be extended by an application

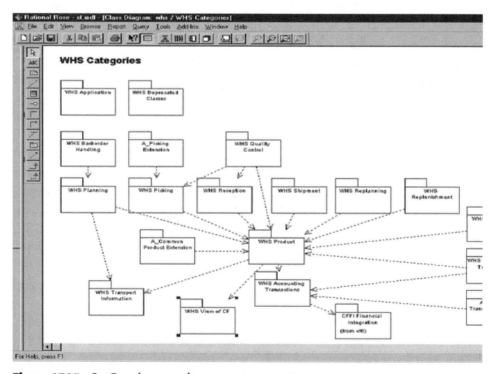

Figure 17.23 SanFrancisco warehouse management.

or another framework. Typically, an application or framework that uses warehouse management will combine these processes in specific ways to support higher-level business processes (such as a sales order).

Following are descriptions of the key business objects and processes involved in warehouse management.

Product

Product is the focal point of the warehouse management core business process. It provides support not only for the product definition and descriptive information, but also incorporates many functions related to inventory handling (e.g., balance update and retrieval, costing, lot and serial number handling, availability checking, lead time calculation). These functions reside on the product interface but are typically delegated to other objects that are easily extendable and replaceable. Specific products can be specified as lot-controlled or serial number–controlled, which makes those respective attributes mandatory for all handling of inventory that is related to that product. Many product costing approaches are supported, both transaction-based (last in, first out or first in, first out) and non–transaction based (average, standard, latest inbound). The application end user will specify one costing approach as the system costing approach, but other costing approaches can be used for what-if scenarios. For example, a customer sets up an application to use standard cost for accounting purposes, but can also ask the application what the average cost is for a particular product.

Product takes advantage of the common business object (CBO) function for conversion of units, specializing the generic behavior provided by the CBOs with product-specific behavior. Each product defines a base unit and the other units in which it can be stocked. It is possible to define a generic set of units and conversion factors (for example, single items, cases, and pallets) but selectively enable only some of those units (for example, cases and pallets) for a particular product. Warehouse management processes can take advantage of units handling to automatically convert goods in stock from one unit to another as part of a process. For example, an availability checking algorithm could take into account the goods that are currently being stored in pallets even though a customer may be requesting a quantity of that product in cases.

Warehouse management also supports single-level kit definitions (a product can be a kit, a kit component, or neither) on a unit-by-unit basis.

The framework does not support multilevel kits because this behavior is akin to manufacturing rather than warehousing.

Warehouse

Warehouses can be selectively location-controlled, which forces all inventory to be associated with a specific location. In other words, if a warehouse is location-controlled, any inventory associated with that warehouse must have a location specified. Stock zones introduce an additional optional level of organization within a warehouse. Zones could be used, for example, to distinguish different areas of the warehouse, such as a frozen goods section of a food warehouse. Stock locations optionally contain measurement information (for example, volume and weight capacity of a location) which can be used (along with other zone and location information) by the location-handling algorithms incorporated into the framework. By using these stock locations, you can make intelligent business decisions when storing and retrieving stocked goods. Again, these algorithms have been implemented in such a way to make them easily extendable and replaceable.

Inventory

SanFrancisco has a broad-reaching definition of inventory, which includes goods in stock, product reservations, and future receptions. The inventory business object is used to represent only the goods that are currently in stock. Inventory is tracked at the most granular level appropriate for the product/warehouse combination (for example, if a product is lot-controlled, the lot is required for inventory tracking). Multiple stock types are defined to allow differentiation within a product (for example, normal versus rejected stock). Products can be selectively designated to allow inventory to be maintained in some warehouses and not in others. Balance summaries at higher levels of granularity (for example, stock type and unit of measure only) are supported based on the cached balances function provided by CBOs. Balances are also defined for future receptions (goods that are going to be delivered by a supplier, from manufacturing, and so on) and eventual reservations (goods that are reserved for a certain purpose, such as a sales order). Such information is often used when calculating product availability. For example, if a customer calls in a sales order with product delivery four weeks in the future, availability checking can take into account a planned delivery of stock three weeks in the future, even though those goods are not currently in inventory.

Stock Transactions

Stock transactions are used to record all increases and decreases to stock. Whenever a stock transaction is created, the framework also ensures that all other necessary operations occur, such as updating the product balances and costing information and creating the necessary financial dissections to record the stock increase or decrease in the General Ledger. Various processes that create stock transactions introduce specialized stock transactions. A specialized stock transaction is also provided for manual stock transactions (transactions not associated with any business process directly supported by the application).

The information contained within stock transaction objects can be used as a source for sophisticated management analysis tools. This is one of the many areas where application developers can provide significant product differentiation and value-add to the frameworks.

Warehouse Business Processes

Many business processes are introduced by warehouse management. The processes defined by warehouse management are those that are needed to serve a wider, more diverse market (for example, distribution and manufacturing applications). These processes are designed to be completed by code using the framework (either applications or other frameworks). They are introduced in warehouse management so that generic processing can occur regardless of the source domain of the process. For example, picking details generated by both distribution and manufacturing processes can be merged into a single consolidated collection at the warehouse management level, and that collection can be used to generate a consolidated pick list. This approach also defines a common base for extensions in various domains. For example, various processes might be extended differently when implementing a manufacturing application rather than when doing order entry.

Planning, Replanning, Reception, Quality Control, Picking, Shipment, Back-order Handling, Replenishment, and Stock Take provide the set of basic processes that need to be extended by the application or another framework (for example, by Order Management). Each of these processes will be discussed in more detail as part of the category summarization for warehouse management.

Warehouse Management Framework Categories

A brief description of each of the WMS packages follows.

Transport Information

This category allows the end user to establish transport times based on a flexible and extendable set of criteria, including address, transport zone, and manner of transport. It builds on the key function provided by CBO generalized mechanisms.

Accounting Transactions

This category captures domain information that is needed to successfully create financial dissections for various warehousing activities. It allows domain developers to work with concepts and objects that are familiar to them (such as products and warehouses) rather than having to become familiar with financial terminology.

Product

This category encompasses all of the core business objects of warehouse management along with numerous low-level business processes which are used as building blocks for higher-level processing. The functions that are provided by this category include the following:

- Product and warehouse definition
- Kit definition
- Costing
- Inventory and stock transactions management
- Availability checking
- Lead time retrieval
- Lot, location, serial number, and units handling

Replenishment

This category evaluates inventory in relation to the reorder point and makes recommendations for orders for a supplier or another warehouse. Replenishment sources (such as suppliers or internal warehouses) can be established on a per-product or per-warehouse combination.

Stock Take

This category provides the processes that are used for counting physical stock. This category uses business rules to determine what products should be included in the count. After the results of the count are entered, stock balances are updated and then corresponding updates of costing and accounting can be made. The business rules involved are extendable to make them adaptable to different business practices.

Stock Transactions

This category supports the creation of stock increases and decreases and also creates the necessary financial transactions along with handling product updates. These stock transactions are used to capture both manual changes to stock as well as the changes to stock that result from processes such as stock take, picking, and reception, among others.

Picking

This category manages the picking process, which is defined as picking products from stock. This category also provides the ability to adapt the picking process according to specific business and finance policies. The picking process may select the appropriate locations, lots, or serial numbers for picking products from stock and also adjusts inventory to reflect the correct amount while creating the necessary financial transactions. Pick lists can be selectively generated according to extendable business rules.

Reception

This category manages the reception process, which is defined as the reception of product into the warehouse. This category also provides the ability to adapt the reception process according to specific business and finance policies. The reception process adjusts inventory and creates the necessary financial transactions. Reception notes can be selectively generated according to extendable business rules.

Warehouse management supports the maintenance of serial number assignment and lot handling for both of the picking and reception categories. Support for handling of stock locations within the warehouse is also included as part of both picking and reception.

Planning and Replanning

This category provides structures to determine which warehouse will receive products or supply products. The business rules involved are extendable to make them adaptable to different business practices. This category also introduces the basic structures that allow the replanning process to be incorporated with other business processes as needed based on business rules.

Quality Control

This category defines the basic process that is used to manage the inspection activity of a quality control process by using flexible business rules.

Shipment

This category manages the shipping process and provides the structures that are needed to create the shipping details and ship lists. The business rules involved are extendable to make them adaptable to different business practices.

Back Order Handling

This category supports the ability to selectively incorporate back ordering support with other processes, such as picking, by using extendable business rules.

Order management (see Figure 17.24) provides the core infrastructure needed by order-processing applications. It supports a virtually unlimited number of order types, providing specific examples of various types of sales, purchase, and internal orders. Application developers can use these samples either as is or as a starting point for defining their own order types. These order types are built from combinations of various processes, some of which are introduced by warehouse management and the CBOs, and others that are introduced directly by order management. Because of the way these processes are combined, an application has a great deal of flexibility in defining new order type variations which reuse existing processes in different ways.

Order management also provides support for order-specific business objects. Some of these business objects, like OrderProduct and Order-Partner, extend the capabilities of business objects introduced by warehouse management and the CBOs. Other business objects, like those supporting prices and discounts, are provided solely at the order management level.

Order Business Processes

Order management builds on the processes introduced by warehouse management and the CBOs, as well as introducing its own order-specific

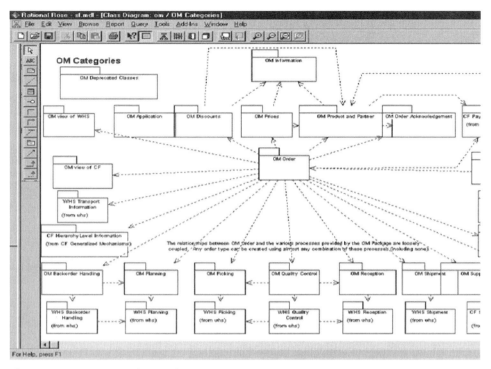

Figure 17.24   SanFrancisco order management.

processes. Each of these processes is designed so that individual processes can be coupled together in very flexible ways. The framework performs this by using the life cycle mechanisms provided by the CBO generalized mechanisms.

Following is a short description of the processes introduced by CBOs and by order management.

The following processes are introduced by CBOs:

- *Invoicing:* Used to record the actual billing related to the order.
- *Supplementary charges:* Used to record charges on an order that are not directly related to products (e.g., freight, special handling charges, invoicing fees, and so on).

The following processes are introduced by order management:

- *Order:* Used to capture customer and supplier information (often known as *order header*).
- *OrderPriceDetail:* Used to capture product and price information (with OrderRequestedDetail, this is part of what is often known as an *order line*).

- *OrderRequestedDetail:* Used to capture quantity, delivery time, and delivery address information (with OrderPriceDetail, this is the remainder of the order line).

- *OrderAcknowledgement:* Used to allow the order to record that an acknowledgement has been processed.

The first three order management processes just listed are used to handle the order entry aspect of an order management application. These processes are typed the same as with OrderPartner; the same design and implementation is used to support sales, purchase, and internal orders. The application chooses how to present these processes to the end user.

Order Management Framework Categories

A brief description of each OM framework categories follows.

Order Product and Order Partner

Order management extends the product and BusinessPartner business objects.

Pricing and Discounts

Order management allows you to establish and maintain sales, purchase, and internal pricing information in an extremely flexible manner.

Replenishment

Order management introduces two specific types of replenishment sources: one that represents external suppliers, and another that represents internal warehouses.

Accounting Transactions

Order management uses the business objects and processes provided in the common business objects layer for financial transactions. This enables interoperability between applications that are built on order management and other applications that use the common business objects layer for financial transactions, such as General Ledger.

Management of Orders

Order management provides the capability to create an order that includes related detail information and the necessary logic (in the form of policies and validation) that ensures the completeness, correctness, and integrity of the order. This order can be maintained and updated during its life cycle as described in the previous sections. The framework provides seven sample order types on which application developers can base their development.

Planning and Replanning

Order management assigns the relation between an order detail and the warehouse where it will be shipped to (or from) by using the process that is defined in warehouse management. It also extends the information available for replanning defined by warehouse management with order-specific information.

Picking

Order management integrates with the picking process that is defined in warehouse management to pick products out of inventory. Order management then associates the information about each stock pick with the order detail. Order management also maintains product reservations against the specific location, lot, or serial number used for the pick.

Reception

Order management integrates with the reception process that is defined in warehouse management to accomplish the reception of products into inventory. Order management provides the linking between order details and receptions into stock and maintains future receptions accordingly.

Quality Control

Order management uses the quality control process that is defined in warehouse management to perform quality inspections on reception.

Shipping

Order management adapts the shipping process that is defined in warehouse management to support the life cycle–based order structure.

Back Order Handling

Order management extends the back order handling process that is introduced by warehouse management so that it can be incorporated into various order types. Specific business policy examples for back order handling are supplied as part of the framework.

Order Acknowledgement

Order management provides the basic structures that are used to mark orders and their details as acknowledged or unacknowledged.

Order Invoicing

Order management identifies the order line or lines which are to be invoiced and generates the inputs to the common invoicing process defined by the common business objects layer. Order management also creates the financial transactions to be posted to General Ledger.

Order Supplementary Changes

Order management extends the business objects and processes that are provided by the common business objects layer to incorporate supplementary charges into order processing. Supplementary charges can be introduced at any detail level of an order.

Common Business Objects (CBOs) Layer

The common business objects (CBO) layer (see Figure 17.25) is built on top of the foundation layer. This layer, together with the foundation and utilities, forms the base as shown. The common business objects layer consists of objects that perform functions commonly needed across business domains.

General Business Objects

This group includes classes that most commercial applications have to deal with, such as a business partner (e.g., customer or supplier), address, currency, and so on. The company class, which is included here, has special importance in SanFrancisco. Most of the objects in an application typically belong to a company, either directly or indirectly. The currently

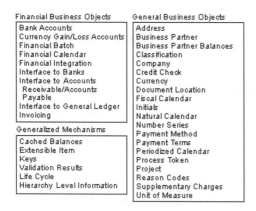

Figure 17.25   CBO: a categorization.

active company object in a SanFrancisco-based application provides the business context in which that application runs, affecting the business objects available to the application and the business algorithms used by that application.

Using the common business objects ensures that SanFrancisco-based applications from different providers can cooperate. The core business processes use CBO classes extensively.

Financial Business Objects

All businesses must deal with money, and virtually all businesses must record financial status in the financial domain or deal with financial business objects, such as bank accounts. The classes in this group enable nonfinancial business processes to work with financial information.

Generalized Mechanisms

This group contains mechanisms that are common to many aspects of business in general. Cached balances, for instance, are totals that can be maintained over inventories or other summarizable information.

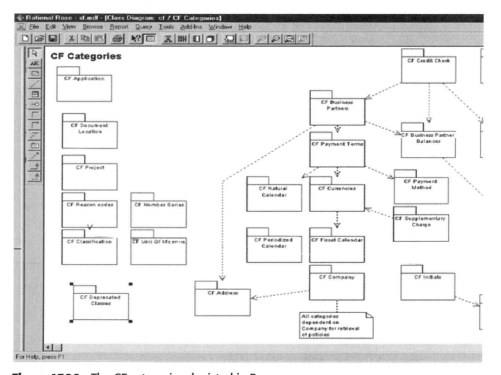

Figure 17.26 The CF categories depicted in Rose.

The foundation layer (see Figure 17.27) is the core technological layer of SanFrancisco and provides fundamental services such as distributed object creation, synchronization, persistence, and a consistent application development model. It encapsulates the technological aspects of cross-platform distributed object management and provides an easy-to-use API. It also includes support for security, provides distributed transaction processing, and forms a middleware layer between a client application and server.

The foundation provides you with the distributed architecture through its set of foundation classes. These foundation classes provide a way to set up a distributed application. The foundation masks the technology differences between platforms and supports multiplatform environments. The foundation also provides classes that form an interface to the different object services.

By using the foundation and complying with the SanFrancisco programming model, you can implement several OO paradigms.

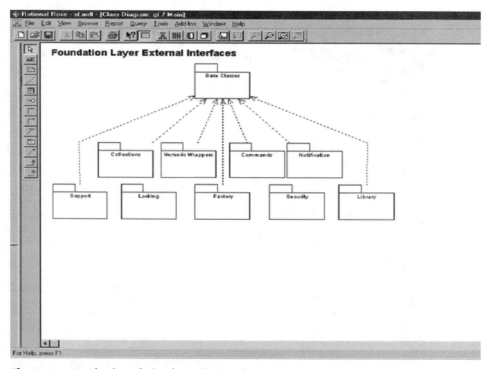

Figure 17.27 The foundation layer depicted in Rose.

The foundation allows you to divide processing between several systems, which gives you control of the performance and scalability of your application.

The foundation is the control tower of SanFrancisco; most of your requests are accepted and routed by the foundation layer. The foundation is your interface to the different services. It deals with the persistent data stores and makes it easy to switch between different methods of persistence without having to recode your application or modify your business objects. Changes are made through the configuration data, which can be updated at priming time.

The foundation layer is also the interface to the Base Factory mechanism that plays an important role in managing distributed objects. We discuss the Base Factory in more detail in The BaseFactory, but remember that all object maintenance (create, delete, copy, and so on) must be done through the Base Factory.

Summary

One of the things that challenged us at WNS right from the beginning was trying to get our arms around the capabilities inherent in the objects. Certainly there is a great deal of SanFrancisco documentation, and we sent several people on training for weeks on end. But toward the end of the training and familiarization process (and in many ways driven by the need to complete this book), we began to look for ways to quickly get up and running using SanFrancisco. Internally we called it *Project: Instant Java.*

This is completely consistent with the literature and strategic positioning of SanFrancisco. The difference between what we had been doing and what we ended up taking on was in the emphasis.

Previously we had emphasized understanding the framework—what is a framework, what is its scope, how does it work, where do we extend it, and so on. These are the big questions, and ultimately they are questions you are only going to address after you have a feeling for what the framework offers right out of the box. Last, since SanFrancisco does provide such a great deal of functionality as shipped, I realized that we had been barking up the wrong tree.

Therefore, instead of focusing on how to extend the framework, we decided to look at what we could build out of the components as shipped. This is what we just covered as the SF Bean–based development from the samples. In the next chapter you will see that we were also able to take advantage of some of the SanFrancisco code through servlets.

CHAPTER 18

Creating Simple SanFrancisco Applications

O ne of the most important breakthroughs we had while working with the Big Blue Java tool set was finally figuring out how to jumpstart SanFrancisco development. This is something that the SF development team obviously knew it had to provide, but for some reason we all missed its significance when Version 1.4 of the framework came out.

Instead of working from the complexity of the framework out, after our initial efforts with SF faltered we decided to begin again with small steps. I hope this will help you come to grips with what use SF can be for you. I know it certainly helped my group.

SF Development

Developers of SanFrancisco generally fall into three categories: framework developers, bean builders, and bean assemblers. Framework developers create business interfaces, and the factory and foundation classes that go with it. The bean builder then builds the bean, based on the interface and some information from the foundation and controller while bean assemblers wire working beans to user interface screens.

From the preceding description of the roles of developers one can see that a bean is separated into three logical sections. This is shown in Figure 18.1

SF Beans do not exist by themselves but are generally created as a three-bean set consisting of one nonvisual bean and two visual beans. This is not always true, however; there may be many visual beans, or only one. The only rule that holds true is that there is always one nonvisual bean.

The SanFrancisco Framework

There is a hierarchical architecture for the framework, based on business-stakeholder relationships. (A stakeholder is any individual or entity that has a stake in the company, e.g., stockholders, customers, vendors, and employees.) This framework is depicted in Figure 18.2.

There is only one company object that isn't owned by any other company objects. This is loosely called the *enterprise*, and this object owns all other objects. There is a one-to-many relationship between the company and its subcompanies (actually you can have sub-sub and sub-sub-sub and so on). The subcompanies can be thought of as geographical or logical divisions of a large international business. The subcompanies have

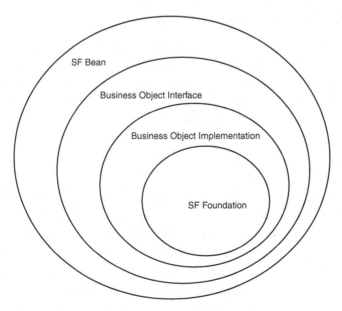

Figure 18.1   Logical division of an SF Bean.

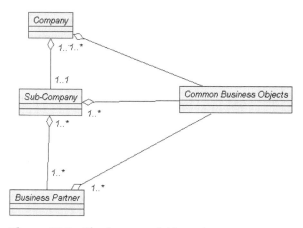

Figure 18.2 The framework hierarchy.

business partners that have their common business objects. Every object in SF is owned by another object except for the company (also called the enterprise). Also, every object has a controller associated with it.

When you query objects you can specify if you will also see the parent's controller's objects. This is described as a *chain of responsibility*. The controllers have a hierarchical relationship, leading to a hierarchical relationship with all the objects and data. This is a business-based architecture; when you cannot find an item in one warehouse, then you look to another nearby division, and if you can't get it there, you order it from the main warehouse. As you can see by this simple example, SF provides an ideal architecture for business applications.

Now let's look at the basis for a nonvisual bean in SF. These beans are central to an understanding of the architecture and how the common business objects fit into the architecture.

Nonvisual SF Beans

A nonvisual bean implements three interfaces, depending on the mode of the bean. These interfaces are the business object interface of a single object, the life cycle interface for creating and deleting business objects, and the collection interface used to access a collection of the business objects.

The modes of a business object were developed to reduce the amount and complexity of coding in the SanFrancisco framework. This reduction in the complexity of using the framework comes at the expense of increased complexity at the framework developer level. However, this is an appropriate model for the SF framework as a few programmers can develop and extend the framework, while less-experienced programmers can develop applications.

Some of the important points to recognize at all levels of development and implementation for the modal architecture are:

- Nonvisual beans can only be run in one mode at a time.
- Some nonvisual beans only support one mode.
- Visual beans do not have modes.
- The mode can be changed at run-time.
- There are four modes that a bean can assume:

  Controller

  Owned collection

  Collection

  Owned business object

Descriptions of the Four Modes

Controller mode. The bean is a collection of objects of a certain class. You can then use the collection methods to manipulate the objects in a controller by iteration throughout the objects and adding, deleting, or manipulating objects. The controller is retrieved from the current active company object. Of important note is the Directly-Owned property. If this property is set to True, only the objects that the controller directly owns are available. However if this property is set to False, all objects that the controller and its parent owns are available for access.

Owned collection mode. This mode assumes that the business objects implement the business object interface and are stored in an SF collection, and that another business object owns the collection object. In this mode the collection changes are routed through the owner's methods. Thus the owner's methods are used to iterate over the collection and add and delete objects.

Collection mode. This is similar to the owned collection mode; however it assumes that the collection isn't owned and thus its methods are used to access the collection. This mode should be used when the collection doesn't have any owners.

Owned object mode. When a business object (X) owns or references another business object (R), the owner provides methods to retrieve the owned business object. Owned object mode assumes that business objects that implement the business object interface X are (or can be) owned by another business object R (shown in Figure 18.3).

To implement this relationship, the owned nonvisual bean (R) has property businessObjectOwner:

- The nonvisual bean X routes getX() and setX() method calls to the owner R.

- Owned entities are a good example of the owned object mode. For example, PrimaryAddress in Company is an owned object. The address bean uses the following methods to get and set the primaryAddress:

- company.getPrimaryAddress()

- company.setPrimaryAddress(addr)

- *Object mode.* This mode is used when an object is self-owned and thus all actions on the business object are self-contained. This is used extensively in user-written code. The mode of an object can be switched at runtime by using the methods shown in Table 18.1.

One selects the modes to implement by inspecting the UML diagram. You should look for the modes that an object interface employs, along with other modes that might be used by other objects. All of the modes should be created in the nonvisual bean.

Nonvisual beans fire events that can be used to identify nonvisual bean state changes. These events are:

Figure 18.3   UML diagram of an owned object.

Table 18.1 Object Methods Associated with Changing Modes

METHOD	SWITCHES TO MODE
setController()	Controlled mode
setCollectionOwner()	Owned collection mode
setCollection()	Collection mode
setBusinessObjectOwner()	Owned business object mode
setBusinessObject()	Business object mode

CollectionChangeEvent. Fired whenever:

- A new collection is set on the bean.
- refreshData is called.
- A new query is run.

CreateBusinessObjectEvent. Fired whenever a new business object instance is created.

DeleteBusinessObjectEvent. Fired whenever a business object is deleted.

PropertyChangeEvent. Fired whenever a business object property is changed.

SelectionChangeEvent. Fired whenever the collection cursor is moved.

VetoableChangeEvent. Fired before a business object property is changed, allowing listeners to veto the change. Nonvisual properties are not (usually) constrained properties (properties that fire VetoableChangeEvents). Nonvisuals fire this event only before commit is called.

The SanFrancisco business model is based on hierarchy of companies. SanFrancisco beans require one company in the hierarchy to be designated as the active company. The active company allows you to work with controllers from different companies. The active company also determines which controller is used for controlled mode objects, and dynamic properties.

WNS Currency Example

Our currency example provides a list of currencies available to the company. This is a real-world example which when run displays a screen as shown in Figure 18.4.

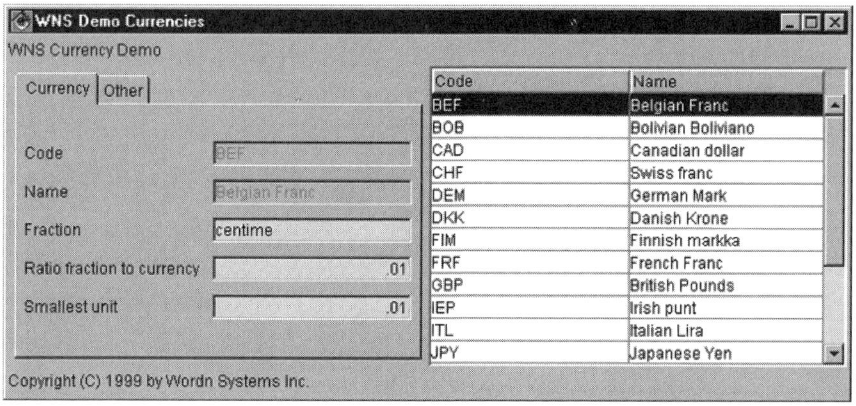

Figure 18.4 The demo SF currency screen.

The data is based on the sample data provided by SF. Currency is an SF business object; the class which creates this object is located at com. ibm.sf.cf.Currency. Currency is stored in a currency controller, represented by class com.ibm.sf.cf.CurrencyController, which is retrieved from the active company. This applet was quite easy to construct, as you will see from the code.

```
package wns.com.VisualExamples;

import java.awt.*;
import java.awt.event.*;
import com.ibm.sf.beans.cf.*;
import com.ibm.sf.beans.base.*;

/**
 * This Class was created by James Carlson for WNS, Inc.
 * This is the sole property of WNS, Inc. Do Not redistribute.
 */
public class CurrencyDemo extends java.awt.Frame implements WindowListener
{
  Panel myPanel = new Panel();
  GridLayout gridLayout1 = new GridLayout();
  Label myLabel1 = new Label();
  Label myLabel2 = new Label();
  CurrencyObjectForm myCurrencyObjectForm = null;
  CurrencyCollectionForm myCurrencyCollectionForm = null;
  CurrencyBean myCurrencyBean = null;
/**
 * CurrencyDemo constructor comment.
 */
public CurrencyDemo() {
    super();
    try {
```

```java
            this.frameInit();
        } catch (Exception e) {
          e.printStackTrace();
        }
    }
/**
 * This method was created in VisualAge.
 */
public void frameInit() throws Exception{
        addWindowListener(this);
        this.setLayout(new BorderLayout());
        this.setSize(new Dimension(650, 300));
        this.setTitle("WNS Demo Currencies");
        myLabel1.setText("Copyright (C) 1999 by WNS, Inc.");
        myLabel1.setBackground(Color.lightGray);
        myPanel.setLayout(gridLayout1);

        ApplicationContextBean.setAliveMode(false);
        java.beans.Beans.setDesignTime(true);

        myCurrencyBean = new CurrencyBean();
        myCurrencyCollectionForm = new CurrencyCollectionForm();
        myCurrencyObjectForm = new CurrencyObjectForm();

        this.add(myPanel, BorderLayout.CENTER);
        myPanel.add(myCurrencyObjectForm, null);
        myPanel.add(myCurrencyCollectionForm, null);
        this.add(myLabel1, BorderLayout.SOUTH);

        myLabel2.setText("WNS Currency Demo");
        myLabel2.setBackground(Color.lightGray);
        this.add(myLabel2, BorderLayout.NORTH);

        myCurrencyCollectionForm.setBusinessObjectBean(myCurrencyBean);
        myCurrencyObjectForm.setCollectionForm(myCurrencyCollectionForm);
        ApplicationContextBean.setAliveMode(true);
        myCurrencyBean.doSetActiveContextController();
        myCurrencyCollectionForm.reload();
        myCurrencyCollectionForm.select(0);
    }
/**
 * This method was created in VisualAge.
 * @param args java.lang.String[]
 */
public static void main(String args[]) {
        ApplicationContextBean.setExceptionHandle(false);
        try {
          ApplicationContextBean.getActiveCompany(null);
          CurrencyDemo frame = new CurrencyDemo();
          frame.setVisible(true);
          frame.toFront();
        }
        catch (Exception e) {
          ApplicationContextBean.printException(e);
```

```
            System.exit(-1);
        }

    }
    /**
     * windowActivated method comment.
     */
    public void windowActivated(java.awt.event.WindowEvent e) {
    }
    /**
     * windowClosed method comment.
     */
    public void windowClosed(java.awt.event.WindowEvent e) {
    }
    /**
     * windowClosing method comment.
     */
    public void windowClosing(java.awt.event.WindowEvent e) {
            System.exit(0);
    }
    /**
     * windowDeactivated method comment.
     */
    public void windowDeactivated(java.awt.event.WindowEvent e) {
    }
    /**
     * windowDeiconified method comment.
     */
    public void windowDeiconified(java.awt.event.WindowEvent e) {
    }
    /**
     * windowIconified method comment.
     */
    public void windowIconified(java.awt.event.WindowEvent e) {
    }
    /**
     * windowOpened method comment.
     */
    public void windowOpened(java.awt.event.WindowEvent e) {
    }
}
```

Comments on the Code

As you compare this to the code from the ComicBookApplet you will realize that it is much smaller than that code. This is due to the use of CurrencyBean, CurrencyCollectionForm, and the CurrencyObjectForm objects. These are objects that are shipped with SF and demonstrate the power of the beans and framework provided in some of the 12,000 beans and accompanying 54,000 methods.

Configuring the Environment

One of the trickiest aspects of building applets is the proper setup of the programming environment. First, you must configure SF to allow other applications, including VAJava, to access its data. The problem stems from the use SF makes of the string class. In order to provide compatibility with Java 2 code, the SF developers used the string class from Java 2. This makes the data SF creates inaccessible to other Java 1 applications.

To get around this you must alter SF to have all the Java applications read and understand the same data. This is accomplished by renaming the following file d:\SF\SF140\JAVA\LANG\String.class and d:\SF\SF140\com\ibm\sf\gf\StringValidate.class to any other name (don't delete them though you will need them in the future).

Now you will have to reinitialize your NameSpace and data. You then must modify VAJava's class path to include d:\sf\sf140\, and then restart VAJ. When it comes time to run your applet you must specify on which port you will connect to the LSFN. First you must change your d:\sf\sf140\sfconfig.ini file; on the line which says GSM_port you must set it to GSM_port=9896. Additionally you must set the port in VAJava, as shown in Figure 18.5.

Now you must stop all SF servers and run the samples from the START->Programs->IBM SanFrancisco 1.4.0->Samples->Run Samples. After this has set up, your desktop will look like Figure 18.6.

Now select Business Object Samples and then Launch Samples. This will prime your workspace with sample data and start the LSFN on port 9896. Finally you can run your applet.

This is fine when you get your environment set up; however it can prove to be frustrating to get the LSFN working with the sample data. The only suggestion I can make here is to try installing IBM's 1.1.7 JDK and make sure your classpath is set up correctly to both Swing(JFC) and the JDK.

Now let's look another example, which demonstrates WebSphere integration with SF and a CBO. The output of this sample as shown is not ready for production; however it demonstrates the ease of creating a servlet gateway to a LSFN.

As you can see, this servlet simply displays the name and ratio of all the currency objects in the LSFN. We use the controller to iterate though the objects and simply use accesor methods to get the name and ratio. As

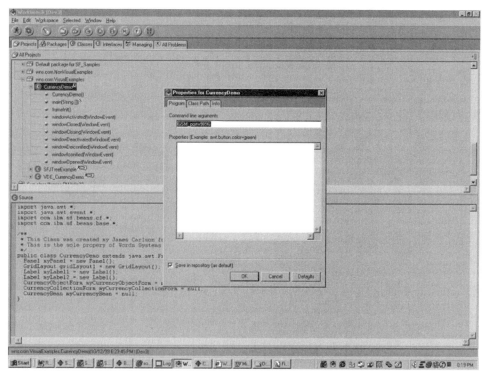

Figure 18.5 Setting the server port in VisualAge for Java.

mentioned earlier, this code has certain shortcomings; namely it isn't thread-safe, it lacks security, and it doesn't use the base factory. Despite these relatively easy-to-overcome weaknesses, our servlet demonstrates the ease of integration with SF.

The code that generates this servlet is shown here:

```
package WNSSF;

import javax.servlet.*;
import javax.servlet.http.*;
import com.ibm.sf.gf.*;
import com.ibm.sf.cf.*;
import com.ibm.sf.beans.base.*;
import com.ibm.sf.beans.cf.*;

/**
 * This Class was created by James Carlson for WNS, Inc.
 * This is the sole propery of WNS, Inc. Do Not redistribute.
 * Note this sample is based on IBM Sample - IBM SanFrancisco/WebSphere
 * Integration Sample.
 * There are many good samples for programmers that extend the
 * functionality of servlets
 */
```

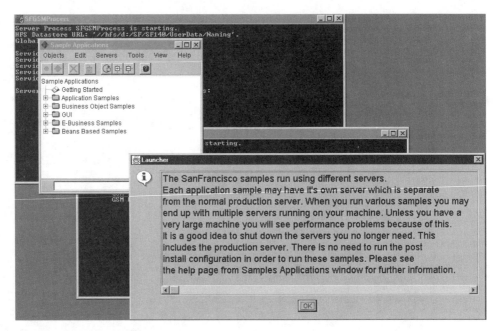

Figure 18.6 Running SF samples.

```java
public class WNSCurrencyServlet extends javax.servlet.http.HttpServlet {
/**
 * This method was created in VisualAge.
 */
public void destroy() {
    // This method gets called each time you destroy the servlet.
    // Depending on your configuration this may happen on when the
    // server is shut-down.
    try {
        Global.uninitialize(); //frees up SF resources
        super.destroy();
    } catch (GFException e) {
        log("The WNSCurrency Servlet has thrown an exception in the
destroy method :" + e.getMessage());
    }

}
/**
 * This method was created in VisualAge.
 * @param req javax.servlet.http.HttpServletRequest
 * @param res javax.servlet.http.HttpServletResponse
 * @exception javax.servlet.ServletException The exception description.
 * @exception java.io.IOException The exception description.
 */
public void doGet(HttpServletRequest req, HttpServletResponse res ) throws
ServletException, java.io.IOException {
```

```
        java.io.PrintWriter pOut = null; //setup a output stream to the
                                  browser

    res.setContentType("text/html"); //setup the content type

    pOut = res.getWriter(); //get a connection to the response stream
    //Now I start Forming the Webpage
    pOut.println("<HTML><HEAD><TITLE>");
    pOut.println("Currency Common Business Objects from the Logical
SanFrancisco Network");
    pOut.println("</TITLE></HEAD>");
    pOut.println("<H1>The Samples Currency Display Page version
1.0.4</H1>");

    try {

        CurrencyBean cb = new CurrencyBean();

        //This section will be used in the next version to write to the
        // objects
        // Global.factory().begin();
        // cb = (CurrencyBean)
Global.factory().getEntity("Currency",AccessMode.createPlusWrite());

       // reset the iterator to the beginning of the collection
        cb.reset();
        // Now we will simply write all the codes to the output stream
        // (ie the browser)
        while ( cb.getNext() != null ) {
            pOut.print("The Currency name is : " +
cb.getCurrencyName() );
            pOut.println(" The ratio of the currency to the companies
currency is : " + cb.getRatioOfFractionToCurrency());

            pOut.println("<BR>");
            }

    } catch (Exception e) {
        pOut.println("SF has thrown an exception!");
    }

    pOut.println("</HTML>");

    pOut.close();

}
/**
 * This method was created in VisualAge.
 * @param config javax.servlet.ServletConfig
 * @exception javax.servlet.ServletException The exception description.
 */
public void init(ServletConfig config) throws ServletException {
    // this method is called when you first initalize the servlet. It
    // is only fired once (each time the servlet is started!)
    super.init(config); // Must call if you are overriding
```

```
init(ServletConfig)
    try {
        Global.initialize();
         // this creates the resources needed by our servlet!
    }
    catch (Exception e)
    {
         log("The initalization method of WNSCurrencyServlet has failed
:" + e.getMessage());
    }

}
}
```

This code was generated in VAJava and exported to the WebSphere directory. The setting up of WebSphere to accomodate the SF code was accomplished in two steps. The first step is to modify the classpath as shown in Figure 18.7.

The classpath must include the SF install directory and the JDK117 classes. The second step is to disable the JIT compiler; this is shown in Figure 18.8.

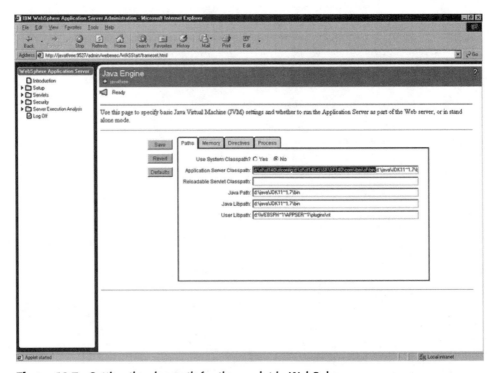

Figure 18.7 Setting the classpath for the servlet in WebSphere.

Once both steps are taken, you must restart the WebSphere application server (and consequently the IBM HTTP server) to update the JVM. Now that you have servlet access to the SFLN you can easily produce very lightweight reporting tools accessible by any browser anywhere in the world. This technology puts the entire weight of the LSFN and the application logic on the server side. This is an ideal solution for a widely distributed enterprise with existing legacy.

Further SF Information and Documentation

It can be very difficult to find information on the framework, as there is no documentation on the documentation. There are three good locations for information, including:

- The peer-to-peer support group and the local documentation. The peer-to-peer support group provides good knowledge on installation and configuring SF (located at http://www.networking.ibm.com/ SanFrancisco/forum.html).

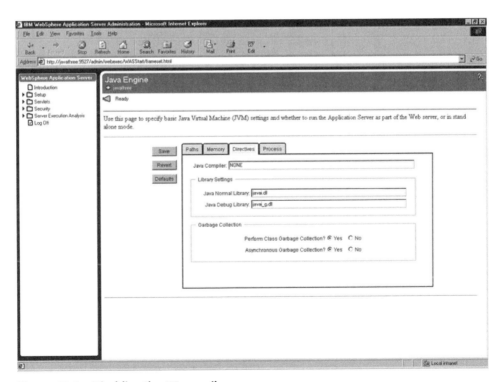

Figure 18.8 Disabling the JIT compiler.

- Another source of information is the E:\SF\SF140\com\ibm\sf\doc\ doc_en\ibmsf.sf.FS_DocumentationEntry.html document (where e:\ is the drive where you installed SF). The samples and application framework are comprehensive and well explained, although it is sometimes difficult to find exactly what you need.

- The Javadocs accompanying the framework provide a wealth of very low level knowledge on the methods and classes that make an object. These are located in D:\SF\SF140\com\ibm\sf\doc\doc_en\gl\javadocs\ ibmsf.gl.FS_Packages.html.

Taken together, these provide a good reference for extending the framework, as well as an excellent treatment of the complexity associated with the framework. From this chapter you should be able to appreciate the simplicity offered by SanFrancisco Beans (such as CurrencyBean, which we showcased in the currency applet in this chapter).

CHAPTER 19

Component Transaction Brokering

The IBM white paper on component transaction brokering has been making the rounds since October 1997. This hoary and venerable paper is still the best introduction to the TXSeries that I've found, and rather than rewrite it, adding little value, I thought I'd simply include it. (Okay, actually I'm going to lend a little value here by editing it somewhat.) It's still a pretty good piece of work, and it does describe the technology at a level appropriate for this book.

If you work with CICS and other established IBM environments, you should probably have a quick look at this to get an idea of how pervasive IBM/Java integration is going to be.

Introduction

When customers deposit money at a bank, they trust that the correct amount will be credited to their accounts. Likewise, travelers who make a hotel reservation expect to find rooms when they reach their destination. Net users, too, need to be assured that the data they download is intact and uncorrupted. These examples simply illustrate how much trust we put into the systems that manage our daily affairs.

Indeed, system trust is the cornerstone of building and deploying all business applications. All over the world, businesses rely on their computers to carry out billions of transactions each day to meet the needs of their customers and employees. Businesses must trust their systems to complete every transaction without fail. If they can't, they will not survive.

IBM's TXSeries has been designed with system trust in mind. It does so by fully integrating the industry's most powerful transaction middleware: CICS (Customer Information Control System), Encina, and Component Broker. In this overview, we will describe how TXSeries builds system trust through its rich collection of features. We will also describe how TXSeries enables enterprises to harness the valuable resources of the Internet and stay in step with the constantly evolving technologies of transactions systems.

The Key Features of TXSeries

IBM believes that a transaction processing system must excel in five key areas if it is to deliver system trust. These are: *availability*, *integrity*, *investment protection*, *scalability*, and *security*. Let's look at exactly what these entail.

Availability

No matter what a system does or how much it costs, its value is compromised if the system is not available when you need it. That means full-time availability, regardless of hardware, software, or network failures—no excuses.

TXSeries ensures system availability through replication, by executing copies of the application on many servers. But simple application replication is not enough. True availability needs both operations support and automation. That is why TXSeries provides administrators with the ability to easily define groups of servers that can be managed, replicated, and relocated within a single administrative task, from a centralized location. Reconfiguration can take place while the system is running, without loss of service to the end user. Best of all, potential failures can be anticipated and preventive measures put in place instead.

When a reconfiguration occurs, either through explicit administrative action or through a failure in some environmental component, TXSeries automatically causes any partially performed work to be made consistent and reroutes requests from inaccessible facilities to the remaining servers. TXSeries will attempt to correct failures by restarting affected servers automatically. Within the graphical administrative console, the status of changed servers is highlighted, thereby notifying the operations staff that a failure has occurred and rerouting is taking place.

Integrity

In transaction processing, availability is pointless without system integrity. Services must maintain accurate records of any actions performed. For example, if money is transferred from one bank account to another, both balances must match to reflect the change. Anything less than that would result in utter chaos.

The TXSeries transaction engine is the most powerful, most reliable, and highest performance engine available. It delivers system integrity through a number of unique features. Its dynamically assigned transaction coordinators, for example, eliminate network bottlenecks. Its distributed and nested transactions mitigate failure points. The operational and physical logging provide fast-commit processing. In addition, TXSeries guarantees full transactional integrity across heterogeneous servers connected by DCE Remote Procedure Call (RPC), Internet Inter Orb Protocol (IIOP), and LU 6.2. TXSeries also supports all of the major transaction interfaces: Open Group's TX and XA, Object Management Group's CORBA Services OTS, IBM's CPI-RR, and Encina's Transactional-C and Transactional-C++ systems.

Longevity

Corporations have invested billions of dollars on IT hardware and software. A key factor in maximizing the return on their investment will be keeping applications running productively for as long as possible. TXSeries delivers longevity in two important ways. First, it lets you build on the applications you already have by focusing on reuse of existing applications. For example, it allows you to extend the reach of an application by providing new access methods, such as the Web, and allows you to build new applications and services that require information and services from existing applications. Second, new applications built on TXSeries are easily adapted for future needs. TXSeries gives companies the flexibility to adjust to business and technology changes. Ultimately,

TXSeries provides the ability to continuously improve and expand services without disruptions, which is critical for system trust.

Scalability

Demands on network service can vary over time. The changes could be short-term, such as when a bank experiences a rush of customers during lunchtime. Or, they could be long-term, such as when a business simply grows. Moreover, as more companies extend services on the Internet, network resources face greater, often unpredictable, demands. These factors make scalability an important issue—now and in the future.

TXSeries solves the scalability problem in two ways. First, it uses replication mechanisms, which have become the industry standard for defining and managing scalability. Second, it uses workload management, which distributes client requests among servers. TXSeries contains a variety of workload management algorithms, including capacity distribution, most recently used, and round-robin. In the near future, data-dependent routing will also be added as a built-in choice.

TXSeries also provides interfaces by which sophisticated users may attach their own workload distribution algorithm. Because TXSeries implements both replication management and workload management, no single failure can bring down a system. Through its internal distributed architecture, TXSeries offers linear scalability that grows to meet new business needs, ensuring the system trust for transaction processing.

Security

Is your company's data safe from prying, unauthorized eyes? Are the people you deal with on the Web really who they say they are? A *maybe* answer to either of these questions could spell big trouble for any enterprise. That is why the ability to protect resources is a key part of TXSeries. The key features of TXSeries provide customers with the most comprehensive security functionality in the industry:

Authentication control. Authentication is how TXSeries ensures that both users and servers are legitimate. Based on Kerberos technology provided by DSSeries, authentication control features the ability to verify the identity of both users and servers. This prevents impostors from using the system and rogue servers from pretending to be the legitimate business providers to the public.

Authorization control. Authorization specifies how services may be accessed and by whom. Unlike other systems, TXSeries attaches security information to services rather than to servers. Hence, it's possible to move a server from one machine to another without further reconfiguration of the security definitions. Security mechanisms tied to a machine make dynamic reconfiguration either impossible or very difficult, and risk opening security vulnerabilities during reconfiguration.

Session security. TXSeries uses two levels of session security—integrity and privacy—to ensure that communications between a client and a server are secure. Integrity ensures that no packet information is altered as it travels between client and server. Privacy goes a step further, encrypting all of the data sent between client and server, thereby preventing inspection of the data as it travels through networks. Both integrity and privacy are based on DES algorithms.

Web security. The authentication facilities of TXSeries are supported by IBM's Global Sign-On product. TXSeries also uses public key technology (SSL) to secure communications from the browser to the entry point of the transaction processing server. When the session transfers from the Web environment to the transaction processing environment, TXSeries automatically converts the security information. This enables TXSeries to provide end-to-end security from the Web browser to the server to the mainframe.

Web and Internet connectivity. By its very name, the Web encourages connectivity and the reuse of services to provide more services. As more enterprises become global, they will need to fuse their information technology infrastructure with the Web in order to build and enhance their businesses. This is what IBM calls *e-business*. E-business is why the Internet matters to the business world.

For e-business to grow, effective transaction processing driven by reliable and secure network connectivity must be in place. Businesses rely on middleware such as TXSeries to support and simplify connections across increasingly diverse and complex networks. Why? Because middleware is the most practical way to provide fail-safe processing across heterogeneous environments. TXSeries delivers secure cross-enterprise integration, reliable electronic communications with third parties, and maximum flexibility to scale. TXSeries is one of the five application servers within IBM's Network Computing Framework, along with Domino Go, Domino Mail, Domino, and DB/2 Universal Database. TXSeries, especially, facilitates system trust on the Internet with the following features:

Browser support. TXSeries users can access transactions directly from the most popular browsers, including Lotus Notes Client, Microsoft Internet Explorer, Netscape Navigator and Communicator, and Mosaic. Two approaches are supported: Java Applets and IIOP.

Java applets. TXSeries supports Web integration by providing applets for both the CICS and Encina components. In both cases, code that represents the client interfaces for CICS (ECI and EPI) and Encina (call invocation) is written in Java and can be loaded onto Web pages. On demand, the Java can be downloaded into the browser and executed within the browser. The browser then accesses transactions through an intermediary, which accepts the protocol used by the Java applet and converts it into a protocol acceptable to a TXSeries server. For example, the CICS Java applet protocol is converted into CICS client calls, while the Encina Java applet protocol is converted into DCE RPCs.

Two unique features supported by TXSeries Java applets are multistep transactions and end-to-end security. Unlike other approaches to browser support, the TXSeries Java applet can contain calls to begin and commit transactions that bracket a collection of requests to multiple servers. Therefore, a browser can access multiple sources of data and services in support of its transaction. In addition, the Java applet can exploit Internet-standard SSL to provide secure communications.

With the inclusion of an ORB into a browser, Java applets can make IIOP calls from the browser to any IIOP-enabled server. TXSeries can accept IIOP calls to execute transactions when configured with Iona's Orbix.

Web Server Support

TXSeries offers a full range of features that enable developers and administrators to provide transactional Web servers. Capabilities range from quick and easy to use to more sophisticated, better performing and highly-secure architectures. TXSeries is shipped with the Domino Go Web server integrated, but it also supports Netscape and Microsoft Web servers:

Common gateway interface (CGI) support. TXSeries supports CGI, the standard interface provided by essentially all Web servers. Using this interface, developers can build applications that act as a client to a TXSeries server. The applications are invoked using the standards specified by CGI for mapping URLs to executable binaries. This approach is very useful for low-volume, simple applications. The transactional applications have the full range of TXSeries facilities available to them.

Java and servlets. Servlets are Java programs that are executed within the Java Virtual Machine of a Web server. With the inclusion of a Java Virtual Machine in Web servers, TXSeries uses servlets to build transactional servers through both independently running and integrated business functions (see next list entries).

Independently running business functions. These functions separate the processing of the Web request, such as HTTP request processing, from the business logic needed to fulfill the request. A Web server retrieves a request and starts executing a Java servlet. The servlet uses TXSeries Java routines for accessing TXSeries servers running in another process (typically on the same machine, but configurable to be on other machines). In addition to handling servlet requests, the transaction server continues to accept requests using its native protocols from other clients. By separating the processing of Web requests from business functions, users can match the resource requirements needed for each activity. The separation also allows developers to choose an appropriate language, from COBOL to C++, for development the business logic. The business logic used in the Web environment can be remotely administered using the existing TXSeries administration tools, allowing for simplified management and configuration of the TXSeries servers.

Integrated business functions. A later release of TXSeries will support fully integrated business functions within Domino Go. Fully integrated business functions are executed completely within the Web server's Java Virtual Machine. Here, the business logic is written in Java and retrieves data from one or more sources. It selectively calls upon other transactional servers and processes the collected information to implement a business process. Typically, these business functions would be transactional to ensure that ACID properties (atomicity, consistency, isolation, and durability) are applied. The OTS and OCCS facilities of TXSeries are already callable from Java, ensuring transactional updates to data sources. As a result of IIOP support within Java and TXSeries, a Java program running in a Web server can transact with other servers that can accept IIOP calls. This applies whether they are Web servers running Java programs; stand-alone

ORBs, such as Iona's Orbix or the Component Broker ORB within TXSeries; or other Java Virtual Machines supporting IIOP.

TXSeries and the Reuse of Current Applications

TXSeries has the broadest range of capabilities in the industry to ensure longevity of applications, both in reusing existing applications and skills, and in building new applications for reuse. The wealth of existing applications on the mainframe written in CICS provides a rich field that offers exceptional potential for reuse. Thus, a key requirement for reuse of existing applications is interoperability with the mainframe. TXSeries provides unparalleled function for connecting the UNIX and Microsoft Windows NT environments with the mainframe. TXSeries provides the following methods to connect to CICS:

CICS ISC. The Inter-System Communication (ISC) interfaces of CICS are a proven, established method to interconnect all CICS systems. TXSeries contains a complete implementation of CICS, including ISC's support for function shipping, remote file access, transaction routing, and distributed program link. The natural connectivity between CICS systems is the simplest, most effective way to integrate new applications with existing applications. On UNIX and Microsoft Windows NT machines, the CICS programs can integrate the new access methods associated with those environments, such as the Internet, and provide connection to existing mainframe systems.

CPI-C. The CPI-C (and CPI-RR) interfaces are the leading conversational interfaces defined by IBM and adopted as open group standards. These conversational interfaces are supported by mainframe systems, as well as within TXSeries. Normally, CPI-C and CPI-RR are implemented using the LU6.2 protocol on top of an SNA network stack. Using the TCP-IP protocol, TXSeries contains support for CPI-C and CPI-RR using LU6.2 over the Internet. TXSeries also contains a protocol converter which can convert LU6.2 carried on either TCP-IP or SNA network protocols to LU6.2 carried on the other. In this way, TXSeries provides the ability to interact with mainframe systems using an established, open interface via established, open protocols.

Distributed program link (DPL). DPL is the capability of one program to invoke a CICS transaction simply by name. As mentioned earlier, the ISC facilities of CICS contain a DPL facility modeled after the CICS transaction invocation syntax. A recent addition to TXSeries is

DPL for Encina. With this capability, a CICS transaction on the mainframe can be accessed as a simple procedure call from the client program, just like any other call between a client and a server. With the support in IBM's VisualAge for automatically processing communications area definitions, developers using DPL within CICS' ISC and Encina's RPC can quickly and effectively create programs for accessing existing mainframe applications.

MQSeries. MQSeries, the industry's leading messaging middleware, is now an integral part of TXSeries. This integration permits transactional and nontransactional messaging to be combined with transactional application servers. Queuing and messaging are essential pieces of transaction processing architecture, and TXSeries features a queuing system that can be used to integrate TXSeries applications. The addition of MQSeries dramatically enhances the connectivity of TXSeries to many other existing systems and applications—both on the mainframe and elsewhere.

Application adapters. Application adapters are objects that encapsulate and abstract connections to existing applications. As part of the support for component broker interfaces, TXSeries will contain application adapters that can be called from component broker applications. These adapters will permit easy access to many systems, including DB/2, CICS, IMS and SAP.

TXSeries Builds in the Future

TXSeries capabilities for reusing and integrating existing applications far surpass other offerings in the industry. TXSeries can also be used to build systems that can be reused in the future, particularly in the CICS and object environment. Here's how:

Customer Information Control System (CICS). Historically, more transactions are run on CICS than any other single platform. The TXSeries' CICS interface has demonstrated its value as a robust, reusable, available, and secure method for reusing applications. TXSeries contains full support for the CICS interfaces. These interfaces are especially valuable for enterprises already staffed with fully trained CICS specialists. The CICS interfaces can be used, for example, to build portable applications among CICS systems. Another benefit is that client interfaces, such as ECI and EPI, can be used from conventional languages, such as C and COBOL.

Java forms. Java forms, which when used with the CICS Gateway for Java, permit access to CICS applications from browsers and other Java-enabled programs. Full support is provided for function shipping, transaction routing, and distributed program link, which together enable distributed applications in this environment. As the CICS API evolves, TXSeries for UNIX and Microsoft Windows NT will continue to incorporate updated features and functions, preserving customers' investments across platforms and ensuring the future evolution of the CICS in the UNIX and NT environments.

Objects. Object technology is the industry's leading approach for building applications for reuse. TXSeries supports the latest innovations in object technology while letting customers choose when to introduce each innovation into their mix. It allows customers to take many approaches to using object technology.

TXSeries contains the ability to define objects based on the distributed computing environment (DCE) IDL, an open group standard, and the protocol for communicating between them.

TXSeries Encina++ component not only allows users to define objects with C++ syntax, but offers the methods for exchanging distributed object references. This allows one object to refer to a second object in another machine.

TXSeries also supports CORBA Services OTS and OCCS interfaces. It also allows the use of Iona's Orbix Object Request Broker (ORB) to provide CORBA IDL definitions of objects and for IIOP communications between client and server. Future versions of TXSeries will contain the component broker ORB—an integrated ORB for IIOP communications and CORBA object services.

Future versions of TXSeries will support the component broker programming methodology, model, and tools for building advanced business applications out of reusable components.

From this discussion, you should be able to see how TXSeries builds and ensures system trust through its availability, integrity, longevity, scalability, and security features. We have also looked at how TXSeries allows companies to link IT infrastructures to the Internet to build and enhance their businesses—their e-business. And finally, we saw the innovative ways by which TXSeries helps enterprises reuse their network resources to get the most for their IT dollars. However, this is only a beginning. Just as new technologies, the growth of the Web, and other factors continue to change the global marketplace, TXSeries too, will evolve to ensure that IBM customers always get the most from their IT investments.

WebSphere Enterprise Management Tools

In the same way that we left Lotus pretty much out of the scope of Big Blue Java, we have also ignored the Tivoli systems management products. This was not because of any lack or weakness on their part, but because developers typically don't have that much interest in systems administration, which could form a good-sized book in its own right. At the same time, while we were wrestling with an understanding of what WebSphere Enterprise was all about, it came out that integrated management of the server environment is a key feature and benefit of the product line. Tivoli is, of course, integral to the full IBM solution for large e-business environments. In the interest of not completely overlooking systems management, I am including a description of Tivoli from IBM.

Tivoli E-business Management for WebSphere

The power of Tivoli's e-business management products enables customers to speed deployment, ensure security, maintain availability, and optimize performance of their internal and Internet-enabled business systems.

Understanding the Health of Your E-business Websphere Applications

Many companies face the daily challenge of ensuring that large and complex e-business systems, based on WebSphere Encina, Distributed CICS, or Enterprise JavaBeans (EJB) servers and other related components, are operating efficiently and effectively. The Tivoli enablement of WebSphere provides a comprehensive, reliable, and cost-effective management solution for integrated business systems. It monitors WebSphere resources, manages alerts, automates routine tasks, and provides inventory information and user administration across multiple platforms. The WebSphere Manager Tivoli modules maximize operations investments by building on the Tivoli Enterprise System, a common infrastructure and set of tools for consistent enterprise management.

Single Point of Control

Through the use of Tivoli Global Enterprise Management (GEM), the Tivoli management in WebSphere can consolidate management of multiple CICS regions or Encina cells, and integrate this information with the rest of the data from other system components being used, such as networks, databases, message queues, and host connections. It provides monitoring and operational tasks for production, testing, and development environments from one central location. Through the GEM console, operators can see the overall view of how the WebSphere environment is performing and can quickly identify and resolve performance or availability problems.

Powerful Management Functionality

Websphere Manager for Tivoli supports Tivoli GEM management functions such as discovery of CICS regions or Encina monitor cells, comprehensive monitoring with associated operations, event management, and visual aggregation of information from important resources such as:

- Structured file server (SFS)
- Peer-to-peer communications (PPC) gateways
- Other CICS regions via direct SNA links
- Other Encina node managers
- Recoverable queuing system (RQS) servers.

WebSphere customers will be able to locally monitor availability and performance criteria, such as active transaction count and log volume free space, against a critical threshold and take the appropriate action to prevent system and performance problems.

WebSphere User Security tightly integrates with Tivoli User Administration and extends its functionality to include DCE-related user, groups and organization attributes (see Table 19.1).

Component Broker as Part of WebSphere Enterprise

In the mid-1990s IBM offered a product called Distributed Object Systems Model (DSOM), which was folded into Component Broker in 1997. Well, at least that's what some of the industry analysts suspected. In 1999 IBM decided that these services actually belonged as part of WebSphere Enterprise, and this integration has been going on since.

Table 19.1 Tivoli Features and Benefits

MANAGEMENT SERVICE	WHAT IT DOES	WHAT IT MEANS TO YOU
Comprehensive monitoring	Provides critical out-of-band monitoring to ensure the availability of WebSphere Enterprise Edition application servers.	Comprehensive monitoring, ensuring the availability of WebSphere Distributed CICS and Encina environments upon which business-critical applications depend.
Centralized WebSphere management	Allows administrators to manage multiregion/multicell, cross-platform and enterprise-scale distributed CICS, Encina, or EJB systems from one centralized point.	Simplifies and reduces labor required to manage WebSphere environments.
Rules-based event correlation	Correlates WebSphere events with other sources (network devices, operating systems, etc.) based on user-defined rules.	Allows events to be evaluated in context with one another for accurate problem diagnosis and resolution.
Automated operations	Actions can be automated to execute on a scheduled basis or as the result of event occurrences.	Provides lights-out management.
End-to-end WebSphere management	Manages distributed CICS and Encina regions or cells on multiple platforms and operating systems.	A complete view and manageability of your entire WebSphere network.
Tivoli Global Enterprise Manager Integration	Allows WebSphere Application Server to be managed as a component in a larger business system.	Higher availability of the business systems that drive your business.

Products

The Component Broker Toolkit and Component Broker Connector allow distributed object and component-based applications to be built with direct integration to existing systems. In this case, the existing systems are expected to be CICS and other IBM legacy environments; however, they are not limited to working with IBM products.

The CB Connector and CB Toolkit are fully compliant with the Common Object Request Broker Architecture (CORBA), the Common Object Services (COS) and Internet Inter-ORB Protocol (IIOP). They implement services such as naming, security, transactions, lifecycle, and concurrency.

The CB Toolkit works with VisualAge for Java and with the SanFrancisco components. It runs on AIX, NT, and OS/390, as well as with other Unix platforms.

MQ Series

The following is a collection of materials I siphoned off from IBM's Web site to give you a quick overview of what IBM is doing with MQ Series and how it extends your existing systems to work with Big Blue Java solutions.

IBM is introducing a new framework of products based on MQSeries which aims to address integration from a business as well as an information technology (IT) perspective. The new product family means having information systems that support the way you work; fit in with your business processes and workflow; and deliver real business advantage.

The family of business integration solutions, based around IBM's award-winning MQSeries software, consists of:

MQSeries. The base MQSeries product connects any application or system to any other, totally and reliably. You can begin to think of applications as if they were building blocks that can be connected in any way you like.

MQSeries Integrator. Message brokering that centralizes knowledge of the enterprise (like business rules and application data formats) in a central hub. It accelerates and simplifies the distribution of data relating to business events, and connects applications to build new business processes.

MQSeries Workflow. Aligns and integrates your organization's resources and capabilities with your business strategies, accelerating process flow, cutting costs, eliminating errors, and improving workgroup productivity. Workflow supports business process reengineering: Use it to design, refine, document, and control your processes, while you can focus on the work at hand.

Listing of all platforms supported by MQSeries Integrator:

- Version 2 Release 0

    MQSeries Integrator for AIX

    MQSeries Integrator for Windows NT

- Version 1 Release 1

    MQSeries Integrator for AIX and DB2

    MQSeries Integrator for AIX and Oracle

    MQSeries Integrator for AIX and Sybase

    MQSeries Integrator for AS/400 and DB2

    MQSeries Integrator for HP-UX and DB2

    MQSeries Integrator for HP-UX and Oracle

    MQSeries Integrator for HP-UX and Sybase

    MQSeries Integrator for Windows NT and DB2

    MQSeries Integrator for Windows NT and Oracle

    MQSeries Integrator for Windows NT and SQL Server

    MQSeries Integrator for Windows NT and Sybase

    MQSeries Integrator for OS/390 and DB2

    MQSeries Integrator for Sun Solaris and DB2

    MQSeries Integrator for Sun Solaris and Oracle

    MQSeries Integrator for Sun Solaris and Sybase

The specifics of each one of these products is available on the Web site as well. However, I thought it was worth noting the details on the integrator products. Even the sales information has some value in describing the capabilities of this product. Since I have not worked with it myself, it seemed the best idea to just let IBM have its say.

MQSeries Integrator for AIX and DB2

With MQSeries Integrator, MQSeries users can quickly and easily implement powerful, real-time, application-to-application message transformation and intelligent message routing.

The flexibility and scalability of MQSeries Integrator lets you rapidly add, extend, or replace applications within information flows to achieve business integration. It enables the business intelligence of the enterprise to be captured as rules.

MQSeries Integrator supports custom-built or predefined application libraries. It offers scalable data transformation and intelligent transaction routing to integrate applications, databases, and networks.

You can achieve business effectiveness across the enterprise with MQSeries Integrator by tighter integration with leading enterprise resource planning (ERP) systems, existing applications, and shrink-wrapped software.

Using MQSeries messaging middleware (which runs on 35-plus platforms) and MQSeries Integrator, you can establish community messaging standards for cross-enterprise trading systems.

Highlights of MQSeries Integrator

- Forms the message-brokering layer of the IBM business integration framework
- Makes adding, extending, or replacing applications in an MQSeries network simple and easy
- Applies intelligent routing to seamlessly integrate applications, databases, and networks
- Enables application-to-application message transformation
- Supports custom-built and predefined application libraries
- Supports PeopleSoft GL, SAP R/3, and S.W.I.F.T. templates from New Era of Networks (NEON) Inc.
- Includes new usability features and improved graphical user interfaces

Software for Server Product

- IBM AIX V4.2 or V4.3
- IBM DB2 Universal Database V5.0 or V5.2

Messaging Connectivity

The following list shows the platforms supported by MQSeries products or platforms for which message queue interface (MQI) support is available:

- IBM OS/390–Server
- IBM VSE/ESA–Host
- Tandem NSK–Server
- IBM TPF 4.1–Server/Client
- IBM VM/ESA V2.3–Client
- Pyramid DC/OSx–Server/Client
- DYNIX/ptx–Server/Client
- IBM AS/400 IMPI and RISC–Server
- Siemens Nixdorf SINIX–Server/Client
- DIGITAL OpenVMS VAX–Server/Client
- DIGITAL OpenVMS AXP–Server/Client
- Compaq DIGITAL UNIX–Server/Client
- Stratus VOS–Client
- AIX and MVP compliant systems–Server/Client
- HP-UX–Server/Client
  - Stratus Continuum
- NCR (AT&T GIS) UNIX–Server/Client
- Sun Solaris–Server/Client
- SCO OpenSrvr UNIX–Server/Client
- Linux–Client
- Microsoft Windows NT–Server/Client
- Windows–Host (small footprint)
  - Windows 3.1
  - Windows 95
  - Windows 98
  - Windows NT
- Windows–Client
  - Windows 3.1
  - Windows 95
  - Windows 98

- OS/2 Warp–Server/Client
- DOS–Client
  - WinOS/2
- MacOS–Client
- Java–Client
- Unisys A–Client
- Data General DG/UX–Client
- Silicon Graphix IRIX–Server/Client

Application Integration Libraries

Application integration libraries, with their U.S. feature number codes, are as follows:

S.W.I.F.T.

- Securities Settlement and Reconciliation (w/ISITC) 0013
- Securities Trade Initiation and Confirmation 0014
- Corporate Actions 0015
- Securities Lending 0016
- Foreign Exchange 0017
- Loan/Deposits (Money Market) 0018
- Interest Rate Swaps 0019
- Forward Rate Agreements (FRAs) 0020
- Basic Payments 0021
- Systems Messages 0022

SAP

- MQIntegrator SAP A.I.L. Pkg 0033

PeopleSoft GL

- General Ledger 0036

MQSeries Integrator Capacity Groups

The price model is linked to the processor group machine or node on which the MQSeries integrator program(s) run. The machines relate to a required number of MQSeries integrator capacity units. Additional capacity units are required as you move to larger systems, or add new systems, to accommodate your business use of MQSeries Integrator. A similar price model is used on the MQSeries messaging products.

MQSeries Family of APIs

With MQSeries, you receive a family of four APIs designed to make programming straightforward for any messaging task, from the simple to the most advanced. Three APIs can be used for exchanging messages: MQI is the API that provides full access to the underlying messaging implementation, available for all key languages and environments. JMS or Java Message Service is the Java standard, providing much of the function available through the MQI. AMI, or Application Messaging Interface, simplifies the handling of messages with a higher level of abstraction that allows policy handling and many messaging features to be provided by the middleware The fourth API, the CMI or Common Messaging Interface, simplifies the creation of message content. All four of the APIs can interoperate.

The Original MQSeries Message Queue Interface

The Message Queue Interface (MQI) is an easy-to-use programming interface that allows applications to communicate transparently across the various platforms that make up the enterprise-wide computing environment. The MQI allows full access to MQSeries messaging support.

Portable Standards with the Java Message Service

Java Message Service (JMS) is a specification of a portable API for asynchronous messaging. JMS has been developed by Sun Microsystems in collaboration with IBM and other vendors interested in promoting industry-wide standard frameworks.

Many aspects of Java API implementation are the responsibility of the vendor developing the product, and naturally IBM will provide a robust JMS service using MQSeries core technology.

JMS is an object-oriented Java API with a set of generic messaging objects for programmers to write event-based messaging applications. JMS supports both request/reply and publish/subscribe models as separate object models.

Application developers can be assured that their JMS applications will communicate with applications written to the Message Queue Interface (MQI), and to the new Application Messaging Interface (AMI).

New Application Messaging Interface for MQSeries Now Available

Now, MQSeries is making messaging programmers even more productive. The new Application Messaging Interface (AMI) is a high-level API that greatly simplifies programming for application messaging and publish/subscribe. IBM specified and developed the API, which has now been adopted as a standard by the Open Application Group Inc. (OAGI).

The AMI, with bindings for standard programming languages including Java, C, C++, and COBOL, reduces the amount of code required to be written for new applications. It provides a high level of abstraction, moving message-handling logic from the application into the middleware. Previously, programmers coding messaging applications needed to select queue names and decide message characteristics like priority, retries, or expire time. Now, they can register sets of standard characteristics as policies for message handling, and use the AMI to set the appropriate policy for a message.

IBM will provide a suite of common policies, and an open policy-handler framework that encourages additional policies to be created by the enterprise or third-party software vendors.

In addition to providing policy, the AMI also allows programmers to associate a service name with a message. The service is a high-level of abstraction that represents an MQSeries queue, but can also be implemented to communicate with a database, printer, or e-mail, for example.

An important benefit of the AMI is that programmers can focus on business logic and message content. Connectivity code is reduced to specifying a service and a policy to be used when sending or receiving messages. IT administrators can set up policies easily using the AMI's graphical tools, which shields them from the complexities of individual platforms and minimizes the need for expensive, whole-system testing every time they make a small change. These capabilities translate into lower costs at practically every link in the IT chain.

Message Construction with CMI

The Common Message Interface (CMI) is a logical message construction API, used in conjunction with a message delivery API, like the Message Queue Interface (MQI), the Application Messaging Interface (AMI), or MQSeries Support for JMS (Java Message Service).

With CMI, programmers will be able to dynamically construct and parse messages, and provide query and update facilities on constructed messages regardless of their physical representation. CMI will provide programming support for both language-dependent and language-independent data structures in a consistent manner. It will handle tagged value data such as XML, and language-dependent structures found in C, COBOL, and Java, used in conjunction with the message dictionary support provided in MQSeries Integrator V2. CMI will provide a powerful tool for manipulating both simple and complex data as a single entity.

CHAPTER 20

Integrating Legacy Systems

This topic is one that could easily fill not just one book, but an entire shelf of books in the world's biggest bookstore. Enterprise application integration was touched on as one of the drivers towards Java and objects, but in this chapter I would like to take a quick look at how we can leverage integration of legacy data stores and the applications that manage them.

One of the biggest problems with the object-oriented approach is the insistence that data must be tightly coupled with the methods in an object. Although this provides benefits, it also causes a great deal of difficulty when considering the integration of traditional data sources.

CICS applications that use VSAM file sets can be accommodated through component broker, while TX Series and MQ Series can be configured to combine traditional applications and databases within object-oriented transactions.

Another point to consider is that SanFrancisco itself has a means of integrating external data with SF objects through the external mapping tool.

Last, there are translation tools available as part of the DB2 family that will allow access to multiple heterogeneous sources of data. The purpose of this chapter is to discuss these architectural options at a conceptual level and to identify tools and techniques that either have been or can be used.

When looking at the linkages from an object or application server perspective, you can see that the application server must negotiate with a middleware service to broker the request out to the desired data source.

Issues such as data type mapping and security are managed by the middleware. In some cases, the application user will have no idea that the data being presented has been garnered from multiple distributed sources.

At the highest level, the areas of responsibility are assigned as shown in Figure 20.1.

In the diagram represented by Figure 20.1, the objects inside the SanFrancisco framework are mapped to a component transaction server or object request broker, which in turn talks to the legacy database. This may be a direct call to a database engine, which is appropriate for a client/server application, or it may require invoking an application that in turn calls the dataset. This application integration approach would be more likely handled by a CICS transaction and brokered through a CB connector.

One of the key themes in this book is that while object-orientation is wonderful, excellent, and terrific, it is simply not going to replace all of the other applications and system architectures that exist out here in the big bad world. We have to be inclusionary, not exclusive in order to bring all this good stuff together.

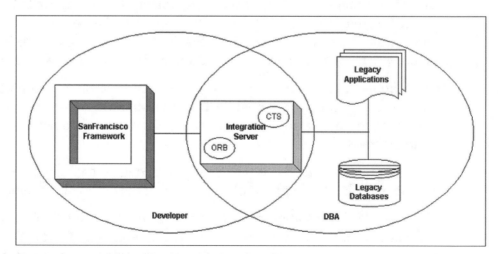

Figure 20.1 Middleware roles and responsibilities.

With that philosophical statement out of way, we can now move on to see just how this might be accomplished.

One approach we wanted to pursue in 1998 was to map the objects to a relational store and then subsequently map that database representation to other data sources, relational, traditional, and otherwise. I am including it here as an example of one of the means of integrating legacy data, expressed as a business case.

We actually submitted this approach for funding under a research grant, and it was approved. Unfortunately, as sometimes happens with grants the funding was cut to the point that undertaking it didn't make sense. As a result, this is still only a concept, as opposed to a tried and true approach to integrating specifically SanFrancisco objects with existing real-time, third-party data stores.

SanFrancisco Database Integration Proposal

The following proposal was developed by Daniel J. Worden, WNS, Inc., December 17, 1998.

Objective

To identify a technically sound, quick to implement, and reasonably priced means of integrating applications developed using the SanFrancisco Application Development components with external data sources, specifically Sybase and Microsoft SQL Server.

Terms of Reference

Any proposed solution will:

- Allow objects developed in SanFrancisco to transparently access data held in a variety of existing data stores, but specifically relational and other legacy data.
- Provide access to these data stores without materially diminishing performance of the SFP objects beyond the levels experienced in accessing DB/2 or Oracle persistent data stores.
- Minimize the need by the SanFrancisco development team to support the third-party integration utilities.

- Identify the source of domain and database technical expertise needed to develop and implement the third-party data store connectivity.

- Mask from the customer any proprietary technology acquired from a vendor other than IBM or the customer's third-party data store

- Support scalability to large numbers of concurrent users (i.e., 5,000)

- Plan for validation of the solution through a short-term proof of concept test

- Fit within the budget model of SanFrancisco TLAs and their customers for development and deployment of scalable solutions incorporating the external database connector.

Introduction

WNS, Inc. is a SanFrancisco TLA, IBM Business Partner, and a Sybase System Integrator. Incorporated in 1991, the company has a staff of 20, and specializes in database administration, integration, and custom application development. In discussions with our SanFrancisco marketing representative regarding a specific customer opportunity for SFP, the need for support of additional access to external data stores was covered. During the SanFrancisco conference (August 25–28), another specific customer opportunity was identified with Endura Systems of Seattle, but again the need for support of a third party relational database (Informix) was a major hurdle. In meetings with responsible IBM managers, the opportunity and requirements were discussed in general terms. As an action item from these meetings, WNS was tasked with proposing a specific means of overcoming the integration issues within the constraints faced by each of the concerned parties.

Subsequently, Customer E was acquired by another organization and postponed adoption of SanFrancisco. This has reduced the requirement to integrate Informix. However, further discussions with SanFrancisco consultants in the UK and Hong Kong respectively indicated that there are very large Sybase accounts in the financial services sector who have interest in SanFrancisco and significant existing investments in Sybase technology. Adoption of SanFrancisco for these accounts is dependent on interfacing to Sybase. The approach recommended in this proposal specifically addresses integration of SanFrancisco with Sybase, Informix, and other data stores.

Requirements

While object-oriented Java development tools are very appealing to development shops and large internal IT departments, there are a large number of prospective customers who are unable or unwilling to migrate control over their enterprise data from current relational or nonrelational data stores. Other applications using data stores such as CICS/VSAM or ISM are very tightly integrated with the applications and require wholesale replacement of the application in order to support a move to applications using SanFrancisco components. In either case, the net effect is to discourage prospective customers with these environments from moving to the SanFrancisco Java development framework.

The SanFrancisco application framework is integrated with DB/2 and Oracle databases at the CLI (call level interface) level. Integration through ODBC does not typically perform sufficiently enough to be a usable option, and JDBC implementation differs widely from each vendor. This means that any new data source to be integrated must have its own access layer using CLI or native drivers. One approach under consideration by the SFP development team in Rochester was to create a Microsoft SQL Server native interface using DB-Library and Transact SQL.

Ultimately, SFP will support the Enterprise JavaBean architecture, and it is likely that most, if not all, third-party vendors will also move in this direction as well. Any native database drivers written now would have to continue to be supported by future versions of SFP, which builds in ongoing support costs and complexity.

The main requirement to be addressed by this proposal is to create a means of integrating applications developed using SanFrancisco components with a variety of legacy data stores, while minimizing any downstream support liability. Any proposed solution would have to meet the terms of reference which define the rules of engagement as defined by all involved parties.

Proposed Solution

Sybase provides a database middleware product called DirectConnect that supports integration of applications or servers capable of issuing DB-Library or CT-Library calls with several other database environments, including:

- Informix
- Ingres
- CICS/VSAM
- CICS/ISM
- AS/400
- MVS

Extension of this connectivity can be achieved through additional middleware offerings to include 25 legacy and competitive relational database products.

DirectConnect for Informix has been installed in production (on HP-UX) for environments with as many as 9,000 concurrent users. DirectConnect translates T-SQL from DB-Library into Informix calls under INET. These calls include support for Binary Large Objects, among other features supported by Informix.

It is already planned that the SanFrancisco External Data Mapper be extended to support Microsoft SQL Server. By definition this means support from SanFrancisco containers for DB-Library. Microsoft acquired DB-Library, along with the rights to SQL Server as part of its original licensing with Sybase. To provide compatibility with DirectConnect, certain MS SQL Server DB-Library calls will have to be avoided, but WNS can provide the expertise needed to ensure this. A senior WNS resource was provided to the SF development team for a two-week engagement to resolve the deadlocking issue they experienced when connecting to Microsoft SQL Server 6.5 using ODBC. While doing this, we demonstrated the ability to connect to Sybase SQL Server 11.5, through the same ODBC connection. This validates the idea that MS-SQL Server 6.5 and Sybase SQL Server can be treated identically from a client connection standpoint.

The recommended topology for this interconnection is shown in Figure 20.2.

The key concept underlying this topology is that the meta data catalog is represented as the only link between the SanFrancisco objects and the legacy data. In other words, everything presented to SanFrancisco looks like a SQL Server database.

As it turns out, DB2 supports similar functionality through DataJoiner. Please look on the Web site www.BigBlueJava.com for more informa-

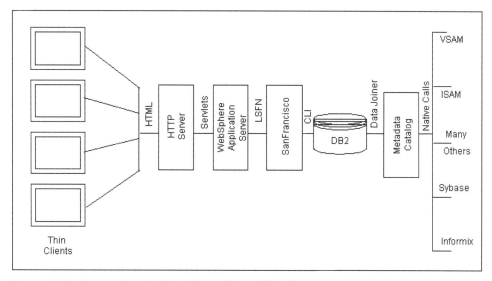

Figure 20.2 Integrating SanFrancisco with multiple data stores.

tion about this product. We didn't have an opportunity to test it prior to going to print. This should mean that for those of you who want to maintain a Blue tool set, the same approach can be adopted as we recommended for SQL Server, Sybase, and Informix. If any of you has any interest in following up on this approach, please feel free to e-mail me at djworden@wns.com.

Two-Phase Commit

One of the more significant technologies that must be incorporated into managing updates across multiple applications is two-phase commit. In essence, a two-phase commit allows a target server to mark a transaction as committed, but to be able to roll back that committed transaction in the event that one of the parties involved in the transaction cannot actually complete.

Two-phase commit is incorporated into the native driver support that SanFrancisco offers for DB2 and Oracle. Since the SF objects do not have actual ownership of the data, there is a potential problem of the object-based transaction being committed while the underlying data in the database does not change. Two-phase commit addresses this issue by managing the requirement to commit the transaction first on the object side, but only actually making the final commitment after the database has reported that the data changed successfully.

There is obviously a good deal more to writing two- (or three-) phase commit transactions than we are covering here. My intent is only to note that distributed databases have supported synchronization through multiphase commit services and that integration of legacy systems with object-based applications will likely need to incorporate this technique.

Enterprise JavaBean Wrappers

If the distributed integration architecture involved connecting disparate databases through calls somewhat like JDBC or ODBC, the Enterprise JavaBean approach is to make existing data EJB-aware and use those methods to get at the data.

Similar to the approach of writing a CORBA wrapper around the legacy application and then coding transactions to write to the CORBA specification, EJB wrappers offer the same potential.

As Enterprise JavaBeans gain acceptance in the marketplace, more vendors will support EJB representation of their applications and tools. This should allow us to treat applications as if they are all EJB components; integrate them into a larger distributed architecture; and not worry about the underlying implementation.

Enter XML

Approved by W3C in early 1998, the Extensible Markup Language standard is designed to make it easier to link client applications and viewers to diverse backend systems. Lotus and Microsoft have both announced their intentions to incorporate XML support into their Office suites. This should provide even more momentum for XML integration.

Where HTML is useful for portraying text and graphic images to a browser, the role XML plays is more data oriented. HTML handles the presentation of information, but provides little functionality for validation and data handling.

The key service provided by XML is the representation of data and document type along with the presentation of the data at the field level. Customer_id might be described through XML as a 10-digit numeric field, allowing the receiving ERP system to accept this field as the key on which to search. By defining an XML import standard, any application can accept input from browsers that incorporate XML.

More than just accepting data as entered, the XML screens allow browser users to interact with the system as if they had the fat client application installed on their desktop.

The value of using an XML-based integration is that it allows previously closed systems that once relied on electronic data interchange (EDI) for system-to-system communication to use the internet to exchange data.

Approaches and Techniques

Clearly there are at least two ways to integrate existing systems; at the database level, or through the application that reads and writes the data.

Just as clear should be the need to interject a third-party representation, to which the new application talks and the legacy application listens. At this point in the evolution of Big Blue Java development it is impossible to predict which technique or approach will become dominant. However, to me it seems inevitable that systems will either support XML, provide API access to Java applications, present an EJB- or CORBA-compliant interface, or be candidates for replacement.

Summary

Distributed objects represent the future of applications development. The challenge will be to represent existing systems as objects in a consistent architecture allowing us to treat the enterprise as a single system.

The largest gains from the ability to represent disparate systems in a similar manner, and to manage updates across multiple distributed databases, is in creating value chains of integrated enterprises.

E-business demands greater efficiencies in communication and coordination of organizational processes. In order to work, this has to be supported by information systems. That driver will ensure that people who have invested in legacy systems and wish to maintain them will also be looking for secure and manageable ways to present those systems to the world.

Without knowing the specifics of any given legacy application, it is impossible to discuss ways of integrating with it. At the same time, it is worth noting that IBM is making every effort to ensure that if you created that application with their tools, it will support Java integration on some level. And if you created it with other tools, IBM offers translators and adaptors that will help you to bring it into the fold.

CHAPTER 21

Pulling It All Together

A t this point I hope that you have an appreciation for the scope of what IBM is trying to accomplish by incorporating Java into its product offerings. I know that at the outset of IBM's strategic migration it was not exactly clear what the company was setting out to do. However, by now it should be clear that a top-to-bottom reinvention of IBM's technology and focus is and has been on the agenda for several years.

Technology is merely a slightly bigger word for tool. As we know, humans are both toolmakers and tool users. When it comes to computers for e-business, IBM has set out to make itself by far the premier supplier of tools with which to do business.

Which leaves us, the tool users, to judge how successful they have been at achieving this ambitious goal.

It should be no surprise that this book only introduces the IBM approach to Java technology and how its products support that technology. Our intention from the outset has been to show how the entire tool set fits together into a single strategy for the future.

In the first section we looked at how Java has created an opportunity for IBM to undo the Tower-of-Babel effect spawned by IBM's traditional product line segmentation. The dream of write once–run anywhere programming is fast becoming a reality. IBM has made it possible for a development shop to commit to a language and to thereafter rest assured that the applications developed with it will run on any product IBM provides.

I hope the description of why this is a win/win proposition has in some measure sold you on working with Java. When WNS made the leap in 1997, we were not quite sure whether this was a gigantic risk or merely a huge one. The reason for the coverage on IBM's strategy has been to set the stage for why this approach is not really risky at all—unless you suspect that the Internet doesn't have much of a future for business.

Development Tools

It is apparent now that with IBM having standardized on Java as a language, the company is leaving no stone unturned in the provision of tools with which to develop applications. Visual Age, WebSphere Studio, and NetObjects Fusion provide a complete set of tools for e-business client application development. There are overlaps in the coverage provided by these tools, as we demonstrated with the approaches to developing the comic book applet. I believe this is a very good thing, inasmuch as it will allow you as a developer to stretch your tool of choice into new directions. At the same time, we covered applets, servlets, Java server pages, and beans. It should be apparent that even by standardizing on Java, there is still a great deal of design work that needs to be done in order to map the right technique to the requirement.

Servers

To my way of thinking, with IBM's move to creating a family of Web application servers under WebSphere, the company made it clear that it was serious about this direction. It pulled together previously unrelated technology like Component Broker and MQ Series, thereby mandating that today and tomorrow these products would work together in a cohesive architecture.

Undeniably, there is a tremendous technical challenge in making that mandate a reality. It is one thing to tie an HTTP server to a Java store to a database. I hope that our coverage of the HTML, Web, and database servers, as well as showing how they actually connect, clearly pointed at how IBM expects n-tier client/server systems to be developed with its tools. WebSphere is the standard application server of the future, at least if you want to work with IBM's view of e-business tools.

Components

As we moved into tools for modeling the enterprise, like EMT and Rose, this book should have put a spotlight on the need to model your requirements, as well as practical suggestions for how to go about doing that. For years anyone working as a professional IT developer has been saying, talk to the users and understand their requirements. The e-business revolution is about more than just technology. It is about the way we apply technology to commercial practices. It is revolutionizing the supply chain itself, as well as each organization that participates in that chain, from manufacturers to end customers. E-business applications support that order-of-magnitude gain in efficiency, but like all highly leveraged opportunities, that comes at a cost. Moving through the chapters on SanFrancisco, I hope we made it clear that the cost of this efficiency is complexity. That, and a Mount Everest–sized learning curve.

Major Lessons

We made several key discoveries as we moved WNS's operation from a traditional client/server shop focused on databases to an e-business development shop focused on Enterprise JavaBeans. These have been shared with you over the course of the book, but since I have been told that few people sit down and read technical books from cover to cover, I will recap them here.

Model, Model, Model

When you use VisualAge for Java, and you are connecting controllers to visual objects, connecting the model is one of the options. The development paradigm incorporated by IBM is model-view-controller; the object model must be created in Rose prior to generating code; the Enterprise business processes are modeled using Enterprise Modeling Tool. Everywhere in this process we create and refer to models. The organization is modeled, the objects are modeled, the data is modeled, and the model is modeled.

The emphasis on understanding and planning your work is no longer the sign of a superior shop. Over the course of *Big Blue Java*, I have made the case that is not possible to succeed with this technology by jumping into coding and iterating your way through to a finished product. Yes, that will work for the creation of prototypes, or proof-of-concept, or demonstrations of technical mastery–type subprojects. To use this technology correctly, you must have the top, side, and end view of the organization designed. You must understand it to the nth degree. That is a critical success factor. Luckily for us, there are tools to help us get the job done.

Visual Programming

Stop writing code. That is a cornerstone message that I would like to reinforce. Writing code means rewriting code. The models we create are visual in nature; they help to depict the organization and the application in ways that can easily be grasped by nontechnical and new technical resources alike. To write code is to require someone be able to read code in order to support it. This is not the way to develop Big Blue Java applications. (Okay, so that might be overstating the case a little.) Of course we will always have to wrestle with syntax, and coding applications will never be replaced entirely by code generators. The real point is to avoid writing code that doesn't directly reference a visual model for process or requirements. Using VisualAge for Java means coming to understand the need to dance with the tool and deal with its overhead even when you feel that it would be faster to write the application by hand.

The reason for this is the other major lesson I hope this book taught.

Team Java

The applications we are developing for e-business are too complex to be developed by just one person. Even when we are talking about a single Web site that talks to a straightforward relational database, more than one person is required, because inevitably someone is going to have to support that application. You might not share the work with another developer today, but be assured that at some point your beautiful self-contained application will be somebody else's headache. Taking a Team Java approach is effective even for simple NetObjects Fusion projects.

At the other end of the spectrum, any application that uses the word enterprise in its scope definition requires a team of people to handle the distribution of labor. Nobody does it all, and when it comes to developing Java applications, it can be fatal to try. This is old news for those of you who work on big applications. There is just too much work for any individual, so you use structures for sharing work across a multidisciplinary team. Source code management is just part of it. The separation of concerns is a critical component to the way IBM is architecting Java solutions. It also plays to the strong side of object oriented programming—encapsulation. It shouldn't be necessary to understand the inner workings of the entire application top to bottom. By the time we add in legacy systems integration, the database, and the network, it is doubtful that anyone can be familiar with all of the acronyms that are employed, let alone maintain an in-depth understanding of how all of the technologies work.

In an earlier book, I said it was important that developers understand the end-to-end process of development for a client/server project. But that was then. Today it seems clear—from working with the creation of even a basic decision-support application using IBM's Java toolset—that teamwork, and the attendant reliance on other people to get their jobs done, is the winning approach. No one beats everyone.

Think Distributed Objects

I don't believe that many of us are going to dive right into rewriting our enterprise systems as object-oriented applications, throw out DB2 in favor of an object-oriented database, or never speak another dialect besides UML. I also believe that the key to understanding what IBM is doing with this technology is to look past the tools and into the future of applications development. To me, this means distributed objects.

When we at WNS were wrestling our SanFrancisco-based application into submission, we found that even a team of bright young developers with no preconceived notions had difficulty understanding why all that overhead was required. As we talked it through, it became increasingly clear that the idea that several distinct development teams could use the same objects to develop applications was the central value proposition for SanFrancisco. These development teams could be internal, or they could be sequential iterations of third-party developers. The notion that not only does the code representing a customer get maintained in a single place, but that it can be incorporated into vastly different applications created by different folks at different times, got the team to *grok* SanFrancisco. Grok is the term coined by Robert A. Heinlein in *Stranger in a Strange Land.* It means *to get, gestalt, understand,* and a little bit more.

The tremendous amount of overhead incurred by SanFrancisco is like the overhead needed for a public transit system. It may seem like overkill when you just want to take the bus across town, but it makes a whole lot more sense when you start looking at millions of people transported all over the area for a year. SF is big stuff. It is going to take a while before its impact is really clearly demonstrated, although we are in the introductory and conceptual phases of that process now. That's why I say *think* distributed objects. It may actually be too early for a full-fledged commitment to nothing but SF development. At the same time, Enterprise JavaBeans has all the makings of a unifying architecture, especially as implemented by IBM in products like WebSphere Enterprise. My guess is that by the time we get to Version Five of these products, the trickle will become a juggernaut, and the path to the future will be very clear indeed.

Easing into IT

Some people believe that the best way to get into a cold pool is to dive right in. On the other hand, if you have ever taken a Japanese bath, you know that sometimes the best way to get into hot water is to ease into it. At this point, I'm not entirely sure which one is the best representative of working with Big Blue Java technology. Like all metaphors, both comparisons break down at some point.

Still, one of the major objectives I had when I set out to write this book was to appeal to those of you who had a long-standing tradition of providing information services to your organizations with technology you knew had to change. In particular, I was mindful of the huge number of AS/400 shops out there in the world, with highly functional RPG applications. This book was not written for object-oriented gurus or people who have been working with Java for years. It was intended all along as a document of the path my company took when we made the radical transition to developing applications in Java. My hope is that it achieved the goal of making some choices easier for you.

In my mind's eye, I see this technology as being especially well-suited for organizations of 100 employees and more, especially if a good percentage of those people work with information. There is no upward limit on the scalability of Big Blue Java applications. By incorporating the mainframe solidly into the strategy, IBM has ensured that you won't be left stranded.

As you will have taken away from the chapters on NetObjects Fusion and WebSphere Studio, you can begin to work with Big Blue Java to database-enable your basic browser application without making the move into Java components and beans, enterprise or otherwise.

The kicker is that moving toward Java in any fashion will be beneficial for your shop. Getting started with the syntax while you build your appreciation for objects but starting by delivering browser-based applications is one viable way to go. The problem with this approach is that you will end up with legacy Java applications that need to be supported or replaced. This doesn't have to be a problem, as long as you are prepared to discard the initial set of applications when the time comes. That turned out to be very difficult with COBOL applications, so it bears consideration.

In terms of pulling it all together, you should consider what IBM is enabling and how that appeals to your organization or to you as a developer.

Implications and Ramifications

I am convinced that the move to e-business computing by way of Java and Enterprise JavaBeans is as significant a move for the IBM corporation as it was for Thomas Watson Jr. to move the company to computers and away from tabulating machines.

One of the key implications as covered in the first section of the book is the unification of the hardware line. Every system produced by IBM will support Java. This is a significant first. In fact, it opens up the ability for AS/400 programmers to move to mainframe shops, for PC gurus to migrate over to midrange environments, and for Unix hacks to go anywhere they want. (Well, at least as Java developers.)

This might also have been somewhat applicable to C++ developers, with the notable exception that Java is much more platform-independent. The hardware and operating system are much more a commodity to power the application, where the focus needs to be.

The Developer's Opportunity

As I have previously noted, becoming a Big Blue Java developer can give you increased mobility. Your applications are not simply for a single operating environment. Ironically, while the Big Blue Java programmers are enjoying greater freedom of movement, anyone making the commitment to Microsoft tools will be finding themselves stranded in a one-operating-system world—the opposite to the new IBM approach.

Visual programming might generate chunkier code than you can hand-craft yourself, but it allows you to focus on building applications that do what you need them to do. IBM has made great strides in moving infra-structure programming out of the hands of the developer. Let's face it, wrestling with explicit CLI calls wasn't a lot of fun anyway. For most application developers, it's the gleam in the eyes of the user who can do something with your program that he or she was never able to do before that makes it all worthwhile.

Beyond being able to finally take some things for granted (like database access or screen-handling characteristics), developing in Java means that you can take advantage of other people's beans. Sharing code (meaning making use of other people's code) becomes straightforward. This leads to a very different experience than cutting and pasting code from examples or modifying a code fragment to do something close.

In a strategy similar to the leverage that developers have gained from using ActiveX controls in Visual Basic or frameworks and controls shipped with environments like PowerBuilder and Delphi, IBM is making Java its platform of choice for new applications development. This means it is easier, faster, and more fun for you, the developer, to get your job done. Not a bad deal, eh?

The Development Manager's Opportunity

Anyone responsible for managing a software development group can appreciate the value of having developers who want to work with a particular environment or tool set. It's easier to motivate people to work hard with tools they like than tools they hate.

Still, there are other concerns beyond acquiring a tool set that people want. IBM has made sure that its existing customer base will enjoy the benefits of interoperability with Java and the company's current systems. Imagine a million developers all working on code that you can incorporate into your solutions. Imagine a catalog of beans that you can acquire for limited or enterprise deployment. Then picture your users leveraging Web browsers to get access to corporate data and applications. Be deafened by the silence of end user support for clobbered DLL's, flaky network connections, and fat-client administration issues.

Okay, it's not likely to be that close to Nirvana, but by moving your development efforts to Java, you get access to these resources and these benefits. This is quite a bit different than the closed shop lock-in that has been an attribute of many IBM-based environments in the past.

Of course this openness has its own set of drawbacks. People you've had on staff for years may be lured away by myriads of other firms. Increased competition for resources and so on. But taken on balance, the benefits outweigh the risks. Your shop will be able to deploy and support Web-based applications, accessing your corporate data much faster than ever before. The potential to create an architecture for object-oriented systems has been unlocked by IBM's commitment to this strategy. It's no longer pie in the sky, but something you can munch on right now.

The User Benefits

If you haven't asked your user population how they like the Web, don't wait. It has been amazing to me to sit down in front of middle managers and executives responsible for sales, purchasing, warehouse operations, and so on to find out what kind of experience they have had with the Internet. As we covered in the first section, the world is adopting this technology in the same way that fax machines and cell phones caught on—in a hurry.

There is an increasing backlash to having to reinstall Windows on a regular though unpredictable basis. Browser technology is much more stable, and when connected over a high-speed link, performs very well, thank you very much.

The number of people conducting Web-based banking and other financially sensitive functions is increasing. Along with this comes a higher level of confidence that the technology isn't going to fall prey to maladjusted hackers with mayhem on their minds.

In the past two years I have seen a perceptible increase in the acceptance of the Web. Grandparents are more comfortable getting e-mail, looking up the performance of their mutual funds, printing color gif files, and checking out that Christmas cruise. This is the move to the Internet appliance, and Java has a strong role to play in this.

From a user perspective it just makes sense to have a single way to interact with a computer—just as you have a single way to interact with an automobile (well, two ways if you count automatic transmissions). Extending that model means that people can connect to data stores without having to have a unique application installed on their system. Not only is this a time-saver for the central IT administration; it is actually easier and less confusing for the user. Again, it just makes sense.

Whether your user is corporate or personal, you can gain tremendous benefits from moving toward Java. IBM has seen this widespread opportunity for winning and has commandeered center stage. As they say, the race does not always go to the swift—but the smart money bets that way.

I Have Seen the Future

Crystal-ball-gazing is one of the least-likely activities to pay off. Still, at some level that is what anyone who works with Information Technology is called on to do. Look into the future and place some bets.

I once attended a vendor briefing where the technology company in question had fallen on hard times. It had moved from a number-one market position to somewhere around fifth or sixth, and its stock had dropped from the high $50s to below $10 per share. This was not a happy group of people. But the point that came out the loudest was not the quarterly results. It was the bitterness of those people who had invested more than dollars in the technology. They had invested time that they couldn't get back.

The month before the Y2K date rollover, everyone in my world was pretty quiet. It was not that we expected everything to break loose, but there was a sense of wait and see. People were not doing all that much leading into the year 2000. At the same time, we were having very enthusiastic discussions with what people wanted to do in the new year.

Big Blue Java represents a lot more than just a repositioning of products from a tried-and-true computer company. It represents the future of applications development. IBM has jumped ahead of the pack in the commercialization of Java and the inclusion of that technology into its existing products.

Increasingly, in the next few years the early adopters will enjoy the benefits, and the early majority will join in. There is simply too much to be gained by making the move and too much to be lost by not doing so. The question is not *whether* you will Web-enable your applications—it is *when*.

Get experience with the tool set, take it for a test drive, and see what it can do. This has been the most exciting 36 months in the technology business that I can remember. I am delighted to be able to give IBM an A grade for its implementation of Java and to recommend it to all IT practitioners without reservation. Go for it!

Product and Resource List in SanFrancisco OM and WHS Towers

This appendix lists all of the business process functions that are supported by the SanFrancisco objects for Order Management and Warehouse Management.

WNS has modeled these functions and identified the products and resources they use to help you gain an appreciation for the level of detail incorporated into the SF Towers. The models are defined in the E-business Modeling Tool described in Chapter 15. The acronyms are defined to make the models more legible at a glance, and in small part because as systems people, we depend on three-letter acronyms (TLAs) to communicate. The upper- and lower-case letters are used in EMT to differentiate functions and subfunctions.

NAME	ACRONYM	DESCRIPTION
Receive Product	AP/RP	Referred to as reception; the physical receipt of products at the warehouse.
Pick Items	PO/PI	The formal process of retrieving items from inventory for use in outbound orders, stock transfers, or inventory adjustments (i.e., kit creation).
Value-Added Processing	PO/VAP	Kitting, labeling, packaging, and/or light final assembly of new products (not manufacturing).

SHIP ORDER	SO	The process of shipping an outbound order from a warehouse to an order partner (i.e., a customer, a vendor, or another warehouse).
Putaway Product	AP/PP	The process of formally committing received products into inventory.
MAINTAIN ORDER INFORMATION	MOI	Maintains current order information (delivery dates, damaged goods lists, order status, etc.) to be made available for company or order partner queries.
MANAGE INVENTORY	MI	Maintains and provides inventory-specific information to other company processes.
CONTROL QUALITY	CQ	Process sets out inventory inspection schedules, inspection procedures, records results of inspections, and so forth.
Cross-Reference Documentation	rp/CCD	The process of determining any discrepancies between the vendor-supplied shipping manifest and the inbound order supplied by order management.
Inspect Products	rp/IP	The initial inspection of received products to verify their condition, type, and quantity.
Assign Destinations	rp/AD	The process of determining where products are to be placed after they have been received (i.e., putaway as inventory, send to a quality control area, etc.).
Prepare Putaway Locations	pp/PPL	The process of preparing storage locations within a warehouse for the receipt of additional products.
Putaway Product	pp/PP	The process of putting received products into their designated storage areas.
Create/Update Inventory	pp/CUI	The process of updating the inventory status of products.
Assemble Items	vap/AI	Gather picked items together in preparation for kit creation.

Create Kit	vap/CK	The process of packaging and labeling component items together to form a new inventory product.
Package Order	SO/PO	The process of collecting together, packaging, and labeling the required products for a single order.
Consolidate Orders	SO/CO	The process of grouping together all the orders to be included on a single shipment (i.e., shipments could be based on carrier type, mode of transport, etc.).
Hand-Off to Carriers	SO/HOC	The process of passing a prepared shipment to the appropriate carrier.
COURIER	C	The couriers used by the warehouse to pick up and deliver shipments.
CREATE CATALOGUE	CC	Creation of either a hardcopy or a Web-based catalogue containing product identifications and prices.
Record Order Details	CO/ROD	The process of gathering information needed to create an order; information will typically be provided by a customer, or, in the case of a stock movement, another warehouse.
Record Special Requests	CO/RSR	The process of gathering information related to requests for an order, such as special handling, delivery, and so forth.
Check Product Availability	CO/CPA	Provides the quantity of a product that is available to be included in an order; takes into consideration product reservations and future receptions.
Check Credit	CO/CC	Checks a customer's credit limit and balance to determine whether they have enough to initiate a new order.
Calculate Delivery Time	CO/CDT	Determines length of time required before a customer receives an order.
Calculate Order Cost	CO/COC	Calculates the total cost of an order; includes product prices, discounts, and supplementary charges.

Create Order	CO/CO	The process of formally initiating a order.
ALLOCATE PRODUCT	GP	The process of allocating specific products to fill an order.
Create Reception Details	AP/CRD	Creation of a reception note that specifies the details of an anticipated inbound order.
Create Pick List	PO/CPL	Creation of the list that details the items to be picked to fill orders; initiates the picking process.
Initiate Backorders	MI/IB	Initiates an order for a product when there is not enough product on hand to satisfy an order.
Create Ship List	PO/CSL	Creates a ship list used to initiate the shipping process; details orders that must be packaged, labeled, and shipped.
Initiate Invoicing	SO/II	Notifies the accounting process that an invoice must be issued for a shipped order.
MAINTAIN ORDER PARTNERS	MO	Designates and holds information specific to partners who may place orders; typically will be a customer or another warehouse within the company.
Set Prices, Discounts, Supplementary Charges	DP/SPD	Establishes prices and/or discounts that may be product- or group-specific; establishes supplementary charges; also designates possible price groups.
ESTABLISH COMPANY POLICIES	ECP	Establishes companywide policies on base currencies, exchange rate factors, allowable order types, and so forth.
ACCOUNTING	A	Process that tracks financial information.
Valuate Stock	A/VS	The process of determining the net worth of specified types and quantities of inventory.

Create Product	DP/CP	Products form the basis of order products and inventory items; defined by attributes such as ID, description, units of measure, substitutions, and so forth.
Create Warehouse	MI/CW	The process of creating the area in which inventory is stored.
MANAGE RESERVATIONS/ FUTURE RECEPTIONS	MR	The process of creating, updating, and maintaining information pertaining to product reservations and future receptions.
Establish Costing Methods	A/ECM	The process of setting out the permissible costing methods to be used within the company.
Replenish Inventory	MI/RI	The mechanisms in place to identify what items need to be replenished, when to order more products, and the most economical quantity to order.
Create Order Partner	MO/COP	Defining a business partner who will either place orders with, or receive orders from, the company.
Maintain Partner Information	MO/MPI	Maintains current order partner information to be available to queries from other company processes.
CREATE ORDERS	CO	Outlines step-by-step the mechanism of creating an order to be filled by a warehouse.
ACQUIRE PRODUCT	AP	Details the processes that occur when a warehouse receives product.
PREPARE ORDER	PO	Outlines in a step-by-step manner the mechanism used to prepare an outbound order for shipment.
DEFINE PRODUCTS	DP	Sets out parameters for the products to be used by the company, establishes prices, product IDs, identifies supplying order partners and warehouses, and so forth.
SELL PRODUCTS Manage Inventory	SP MI/MI	Maintains and provides inventory-specific information to other company processes.

RESOURCE	NAME	DESCRIPTION
RESOURCE	ADDITIONAL COSTS	Costs such as those associated with warehousing, and so forth.
PRODUCT	ADDITIONAL COSTS	Costs such as those associated with warehousing, and so forth.
RESOURCE	ADVANCED SHIPPING NOTICE	Notification to the warehouse from an order partner to advise of the imminent arrival of ordered products; preliminary notification of the types and quantities of products to be delivered.
PRODUCT	ADVANCED SHIPPING NOTICE	Notification to the warehouse from an order partner to advise of the imminent arrival of ordered products; preliminary notification of the types and quantities of products to be delivered.
RESOURCE	ADVANCED SHIPPING NOTICE	Notification to the warehouse from an order partner to advise of the imminent arrival of ordered products; preliminary notification of the types and quantities of products to be delivered.
PRODUCT	ALLOWABLE ORDER TYPES	The types of orders that are handled by the company (i.e., quotation, full sales order, full purchase order, full credit order, direct sales order, direct sales back-to-back order, stock movement order, etc.).
RESOURCE	ALLOWABLE ORDER TYPES	The types of orders that are handled by the company (i.e., quotation, full sales order, full purchase order, full credit order, direct sales order, direct sales back-to-back order, stock movement order, etc.).
RESOURCE	ALLOWABLE REPLACEMENT	A product designated to replace another which is no longer obtainable.
PRODUCT	ALLOWABLE REPLACEMENT	A designated product to be used to replace another product which is no longer obtainable.

RESOURCE	ALLOWABLE SUBSTITUTION	A product that may be substituted for another in the event that the requested product is not currently available.
PRODUCT	ALLOWABLE SUBSTITUTION	A different product that may be substituted on an order in the event that the requested product is not currently available.
PRODUCT	AS-PUTAWAY INFORMATION	Information resulting from the put-away process that specifies product type, where products were stored in the warehouse, how many were stored, and so forth.
RESOURCE	AS-PUTAWAY INFORMATION	Information resulting from the put-away process that specifies product type, where products were stored in the warehouse, how many were stored, and so forth.
PRODUCT	ASSEMBLED ITEMS	Items gathered together to be included in a kit.
RESOURCE	ASSEMBLED ITEMS	Items gathered together to be included in a kit.
RESOURCE	AVAILABLE CREDIT	The amount of credit currently available to an order partner.
PRODUCT	AVAILABLE CREDIT	The amount of credit currently available to an order partner.
PRODUCT	AVERAGE COST	Costing method that assigns an average inventory cost as the price of a product.
RESOURCE	AVERAGE COST	Costing method that assigns an average inventory cost as the price of a product.
PRODUCT	BACKORDER	That unfulfilled portion of an original order which is designated for future fulfillment; also the actual order placed to obtain products to satisfy the remainder of an order.
RESOURCE	BACKORDER	That unfulfilled portion of an original order which is designated for future fulfillment; also the actual order

		placed to obtain products to satisfy the remainder of an order.
PRODUCT	BACKORDER REQUEST	A request sent to the order management system to backorder a specified type and quantity of products.
RESOURCE	BACKORDER REQUEST	A request sent to the order management system to backorder a specified type and quantity of products.
PRODUCT	BACKORDERABLE DETAIL	A product which does not have a sufficient balance in inventory to fill an order; a product for which the need for a backorder has been confirmed.
RESOURCE	BACKORDERABLE DETAIL	A product which does not have a sufficient balance in inventory to fill an order; a product for which the need for a backorder has been confirmed.
PRODUCT	BASE CURRENCY	The default currency used by the company.
RESOURCE	BASE CURRENCY	The default currency used by the company.
RESOURCE	BASE CURRENCY	The default currency used by the company.
PRODUCT	BILL OF LADING	A document or receipt prepared by the shipping warehouse to be signed by the owner of a shipment or a common carrier; lists the goods which comprise the shipment.
RESOURCE	BILL OF LADING	A document or receipt prepared by the shipping warehouse, to be signed by the owner of a shipment or a common carrier; lists the goods which comprise the shipment.
RESOURCE	BILL OF LADING	A document or receipt prepared by the shipping warehouse, to be signed by the owner of a shipment or a common carrier; lists the goods which comprise the shipment.
RESOURCE	BILL OF LADING	A document or receipt prepared by the shipping warehouse to be signed

		by the owner of a shipment or a common carrier; lists the goods which comprise the shipment.
PRODUCT	CATALOGUE	A hardcopy or a Web-based catalogue containing product identifications and prices.
RESOURCE	CATALOGUE	A hardcopy or a Web-based catalogue containing product identifications and prices.
PRODUCT	COMPANY	The business entity that owns the warehouse; defined by its policies and associations with order partners, warehouse, and products.
RESOURCE	COMPANY	The business entity that owns the warehouse; defined by its policies and associations with order partners, warehouse, and products.
RESOURCE	COST TYPE	A subset of the value of goods in stock. The total value of goods in stock, for example, may be divided into normal goods, goods in quality control, and goods in transit.
PRODUCT	COST TYPE	A subset of the value of goods in stock. The total value of goods in stock, for example, may be divided into normal goods, goods in quality control, and goods in transit. Each cost type is related to a stock type.
RESOURCE	COSTING LEVEL	The level at which the costing method will be set (i.e., enterprise-wide costing methods, or applicable on a per-warehouse/per-product basis).
PRODUCT	COSTING LEVEL	The level at which the costing method will be set (i.e., enterprise-wide costing methods, or applicable on a per-warehouse/per-product basis).
PRODUCT	COSTING METOD	Defines five possible costing methods that can be applied at a product, warehouse, or general level.

RESOURCE	COSTING METOD	Defines five possible costing methods that can be applied at a product, warehouse, or general level.
RESOURCE	COSTING POLICY	The type of costing method used to determine the price of a particular inventory item; default methods are standard fixed cost, average cost, latest inbound cost, FIFO, LIFO.
PRODUCT	COSTING POLICY	The type of costing method used to determine the price of a particular inventory item; default methods are standard fixed cost, average cost, latest inbound cost, FIFO, LIFO.
RESOURCE	COURIER	Name of the preferred courier to use for orders placed by a specific order partner.
PRODUCT	COURIER	Name of the preferred courier to use for orders placed by a specific order partner.
RESOURCE	CREDIT LIMIT	The maximum amount of credit extended to an order partner.
PRODUCT	CREDIT LIMIT	The maximum amount of credit extended to an order partner.
PRODUCT	CREDIT STATUS	Indicates whether an order partner has enough available credit to initiate a new order.
RESOURCE	CREDIT STATUS	Indicates whether an order partner has enough available credit to initiate a new order.
RESOURCE	CREDIT STATUS	Indicates whether an order partner has enough available credit to initiate a new order.
PRODUCT	DAMAGED GOODS LIST	List of items received from an order partner that were damaged upon arrival at the warehouse.
RESOURCE	DAMAGED GOODS LIST	List of items received from a vendor that were damaged upon arrival at the warehouse.
PRODUCT	DELIVERY ADDRESS	The address to which an order will be delivered.

RESOURCE	DELIVERY ADDRESS	The address to which an order will be delivered.
PRODUCT	DELIVERY DATE	The date on which an order can be delivered to an order partner.
RESOURCE	DELIVERY DATE	The date on which an order can be delivered to an order partner.
RESOURCE	DELIVERY DATE	The date on which an order can be delivered to an order partner.
RESOURCE	DELIVERY DATE	The date on which an order can be delivered to an order partner.
PRODUCT	DELIVERY DATE	The date on which an order can be delivered to an order partner.
RESOURCE	DELIVERY DATE	The date on which an order can be delivered to an order partner.
RESOURCE	DELIVERY DATE	The date on which an order can be delivered to an order partner.
PRODUCT	DELIVERY TIME	The length of time it will take to deliver an order to an order partner.
RESOURCE	DELIVERY TIME	The length of time it will take to deliver an order to an order partner.
RESOURCE	DELIVERY TIME	The length of time it will take to deliver an order to an order partner.
RESOURCE	DESTINATION LIST	Specifies where products are to be placed after they have been received. (i.e., putaway as inventory, sent to quality control area, etc.)
PRODUCT	DESTINATION LIST	Specifies where products are to be placed after they have been received. (i.e., putaway as inventory, sent to quality control area, etc.)
PRODUCT	DISCOUNTS	Discounts available on a per product, group, order, or customer basis.
RESOURCE	DISCOUNTS	Discounts available on a per product, group, order, or customer basis.
RESOURCE	DISCOUNTS	Discounts available on a per product, group, order, or customer basis.
RESOURCE	DISCOUNTS	Discounts available on a per product, group, order, or customer basis.

PRODUCT	DISCOUNTS	Discounts available specifically for a particular order partner.
RESOURCE	DISCOUNTS	Discounts available on a per product, group, order, or customer basis.
PRODUCT	ECONOMIC ORDER POINT	The quantity of a product which should be purchased or manufactured at one time in order to minimize the combined costs of acquiring and carrying inventory.
RESOURCE	ECONOMIC ORDER POINT	The quantity of a product which should be purchased or manufactured at one time in order to minimize the combined costs of acquiring and carrying inventory.
PRODUCT	EXCHANGE RATE FACTORS	Exchange rates offered on currencies different from the base currency.
RESOURCE	EXCHANGE RATE FACTORS	Exchange rates offered on currencies different from the base currency.
RESOURCE	EXTRANEOUS COSTS	Indicates whether other costs, such as those associated with purchasing, handling, and so forth, will be considered when establishing a costing policy.
PRODUCT	EXTRANEOUS COSTS	Indicates whether or not other costs, such as those associated with purchasing, handling, and so forth, will be considered when establishing a costing policy.
PRODUCT	FIFO	First-In/First-Out costing method.
RESOURCE	FIFO	First-In/First-Out costing method.
RESOURCE	FUTURE RECEPTIONS	Information about products that are expected to be taken into inventory in the near future; can include storage locations, serial numbers, and so forth.
PRODUCT	FUTURE RECEPTIONS	Information about products that are expected to be taken into inventory in the near future; can include storage locations, serial numbers, and so forth.

RESOURCE	FUTURE RECEPTIONS	Information about products that are expected to be taken into inventory in the near future; can include storage locations, serial numbers, and so forth.
RESOURCE	FUTURE RECEPTIONS	Information about products that are expected to be taken into inventory in the near future; can include storage locations, serial numbers, and so forth.
RESOURCE	FUTURE RECEPTIONS	Information about products that are expected to be taken into inventory in the near future; can include storage locations, serial numbers, and so forth.
RESOURCE	FUTURE RECEPTIONS	Information about products that are expected to be taken into inventory in the near future; can include storage locations, serial numbers, and so forth.
PRODUCT	GROUP	A category of products that are grouped together on the basis of some predetermined commonality.
RESOURCE	GROUP	A category of products that are grouped together on the basis of some predetermined commonality.
RESOURCE	INVENTORY	Formal collection of products or items held in a warehouse and available for outgoing order.
PRODUCT	INVENTORY	Formal collection of products or items held in a warehouse and available for outgoing order.
RESOURCE	INVENTORY	Formal collection of products or items held in a warehouse and available for outgoing order.
PRODUCT	INVENTORY	Formal collection of products or items held in a warehouse and available for outgoing order.
RESOURCE	INVENTORY ID	An identifier, usually a number, that uniquely identifies an item in inventory.

RESOURCE	INVENTORY INSPECTION SCHEDULE	A predefined schedule for quality control checks of inventory items.
PRODUCT	INVENTORY INSPECTION SCHEDULE	A predefined schedule for quality control checks of inventory items.
RESOURCE	INVENTORY LOCATIONS	Designated areas in the warehouse for the storage of specific inventory items.
PRODUCT	INVENTORY LOCATIONS	Designated areas in the warehouse for the storage of specific inventory items.
RESOURCE	INVENTORY LOCATIONS	Designated areas in the warehouse for the storage of specific inventory items.
PRODUCT	INVENTORY LOCATIONS	Designated areas in the warehouse for the storage of specific inventory items.
RESOURCE	INVENTORY LOCATIONS	Designated areas in the warehouse for the storage of specific inventory items.
RESOURCE	INVENTORY LOCATIONS	Designated areas in the warehouse for the storage of specific inventory items.
RESOURCE	INVENTORY LOCATIONS	Designated areas in the warehouse for the storage of specific inventory items.
RESOURCE	INVENTORY LOCATIONS	Designated areas in the warehouse for the storage of specific inventory items.
RESOURCE	INVENTORY LOCATIONS	Designated areas in the warehouse for the storage of specific inventory items.
RESOURCE	INVOICE ADDRESS	The address to which the invoice for an order should be sent.
PRODUCT	INVOICE ADDRESS	The address to which the invoice for an order should be sent.
PRODUCT	INVOICE NOTICE	A notice sent to the accounting process alerting to the need to issue an invoice for a shipped order.

RESOURCE	INVOICE NOTICE	A notice sent to the accounting process alerting to the need to issue an invoice for a shipped order.
PRODUCT	KIT	A new product composed of two or more separate items picked from inventory.
RESOURCE	KIT	A new product composed of two or more separate items picked from inventory.
RESOURCE	KIT DEFINITION	The list of separate inventory items to be grouped as a new product.
PRODUCT	KIT DEFINITION	The list of separate inventory items to be grouped as a new product.
RESOURCE	LABELING INFORMATION	Information to be included on labels applied to items while they are being kitted, packaged, and so forth.
PRODUCT	LABELING INFORMATION	Information to be included on labels applied to items while they are being kitted, packaged, and so forth.
RESOURCE	LABELING INFORMATION	Information to be included on labels applied to items while they are being kitted, packaged, and so forth.
PRODUCT	LATEST INBOUND	Costing method that assigns the cost of the latest inbound shipment of an order product as its price.
RESOURCE	LATEST INBOUND	Costing method that assigns the cost of the latest inbound shipment of an order product as its price.
PRODUCT	LIFO	Last-In/First-Out costing method.
RESOURCE	LIFO	Last-In/First-Out costing method.
PRODUCT	LOT	A means of grouping a collection of products (typically received on the same date) whose balances and value are usually considered collectively.
RESOURCE	LOT	A means of grouping a collection of products (typically received on the same date) whose balances and value are usually considered collectively.
PRODUCT	LOT NUMBER	A number that uniquely identifies a collection of items in inventory that

		have been grouped together, typically having the same receive date.
RESOURCE	LOT NUMBER	A number that uniquely identifies a collection of items in inventory that have been grouped together, typically having the same receive date.
RESOURCE	LOT NUMBER	A number that uniquely identifies a collection of items in inventory that have been grouped together, typically having the same receive date.
RESOURCE	LOT NUMBERS	An identifier, usually a number, which uniquely identifies a lot.
PRODUCT	LOT NUMBERS	An identifier, usually a number, which uniquely identifies a lot.
RESOURCE	LOT NUMBERS	An identifier, usually a number, that uniquely identifies a group of products or orders that have been grouped according to a predefined criteria; one of the ways by which inventory can be stored and controlled in a warehouse.
PRODUCT	LOT NUMBERS	An identifier, usually a number, that uniquely identifies a group of products or orders that have been grouped according to a predefined criteria; one of the ways by which inventory can be stored and controlled in a warehouse.
RESOURCE	MANNER OF TRANSPORT	Indicates the type of transport to be used to ship an order to its destination.
PRODUCT	MANNER OF TRANSPORT	Indicates the type of transport to be used to ship an order to its destination.
PRODUCT	MISSING PRODUCTS LIST	List of items that had been expected on the basis of a purchase order but were missing from a received shipment from a vendor.
RESOURCE	MISSING PRODUCTS LIST	List of items that had been expected on the basis of a purchase order but

		were missing from a received shipment from a vendor.
PRODUCT	ORDER	A fully-attributed formal request for products.
RESOURCE	ORDER	A fully-attributed formal request for products.
RESOURCE	ORDER	A fully-attributed formal request for products.
RESOURCE	ORDER	A fully-attributed formal request for products.
RESOURCE	ORDER	A fully-attributed formal request for products.
PRODUCT	ORDER COST	The total cost of an order.
RESOURCE	ORDER COST	The total cost of an order.
RESOURCE	ORDER DATE	The date and time on which the order was placed.
PRODUCT	ORDER DETAILS	Information such as requested items and quantities, general order partner information, delivery addresses and dates, and so forth.
RESOURCE	ORDER DETAILS	Information such as requested items and quantities, general order partner information, delivery addresses and dates, and so forth.
PRODUCT	ORDER INFORMATION	Order-dependent values such as order number, order time, order cost, and so forth.
RESOURCE	ORDER INFORMATION	Order-dependent values such as order number, order time, order cost, and so forth.
RESOURCE	ORDER NUMBER	An identifier, usually a number, that uniquely identifies an order.
PRODUCT	ORDER NUMBER	An identifier, usually a number, that uniquely identifies an order.
PRODUCT	ORDER PARTNER	A business partner who either places or receives orders; also holds general information and policies such as whether backorders are permitted with this partner.

RESOURCE	ORDER PARTNER	A business partner who either places or receives orders; also holds general information and policies such as whether backorders are permitted with this partner.
RESOURCE	ORDER PARTNER	A business partner who either places or receives orders; also holds general information and policies such as whether backorders are permitted with this partner.
PRODUCT	ORDER PARTNER	A business partner who either places or receives orders; also holds general information and policies such as whether backorders are permitted with this partner.
RESOURCE	ORDER PARTNER	A business partner who either places or receives orders; also holds general information and policies such as whether backorders are permitted with this partner.
RESOURCE	ORDER PARTNER	A business partner who either places or receives orders; also holds general information and policies such as whether backorders are permitted with this partner.
RESOURCE	ORDER PARTNER	A business partner who either places or receives orders; also holds general information and policies such as whether backorders are permitted with this partner.
RESOURCE	ORDER PARTNER	A business partner who either places or receives orders; also holds general information and policies such as whether backorders are permitted with this partner.
RESOURCE	ORDER PARTNER	A business partner who either places or receives orders; also holds general information and policies such as whether backorders are permitted with this partner.

RESOURCE	ORDER PARTNER	A business partner who either places or receives orders; also holds general information and policies such as whether backorders are permitted with this partner.
PRODUCT	ORDER PLANNING DETAILS	Specifies the detailed planning information—such as warehouse, manner of transport, shipping time, delivery date, stock identification and type—for part or all of the quantity of a product specified by a single order requested detail.
RESOURCE	ORDER PLANNING DETAILS	Specifies the detailed planning information—such as warehouse, manner of transport, shipping time, delivery date, stock identification and type—for part or all of the quantity of a product specified by a single order requested detail.
RESOURCE	ORDER PLANNING DETAILS	Specifies the detailed planning information—such as warehouse, manner of transport, shipping time, delivery date, stock identification and type—for part or all of the quantity of a product specified by a single order requested detail.
RESOURCE	ORDER PLANNING DETAILS	Specifies the detailed planning information—such as warehouse, manner of transport, shipping time, delivery date, stock identification and type—for part or all of the quantity of a product specified by a single order requested detail.
PRODUCT	ORDER STATUS	The current processing stage of an order. Typically, an order will be in the process of being picked, kitted, packed, or shipped.
RESOURCE	ORDER STATUS	The current processing stage of an order. Typically, an order will be in the process of being picked, kitted, packed, or shipped.

PRODUCT	ORDER TIME	The date and time on which the order as placed.
RESOURCE	PACKAGING INFORMATION	Information detailing how items or an order should be packaged for outbound shipment.
PRODUCT	PACKAGING INFORMATION	Information detailing how items or an order should be packaged for outbound shipment.
RESOURCE	PACKING POLICIES	Policies, which can be product-specific and/or general, that determine how products should be packaged as part of a shipment.
PRODUCT	PACKING POLICIES	Policies, which can be product-specific and/or general, that determine how products should be packaged as part of a shipment.
PRODUCT	PACKING POLICIES	Policies, which can be product-specific and/or general, that determine how products should be packaged as part of a shipment.
RESOURCE	PACKING POLICIES	Policies, which can be product-specific and/or general, that determine how products should be packaged as part of a shipment.
RESOURCE	PAYMENT METHOD	Payment method used by an order partner to pay an order invoice.
PRODUCT	PAYMENT METHOD	Payment method used by an order partner to pay an order invoice.
RESOURCE	PAYMENT TERMS	Terms which may be offered to an order partner if an invoice is paid in a timely fashion.
PRODUCT	PAYMENT TERMS	Terms which may be offered to an order partner if an invoice is paid in a timely fashion.
PRODUCT	PHYSICAL MEASUREMENTS	The measured, physical dimensions of the product.
RESOURCE	PHYSICAL MEASUREMENTS	The measured, physical dimensions of the product.
PRODUCT	PICK LIST	A list created through the order process that directs the picking of specific products to fill orders.

RESOURCE	PICK LIST	A list created through the order process that directs the picking of specific products to fill orders.
PRODUCT	PICKED ITEMS	Items that have been picked from inventory as specified in a pick list; these items will be grouped by individual order.
RESOURCE	PICKED ITEMS	Items that have been picked from inventory as specified in a pick list; these items will be grouped by individual order.
RESOURCE	PICKED ITEMS	Items that have been picked from inventory as specified in a pick list; these items will be grouped by individual order.
PRODUCT	PICKING DATES	The dates on which specific orders are to be picked.
RESOURCE	PICKING DATES	The dates on which specific orders are to be picked.
RESOURCE	PLANNED LOCATION LIST	Locations within a warehouse in which it is intended to store specific products.
PRODUCT	PLANNED LOCATION LIST	Locations within a warehouse in which it is intended to store specific products.
PRODUCT	PREPARED ORDER	An outbound order (stock transfer or sales order) that has been assembled, packaged, and labeled and is ready to be included in a shipment.
RESOURCE	PREPARED ORDER	An outbound order (stock transfer or sales order) that has been assembled, packaged, and labeled and is ready to be included in a shipment.
PRODUCT	PREPARED PUTAWAY LOCATIONS	Storage locations that have been prepared for the receipt of additional products.
RESOURCE	PREPARED PUTAWAY LOCATIONS	Storage locations that have been prepared for the receipt of additional products.

PRODUCT	PREPARED SHIPMENT	A shipment that is ready to be handed off to the appropriate carriers and removed from the warehouse.
RESOURCE	PREPARED SHIPMENT	A shipment that is ready to be handed off to the appropriate carriers and removed from the warehouse.
RESOURCE	PREPARED SHIPMENT	A shipment that is ready to be handed off to the appropriate carriers and removed from the warehouse.
PRODUCT	PRODUCT	An individual item or type of item held in a warehouse and available for orders; Products in inventory will have IDs, quantities, costs, and may be allocated to specific storage locations and zones, an associated order partner and supplying warehouse, and so forth.
RESOURCE	PRODUCT	An individual item or type of item held in a warehouse and available for orders; Products in inventory will have IDs, quantities, costs, may be allocated to specific storage locations and zones, an associated order partner and supplying warehouse, and so forth.
RESOURCE	PRODUCT	An individual item or type of item held in a warehouse and available for orders; Products in inventory will have IDs, quantities, costs, may be allocated to specific storage locations and zones, an associated order partner and supplying warehouse, and so forth.
PRODUCT	PRODUCT BALANCE	The quantity of product available to fill an order; indicates whether or not there is sufficient quantity on hand and in the future receptions, or if a backorder is required.
PRODUCT	PRODUCT BALANCE	The quantity of a product currently available to be used to fill an order.
RESOURCE	PRODUCT BALANCE	The quantity of a product currently available to be used to fill an order.

RESOURCE	PRODUCT BALANCE	The quantity of a product currently available to be used to fill an order.
RESOURCE	PRODUCT BALANCE	The quantity of a product currently available to be used to fill an order.
PRODUCT	PRODUCT BALANCE	The quantity of a product currently available to be used to fill an order.
RESOURCE	PRODUCT BALANCE	The quantity of a product currently available to be used to fill an order.
RESOURCE	PRODUCT BALANCE	The quantity of a product currently available to be used to fill an order.
RESOURCE	PRODUCT BALANCE	The quantity of a product currently available to be used to fill an order.
RESOURCE	PRODUCT BALANCE	The quantity of product available to fill an order; indicates whether there is sufficient quantity on hand and in the future receptions, or if a back-order is required.
PRODUCT	PRODUCT DESCRIPTION	Description of a product; includes product-specific values for ID, units of measure, order partner, price, discounts, lead time, and so forth.
RESOURCE	PRODUCT DESCRIPTION	Describes what a product is, gives units of measure, and so forth.
RESOURCE	PRODUCT DESCRIPTION	Description of a product listed in a catalogue for sale.
PRODUCT	PRODUCT DESCRIPTION	Description of a product listed in a catalogue for sale.
PRODUCT	PRODUCT DESCRIPTION	Description of a product; includes product-specific values for ID, units of measure, order partner, price, discounts, lead time, and so forth.
RESOURCE	PRODUCT DESCRIPTION	Description of a product; includes product-specific values for ID, units of measure, order partner, price, discounts, lead time, and so forth.
RESOURCE	PRODUCT DESCRIPTION	Description of a product; includes product-specific values for ID, units of measure, order partner, price, discounts, lead time, and so forth.

PRODUCT	PRODUCT ID	An identifier, usually a number, that uniquely identifies an item inbound from an order partner, held in inventory, or outbound as part of an order.
RESOURCE	PRODUCT ID	An identifier, usually a number, that uniquely identifies an item in inventory.
RESOURCE	PRODUCT ID	An identifier, usually a number, that uniquely identifies an item in inventory.
RESOURCE	PRODUCT ID	An identifier, usually a number, that uniquely identifies an item in inventory.
RESOURCE	PRODUCT ID	An identifier, usually a number, that uniquely identifies an item in inventory.
RESOURCE	PRODUCT ID	An identifier, usually a number, that uniquely identifies an inventory item listed in the catalogue.
PRODUCT	PRODUCT ID	An identifier, usually a number, that uniquely identifies an inventory item listed in the catalogue.
RESOURCE	PRODUCT ID	An identifier, usually a number, that uniquely identifies an item in inventory.
PRODUCT	PRODUCT ID	An identifier, usually a number, that uniquely identifies an item in inventory.
RESOURCE	PRODUCT ID	An identifier, usually a number, that uniquely identifies an item in inventory.
RESOURCE	PRODUCT ID	An identifier, usually a number, that uniquely identifies an item inbound from an order partner, held in inventory, or outbound as part of an order.
RESOURCE	PRODUCT ID	An identifier, usually a number, that uniquely identifies an item inbound from an order partner, held in inventory, or outbound as part of an order.

RESOURCE	PRODUCT ID	An identifier, usually a number, that uniquely identifies an item inbound from an order partner, held in inventory, or outbound as part of an order.
RESOURCE	PRODUCT PRICE	The cost for product; typically a fixed dollar amount per unit.
PRODUCT	PRODUCT PRICE	The cost for product; typically a fixed dollar amount per unit.
RESOURCE	PRODUCT PRICE	The cost for product; typically a fixed dollar amount per unit.
PRODUCT	PRODUCT PRICE	The cost for product; typically a fixed dollar amount per unit.
RESOURCE	PRODUCT PRICE	The purchase price of a product listed in the catalogue.
PRODUCT	PRODUCT PRICE	The purchase price of a product listed in the catalogue.
RESOURCE	PRODUCT PRICE	The cost for product; typically a fixed dollar amount per unit.
PRODUCT	PRODUCT PRICE	The cost for product; typically a fixed dollar amount per unit.
RESOURCE	PRODUCT PRICE	The cost for product; typically a fixed dollar amount per unit.
RESOURCE	PRODUCT PRICE	The cost for product; typically a fixed dollar amount per unit.
RESOURCE	PRODUCT RESERVATIONS	Identifies the types and quantities of products that have been set aside to fill an order; initially comprises a soft allocation but, just prior to picking, details specific IDs, quantities, storage locations, and so forth for items that have been designated to.
RESOURCE	PRODUCT RESERVATIONS	Identifies the types and quantities of products that have been set aside to fill an order; initially comprises a soft allocation but, just prior to picking, details specific ID's, quantities, storage locations, etc. for items that have been designated to.

PRODUCT	PRODUCT RESERVATIONS	Identifies the types and quantities of products that have been set aside to fill an order; initially comprises a soft allocation but, just prior to picking, details specific ID's, quantities, storage locations, etc. for items that have been designated to.
RESOURCE	PRODUCT RESERVATIONS	Identifies the types and quantities of products that have been set aside to fill an order; initially comprises a soft allocation but, just prior to picking, details specific ID's, quantities, storage locations, etc. for items that have been designated to.
RESOURCE	PRODUCT RESERVATIONS	Identifies the types and quantities of products that have been set aside to fill an order; initially comprises a soft allocation but, just prior to picking, details specific ID's, quantities, storage locations, etc. for items that have been designated to.
RESOURCE	PRODUCT RESERVATIONS	Identifies the types and quantities of products that have been set aside to fill an order; initially comprises a soft allocation but, just prior to picking, details specific ID's, quantities, storage locations, etc. for items that have been designated to.
PRODUCT	PUTAWAY PRODUCT	A product that has been put in its designated storage location but whose inventory status has not yet been updated.
RESOURCE	PUTAWAY PRODUCT	A product that has been put in its designated storage location but whose inventory status has not yet been updated.
PRODUCT	QUOTE	Given in response to an order partner request for a quoted price on an order; not considered a formal order until it is committed to the system.

RESOURCE	QUOTE	Given in response to an order partner request for a quoted price on an order; not considered a formal order until it is committed to the system.
RESOURCE	RECEIVED PRODUCTS	Products that have been delivered to a warehouse but have not gone through the receiving process.
PRODUCT	RECEIVED PRODUCTS	Products that arrived at a warehouse as part of an inbound order and have gone through the receiving process.
RESOURCE	RECEIVED PRODUCTS	Products that arrived at a warehouse as part of an inbound order and have gone through the receiving process.
RESOURCE	RECEIVED PRODUCTS	Products that arrived at a warehouse as part of an inbound order and have gone through the receiving process.
PRODUCT	RECEIVED PRODUCTS	Products that have been delivered to a warehouse but have not gone through the receiving process.
PRODUCT	RECEIVING REPORT	Documents the result of the receiving inspection and count.
RESOURCE	RECEIVING REPORT	Documents the result of the receiving inspection and count.
RESOURCE	RECEIVING WAREHOUSE	The warehouse that will receive products to fill an order.
RESOURCE	RECEIVING WAREHOUSE	The warehouse designated to receive all or part of an order.
PRODUCT	RECEIVING WAREHOUSE	The warehouse designated to receive all or part of an order.
RESOURCE	RECEIVING WAREHOUSE	The warehouse designated to receive all or part of an order.
RESOURCE	RECEIVING WAREHOUSE	The warehouse designated to receive all or part of an order.
PRODUCT	REORDER POINT	The inventory level at which action is taken to replenish stock. The reorder point is normally calculated as the quantity forecasted to be used during the lead time plus a quantity of safety stock.

RESOURCE	REORDER POINT	The inventory level at which action is taken to replenish stock. The reorder point is normally calculated as the quantity forecasted to be used during the lead time plus a quantity of safety stock.
PRODUCT	REPLENISHMENT FLAG	Designates whether the warehouse is replenished from either another warehouse, an OrderPartner, or both.
RESOURCE	REPLENISHMENT FLAG	Designates whether or not the warehouse is replenished from either another warehouse, an OrderPartner, or both.
PRODUCT	REPLENISHMENT REQUEST	A request for a replenishment order to be placed.
RESOURCE	REPLENISHMENT REQUEST	A request for a replenishment order to be placed.
RESOURCE	REQUESTED DETAILS	Special requests made by an order partner when creating an order (i.e., request to deliver requested products to two separate delivery addresses).
PRODUCT	REQUESTED DETAILS	Special requests made by an order partner when creating an order (i.e., request to deliver requested products to two separate delivery addresses).
PRODUCT	REQUESTED DETAILS	Special requests made by an order partner when creating an order (i.e., request to deliver requested products to two separate delivery addresses).
RESOURCE	REQUESTED DETAILS	Special requests made by an order partner when creating an order (i.e., request to deliver requested products to two separate delivery addresses).
RESOURCE	REQUESTED QUANTITY	The quantity of a product requested by an order partner.
PRODUCT	REQUESTED QUANTITY	The quantity of a product requested by an order partner.
RESOURCE	REQUESTED QUANTITY	The quantity of a product requested by an order partner.

RESOURCE	SERIAL NUMBER	A unique identifier used to identify a single instance of an inventory product; one of three ways in which warehouses can be stock controlled (location, lot, or serial-number controlled).
PRODUCT	SERIAL NUMBER	A unique identifier used to identify a single instance of an inventory product; one of three ways in which warehouses can be stock controlled (location, lot, or serial-number controlled).
RESOURCE	SERIAL NUMBER	A unique identifier, provided either by the vendor or assigned by the warehouse, to identify and track a single inventory item.
PRODUCT	SERIAL NUMBER	A unique identifier, provided either by the vendor or assigned by the warehouse, to identify and track a single inventory item.
RESOURCE	SERIAL NUMBER	A unique identifier used to identify a single instance of an inventory product; one of three ways in which warehouses can be stock controlled (location, lot, or serial-number controlled).
PRODUCT	SHIP LIST	A collection of information for a particular shipping task, specifying the items to be shipped and other relevant information about the shipment.
RESOURCE	SHIP LIST	A collection of information for a particular shipping task, specifying the items to be shipped and other relevant information about the shipment.
PRODUCT	SHIPPED ORDER	An order that has been picked up by a carrier and has left the warehouse.
RESOURCE	SHIPPED ORDER	An order that has been picked up by a carrier and has left the warehouse.
RESOURCE	SHIPPING MANIFEST	Documentation from a vendor that accompanies an order, detailing the types and quantities of items.

PRODUCT	SHIPPING MANIFEST	Documentation from a vendor that accompanies an order, detailing the types and quantities of items.
PRODUCT	SHIPPING NOTIFICATION	A notice sent to order management advising of an order's shipped status; also triggers the invoicing process for the shipped orders.
RESOURCE	SHIPPING NOTIFICATION	A notice sent to order management advising of an order's shipped status; also triggers the invoicing process for the shipped orders.
RESOURCE	SHIPPING WAREHOUSE	The warehouse designated to ship all or part of an order.
PRODUCT	SHIPPING WAREHOUSE	The warehouse designated to ship all or part of an order.
PRODUCT	SIGNED WAYBILL	Document signed by warehouse personnel to confirm receipt of items from a vendor.
RESOURCE	SIGNED WAYBILL	Document signed by warehouse personnel to confirm receipt of items from a vendor.
PRODUCT	SOFT ALLOCATION	A quantity of a particular product to reserve.
RESOURCE	SOFT ALLOCATION	Usually created simultaneously with a new order and represents an initial assignment of a quantity of a particular product to reserve.
RESOURCE	SOFT ALLOCATION	A quantity of a particular product to reserve.
RESOURCE	SPECIAL HANDLING POLICIES	Customer-specific handling policies which must be considered when handling products or inventory.
PRODUCT	SPECIAL HANDLING POLICIES	Customer-specific handling policies which must be considered when handling products or inventory.
RESOURCE	SPECIAL HANDLING POLICIES	Customer-specific handling policies which must be considered when handling products or inventory.

PRODUCT	STANDARD FIXED COST	Costing method which assigns a fixed dollar amount as the price of an order product.
RESOURCE	STANDARD FIXED COST	Costing method which assigns a fixed dollar amount as the price of an order product.
PRODUCT	STOCK CONTROL OPTIONS	The permitted means of stock control (i.e., location, lot, or serial-number controlled).
RESOURCE	STOCK CONTROL OPTIONS	The permitted means of stock control (i.e., location, lot, or serial-number controlled).
PRODUCT	STOCK VALUE	The monetary value of specified types and quantities of inventory.
RESOURCE	STOCK VALUE	The monetary value of specified types and quantities of inventory.
PRODUCT	STOCK ZONES	Designated zones in the warehouse for storing specified inventory (i.e., there may be a specific zone for all frozen foods).
RESOURCE	STOCK ZONES	Designated zones in the warehouse for storing specified inventory (i.e., there may be a specific zone for all frozen foods).
RESOURCE	STOCK ZONES	Designated zones in the warehouse for storing specified inventory (i.e., there may be a specific zone for all frozen foods).
RESOURCE	STOCK ZONES	Designated zones in the warehouse for storing specified inventory (i.e., there may be a specific zone for all frozen foods).
RESOURCE	STOCK ZONES	Designated zones in the warehouse for storing specified inventory (i.e., there may be a specific zone for all frozen foods).
RESOURCE	STORAGE POLICIES	General policies and procedures that detail where items should be stored in a warehouse and any specific pre-

		cautions or considerations that must be taken into account when committing an item to inventory.
PRODUCT	STORAGE POLICIES	General policies and procedures that detail where items should be stored in a warehouse and any specific precautions or considerations that must be taken into account when committing an item to inventory.
PRODUCT	SUPPLEMENTARY CHARGES	Charges included on an order invoice for things other than purchase price, taxes, and so forth.
RESOURCE	SUPPLEMENTARY CHARGES	Charges included on an order invoice for things other than purchase price, taxes, and so forth.
RESOURCE	SUPPLEMENTARY CHARGES	Charges included on an order invoice for things other than purchase price, taxes, and so forth.
RESOURCE	SUPPLYING WAREHOUSE	The warehouse supplying the products used to fill a order.
PRODUCT	SUPPLYING WAREHOUSE	The warehouse supplying the products used to fill a order.
RESOURCE	TERMS OF DELIVERY	Any applicable terms of delivery specific to the order partner.
PRODUCT	TERMS OF DELIVERY	Any applicable terms of delivery specific to the order partner.
PRODUCT	TRANSACTION REQUEST	A request from some other warehouse process to move stock in the inventory; could be either adding new inventory, moving items within inventory, or removing items from inventory; defined by the product, quantity, and warehouse involved.
PRODUCT	TRANSACTION REQUEST	A request from some other warehouse process to move stock in the inventory; could be either adding new inventory, moving items within inventory, or removing items from inventory; defined by the product, quantity, and warehouse involved.

RESOURCE	TRANSACTION REQUEST	A request from some other warehouse process to move stock in the inventory; could be either adding new inventory, moving items within inventory, or removing items from inventory; defined by the product, quantity, and warehouse involved.
RESOURCE	TRANSACTION REQUEST	A request from some other warehouse process to move stock in the inventory; could be either adding new inventory, moving items within inventory, or removing items from inventory; defined by the product, quantity, and warehouse involved.
RESOURCE	TRANSACTION REQUEST	A request from some other warehouse process to move stock in the inventory; could be either adding new inventory, moving items within inventory, or removing items from inventory; defined by the product, quantity, and warehouse involved.
RESOURCE	TRANSPORT TIME	The amount of time required to ship a product from its supplying warehouse or vendor to the receiving order partner; typically dependent on the *ship from* and *ship to* locations as opposed to being product-dependent.
PRODUCT	TRANSPORT TIME	The amount of time required to ship a product from its supplying warehouse or vendor to the receiving order partner.
RESOURCE	TRANSPORT TIME	The amount of time required to ship a product from its supplying warehouse or vendor to the receiving order partner.
PRODUCT	UNITS OF MEASURE	The units of measure which are valid to use with a specific product.
PRODUCT	UNITS OF MEASURE	The official listing of units of measure which are valid to use within the company.

RESOURCE	UNITS OF MEASURE	The official listing of units of measure which are valid to use within the company.
RESOURCE	UNITS OF MEASURE	The units of measure which are valid to use with a specific product.
RESOURCE	UNITS OF MEASURE	The official listing of units of measure which are valid to use within the company.
PRODUCT	UPDATED FUTURE RECEPTIONS	Updated information on future product receptions.
PRODUCT	UPDATED FUTURE RECEPTIONS	Updated information on future product receptions.
RESOURCE	UPDATED FUTURE RECEPTIONS	Updated information on future product receptions.
RESOURCE	UPDATED FUTURE RECEPTIONS	Updated information on future product receptions.
PRODUCT	UPDATED INVENTORY STATUS	Updated quantity of an item in inventory after a stock transaction.
RESOURCE	UPDATED INVENTORY STATUS	Updated quantity of an item in inventory after a stock transaction.
PRODUCT	UPDATED INVENTORY STATUS	Updated quantity of an item in inventory after a stock transaction.
PRODUCT	UPDATED ORDER STATUS	Information provided to order management to indicate the current processing stage of an order. Typically, an order will be in the process of being picked, kitted, packed, or shipped.
RESOURCE	UPDATED ORDER STATUS	Information provided to order management to indicate the current processing stage of an order. Typically, an order will be in the process of being picked, kitted, packed, or shipped.
PRODUCT	UPDATED RESERVATIONS	Updated product reservations.

PRODUCT	UPDATED RESERVATIONS	Updated product reservations.
RESOURCE	UPDATED RESERVATIONS	Updated product reservations.
RESOURCE	UPDATED RESERVATIONS	Updated product reservations.
RESOURCE	WAREHOUSE	The area in which inventory is stored.
PRODUCT	WAREHOUSE	The area in which inventory is stored.
RESOURCE	WAREHOUSE	The area in which inventory is stored.
RESOURCE	WAREHOUSE	The area in which inventory is stored.
PRODUCT	WAYBILL	A document prepared by the carrier of a shipment of goods that contains details of the shipment, route, charges, and so forth.
RESOURCE	WAYBILL	A document prepared by the carrier of a shipment of goods that contains details of the shipment, route, charges, and so forth.

SanFrancisco Warehouse Code Listing

The real introduction of WNS, Inc., to the future and power of Java came about through a chance meeting between myself and Joe Damassa, the then-director in charge of SanFrancisco and now vice president responsible for IBM's Application Integration Middleware. We were both attending a session on IBM NetStation hardware, and when he mentioned that he was giving the next session, I tagged along.

At this point, I am very glad that I did.

It's important to recognize that the SanFrancisco project has driven much of the understanding of the power and future of Java for IBM. SF was the first Java project undertaken by Big Blue, and the Enterprise JavaBeans specification has come about largely because of the work done by the development team in Rochester, Minnesota. This is big stuff, and there are some very bright and talented folks hard at work at it.

That compliment is without qualification. That being said, I have some arguments with the product itself. SanFrancisco was originally marketed as a complete set of business objects that customers could use to construct fast, flexible, and robust Java applications.

It turns out that the whole process is much, much, more complicated than that.

This section is devoted to SanFrancisco business objects because at WNS we believe it is the cornerstone of our future software development efforts. Every bump, bruise, and difficulty we encountered will be documented in this section from the standpoint of a shop that is relatively new to distributed objects, though experienced at developing software.

When I say relatively new, I mean that WNS cycled through a number of so-called object-oriented gurus, only to find that they lacked any appreciation for solving real-world problems through software. The process of practicalizing objects in the form of SanFrancisco has been a real challenge—but one from which I believe we are finally beginning to see benefits.

Understanding the Paradigm

Distributed objects are different, though many of the things I was warned about are overstated. First, let's understand what we get when we develop an application using SFP. We get pretested, prebuilt application objects that do a bunch of very specific things. I do mean *specific*.

In customizing the objects to do what you want them to, chances are you are going to run afoul of the assumptions that underly the SF framework. I've spent some time with the folks in Rochester, and to be absolutely candid, pulling no punches, they seem to only reluctantly accept that we are not going to throw out all our existing technology and reinvent the world as an object-oriented model.

This appalling lack of sensitivity to the real-world difficulty of securing funding for IT projects makes it particularly challenging when providing feedback. The bottom line is that a tremendous amount of work has gone into SF, and you can take advantage of it, but you're going to have to do it *their* way, rather than just nip off a few snippets of code for your own purposes.

That being said, let's go through the process of installing SanFrancisco 1.4, which is the production release available as I write this. We will cover what to expect from the EJB-compliant release of SF in 2000, but based on the track record, you'll want to start working with 1.4, keep with the development model, and use the migration utilities to move your code from one version to the next.

As I have already indicated ad infinitum (and nauseum?), you *must* work with the SF programming model in order to maintain migratibility.

I know there is a lot of code here, but I really think it's important to demonstrate at least a little of the functionality provided by the visual programming approach recommended here in *Big Blue Java*, as opposed to trying to write the stuff yourself. Yes, the code generator did spew out a lot of this, but I hope you can compare it to the code we create out of linked EMT, Rose, and SF Bridge tools to get an idea of the clarity of the code.

This code should begin to give you an idea of the SF-specific syntax that is used for handling warehouse activities within the framework. However, there are several other steps that must be taken in order to populate an actual warehouse. Keep in mind that some of this code will require handcrafting (which we'll go into later) and that by using the default code generator you end up having to check the differences between the SF-generated code and your modified version. Then you must cut and paste the changes into the newly generated code. If this isn't proof positive that you need to stay with the visual programming model, I don't know what is.

In any case, I thought it was well worth showing in all it's glory a command—to perform a straightforward function within SanFrancisco. The point is that prior to adding any products to a warehouse, you must first initialize a company to own those products. While on some level this might seem commonsensical, remember that is the nature of dealing with the framework. You can't just grab a function or a do a simple transaction. Your transaction exists in the context of the entire framework. Products must belong to a company; therefore before you can add products to a warehouse you must start at the top and work down.

This handles the creation of initial SF warehouse objects and handles any exceptions thrown in during the process. Even with that, however, we still don't have a working warehouse inventory listing or object to handle that business function. We chose to implement that support by using SF commands.

Figure B.1 shows the flow of object creation in this SF command for product warehouse link. This is a subset of the inventory initialization command. The source code for this command is included in this appendix.

Figure B.2 shows the flow of object creation in the SF command for product unit link. Like product warehouse link this is a subset of the inventory initialization command.

Figure B.3 shows the flow of object creation in the SF command for lots. This too is a subset of the inventory initialization command.

Figure B.4 shows the flow of object creation for product serial numbers. The entire set of models for the product initialization command can be found on the companion CD. Or you can check www.bigbluejava.com for an Adobe Acrobat version. The code for the entire inventory initialization command follows.

Code representing a sample warehouse product inventory command is depicted in Figure B.1.

```
package com.big.wms;

import java.io.*;
import java.util.*;
import com.ibm.sf.gf.*;
```

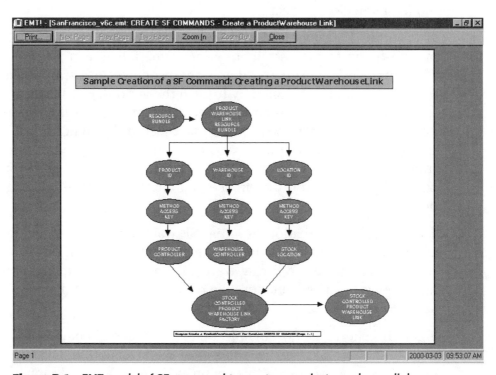

Figure B.1 EMT model of SF command to create a product warehouse link.

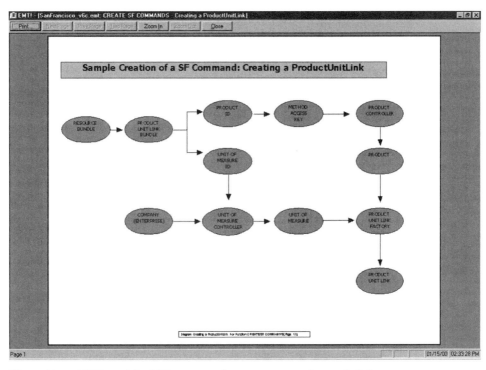

Figure B.2   EMT model of SF command to create a product unit link.

```
import com.ibm.sf.cf.*;
import com.ibm.sf.whs.*;

/*===================================================================*/
/**
 * This command is used to initialize product quantities for initial
 * product data.
 * <p><strong>Generated By:</strong> San Francisco Code Generator, Version
 * 1.3, 11 April 1999
 */
/*===================================================================*/

public class WNSInventoryInitializeCmdImpl extends CommandImpl implements
WNSInventoryInitializeCmd {

    public static final String IMPLEMENTATION_NAME =
"big.WNSInventoryInitializeCmdImpl";
    final static int versionNumber = 1;

    /** <p>not owned and mandatory attribute </p>*/
    protected Handle ivCompanyHdl;   // for Company entity

    /*-----------------------------------------------------------*/
    /*    Protected methods and Variables */
```

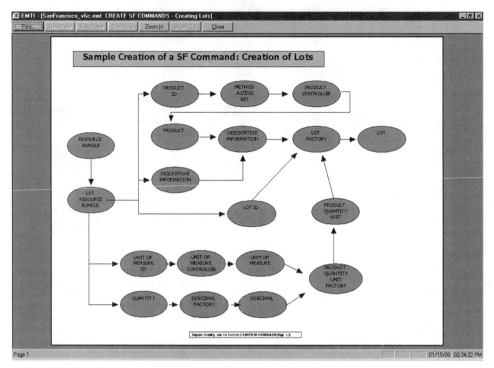

Figure B.3 EMT model of SF command for creation of lots.

```
/*--------------------------------------------------------------*/
/*--------------------------------------------------------------
*/
/**
 * Deletes any owned objects. <p>For more information, see the
 * <i>"SanFrancisco Programming Model"</i>.
 * <p>
 * <strong>PreConditions:</strong> None
 * <br><strong>PostConditions:</strong> Object's state destroyed
 * <br><strong>Object Changed:</strong> true
 *
 * @return void
 * @exception com.ibm.sf.gf.SFException San Francisco Framework
 * Exception
 */
/*--------------------------------------------------------------
*/
protected void destroy() throws com.ibm.sf.gf.SFException {
    // first, delete any objects added by this subclass
     // Company entity is not owned, just delete handle
     deleteHandle (ivCompanyHdl);
```

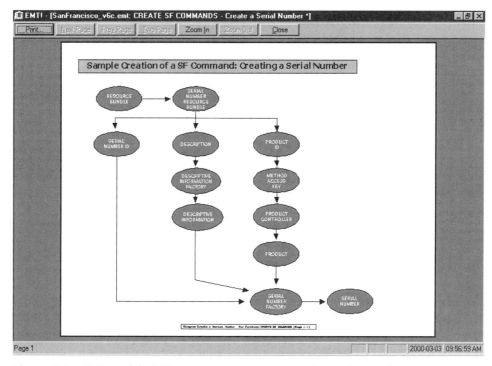

Figure B.4 EMT model of SF command to create a product serial number.

```
        // call parent to destroy its contained objects
        super.destroy();

    }
    /*----------------------------------------------------------------
*/
    /**
     * Checks if the instances are equal. <p>For more information, see
     * the <i>"San Francisco Programming Model"</i>.
     * <p>
     * <strong>PreConditions:</strong> None
     * <br><strong>PostConditions:</strong>
     * <br><strong>Object Changed:</strong> false
     *
     * @param anObject class instance to compare this to
     * <i>(Optional)</i>
     * @return boolean - true if instances are equal
     */
    /*----------------------------------------------------------------
*/
    public boolean equals(Object anObject) {
        try {
```

```
                    // check to make sure object being compared is same type
                    // and if so, call parent to check inherited state
                if ((anObject instanceof WNSInventoryInitializeCmd) &&
super.equals(anObject)) {
                    // cast object to type WNSInventoryInitializeCmd
                    WNSInventoryInitializeCmd bDSInventoryInitializeCmd
= (WNSInventoryInitializeCmd)anObject;

                    // now compare state added by this subclass
                    if (                          // non-collection entites
                                                  need to have equal handles
                        (Helper.equals(ivCompanyHdl,
WNSInventoryInitializeCmd.getCompanyHdl())) )
                        return (true);
                }
                return (false);
            }
        catch (Exception ex) {
            throw (new SFRuntimeException(ex, new
TextResource("MSG_RMTSFEXCEP_DEFAULT",
"com.ibm.sf.gf.resources.SFExceptionResources", (Object[])null, "Runtime
Exception has Occurred")));
            }
    }
    /*----------------------------------------------------------------
*/
    /**
     * Writes the object's state to the specified stream.
     * <p>For more information, see the <i>"San Francisco Programming
     * Model"</i>.<p>
     * <strong>Restriction:</strong> This method is implemented by the
     * class developer and is
     * NOT typically called by anything outside the Foundation Layer.
     * <br><strong>PreConditions:</strong> None
     * <br><strong>PostConditions:</strong>
     * <br><strong>Object Changed:</strong> false
     *
     * @param stream stream to read from <i>(Mandatory - object may be
     * changed)</i>
     * @return void
     * @exception java.io.IOException if an I/O error occurs
     */
    /*----------------------------------------------------------------
*/
    public void externalizeToStream(BaseStream stream) throws
java.io.IOException {
        //externalize the version number
        stream.writeInt(versionNumber);
        // write the parent's state
        super.externalizeToStream(stream);
        stream.writeHandle(this,ivCompanyHdl);
```

```
    }
    /*------------------------------------------------------------*/
    /*    Public methods                                          */
    /*------------------------------------------------------------*/

    /*----------------------------------------------------------------
*/
    /**
     * Gets Company.
     * <p>
     * <strong>PreConditions:</strong> None
     * <br><strong>PostConditions:</strong>
     * <br><strong>Object Changed:</strong> false
     *
     * @return Company
     * @exception com.ibm.sf.gf.SFException San Francisco Framework
     * Exception
     */
    /*----------------------------------------------------------------
*/
    public Company getCompany() throws com.ibm.sf.gf.SFException {
        // call inherited method to access the entity and update the
        // handle
        Company company = (Company) getObjectFromHandle(
                        ivCompanyHdl, AccessMode.createNormal());
        return (company);
    }
    /*----------------------------------------------------------------
*/
    /**
     * Gets the Handle to Company.
     * <p>
     * <strong>Restriction:</strong> Not for normal client use. The
     * returned Handle must NOT be
     * modified or saved. See Programmers Guide for additional
     * information.
     * <br><strong>PreConditions:</strong> None
     * <br><strong>PostConditions:</strong>
     * <br><strong>Object Changed:</strong> false
     *
     * @return Handle
     * @exception com.ibm.sf.gf.SFException San Francisco Framework
     * Exception
     */
    /*----------------------------------------------------------------
*/
    public Handle getCompanyHdl() throws com.ibm.sf.gf.SFException {
        return (ivCompanyHdl);
    }
/*------------------------------------------------------------*/
/**
```

```
 * Performs the Command.
 * <p>
 * <strong>PreConditions:</strong> None
 * <br><strong>PostConditions:</strong>
 * <br><strong>Object Changed:</strong> false
 *
 * @return void
 * @exception com.ibm.sf.gf.SFException San Francisco Framework Exception
 */
/*------------------------------------------------------------------*/
protected void handleDo() throws com.ibm.sf.gf.SFException {
    //*** Add begin
    /*..........................
        This command will create:
        1 - Product Warehouse Links
        2 - ProductUnitLinks
        3 - Lots
        4 - Serial Numbers
        ..........................*/
     Company company = getCompany();
     /*......................................
        Step 1 - Creating product warehouse links

        Creating the replenishment source chooser
        policy
        ......................................*/
     DReplenishmentSourceChooserPolicy defaultPolicy =
DReplenishmentSourceChooserPolicyDefaultFactory.createDReplenishmentSource
ChooserPolicyDefault();
     /*.
        Getting the product controller and the warehouse controller
      .*/
     ProductController pc = (ProductController)
company.getPropertyBy("whs.ProductController");
     WarehouseController wc = (WarehouseController)
company.getPropertyBy("whs.WarehouseController");
     try {
         System.out.println("Creating product warehouse links....");
         String pwlBundle = "resources/" + company.getId() +
"ProductWarehouseLink";
         ResourceBundle bundle = ResourceBundle.getBundle(pwlBundle);
         String numpwlsStr = bundle.getString("NUM");
         int numpwls = 0;
          try {
              numpwls = new Integer(numpwlsStr).intValue();
          } catch (NumberFormatException nfe) {
              System.out.println("Could not get number of product-
warehouse links");
              return;
          }
```

```
        for (int i = 0; i < numpwls; i++) {
                String productId = bundle.getString("P" + i);
                String warehouseId = bundle.getString("W" + i);
                String locationId = bundle.getString("L" + i);
                DMethodAccessKey key =
DSimpleMethodKeyFactory.createDMethodAccessKey(productId);
                Product product = pc.getProductBy(key);
                key =
DSimpleMethodKeyFactory.createDMethodAccessKey(warehouseId);
                Warehouse whs = wc.getWarehouseBy(key);
                key =
DSimpleMethodKeyFactory.createDMethodAccessKey(locationId);
                StockLocation sl = ((LocationControlledWarehouse)
whs).getStockLocationBy(key);
                try {
                        StockControlledProductWarehouseLink pwl =
StockControlledProductWarehouseLinkFactory.createStockControlledProduct
WarehouseLink(product, AccessMode.createNormal(), whs, defaultPolicy, null,
true, sl, null);
                } catch (ErrorsException e) {
                        System.out.println("Exception creating a PWL" +
e.getMessage());
                        Iterator it =
e.getResultsCollection().createResultMessageIterator();
                        while (it.more())          {
                                System.out.println(((DResultMessage)
it.next()).format());
                        }
                        SFException sfe = (SFException) e.getPrevious();
                        if (sfe != null && sfe instanceof ErrorsException) {
                                Iterator sfeit = ((ErrorsException)
sfe).getResultsCollection().createResultMessageIterator();
                                while (sfeit.more()) {
                                        System.out.println(((DResultMessage)
sfeit.next()).format());
                                }
                        }
                        throw (e);
                }
            }
    } catch (MissingResourceException mre) {
        System.out.println("Product-Warehouse Links not found");
        return;
    }
    /*.......................................
        Step 2 - Creating ProductUnitLinks

        Getting the UOM controller
        .......................................*/
    UnitOfMeasureController uomC = (UnitOfMeasureController)
```

```
company.getPropertyBy("cf.UnitOfMeasureController");
    try {
        System.out.println("Creating product unit links....");
        String pulBundle = "resources/" + company.getId() +
"ProductUnitLink";
        ResourceBundle bundle = ResourceBundle.getBundle(pulBundle);
        String numPULsStr = bundle.getString("NUM");
        int numPULs = 0;
        try {
            numPULs = new Integer(numPULsStr).intValue();
        } catch (NumberFormatException nfe) {
            System.out.println("Could not get number of
ProductUnitLinks");
            return;
        }
        for (int i = 0; i < numPULs; i++) {
            String productId = bundle.getString("P" + i);
            String uomId = bundle.getString("L" + i);
            DMethodAccessKey key =
DSimpleMethodKeyFactory.createDMethodAccessKey(productId);
            Product product = pc.getProductBy(key);
            UnitOfMeasure uom = uomC.getUnitOfMeasureBy(uomId);
            try {
                ProductUnitLink pul =
ProductUnitLinkFactory.createProductUnitLink(product,
AccessMode.createNormal(), uom, null); //... No measurements
            } catch (ErrorsException e) {
                System.out.println("Exception creating a PUL " +
e.getMessage());
                Iterator it =
e.getResultsCollection().createResultMessageIterator();
                while (it.more()) {
                    System.out.println(((DResultMessage)
it.next()).format());
                }
                throw (e);
            }
        }
    } catch (MissingResourceException mre)  {
        System.out.println("Lots not found for company " +
company.getId());
    }

    /*........................................
        Step 3 - Creating Lots
     ........................................*/
    try {
        System.out.println("Creating lots....");
        String lotBundle = "resources/" + company.getId() + "Lot";
        ResourceBundle bundle = ResourceBundle.getBundle(lotBundle);
        String numLotsStr = bundle.getString("NUM");
```

```
        int numLots = 0;
        try {
            numLots = new Integer(numLotsStr).intValue();
        } catch (NumberFormatException nfe) {
            System.out.println("Could not get number of Lots");
            return;
        }
        for (int i = 0; i < numLots; i++) {
            String productId = bundle.getString("P" + i);
            String lotId = bundle.getString("L" + i);
            String description = bundle.getString("D" + i);
            String uomId = bundle.getString("U" + i);
            String quantityStr = bundle.getString("Q" + i);
            DMethodAccessKey key =
DSimpleMethodKeyFactory.createDMethodAccessKey(productId);
            Product product = pc.getProductBy(key);
            DescriptiveInformation di =
DescriptiveInformationFactory.createDescriptiveInformation(AccessMode.
createNormal(), product.getHandle());
            di.addDefaultDescription(description);
            UnitOfMeasure uom = uomC.getUnitOfMeasureBy(uomId);
            DDecimal quantity =
DDecimalFactory.createDDecimal(quantityStr);
            DProductQuantityUnit pqu =
DProductQuantityUnitFactory.createDProductQuantityUnit(quantity, uom,
product);
            try {
                Lot lot = LotFactory.createLot(product,
AccessMode.createNormal(), lotId, di);
                lot.updateLot(pqu);
            } catch (ErrorsException e) {
                System.out.println("Exception creating a PWL" +
e.getMessage());
                Iterator it =
e.getResultsCollection().createResultMessageIterator();
                while (it.more()) {
                    System.out.println(((DResultMessage)
it.next()).format());
                }
                throw (e);
            }
        }
    } catch (MissingResourceException mre) {
        System.out.println("Lots not found for company" +
company.getId());
        System.out.println("Assuming this company doesn't handle lots -
continuing...");
    }

    /*......................................
        Step 4 - Creating Serial Numbers
```

```
                  ....................................*/
      try {
            System.out.println("Creating serial numbers....");
            String snBundle = "resources/" + company.getId() +
"SerialNumber";
            ResourceBundle bundle = ResourceBundle.getBundle(snBundle);
            String numSNsStr = bundle.getString("NUM");
            int numSNs = 0;
            try {
                 numSNs = new Integer(numSNsStr).intValue();
            } catch (NumberFormatException nfe) {
                 System.out.println("Could not get number of Serial
Numbers");
                 return;
            }
            for (int i = 0; i < numSNs; i++) {
                 String productId = bundle.getString("P" + i);
                 String snId = bundle.getString("S" + i);
                 String description = bundle.getString("D" + i);
                 DMethodAccessKey key =
DSimpleMethodKeyFactory.createDMethodAccessKey(productId);
                 Product product = pc.getProductBy(key);
                 DescriptiveInformation di =
DescriptiveInformationFactory.createDescriptiveInformation(AccessMode.
createNormal(), product.getHandle());
                 di.addDefaultDescription(description);
                 try {
                      SerialNumber sn =
SerialNumberFactory.createSerialNumber(product, AccessMode.createNormal(),
snId, di);
                 } catch (ErrorsException e) {
                      System.out.println("Exception creating a PWL" +
e.getMessage());
                      Iterator it =
e.getResultsCollection().createResultMessageIterator();
                      while (it.more()) {
                           System.out.println(((DResultMessage)
it.next()).format());
                      }
                      throw (e);
                 }
            }
      } catch (MissingResourceException mre) {
            System.out.println("Serial numbers not found for company " +
company.getId());
            return;
      }

      /*....................................
            Step 3 - Creating Inventories

            Getting the stock type controller
```

```
          ....................................*/
      System.out.println("Creating inventories....");
      StockTypeController stc = (StockTypeController)
company.getPropertyBy("whs.StockTypeController");
      try {
          String invBundle = "resources/" + company.getId() +
"Inventory";
          ResourceBundle bundle = ResourceBundle.getBundle(invBundle);
          String numInvsStr = bundle.getString("NUM");
          int numInvs = 0;
          try {
              numInvs = new Integer(numInvsStr).intValue();
          } catch (NumberFormatException nfe) {
              System.out.println("Could not get number of
Inventories");
              return;
           }
          for (int i = 0; i < numInvs; i++) {
              SerialNumber sn = null;
              Lot lot = null;
              StockLocation location = null;
              StockZone zone = null;
              Warehouse whs = null;
              StockTypeValue stv = null;
              String productId = bundle.getString("P" + i);
              String warehouseId = bundle.getString("W" + i);
              String zoneId = bundle.getString("Z" + i);
              String stockTypeId = bundle.getString("T" + i);
              String lotId = bundle.getString("L" + i);
              String uomId = bundle.getString("U" + i);
              String quantityStr = bundle.getString("Q" + i);
              String snId = bundle.getString("S" + i);
              DMethodAccessKey key =
DSimpleMethodKeyFactory.createDMethodAccessKey(productId);
              Product product = pc.getProductBy(key);
              UnitOfMeasure uom = uomC.getUnitOfMeasureBy(uomId);
              key =
DSimpleMethodKeyFactory.createDMethodAccessKey(warehouseId);
              whs = wc.getWarehouseBy(key);
              key =
DSimpleMethodKeyFactory.createDMethodAccessKey(zoneId);
              zone = ((LocationControlledWarehouse)
whs).getStockZoneBy(key);
              stv = stc.getStockTypeValueBy(stockTypeId);
              DDecimal quantity =
DDecimalFactory.createDDecimal(quantityStr);
              DSet locations = product.assignStockLocation(whs, stv,
uom, zone, null, null, // Don't pass a measurement
              ptq, null, null);
              if (locations == null) {
                  System.out.println("Could not retrieve the stock
```

```
location");
                        System.out.println("Product: " + product.getId());
                        System.out.println("Warehouse: " + whs.getId());
                        throw (new ErrorsException());
                }
                Iterator locIt = locations.createIterator();
                location = ((DAssignStockLocationResult)
locIt.next()).getStockLocation();
                locIt.releaseResources();

                /*................................................
                                        Now, update the inventory. Necessary
                                        steps:
                                        1- Create a
                                        DInventoryBalanceAccessKey for update
                                        2- Update the balance on the product,
                                        passing the key
                                            and the
                                        DProductTransactionQuantity

................................................*/
                System.out.println("Updating product balances:");
                System.out.println("\tProduct: " + product.getId());
                System.out.println("\tWarehouse: " + whs.getId());
                DProductTransactionQuantity ptq =
DProductTransactionQuantityFactory.createDProductTransactionQuantity(
quantity, uom, product);
                    if (!lotId.equals("N/A")) {
                        key =
DSimpleMethodKeyFactory.createDMethodAccessKey(lotId);
                        lot = product.getLotBy(key);
                    }
                    if (!snId.equals("N/A")) {
                        key =
DSimpleMethodKeyFactory.createDMethodAccessKey(snId);
                        sn = product.getSerialNumberBy(key);
                    }

    /*................................................
                                        Get the stock location from the
                                        product - to simulate
                                        reception. The default
                                        DStockLocationAssignerPolicy will
                                        be used. The set of locations will
                                        contain only the
                                        default location, as defined in the
                                        pwl

................................................*/
                System.out.println("Receiving Product: " +
product.getId() + " for warehouse: " + whs.getId() + " in zone: " +
zone.getId());
```

```
                System.out.println("\tLocation: " + location.getId());
                DInventoryBalanceAccessKey invKey =
DInventoryBalanceAccessKeyFactory.createDInventoryBalanceAccessKeyForUpdate
Balance(stv, whs, lot, location, sn);
                System.out.println("Access key for updating balances
created");
                System.out.println("Lot controlled? " +
invKey.isLotSet());
                System.out.println("S/N controlled? " +
invKey.isSerialNumberSet());
                System.out.println("Location controlled? " +
invKey.isStockLocationSet());
                product.updateBalance(invKey, ptq);
            }
    } catch (MissingResourceException mre) {
        System.out.println("Inventory not found");
        throw (new ErrorsException(mre));
    }
    /*..............................................................
..............
        Loop through all the inventories which have been created to set
        the last stock take
        date to the current date.
        This step is necessary only to test various scenarios in the
        sample application - would
        not be needed in a real life application

..............................................................................
.........*/
    DTimePrecisionPolicy timePrecisionPolicy = (DTimePrecisionPolicy)
company.getPropertyBy("whs.DTimePrecisionPolicy");
    Set products = (Set) pc.getDirectlyOwnedProducts(); //... Get the
products
    Iterator productsIt = products.createIterator();
    productsIt.setAccessMode(AccessMode.createPlusWrite());
    while (productsIt.more()) {
            Product product = (Product) productsIt.next();
            Iterator pwlIt = product.createProductWarehouseLinkIterator();
            pwlIt.setAccessMode(AccessMode.createPlusWrite());
            while (pwlIt.more()) {
                ProductWarehouseLink pwl = (ProductWarehouseLink)
pwlIt.next();
                Warehouse whs = pwl.getWarehouse();
                // use the whs policy to get a commit time, subtract a
                // day to create initial
                // stock take date
                DTime today =
timePrecisionPolicy.getCurrentTime("WHS_STOCK_TAKE_COMMIT_TIME", product,
whs, (BusinessPartner) null);

        today.subtractFrom(DAmountOfTimeFactory.createDAmountOfTime(0, 1, 0,
```

```
0, 0));
                    if (product.isStockControlled(whs)) {
                        Iterator invIt =
((StockControlledProductWarehouseLink) pwl).createInventoryIterator();
                        invIt.setAccessMode(AccessMode.createPlusWrite());
                        while (invIt.more()) {
                            Inventory inv = (Inventory) invIt.next();
                            inv.setLastStockTakeTime(today);
                        } // End of inventories loop
                    } //end if
                } //end pwl loop
        } //end products loop
        //*** Add end
    }
    /*-------------------------------------------------------------------
    */
    /**
     * Generates a Hash Code for this Object.
     * <p>
     * <strong>PreConditions:</strong> None
     * <br><strong>PostConditions:</strong>
     * <br><strong>Object Changed:</strong> false
     *
     * @return int
     */
    /*-------------------------------------------------------------------
    */
    public int hashCode() {
        //This method implements custom logic and, therefore has no
        // implementation
        //Please provide implementation for this method
        //*** Begin add
        return 1;
        //*** End add
    }
    /*-------------------------------------------------------------*/
    /* Restricted Methods */
    /*-------------------------------------------------------------*/
    /*-------------------------------------------------------------------
    */
    /**
     * This method is invoked by the Factory after Construction of an
     * instance of this class to ensure proper initialization.
     * <p>
     * <strong>Restriction:</strong> This method is only for use by the
     * class factory for this class or it's subclasses.
     * <br><strong>Object Changed:</strong> true
     *
     * @param locationHandle Handle of location to run the Command near
<i>(Optional)</i>
```

```
    * @param returnCommand Specifies whether or not to return the
    * Command <i>(Mandatory)</i>
    * @param companyHandle <i>(Mandatory)</i>
    * @return void
    * @exception com.ibm.sf.gf.SFException San Francisco Framework
    * Exception
    */
    /*----------------------------------------------------------------
*/
    public void initialize(Handle locationHandle,
                            boolean returnCommand,
                            Handle companyHandle) throws
com.ibm.sf.gf.SFException {

        DResultsCollection tempResults =
validateForInitialize(locationHandle,

returnCommand,

companyHandle);

        if (tempResults != null) {
            throw new com.ibm.sf.cf.ErrorsException(tempResults);
        }

        // no matching initialize method found in parent class, calling
        // default
        super.initialize(locationHandle, returnCommand,
"BDSInventoryInitializeCmd", UndoType.NO_UNDO);

        // handles to entities
        ivCompanyHdl = setHandleToHandle(ivCompanyHdl, companyHandle);
    }
    /*----------------------------------------------------------------
*/
    /**
     * Reads object state from the specified stream and sets the
     * object's state equal to it.
     * <p>For more information, see the <i>"San Francisco Programming
     * Model"</i>.
     * <p>
     * <strong>Restriction:</strong> This method is implemented by the
     * class developer and is
     * NOT typically called by anything outside the Foundation Layer.
     * <br><strong>PreConditions:</strong> None
     * <br><strong>PostConditions:</strong>
     * <br><strong>Object Changed:</strong> true
     *
     * @param stream stream to read from <i>(Mandatory - object may be
     * changed)</i>
     * @return void
     * @exception java.io.IOException if an I/O error occurs
```

```
        */
      /*-----------------------------------------------------------------
*/
      public void internalizeFromStream(BaseStream stream) throws
java.io.IOException {
            if(stream.skipThisClass(IMPLEMENTATION_NAME)) {
                super.internalizeFromStream(stream);
                return;
            }
            // Internalize the version number
            int objectIntStreamVersion = stream.readInt();
            // read the parent's state
            super.internalizeFromStream(stream);
            ivCompanyHdl = stream.readHandle(this,ivCompanyHdl);
      }
      /*-----------------------------------------------------------------
*/
      /**
       * Sets Company.
       * <p>
       * <strong>PreConditions:</strong> None
       * <br><strong>PostConditions:</strong>
       * <br><strong>Object Changed:</strong> true
       * <br><strong>Note:</strong> NULL may not be passed since
       * ivCompanyHdl is a mandatory attribute
       *
       * @param newCompany new Company of the WNSInventoryInitializeCmd
       * <i>(Mandatory)</i>
       * @return void
       * @exception com.ibm.sf.gf.SFException San Francisco Framework
       * Exception
       */
      /*-----------------------------------------------------------------
*/
      public void setCompany(Company newCompany) throws
com.ibm.sf.gf.SFException {
            // call inherited method to change handle to specified entity
            ivCompanyHdl = setHandleToObject(ivCompanyHdl, newCompany);
      }
      /*-----------------------------------------------------------------
*/
      /**
       * Sets the values of all this instance's instance variables to the
       * values of the specified instance.
       * <p>For more information, see the <i>"San Francisco Programming
       * Model"</i>.
       * <p>
       * <strong>PreConditions:</strong> None
       * <br><strong>PostConditions:</strong> equals(sourceDependent) ==
       * true
       * <br><strong>Object Changed:</strong> true
```

```
       *
       * @param sourceDependent class instance to set equal to
       * <i>(Optional)</i>
       * @return void
       * @exception com.ibm.sf.gf.SetEqualParameterException San Francisco
       * Framework Exception
       * @exception com.ibm.sf.gf.SFException San Francisco Framework
       * Exception
       */
      /*----------------------------------------------------------------
*/
      public void setEqual(Dependent sourceDependent) throws
com.ibm.sf.gf.SetEqualParameterException, com.ibm.sf.gf.SFException {
            // check if objects are of the same type
            try {
                  if (sourceDependent != null)  {

                        // call parent to set inherited state

                        super.setEqual(sourceDependent);

                        // cast Dependent object parameter to type
BDSInventoryInitializeCmd

                        WNSInventoryInitializeCmd WNSInventoryInitializeCmd
= (WNSInventoryInitializeCmd) sourceDependent;

                        // Entities
                        ivCompanyHdl = setHandleToHandle(ivCompanyHdl,
bDSInventoryInitializeCmd.getCompanyHdl());
                  }
                  else {
                        throw new
com.ibm.sf.gf.SetEqualParameterException();
                  }
            }
            catch (ClassCastException ex) {
                  throw new
com.ibm.sf.gf.SetEqualParameterException(sourceDependent,"com.big.wms.WNS
InventoryInitializeCmd");
            }
      }
      /*----------------------------------------------------------------
*/
      /**
       * Sets the target of the Command.
       * <p>
       * <strong>Object Changed:</strong> true
       *
       * @param target <i>(Mandatory)</i>
       * @return void
       * @exception com.ibm.sf.gf.SFException San Francisco Framework
```

```
     * Exception
     */
    /*------------------------------------------------------------------
*/
    public void setTarget(Base target) throws com.ibm.sf.gf.SFException
{
            // call inherited method to change handle to specified entity
            ivCompanyHdl = setHandleToObject(ivCompanyHdl, (Company)
target);
    }
    /*------------------------------------------------------------------
*/
    /**
     * Represents Object's State in a String.
     * <p>
     * <strong>PreConditions:</strong> None
     * <br><strong>PostConditions:</strong>
     * <br><strong>Object Changed:</strong> false
     *
     * @return String
     */
    /*------------------------------------------------------------------
*/
    public String toString() {
            try {
                    String retVal = super.toString();
                    return (retVal);
            }
            catch (Exception ex) {
                    throw (new SFRuntimeException(ex, new
TextResource("MSG_RMTSFEXCEP_DEFAULT",
"com.ibm.sf.gf.resources.SFExceptionResources", (Object[])null, "Runtime
Exception has Occurred")));
            }
    }
    /*------------------------------------------------------------------
*/
    /**
     * Validation for method initialize.
     *
     * @return DResultsCollection - A collection of messages if
     * validation failed, otherwise null
     * @exception com.ibm.sf.gf.SFException San Francisco Framework
     * Exception
     * @see com.big.wms.WNSInventoryInitializeCmdImpl#initialize
     */
    /*------------------------------------------------------------------
*/
    protected DResultsCollection validateForInitialize(Handle
locationHandle,
                                                       boolean
```

```
returnCommand,
                                                    Handle
companyHandle) throws com.ibm.sf.gf.SFException {
        DResultsCollection tempResults = null;
        // retrieve the validation level from the context
        int validationLevel = ValidationContext.getValidationLevel();

        if ((validationLevel == ValidationLevelEnum.SEVERE_ERRORS_ONLY)
|| (validationLevel == ValidationLevelEnum.ALL)) {
            // insert code to do severe error validation
            // if errors are found create DResultsCollection
tempResults and add DResultMessages
        }
errors are found create DResultsCollection tempResults (if not already
created)
            // and add DResultMessages
        }

        return (tempResults);
    }
} // end of class WNSInventoryInitializeCmdImpl
```

From these examples, you should be able to track through the code and see what value the SF framework provides.

Throughout the development process, we continued to look for ways to make SanFrancisco, UML, object-oriented analysis and design, and Java application development faster and easier to grasp.

The actual chapters are dedicated to a somewhat less elegant but infinitely more practical approach to working with SanFrancisco components. The good news is that you can actually develop Java applications quickly and effectively using Big Blue tools. The bad news is (if you think of this as bad news) that you must stick with the visual programming model; you have to work around the components as delivered; and you have to really understand the problem to be solved.

In my opinion, IBM has done a great job of delivering a set of applications that lets me choose what weapon to use. Anyone who says that SDI (or object orientation) is the only way to deal with the challenge has never been mugged and found themselves wishing they had a good old-fashioned baseball bat close to hand.

Having gotten that off my keyboard, I feel vastly better. Thanks for staying with me.